To William Hospital Library

With Colonel Culverwells
Compliments & Thanks
July/48

50p
W35

D1578232

LORD BOTHWELL

JAMES HEPBURN, 4TH EARL OF BOTHWELL, IN 1566.
(Enlarged from the Boyle Miniature, by permission of the Scottish National Portrait Gallery)
[*Annan, Glasgow*

LORD BOTHWELL

by

ROBERT GORE-BROWNE

*A Study of the
Life, Character and Times of
James Hepburn, 4th Earl of Bothwell*

COLLINS

FORTY-EIGHT PALL MALL LONDON

1937

THIS BOOK IS SET IN FONTANA, A NEW TYPE
FACE DESIGNED FOR THE EXCLUSIVE USE OF THE
HOUSE OF COLLINS, AND PRINTED BY THEM
IN GREAT BRITAIN

FIRST IMPRESSION JANUARY 1937
SECOND IMPRESSION MAY 1937

COLLINS CLEAR-TYPE PRESS·LONDON AND GLASGOW
COPYRIGHT 1937

I am Don Juan, curst from age to age
By priestly tract and sentimental stage:
Branded a villain or believed a fool,
Battered by hatred, seared by ridicule,
Noble on earth, all but a King in Hell,
I am Don Juan with a tale to tell.

FLECKER.

LIST OF ILLUSTRATIONS

MAPS

PREFACE

In the hope of getting Bothwell's case reheard both by the general public that reads history and the experts who write it, this book follows certain cautious rules. Reliance has only been placed on the evidence of people who were alive in Bothwell's day. Though the conclusions of succeeding generations have been studied, they have not been quoted. In recording the assertions of his contemporaries, allowance has been made for the wind of prejudice. What access each witness had to the facts has also been taken into consideration. To spare the eyes of readers from a plague of footnotes, references are only given where a statement in the text might be disputed or where its source is obscure. Many quotations from books and letters of the time have been included to lend an authority that no writer separated from his subject by three and a half centuries can claim. To suit the convenience of the general reader, spelling has been modernised and matter occasionally condensed.

To his friends the author's debt is great and to strangers who have acted as friends. His subject was originally suggested by Lady Helena Carnegie, a sympathiser with Bothwell, who lent her library and constant help and encouragement during the seven years that the book has taken to write. Without Dr. Bøggild Andersen's expert advice the Scandinavian part of the book could not have been written nor the Scandinavian pictures included. Mr. F. Bierbum and Miss Bierbum made a visit to the scene of Bothwell's last years possible and delightful. The late Sir Bruce Seton of Abercorn, the late Mr. J. R. N. Macphail, Dr. H. W. Meikle, Dr. B. Kornerup, Dr. M. Mackeprang, Mr. William Angus, Mr. A. Francis Steuart, Mr. J. K. Milne Home, Mr. P. Buchan Hepburn, Mr. G. P. Johnston, Mr. Alistair Tayler,

Mr. Nigel de Grey, Dr. and Mrs. Edwin Hubble, have been generous with their help. The staffs of the British Museum, the Record Office, the Advocates' Library, the Register House, the Bodleian, the Huntington Library in California, the Rigsarkiv at Copenhagen, the Museums at Malmoe and Bergen have given valuable assistance. Finally the writer's wife has endured and has even pretended to enjoy daily discussion of Bothwell. Her criticism has been acute; her insight into the dark places of his history more penetrating than any man's.

LIST OF CHIEF CHARACTERS

SCOTS

MARY STUART, Queen of Scots.

LORD JAMES STEWART, afterwards EARL OF MORAY, her illegitimate brother, leader of the Protestant, pro-English party.

LORD JOHN STEWART,
  Commendator of Coldingham
LORD ROBERT STEWART,
  Abbot of Holyrood
} also illegitimate brothers.

THE DUKE OF CHATELHERAULT, head of the HAMIL-TONS and next heir to the throne.

THE EARL OF ARRAN, his son; a strong Protestant.

LORD JOHN HAMILTON, another son.

GAVIN HAMILTON, Abbot of Kilwinning, a cousin; Catholic.

JOHN HAMILTON, the Catholic Primate of Scotland.

THE EARL OF LENNOX, a Catholic with pretensions to the throne.

MARGARET DOUGLAS, his wife.

HENRY STEWART, LORD DARNLEY, his son; a Catholic.

THE EARL OF MORTON, acting head of the DOUGLASES; Protestant and pro-English.

GEORGE DOUGLAS, the Postulate.

MR. ARCHIBALD DOUGLAS.

LORD RUTHVEN, whose wife was a Douglas; Protestant.

LORD LINDSAY, whose wife was a Douglas; Protestant.

JOHN KNOX, head of the Kirk party.

SIR WILLIAM KIRKALDY OF GRANGE, soldier and sup-porter of Knox.

13

JOHN COCKBURN OF ORMISTON, another supporter.
HENRY BALNAVES, another keen Protestant.

THE EARL OF ARGYLL,
THE EARL OF GLENCAIRN, } inclined to change sides.
LORD BOYD,

LORD ERSKINE, afterwards EARL OF MAR, usually neutral.
ARABELLA MURRAY, his wife; a Catholic.
JAMES MURRAY of PURDORVIS, her brother.

THE EARL OF HUNTLY, the most powerful Catholic noble
    in Scotland.
GEORGE GORDON, his son and successor.
LADY JEAN GORDON, his daughter and wife to Bothwell.

THE EARL OF ATHOLL,
LORD SETON,
LORD SEMPILL, } leaders of the Catholic, pro-
LORD LIVINGSTONE, French party.
LORD BORTHWICK,

WILLIAM MAITLAND OF LETHINGTON, the Secretary.
DAVID RIZZIO, the Queen's secretary for Foreign Corre-
    spondence.
JOHN LESLIE, Bishop of Ross, a Court official loyal to Mary.
SIR JAMES MELVILLE, a courtier.

SIR JAMES BALFOUR, a lawyer,
SIR JOHN BELLENDEN, Justice Clerk, } opportunists.
ADAM BOTHWELL, Bishop of Orkney,

LORD HOME,
WALTER KERR OF CESSFORD, } Wardens of the
THE MASTER OF MAXWELL, Marches.
    afterwards LORD HERRIES,

MARY BETON, MARY SETON, MARY LIVINGSTONE and
    MARY FLEMING, the Queen's Maries.

JAMES HEPBURN, EARL OF BOTHWELL.
PATRICK HEPBURN, " THE FAIR EARL," his father.
LADY JANET HEPBURN, his sister.
PATRICK HEPBURN, Bishop of Moray, his uncle.
JAMES ORMISTON OF ORMISTON, his right-hand man.
JANET BETON, Lady of Buccleugh, one of his mistresses.
NICHOLAS HUBERT, called French Paris, his page.
BESSIE CRAWFORD, his wife's maid.

FRENCH

MARY OF LORRAINE, Mary Stuart's mother.
THE DUKE OF GUISE, her uncle.
THE CARDINAL OF LORRAINE, another uncle.

CATHERINE DE MEDICIS, Queen Mother of France.
FRANCIS II, her son.
CHARLES IX, her son.

PHILIBERT DU CROC,
CASTELNAU DE MAUVISSIERE, } envoys and ambassa-
COMTE DE BRIENNE, dors.

D'OYSEL,
SARLEBOUS, } soldiers.

ENGLISH

QUEEN ELIZABETH, Mary Stuart's cousin.
SIR WILLIAM CECIL, her Secretary.

THE EARL OF NORTHUMBERLAND, a Border noble.
SIR HENRY PERCY, his brother.
SIR JOHN FORSTER, Warden of the Marches.
SIR WILLIAM DRURY, Marshal of Berwick.
THE EARL OF BEDFORD, Governor of Berwick.

THOMAS RANDOLPH,
SIR RALPH SADLER, } envoys.
SIR NICHOLAS THROCKMORTON,

FREDERICK II, King of Denmark.

PETER OXE, his High Steward.

CHRISTIERN AALBORG, one of his sea captains.

ANNA THRONDSEN, the daughter of one of his admirals.

ERIK ROSENCRANTZ, her cousin, Viceroy of Norway.

COLONEL JOHN CLERK, a Scottish mercenary in the Danish service.

CHAPTER ONE

JAMES HEPBURN, fourth Earl of Bothwell, has enjoyed a sinister reputation for the four centuries that have passed since his birth. "The murderer, the brutal and debauched Bothwell"; "the turbulent, licentious Earl, the worst man at the Court"; "an unmannerly, unlettered scamp who regarded man's life as little as woman's honour"—these are average tributes from the anthology of abuse that has gathered round his name.

As the reader ponders the indignation of historians, he begins to wonder if the urge, which forces them alternatively to blacken or to glorify the memory of the Queen of Scots, has not embittered their judgment of her third husband. Since he shared her downfall, a chorus of reprobation suits both camps. The enemies of the Queen hope to blast her reputation by linking her with the villain of a Hollywood melodrama, while Mariolaters are glad to find a scapegoat. The aim of these pages is to discover whether original sources do not disclose a more credible figure than the bogy with which history has tried to frighten us.

At first sight the opinion of Bothwell's contemporaries seems to warrant the verdict. "I know him," wrote the English agent at Queen Mary's Court, "as mortal an enemy to our nation as any man alive; despiteful beyond measure, false and untrue as the devil, a blasphemous and irreverent speaker and one that the godly of this nation hath cause to curse for ever." This diatribe was supported by an English governor who saw in Bothwell "a fit man to be minister to any shameful act, either against God or man."

Such tributes must not be read without their context. The speakers were Englishmen of a period when England was seeking the disadvantage of her neighbour by any tortuous or corrupt means. In an outspoken age Bothwell, head of the anti-English faction, was unlikely to have a good press across the Border.

Scots, it may be claimed, added their damning testimony. As prominent a figure as James Stewart, the Queen's half-brother, denounced Bothwell as "an assassin of well-known cruelty, a robber condemned by justice, human and divine." However little he knew about justice, James Stewart, say some, could speak as an authority on murder and peculation. Even so he was no impartial witness. When he came to die, Queen Elizabeth *Fenelon iii. 54.* cried out that she had lost "the most useful friend she had in the world," and the evidence of the leader of the Anglophile party is as suspect as any native Englishman's. The same bias distorts the judgment of partisans who call Bothwell "a monstrous beast, of all men that now exist or ever will, the most wicked," "a bog of vice and sink of all horrible sins," or "the vilest of all two-footed beasts."

It is a commonplace of English law that a man shall be tried by a jury of his peers. American justice grants the right to challenge jurors whose impartiality by any reason of religion, race or circumstance is suspect. At the bar of history, where the right of appeal hardly runs, should not similar precaution be taken? Would the annalist of contemporary gang warfare in Chicago (with all its analogy to Scottish history of the sixteenth century) be wise to accept as gospel the sayings of the "big shot" of a contending gang? In England to-day is a modernist bishop sure to come scathless through a cloud of Anglo-Catholic witness? Are the views of newspaper barons on political leaders who differ from them to be taken by future research-workers as beyond mortal error? If the seeker after truth must pick his way carefully across the flats of this sophisticated century, how delicately should he tread the mazes of a society where variety in wording a creed led naturally to the faggot, political discord was stilled by dagger or axe, and legal procedure shortened with the thumbscrew!

No attempt will here be made to palliate the reported wickedness of Bothwell with the stock defence of the criminals of history. The excuse of "other times and other manners" can only be offered to a reader optimistic enough to believe that London, Madrid, New York, Paris or Berlin do not to-day breed treachery, cruelty and lust as rank as in any castle of Queen Mary's Scotland. Certain progress, however, may be claimed for the civilisation of the moment. To-day, in all countries, public men quite commonly display high standards of honesty, honour and humanity. In the second half of the sixteenth century few characters on either side of the Border could be found to retrieve public life from a dead level of infamy. To-day it may be claimed that in many modern countries frank criminal ethics no longer openly direct public policy. Staviskys and Roehms may flourish for a season, but the murderous tactics of Cecil or Lethington would not be tolerated in a minister, hardly in a dictator. Under democracy covert corruption may persist in the purchase of its suffrages with the taxpayers' money; outside municipal affairs, direct bribery has lapsed. In Queen Mary's day, nearly every Protestant noble in Scotland (with the noteworthy exception of "that unprincipled ruffian" the Earl of Bothwell) was in the pay of the hereditary enemy of his country.

Knowledge of the ignominy was general. In the middle of Bothwell's career the Spanish ambassador could *de Silva to* report to Madrid that eight thousand crowns bought *King Philip II, 18 Sept.,* Queen Elizabeth the goodwill and secret information of *1564.* the leading men in Scotland. A later revision of this pension list lies in the British Museum and bears witness to the lamentably low rates at which the Protestant nobility and gentry of Scotland valued their honour. The Regent tops the salary list with five hundred pounds; two earls and a countess reach two hundred; four earls and six barons are content with a hundred pounds apiece. Prices for commoners ruled rather lower, but George Buchanan drew his hundred and must be admitted to have earned it. The gentler sex was not forgotten.

Wives, daughters and sisters, who kept their ears open and their males up to the mark, find their place on the roll of infamy.

The peculiarity of Bothwell in refusing to accept from his country's enemies an income that would have relieved his chronic need stood him in little stead with his less fastidious neighbours. Uneasy conscience finds relief in disparaging innocence, and the pensioners of England tried to cover their shame by attacking the eccentric who did not share it.

Nor did his religious opinions, which struck across the political grouping of the time, count for righteousness. His convictions kept him protestant; his loyalty to the Queen tied him to the catholics. In the eyes of his allies he ranked as heretic, fit fuel for flames here and hereafter. His co-religionists thought that only atheism could explain his connection with their opponents. His moral liberty made him a paradox in the age of Scotland's Reformation, suspected and unfriended by either side. "In the past," said a clerical intimate of Queen Mary's uncle, the Cardinal, "friends and foes were distinguished by the boundaries of provinces and kingdoms. Men were counted English, Germans, French, Italians. To-day one should but speak of catholics and heretics. A catholic prince should reckon as friends all catholics of all lands, just as heretics consider all heretics their friends."

Even if Bothwell's theology had fitted his politics, it might not have contented his associates. Intolerance was expected from the orthodox of either faith. The official catholic voice may be heard in the conversation of Pope Pius IV. "The good man," as an ambassador disrespectfully describes him, "would not change the subject. He said that the King, princes and cardinals of France went out hunting and did not read the trials of heretics. Heresy is so great an issue, that as soon as a man is ever so little stained with it, there is no other remedy but to burn him incontinently."

On the other side of the water, in Protestant Scotland, the stake was not the fashion. But no greater breadth of mind can be claimed for a town council which perceives "the wicked rabble of anti-Christ the Pope" to resort to Edinburgh, and orders "all monks, friars, priests, nuns, adulterers, fornicators and all such filthy persons to remove themselves within twenty-four hours under pain of carting through the town, burning on the cheek and banishing."

That Bothwell was some centuries ahead of this bigotry is proved by the measures of tolerance that he sponsored in his brief weeks of power. A Scottish Jesuit gave a significant account of that gallant failure. "In the assemblies," he wrote despondently, "two decrees were made, whereby both religions (God have mercy on us) were approved, and the followers of both receive her Majesty's favour and are promised her protection. May God send us better and happier news!" *Father Hay to Bishop of Mondovi, 5 June, 1567.*

He had not long to wait. Before the frosts of winter, Bothwell was rotting in a Danish prison, and Scotland was caught fast in the iron gin of Knox's Calvinism.

Philosophy, religion, politics and an intransigent loyalty forced Bothwell into a dangerous isolation. To play a lone hand suited, indeed, his bent. In spite of the culture he had acquired abroad, he remained a Borderer by genius as well as geography. Border blood taught him the value of sudden, independent, audacious action. It did not fit him for struggle in a world of growing sophistication that had left behind the unpractical rules of a chivalry that only lingered on the marches of England and Scotland.

In this sense Bothwell was an anachronism, fated to follow the mammoth and the megatherium into limbo. How could he expect his light-of-day methods to defeat the subterranean treacheries of Cecil, Lethington and their associates? It is the posthumous triumph of their campaign of abuse that excites protest. Our museums do not hold up the private lives of their megatheria to obloquy or ridicule. Bothwell, least plaintive of victims, himself expresses indignation at his enemies' "slanders and the great wrong they have done, as by God's help every one may clearly see."

With this protest, he was content to leave the verdict to "Time, mother of Truth." She has abused his confidence with four hundred years of full-throated execration. It is the hope of this book that his case may be reconsidered. Unexpected witnesses for the defence come forward. An enemy across the Border, when he met Bothwell face to face, declared that he was "very wise and not the man he was reported to be. His behaviour . . . both courteous and honourable."

An extremist on the other side of the religious fence wrote: "He had been all his lifetime a faithful servant of the crown, a man valiant and for magnanimous powers above all others . . . ready to undertake and more ready to put into execution."

Where so much prejudice has been excited, where the evidence of contemporaries conflicts, where so many years have slid by, it is hard to see clear. The best hope of finding out the truth is to discard preconceived ideas and to follow the man's life day by day, until it leads us to an estimate of his character.

Little knowledge of antecedent Scottish history is needed to understand his story. To a small, poor and sparsely populated country the hereditary enmity of England and the traditional friendship of France were equally fatal. In the autumn of 1513 the French alliance had brought James IV and the best manhood of Scotland to their deaths on the field of Flodden. With the consequences of such annihilation Europe is to-day familiar. Thirty years of anarchy followed, marked only by the sanguinary rivalries of the pro-English and pro-French parties. Submission to Henry VIII of England was the panacea of those who hoped to profit by his friendship. The assistance of Francis I of France was the alternative formula by which the independence of Scotland was to be preserved. To the second view James V, when he was old enough to judge, inclined. He marked his preference by marriage with two

22

Frenchwomen in quick succession. Henry VIII's retort was war, quickly ending with the rout of the Scots at Solway Moss. The news broke their King's heart and he died soon after hearing of the birth of his daughter Mary Stuart.

Her great-uncle Henry VIII had almost secured custody of her person under pretext of betrothal to his son Edward when a patriotic revival in Scotland defeated his designs and discredited his assistants. Recourse to the French alliance could not save the Lowlands from Tudor savagery, and the Border, ordinarily desolated by the raiding propensities of its inhabitants, paid the price of the miscalculations and ambitions of the rulers.

The victory of Scottish arms at Ancrum Moor was counter-balanced by England's success in procuring the murder of Cardinal Beton, leader of the pro-French party.

Henry VIII died and the Protector Somerset inflicted the defeat of Pinkie, only to rouse the obstinacy of the Scots and decide them to send their infant Queen to France where she was betrothed to the Dauphin. The government of Scotland devolved on a Hamilton Regent, next heir to the throne, but the real power lay in the capable hands of Mary of Lorraine, the Queen Mother.

Mary of Lorraine had three difficulties to face. The nationalism of her subjects resented foreign methods; the disloyalty of her nobles thwarted her most disinterested efforts; the late arrival of the Reformation in Scotland took from a catholic ruler the support she should have obtained from a great part of the gentry and populace.

In 1557 the Spanish connection of Mary Tudor brought England into war with France, whose hereditary friendship involved Scotland. The later stages of a half-hearted campaign saw Bothwell's entry into public life. This brief summary may help to make his attitude clear.

CHAPTER TWO

IF embryologists can claim that the first weeks of man's earthly existence repeat his laborious ascent from amphioxus to anthropoid, a biographer need not be grudged a glance at more recent family influences. The power of dead ancestors to mould the lives of their descendants is manifest in a country as conscious of history as Scotland, and a *milieu* as conservative as Bothwell's.

The Hepburns, in whose family ran the titles of Hailes and of Bothwell, inherited a pretension which played a baleful part in the history of the most conspicuous of their race. This tradition was first remarked by Sir George Mackenzie of Rosehaugh, founder of the Advocates' Library at Edinburgh, known from his severities to the Covenanters as "bloody Mackenzie."

"It is hereditary to the house of Hailes," he mused, "to be kind to the widow queens. As Patrick, First Lord Hailes, to Queen Joan, widow of James I; his son to Queen Mary of Guelderland; Patrick, Earl of Bothwell, to Queen Mary of Lorraine; his son to Queen Mary." Family history need only be explored to trace this disposition, so fatal to the last-named holder of the title.

The Hepburns are said to have come over the Border from Hebburn in the parish of Chillingham, Northumberland. In the reign of David II the founder of the family was led into Scotland "ane mean captive." There immobilised by a lack of funds that was to pursue his descendant he stayed. Sooner or later he had, it is related, the presence of mind to rescue the Earl of Dunbar from a savage horse and to earn a gift of land in East Lothian. (Rescues of this nature, rare to-day, were a commonplace of early Scottish history. The ancestor, for instance, of the clan Mackenzie founded the family fortunes by

24

saving the King of Scotland from a stag at bay. The memory or origin of these exploits may be found in the stag's antlers of the Mackenzie crest and in the horse's head of the Hepburns.)

The Hepburn lands cluster in a shallow basin that has the Edge of Lothian for its western lip. Smooth hills roll round like waves. The sea is never out of sight. In the middle, like the grey hump of a whale, rises Taprain Law, near whose bulk the Hepburns of the fourteenth century strengthened and enlarged their castle of Hailes. The stronghold stood at the bottom of a steep pitch and guarded a ford of the narrow Tyne, through which travellers passing from Dunbar to Edinburgh had to splash. The other three sides of the fortress were protected by a moat and walls nine feet thick. In those days strong arms, even more surely than ponderous building, won respect and Sir Patrick Hepburn of Hailes was found worthy to be one of the five successive husbands of Robert Bruce's niece. Not to over-tire this experienced lady with his company, Sir Patrick made a pilgrimage to the shrine of St. Thomas at Canterbury and a longer one to the Holy Land. He managed not to miss the Battle of Otterburn, where he and his son (remembered by genealogists as *miles magnanimus et athleta bellicosus*) saved the Douglas banner. His example encouraged descendants to follow the normal traditions of chivalry— travel and fighting. His great-grandson and namesake started the special family tradition, chivalrous in the more modern sense, of being kind to widow queens. Unfortunately details of his benevolence are scanty.

The bare statement of history that Patrick Hepburn was defending the Castle of Dunbar and that Lady Jane Beaufort, widow of James I of Scotland, came to defend it with him leaves the feeling of a good story spoiled. Three letters from Lady Jane's son, the new King, throw little light. They protest against Patrick's "most treasonable taking of our Castle of Dunbar, burning our ships, slaughter of our people and many other detestable enormities," but fail to mention whether the enormities

Buchanan Rer. Scot. Hist. 378.

Exchequer Rolls V, LXVII.

Raine's History of Durham, Appendix 22.

include kindness to the writer's mother. The end of the adventure comes with more pith than colour. "The XV day of July the quene deit in Dunbar and was erdit in the Charterhouse of Perth and incontinent the lord Hailes gaf our the castell of Dunbar thro trety."

Although these tantalising fragments hint at an epic with roots in romance and fruit in death, imagination must be restrained, for Hepburn interest in queens had generally its practical side. For better or worse Patrick had planted the idea that royal widows were accessible. Fifteen years later his son, Adam, was involved in a dubious affair with the next royal relict, when Mary of Guelders found cause to close the lips of an English duke that were as ready to tell as to kiss. She enlisted Adam's help in a solution that she planned to be final. The ambush failed, but she gave the Hepburn his reward—"she became lecherous of her body," says the chronicle frankly, "and took Adam Hepburn, who had a wife of his own." With all the country to choose from, exclaims another indignant annalist, she had to pick a married man. Not until the tolerant eighteenth century did the hot-blooded Netherlander find an apologist. "A widow in the bloom of beauty and vigour of youth," he wrote, "it would not be a matter of surprise that her chastity was dubious. Even this stain would disappear in the splendour of her merits, for nothing can be more unjust than to infer that the loss of feminine modesty is the loss of every virtue."

Patrick, son of the hero of her romance, broke with the past. Believing that the high road to greatness lay through political, not sentimental, intrigue, he joined the conspiracy against the life of James III, the King who "loved solitariness and desired never to hear of war." His instinct was right and his reward the Earldom of Bothwell. Striking out this new line, the first Earl touched heights that the traditionalists of his house had never reached. Master of the new King's Household, Lord High Admiral of Scotland, Sheriff Principal of Edinburgh, Warden of the West and Middle Marches,

Keeper of the Castles of Edinburgh, Dunbar and Hermitage, Lord of Orkney and the Shetland Isles, he rode through England at the head of a hundred horsemen on an embassy to France and Spain. He also acted as plenipotentiary when his master wooed Margaret Tudor and founded the Stewart claim to succeed to the throne of England.

On his own account he contracted an advantageous alliance with the great Highland family of Gordon. Practical considerations ruled his choice, for his marriage contract stipulates "*ane of the twa* douchters, Margaret or Katherine, quhilk of thame sall best ples the said Erle Bothvill." His famous descendant would have done well to learn from his great-grandfather that conspiracy and intrigue carry a man further and more safely in public life than any prowess in the fields of Mars or Venus.

The first Earl's son, Adam, succeeded. Like many in our day, he was sentenced by the date of his birth to short enjoyment of shadow and sun on Border hills. At the age of twenty-one he fell in the battle that saw the disappearance of the flower of his nation and reduced Scotland to the cultural level of her conqueror.

In spite of his early death at Flodden, Adam had time to show a different sense of values from his father's. Marriage with Agnes Stewart, illegitimate daughter of the Earl of Buchan, suggests that romance took a larger place in his philosophy; that it led him to overlook her birth, and closed his eyes to her standing as the King's ex-mistress—unless indeed that position carried some of the glamour of royal widowhood.

An autumn night brought her the news of Flodden. Lover and husband had been killed fighting the English side by side. Two infants squalled fatherless in the palace and hall—James, aged two, that night the Fifth of Scotland, in due course father of the Queen of Scots; and Patrick, aged one, destined to beget James, Earl of Bothwell, the man whose fate was interlocked with hers.

CHAPTER THREE

THE uneasy life of Patrick, third Earl of Bothwell and father to the subject of this memoir, deserves a chapter to itself. Certain writers, taking too literally divine injunction to visit the sins of the fathers on the children, have recklessly confused the acts of Patrick and James. Convinced in advance of the latter's villainy, by a manipulation of dates that no virtue could have forestalled, they have discredited the steady loyalty of the son with the ineffectual treacheries of the father. The family tradition found in Patrick a determined, and at last a well-documented supporter. In other directions the father's career had an influence on the unformed character of his son.

Patrick, known as the Fair Earl, (a sobriquet earned by complexion rather than character) had a bad start. Left fatherless on the night of Flodden, he did not receive the mother's care that his orphaned state demanded. Agnes had other things to think of than the welfare of her baby. To the husband and lover she lost on the battlefield, she was to add three more husbands. The last she grappled to her with bands of holy wedlock at the age of fifty. This bridegroom was Cuthbert Ramsay, whose name will appear again in our story and who, at the time of his marriage to the dowager, had not reached the discreet age of twenty-one.

It was the century of youth. The Fair Earl was seventeen when he made his first public appearance. On 15th May, 1529 he was imprisoned in Edinburgh Castle to pay for the protection he had given robbers in Liddesdale—severe handling for youthful sympathy with the normal occupation of his Border neighbours.

28

Somewhat unruly and very hard to tame,
I would have none think that I call them thieves.
The freebooter ventures life and limb,
Good wife and bairn and everything—
He must do so, or else must starve and die,
For all his living comes of the enemy——

so Satchells rhymed (more or less) of the Armstrongs,
Earl Patrick shared his point of view and the heavy
hand did not intimidate him. As soon as his two
years' captivity was over, he vented his hatred of the
authority that had punished him by starting a treasonable
correspondence with England that continued at intervals
throughout his short life. Retribution followed with
no lame foot. During the next ten years he paid
with a further spell of prison and three periods
of exile. Venice, "the very haven of liberty and the *Leslie.*
common refuge of foreigners," saw him, and England. *History of*
In the intervals he returned to the greyer skies of his *Scotland, 431.*
native land. During one of these respites, before he was
twenty-one, he found leisure to marry Agnes Sinclair,
another Flodden orphan. Lord Sinclair had been a patron
of the arts and had encouraged Gavin Douglas to make
his translation of the Aeneid into Scots. Lady Sinclair had
been a Hepburn, daughter of the lover of Mary of
Guelders, for marriages between cousins were a commonplace in a narrow aristocracy. The plea of consanguinity
gave such alliances the advantages of easy dissolution.
This was a convenience where family fortunes fluctuated
rapidly with favour at Court and wedlock was an instrument of policy.

This is how Patrick looked to the girl he was courting
—"he was fair and white and something hanging- *Lindsay of*
shouldered and went somewhat forward with a gentle *Pitscottie 17.*
and humane countenance." In later years he was to
ripen into "a gentleman of right comely port and stature," *Patten 81.*
and, as an English captain saw it, "of just and honourable
dealing towards the English king." The Scottish king had
another name for this dealing, and it was only after

release from prison that his son James could be begotten. The birth was celebrated in later years by an epigrammatist with a turn for eugenics.

John Dickinson Speculum Tragicum (A.D. 1602)

"Si crimen fuerit genuisse parentibus ullis
  Crimen erat magnum te genuisse tuis."

"If fatherhood a crime could be
  His it was who fathered thee."

James Hepburn was almost certainly born in 1535.[1] He had one sister who lived, a girl called Janet.

From his earliest days, young James suffered the penalty of his father's treasons. Whether the boy was left in Scotland in charge of a kinsman, or whether he accompanied his father to a foreign land, he lost the sense of security that only home can give. In Scotland or abroad he did not fail to recognise the folly of disloyalty and how, to satisfy a grudge, his father lost liberty, lands and country.

Ten bitter years passed, and one day after the battle of Solway Moss news was brought to Patrick, as he dragged out the time in England, that James the Fifth was dead. That "good poor man's king" (vexed, it was said, by some unkindly medicine, which others called an Italian posset), "had turned him upon his back and looked and beheld all his nobles and lords about him and gave a little smile of laughter, thereafter held up his hands to God and yielded up his spirit."

The Fair Earl wasted no time in commiseration. The new sovereign was a girl-baby a few days old. In the troubled waters of a long minority good sport might be anticipated. Pausing in the country of his refuge only long enough to sign a pact that would commit the infant princess to the benevolent keeping of Henry VIII of

[1] The date of his birth can be fixed by the following facts: James Hepburn was over twenty-one when he succeeded to the title in the autumn of 1556 as there was then no dispensation in respect of nonage. (Hailes. Annals iii., XI.) He is called "twenty-four or about" when he gave evidence against the Earl of Arran in February, 1560. (Pollen LXXXVIII.) A birth in 1535 would most nearly fit these dates.

England, and throwing in a promise to serve and aid that Defender of the Faith, he hurried back to his native land.

It must be confessed that his actions on return satisfied neither his reluctant countrymen nor his recent hosts. Any hopes that the English had built on his promises were quickly disappointed. Sir Ralph Sadler, the stormy petrel of anti-Scottish intrigue, then on one of his periodic visits of mischief to the Border, reported him "the most vain and insolent man in the world, full of folly and nothing to be esteemed." He failed as signally to win the golden opinion of the new regime in Scotland. The Hamilton who had been made Governor of the country during Mary Stuart's minority remarked that there would be no good rule in Liddesdale until the Earl of Bothwell should be shut up in a castle and some honest man put in charge of the Border stronghold of Hermitage in his place.

Imprisonment was the only treatment that had been found to cope with the Earl's disaffection, until the French mother of the infant Queen of Scots discovered a surer check. Might not her widowhood, asked the woman's wit of Mary of Lorraine, stir latent Hepburn tradition?

When Patrick had been home a year, "in return for certain great pleasures, grants and gratitudes done by the Queen Dowager, especially because her Grace had granted a yearly pension of one thousand pounds, money of Scotland," he bound himself by the truth and faith of his body, "to be her Grace's man and servant during her and his natural life." *Bond of Manrent by the Earl of Bothwell in Register House, Edinburgh, S.P. 38a.*

The engagement would be more convincing, if he had not made much the same promise a few months before to the King of England. But the Fair Earl had a business head. His ancestors might have been the lovers of widowed queens; they had not collected a yearly pension of a thousand pounds Scots.

The widow was not his dupe. At the age of twenty-five she was fighting to save her daughter and her daughter's inheritance from the greedy clutches of Henry VIII. If she could lure the Fair Earl with hopes of a royal marriage, she could count for the time on his dubious loyalty. Moreover, since the flutterings of one moth seem to attract his fellows to the candle, Patrick's courtship might provoke the jealousy of other unreliable, but susceptible, noblemen. So Cardinal Beton ("no less a statesman than a clergyman") was given the task of raising the hopes of Matthew, Earl of Lennox, owner of certain dangerous claims to the Stewart succession.

His whisper was not ignored. Patrick, that "lusty young gentleman, fair and pleasant in the sight of women," no longer had the field to himself. Both he and Lennox "daily pursued the court and the Queen Mother with bravery, dancing, singing and playing on instruments, arrayed every day in sundry habiliments and prided who should be most gallant in their clothing."

If the reader is reminded of the courtship of the domestic cock, Mary of Guise could afford a smile at a sartorial contest that kept two of her most powerful and treacherous subjects innocently occupied. Tongues at Court might wag. In Sadler's attentive ear, she expressed her pained surprise at "those bruits touching the contention and strife betwixt the Earls for her love. She was little beholden to the people of this nation that raised such tales." Sir Ralph pursed indignant lips, and a few weeks later spread his own scrap of scandal: "Only the 'old' Queen, the Cardinal and the Earl of Bothwell remain in the Castle of St. Andrews. Whereof the people speak largely enough, because in the late King's time he had her in some jealousy for overfamiliarity betwixt her and the Cardinal."

The Fair Earl looked the winner. In after years he used to assert that Mary of Lorraine promised to marry him and even that she fixed a date. To prove this claim *Bannatyne Misc iii. 414.* he professed himself willing "to debate with his body, that is to say a hundred men for a hundred men, or man for man, that the Queen's Grace promised faithfully by her handwrit, at two sundry times, to take him in marriage." To avoid any suspicion of sentimentality he

32

mentioned that he had been promised the Earldom of Orkney.

This "gallant young gentleman, high-minded and aspiring," did not mean to repeat his great-grandfather's mistake of attempting the favours of a royal widow under the handicap of a wife. In the autumn of 1543 the whole of Scotland was scandalised by the news that the Fair Earl had secured a divorce from the mother of his children. Consanguinity formed the pretext, and possibly consoling himself and Agnes with some truism about omelettes and eggs, he did the fair thing with the gift of the lands of Morham.

So, as the Lady of Morham, the Countess of Bothwell retired into the background and the Earl braced himself to receive the reward that generations of Hepburns had failed to achieve.

He was too late. While the Queen Mother was playing Bothwell against Lennox, she solved the harder problem of the Hamilton Governor of Scotland, whose vacillating authority held the key to the dangerous situation. That "good, soft God's man" had shown himself "the most inconstant man in the world, whatsoever he determineth to-day, he changeth to-morrow." In vain Henry VIII tried to buy his support with the promise of the crown of Scotland north of the Forth. "The unhappy man," says Knox, "quietly stole away from the Lords that were with him, subjected himself to the Cardinal, renounced the profession of Christ Jesus his Holy Evangel and violated the oath he had made for the observation of the league with England."

The Fair Earl enjoyed the privilege of holding the ceremonial towel over the Governor's head during the sacrament that celebrated his absolution. Next day he attended the coronation of the infant princess (performed, Sir Ralph sneered, "with such solemnity as they do use in this country, which is not very costly,") and witnessed the temporary rout of English intrigue.

He was also seeing, though he did not know it, the wreck of his aspirations. To no purpose he had sacrificed his time, his fortune and his marriage vows. His suit could now be safely dismissed. Poorer in purse and illusions, Patrick put a good face on his disappointment. "He lacked expenses," so he spread the report, "and passed home when he was tired of Court, and remained for a while till he saw further in the matter."

At home played a boy of nine deprived of the mother who was to cherish his memory to the end of her days. The fatal seed was sown in his receptive mind that a Hepburn had a right to mate royally.

The Queen Mother and the Cardinal relished their subtle policy without thought for the pawns swept off the table, but on the other side of the board sat the bloated figure of the ageing Tudor. His move was true to type, sudden and ferocious.

Hamilton Papers ii. 360.

"Put all to fire and sword!" he instructed his invading general. "Burn Edinburgh town, so rased and defaced when you have gotten what you can of it, as there may remain for ever a perpetual memory of the vengeance of God. Beat down and overthrow the Castle, sack Holyrood house and as many towns and villages as you may conveniently. Sack Leith, burn and subvert it, putting man, woman and child to fire and sword without exception, where any resistance shall be made unto you. Pass over into the Fife land and extend like extremities and destructions in all towns and villages, whereunto you may reach conveniently; not forgetting so to spoil and set upside down the Cardinal's town of St. Andrews, as the upper stone may be the nether and not one stick stand by another, sparing no creature alive . . ."

The appalling deeds that followed left their mark on the memory of young James Hepburn and go far to explain his unrelenting enmity to the country that perpetrated them. His father was less sensitive. Forgetting his vow to serve the Queen Mother, he only saw the wrong she had done him and plunged once more into correspondence with the enemy.

His private life offered his son no better example than his political career. A mile from his favourite seat of

34

Crichton stood the narrow keep of Borthwick. The absence of its lord on the service of his country gave Patrick occasion to provide some "pretie news." He had seen further in the matter of women and decided that there were as good fish in the sea. "Because the Lady Borthwick was fair," a neighbour reported, "the Earl Bothwell came to her for love." But Isobel Borthwick was no more facile than Mary of Lorraine. She lured him to a midnight tryst, "which hour he kept, and by Gavin Borthwick and others he was taken forth and had into the castle." There the hard-hearted *châtelaine* "made him to be handled and kept. And thus," concludes the gossip-writer whose eye for news was better than his spelling, "I comytt your good lordshipe to the tuycion of the Holly Ghoste." *Lord Eure and Lord Wharton to Lord Shrewsbury, Sept., 1544.*

It is not surprising if the Fair Earl's son learnt at Crichton the lax morality that arouses the indignation of historians, most modest of mankind. Another transaction that did the father little credit may have encouraged a more admirable side to James's character and inculcated that tolerance which distinguished his adult mind.

George Wishart, "a man of great knowledge, of pleasant utterance, humble, modest, charitable and patient," was perambulating the countryside, preaching the reformation of religion. On the 15th January, 1545, in a hard frost, he came to Haddington, and found his congregation "so slender that many wondered. The cause was judged to be that the Earl Bothwell had given inhibition that they should not hear him."

The next night, with some foreboding, the preacher walked to the house of John Cockburn of Ormiston. There he supped, preached, prayed and sang the 51st Psalm,

> For Thou desirest not sacrifice,
> Else would I give it:
> Thou delightest not in burnt offering.

The gift of prophecy, with which the future martyr was credited, seems temporarily to have failed him. At midnight the Fair Earl ("made for money," said some, "butcher to the Cardinal," but more charitably because he was Sheriff of the county,) surrounded the sleeping household.

He woke the laird who stoutly refused to surrender a guest without guarantee for his safety. George Wishart faced the Sheriff with no fear in his honest, visionary eyes.

Spottiswood
78.

"My Lord," he said with dignity, "I praise God that so honourable a man doth receive me this night. For I am assured your Honour will not permit anything to be done unto me against the order of the law. I less fear to die openly than to be murdered in secret."

The Earl's glance shifted.

"I shall not only preserve your body from violence," he protested, "but I will promise upon my honour that neither the Governor nor the Cardinal shall be able to harm you. I shall keep you in my own power till either I make you free, or bring you back to the place, where now I receive you."

So he spoke, and "for fashion's sake" took him to his Castle of Hailes.

"As gold and women," moralises John Knox, "have corrupted all worldly and fleshly men from the beginning, so did they him. For the Cardinal gave him gold and that largely; and the Queen, with whom the said Earl was then in the glunders" (the Reformer's scandal was out of date), "promised him favour in all his lawful suits unto women, if he would deliver the said Mr. George. He made some resistance at first by reason of his promise, but an effeminate man cannot long withstand the assaults of a gracious queen, and so was the servant of God transported to Edinburgh."

At the capital the Earl appeared before the Privy Council and promised to keep the preacher safe. This time he kept his word, lowering his captive into the smaller and less sanitary of the two pit prisons that the castle still exhibits.

At the end of February, George Wishart stood his

36

trial at St. Andrews. A priest read the accusation of heresy, and "when this fat sow," says Knox elegantly, "had read through all his lying menaces, his face running with sweat and foaming at the mouth like a boar, he spat in Mr. George's face."

The result of the trial was in no doubt. Politics were at issue, no less than dogma. On the last morning of his life the condemned man was invited to breakfast by the Captain of the Castle of St. Andrews. For half an hour Mr. George exhorted the company to lay aside rancour, envy and vengeance. Then he blessed the bread and wine and gave to every man. The meal finished, he took his leave, saying with a smile that they would drink together no more.

Two executioners were waiting with a coat of black linen and some bags of gunpowder. The bags they tied under the martyr's armpits, buckling the coat with straps. A great post had been planted in the east court of the Castle. By it, for fear of a rescue, stood men in armour and gunners with their artillery. Overhead, the windows were hung with tapestry and spread with velvet cushions for the Cardinal's and the prelates' ease.

Their victim was talking to the kindly captain, taking the air, which smelt sweet after the weeks of dungeon, and looking about him, seeing the country for the last time. Trumpets blew and Mr. George was tied with chains to the post. As the fire was lit, his lips moved in prayer. The captain, "for the love he bore him," came as near the flames as the heat would allow and wished him to be of good courage. Burnt from the waist down, Wishart looked to where Beton sat and is said to have prophesied: "He who in such state feedeth his eyes on my torments, within a few days shall be hanged out at the same window."

The prophecy was fulfilled. Perhaps the martyr's kinsman, Sir John Wishart of Pitarro, one of the conspirators against the Cardinal, had been indiscreet. Within three months Beton was assassinated "to please God, for Christian zeal and for a small sum of money."[1] His body was exhibited on the battlements by his murderers, before being salted and buried in a dung heap.

It is easy to imagine the effect which accounts of eyewitnesses would have on James Hepburn's impressionable years. The boy may well have imbibed his protestantism from the martyr's sermons in villages near his home; his principles bore rather the stamp of Mr. George's moderation than of John Knox's violence. His teacher's cruel death may have taught him hatred of persecution.

Before the end of the year the English had again crossed the Border. Their Scottish sympathisers were suspect and in spite of the Earl's patriotic assurances, a sentence of exile was followed by imprisonment. A bitter moment came when Isobel Borthwick's husband was given the keeping of Hailes—too late, as it proved,

Official Guide to Hailes Castle. J. S. Richardson.

to preserve it from English occupation. The Southerners' compliments on the "excellent beauty within," and their favourable comparison with the castles of their own country offered little compensation.

He relieved the tedium of imprisonment by brooding over the opportunities of the unmarried state. No sooner had the Scottish defeat at Pinkie given him his liberty, than he hastened to put his dreams to the test. A girl princess, he had decided, was better than a widow queen. His nephew carried an ingenuous proposal to the English

Warwick to Somerset 30 Sept., 1547.

general, who passed it on to the Protector Somerset: "If your Grace would help him to wive in England, he would deliver the Hermitage. He names the wife of the late Duke of Suffolk,[2] but the other two he was loath to name. I saw he meant my Lady Mary or my Lady Elizabeth. He asked for your Grace's safe conduct to see them and return, as though, if he liked them, they would not mislike him." In the unprofitable game of imagining the might-have-beens of history, no more

[1] For this murder the Master of Rothes drew £250 and Kirkcaldy of Grange £200. (Keith 60) This is appreciably higher than current prices in America, but rates might be raised for a Cardinal. On the question of Wishart's complicity, see Keith 43, Burton iii. 258, Karl Pearson 4.n., 10.n.

[2] Lady Jane Grey's mother.

agreeable vision can be summoned than the Virgin Queen the reluctant stepmother of James, Earl of Bothwell. But Patrick's proposal met a cool reception. He spent a morose winter at liberty in Edinburgh.

A fresh turn of the political wheel soon made continued residence unsafe. The Scots, harassed beyond endurance, threw themselves unreservedly into the arms of France. Six thousand "as good men of war as may be counted in Christendom" landed at Leith and forced "the facile Earl" to find his disconsolate way to London.

About this time he published Mary of Lorraine's promise of marriage. The only answer to that piece of bravado was a summons of treason "having respect to the great and high attemptates committed and done by Patrick Earl Bothwell and how he had him toward our Sovereign lady."

Patrick answered with the last shot in his locker. In the late summer he formally renounced allegiance to the crown of Scotland and became the pensioner of England against an advance of 3000 crowns. The motive of his retort may have been less pique than debt, which now weighed heavy. A poor relation, a cleric and a Hepburn, offered a less drastic solution. "What profit or fruit," he wrote with irritating justice, "has followed through your labours to your lordship or your house to this hour, your own wisdom may consider. God has done well with you in sundry sorts. None the less, an your Lordship had all the wit of Solomon, together with as great substance and yearly importance as ever had Scottish man, without you have . . ." (*here the pious conclusion that the writer's cloth demands is disappointed*) "without you have one man that you may give trust to, there can nothing go right." That paragon, the parson of Dalry suggested, was himself, available in exchange for a loan of £100.

Five more dreary years passed in exile. At last, in the spring of 1554, Mary of Lorraine took over the regency. She felt a kindness for her old suitor or a qualm over his treatment. Word of "a very foul and unfriendly pact" was carried to the English by a servant of Patrick's, Sandy Pringle, whose son, Dandie, will be seen continuing his family tradition of espionage into the time of the next Earl.

With the Queen Regent ready to forgive the past, nothing prevented the Fair Earl's return. But people had noticed that since the burning of Wishart, Patrick's luck was out. As they said, "he went backward in his affairs." Hardly was he in Edinburgh when an Englishman, "in thiftuous manner, under silence of night, with certain feigned keys, came to his lodging by moyance of a Scottish boy, and broke his coffers, stealing divers stands of precious clothing and ornaments of his person with buttons, horns of gold and other jewels to the value of 10,000 marks, Scottish money." Apart from the sentimental importance of these relics of the famous courtship, Patrick could not afford the loss; a few months later his creditors in England distrained on the goods that he had left behind.

P.C. Reg. XIV, 145.

Q. Mary of England to the Queen Regent, 16 Feb., 1555.

And now, by life's irony, as his sands were running out, his fortunes began to improve. He owed the change to the Queen Regent's philosophy: "I pass over," she could say, "as gently as I can, preventing things from getting worse, waiting for a better time, and until I see what it may please God to appoint." Willing to try poacher as gamekeeper, she made Patrick Lieutenant of her Border.

Through all his vicissitudes, the Fair Earl kept his sense of humour. "Your Grace," he wrote to Mary from his castle of Crichton, "touches me some part sharp remembering me upon my honour and promise made to your Grace. Madame, I trust surely that your Grace well knows that I have more regard to my honour than to all earthly riches or lands and shall faithfully serve your Grace unto the end of my life. . . ."

He spoke truer than he knew. His time was too short to give scope even to so accomplished a turncoat. On the 24th of July, 1556, he led a Franco-Scottish raid and drove a booty of cattle, sheep and horses. Next day he cele-

Ridpath 584, Teulet i. 269.

brated his success by the betrothal of his daughter Janet to Robert Lauder of the Bass. The exertions of the raid had been too much for the Fair Earl's constitution. Those stooping shoulders and red and white complexion hint at a tuberculous tendency encouraged by captivity and exile. In September he lay at Dumfries mortally ill. Janet's engagement was broken off, officially because her fiancé did not fulfil his obligations, conjecturally because her father's illness allowed her to exercise her choice. *Bannatyne Misc. iii. 306. Grote's Protocols 73.*

At the age of forty-four, Patrick, third Earl of Bothwell, lay on his deathbed, looking back on an eventful life with feelings that it is impossible to gauge. Three terms of prison and four periods of exile had led him as far afield as London and Venice . . . marriage, love, divorce . . . allegiance sworn indifferently to the monarchs of two warring countries . . . moreover—and the memory may have eased his last moments—he had offered himself as husband to a widow Queen and to two Royal Princesses.

CHAPTER FOUR

THE year in which James Hepburn succeeded his father was marked (if "that grave and reverend prelate and wise councillor" Bishop Spottiswood may be believed) by several noteworthy portents. A comet of the kind the vulgar call a fiery besom, whales of huge greatness, hailstones the bigness of a dove's egg, and a dragon, flying low and vomiting fire, clearly presaged some event of note. Subsequent opinion held that it was not the succession of the young Earl but the imminent alteration in his country's religion that provoked these unnatural phenomena.

Most people agreed that changes were overdue. It was six years since a convention had met in Edinburgh and required churchmen "to put away their concubines; to dismiss from their houses their children born in concubinage; not to promote such children to benefices nor to enrich them from the patrimony of the Church." At the same assembly prelates were implored not to keep in their households "manifest drunkards, gamblers, whoremongers, brawlers, night-walkers, buffoons, blasphemers and profane swearers." Results were disappointing. A few years later the Dean and Chapter of Aberdeen had to ask their Bishop to "cause the churchmen to reform themselves and to remove their open concubines, as well great as small." They even made bold to suggest "that his Lordship would be so good as to show good and edificative example, in special in removing and discharging himself of the company of the gentlewoman by whom he is greatly slandered."

The Bishop of Aberdeen was not exceptional. The private life of Bothwell's great-uncle, Patrick, was little more severe. Contemporaries, who crossed their t's, called him "the Bishop of Moray, who was a whore-

Herkless and Hannay iv. 52.

42

monger all his days." John Knox describes him as "a true servant of the king of love," and relates, "such a merry jest," at his expense. "He asked," it appears, "after supper of his gentleman, that they should truly declare how many sundry women every one of them had had and how many were men's wives. One answered that he had lain with five and that two of them were married. The other answered: 'I have had seven and three were married.' It came at last to my Lord himself, who making it very nice for a little space, gave in the end a plain confession and said: 'I am the youngest man, and yet I have had the round dozen and seven of them were men's wives.'"

There is documentary proof that the Bishop was not boasting. It was his genial practice to legitimise in batches large numbers of his children by different mothers. The only difficulty he found was to think of names. Thus John and Patrick got their papers in 1533, Adam, Patrick, George, John and another Patrick in 1545, Janet and Agnes in 1550, while the position of a final Agnes was regularised after her father's death. It is perhaps worth mentioning that the motto of this prolific dignitary was *Expecto*.

At Bishop Patrick's palace of Spynie, near Elgin, James Hepburn received some part of his education. In 1575 an elderly priest deposed that he knew him there twenty years earlier or more. This statement gives much needed confirmation to Dr. Thomas Wilson's story of Bothwell's upbringing in the Bishop's "most wicked, corrupt house, in drunkenness and whoredom, among most vile ministers of dissolute misorder." After careful allowance for political prejudice, it must be granted that for a young man who had inherited something of his grandmother's and his father's temperaments, Spynie was an unfortunate choice.

France, too, offered her system of education. It was usual for young Scots nobles to visit the capital of their traditional ally to acquire the culture that French Court or University could impart, and there is evidence that

Evidence of Action of Divorce of Queen Mary against Bothwell, 22 Sept., 1575.

Bothwell followed the fashion. His so-called Testament alludes to actions during "his youth in Paris," and a Frenchman refers (unflatteringly) to "his time at the schools." A letter of Mary Stuart's, which Bothwell certainly saw, mentions "his first entrance to this realm immediately after the death of his father" and implies a youth spent in foreign parts. Spynie and Paris may reconcile their educational claims if it is supposed that, after James had learnt what the Bishop had to teach, he went abroad to finish his education, returning at his father's death to make his first adult appearance in Scotland.

Fenelon to Charles IX. 29 March, 1568.

Queen Mary to the Bishop of Dunblane, 15 May, 1567.

As a boy, his schooling had to be picked up wherever his father's distracted perambulations allowed. The letters of a young contemporary show that boyhood held the same joys and sorrows for the sixteenth century as for the twentieth.

"Most loving Mother"—wrote little Patrick Waus—"After my hearty commendations ye shall wit that I am in good health, praised be God, wishing the same to you. Ye shall wit that I am very scant of linen cloth of shirts and neckcloths. I have written very oft to you about them and you have never sent me an answer. Naught else but commits you to God and my most hearty commendations to yourself and my sister." The boy's accounts follow. He had bought an Ovid and four pairs of shoes, a bow ("which the tutor's son broke") and a New Testament, three pairs of blue hose, "the commenteris of Ceser," Sallust, half a dozen arrows and a "sam buk" (psalm book). These purchases were covered by a remittance that a letter to his "loving Father" acknowledges: "ye shall wit that I have received your letter and I am very sorrowful that you have been held in such a state, and ye shall wit that I have received thirty shillings from the bearer." From this analogy the reader "shall wit" as much as is likely to be known of the boyhood of James Hepburn.

One thing is sure. His standard of learning was not low for a man of action in Scotland of that date. To this the well-kept remains of his library bear witness. Handsomely bound in calf and tooled with the Hepburn rose and lions is his copy of "The Arithmetic and Geometry of Master Stephen de la Roche."

The charges of necromancy and magic that were brought against him suggest a possible interest in natural science, as it was then misunderstood. For the practice of witchcraft ranged from chemical experiment and the discovery of logarithms to overlooking a cow or raising the devil.

Other less equivocal studies that he favoured were military history and theory, which he read in French translations from the Latin. Robert Valturin on *Military Discipline*, Flavius Vegetius on *Martial Exploits and Chivalry*, Sextus Julius on *Stratagems and Subtleties of War*, Aelian on *The Order of Battle*, a collection of *One hundred and twenty Stories of Battle*—these were his delight and from these in later years he was able to quote.

Besides reading French, he spoke it and wrote it easily in a clear Italian hand of considerable beauty, at a date when some of his noble contemporaries were illiterate or scrawled a barbarous gothic character. For all the years he spent out of the country, his Scottish speech, possibly from pride of race, remained broad.[1]

So much had education done for James Hepburn by the autumn of 1556, when at the age of twenty-one he succeeded to the Earldom of Bothwell. He inherited with it the offices and duties of Sheriff of Berwick, Haddington and Edinburgh; of Bailie in Lauderdale with the castles of Hailes and Crichton; of Lord High Admiral of Scotland. He bore the arms of his Earldom: quarterly, 1st and 4th a bend azure, 2nd and 3rd gules on a chevron argent two lions pulling at a rose of the first, with two lions guardant as supporters. His crest was a horse's head and neck bridled; his motto, which during all his life he observed, was *Keip Trest*—Keep Faith.

His lands and rents he found diminished. To meet creditors, the Fair Earl had sold broad acres to various bearers of his name. The Hepburns of Wauchton and of Whitsome in particular had profited by his extravagance.

Estimate of the Scottish Nobility by Alex. Hay (Grampian Club).

[1] "His rude utterance." (Dr. Thomas Wilson in the Actio.)

Acts and
Decreets xiv.
282, 395 xv. 88.
A slice had gone to Cuthbert Ramsay, the stalwart who
had espoused the charms and claims of James's grandmother, Agnes, senior to her husband by a third of a
century.

On succeeding, James Hepburn's first care was to
save what he could out of the wreck. Within a few months
his much-married grandmother followed her son to the
family vault. James, with a keener eye to business than
to the old lady's good name, claimed that she had been
born and had died a bastard and so secured the escheat
of her goods, movable and immovable. Cuthbert Ramsay,
angrily brandishing the letters of legitimation which
shortly after marriage he had induced the departed to
procure, brought an action to recover a property he may
be thought to have earned.

Bothwell's lawyer had tasted blood. His next victim
was Patrick Hepburn of Bolton, the new Earl's great-
uncle and his heir. The venerable laird unwisely obliged
his nephew to sign a bond confirming the liabilities
he had inherited. The lawyers knew an effective retort.
By entailing the earldom on his "chosen cousin," William
Hepburn of Gilmerton, and reserving for himself a life-
rent, Bothwell could disinherit his great-uncle. It is
true that he ascribed the arrangement to "the singular
favour and regard" he had for William. That cadet of
the Wauchton branch had recently been "in trouble"
and driven to seek refuge in England. The two young
men may have met during the Fair Earl's last period of
exile and have found tastes in common. Indeed James
called his only recorded illegitimate son by the name of
his "chosen cousin." But dislike for the great-uncle as
well as affection for the cousin must have dictated
an entail in which the names of four alternative Hepburns
precede the laird of Bolton's.

Soon even family bickerings were forgotten in the
controversy that, slow to reach Scotland, had already
split Europe into fratricidal parties. Within a year of his
succession Bothwell was called to play his part in the
great political-religious drama of the Reformation.

Register
House,
II. 420 b.

Buchan
Hepburn
Charter chest
25 Mar., 1558.

Patrick
Hepburn of
Wauchton's
will. 30 Aug.,
1547.

CHAPTER FIVE

"Calvin in his chamber five years taught a nun
  Till she was great with gospel and swollen with a son,"

sang Peter Fraxin of Antwerp. His rhyme might be
an unwitting allegory of the Reformation in Scotland.
During patient years the secret seed of Geneva was
sown in the minds of the populace and the lower ranks
of clergy. Sermons were preached on farms, ballads were
hummed by labourers, broadsides passed from work-
hardened hand to hand decrying the wealth, luxury and
immorality of the Roman Catholic Church. The preachers, *de Gouda to*
says a papal envoy, were apostate monks, tailors, shoe- *the Father*
makers, tanners. "They raged against the Pope, con- *General, 30*
firmed in their errors the poor who had lost the faith, *Sept., 1562.*
seduced even priests." In the latter task they would
find help from numerous clerical concubines, naturally
anxious to regularise their positions by a change to a
non-celibate ministry.

The presence in the country of the Queen Regent's
French allies, papists to a man, added fuel to the fire.
Key positions had been given to French officials, castles
garrisoned by French men-at-arms, and the nobility
and gentry of Scotland began to debate whether a cause
which the common people had discovered might not
serve the interests of aristocracy. Suppose no post of
importance were allowed to a Frenchman and no worldly
wealth to a Churchman? There would be perquisites
for a necessitous nobility. Almost half the revenue of *Pollen 528.*
Scotland used to fill the pockets of the Church; the
example of England showed how profitably and how
easily it could be diverted.

So at the end of 1557 the Band of the Congregation
of the Lord came into being, whereby certain earls and

47

lairds, with Lord James Stewart and the Earls of Glencairn and Argyll at their head, entered into a Covenant to support the new religion and to oppose the established authority. "Perceiving," they put it, "how Satan in his members, the anti-christs of the time, cruelly do rage, seeking to overthrow the Gospel of Christ and his Congregation," they promised, "before the Majesty of God to maintain the most blessed word of God and his congregation against Satan and all wicked power that doth intend tyranny or trouble."

Bothwell's opinion of the movement, expressed in after years, hit the mark. The Lords, he considered, grew impatient of the obedience they owed their ruler and, anxious to seduce the common people, began a secret agitation. The more easily to rouse their dupes, they used the pretext of religion.

Bothwell's estimate was shrewd, and it was confirmed by the King of France. For when the Queen Regent sought aid in her emergency, Henry II. sent this message: "If it be only religion that moves them, we must commit Scotsmen's souls unto God, for we have enough ado to rule the consciences of our own countrymen. It is the obedience due unto their lawful queen with their bodies that the King desires."

Mary of Lorraine could count on little obedience from her nobles. In March she had summoned to Stirling the few she thought she could trust—Huntly, Argyll and the new Earl of Bothwell. They had grumbled a little at the power of the French, but agreed to confirm her regency and fixed a date for the next meeting of Parliament, when a commission was to be appointed to attend the betrothal of the fifteen-year old Queen of Scots to the boy Dauphin of France. Young Bothwell was present at the session and helped to vote the money the commissioners needed. The youth, the Queen Regent felt, was loyal—but she trusted Argyll, and Argyll's name appeared on the Band of the Congregation. Troubles never come singly; the war was dragging on with England, and the French men-at-arms, whose loyalty could be trusted,

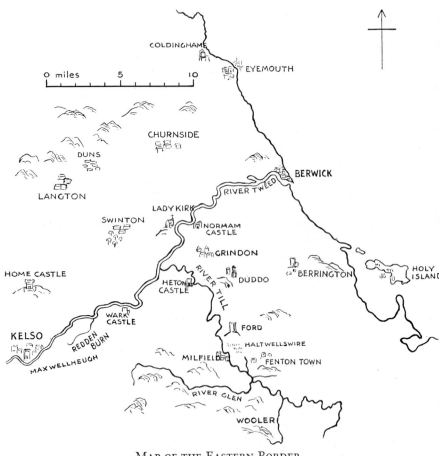

MAP OF THE EASTERN BORDER,
ILLUSTRATING THE LANGTON AND TILL RIVER RAIDS

"were not so cunning in managing Border war, which Sir James Balfour's Annals. 1558. made them oft get well-paid skins." As regular soldiers they enjoyed full-dress battles and sieges and felt lost in a guerrilla war of foray and raid. Border objectives were always points within enemy bounds, where there was property to spoil and not many people to fight. A forced ride under cover of darkness, an hour of burning and plundering with the minimum of killing, and a gallop back to safety, driving sheep and cattle— such was the unfailing routine. With its rules and conventions, Border warfare was almost the prototype of an international sporting fixture to-day.

Shortly after Bothwell's entry into public life, a raid was staged which seems to have had a notable effect on the young man's fortunes.

The Earl of Northumberland "devised with his brother, Sir Henry Percy, to burn a town in the Merse, called Langton, because it was a place of harbour for the Scottish Lieutenant and because there was much corn there." A thousand foot and five hundred horse Mackenzie's, Northumber-land. followed the Percy banner of the Lion and Luces, while the governor of Berwick provided another thousand infantry and a further hundred horse. Before it was light Sir Henry forded the Tweed and rode hard for Langton, ten miles over the Border. Langton with its corn bins went up in flames, and so did Duns hard by. The English troopers almost scored the triumph of capturing the Lieutenant of the Border. But just in time the Earl of Huntly, "heavy through age and asth-matic through corpulence," heaved himself on his horse and clattered out of the startled town.

The raid had achieved its object, and Percy signalled retreat. Collecting livestock took time; Home Castle and Kelso got warning by runner or beacon. Two thou-sand Scottish horse and three bands of foot hurried across country to cut the line of retreat. The straggling herds of cows and sheep slowed the invaders' pace. At dawn the Scots caught the rear guard at Swinton. Footmen with "pikis stark and lang of vi ells of length," and "swords all

L.B. 49 D

notably broad and thin, of exceedingly good temper and universally so made to slice," closed with the English infantry, whose strength lay in "hagbutteris furnished with powdir, flask, morsinghornis and all other geir belonging thairto."

The English had forgotten the mists of early morning. Their gunpowder was damp; their hagbuts missed fire. Hearing the shouting, Percy wheeled his retiring horse and dismounted to meet the pikemen. The fight was bloody by Border standards. One hundred Scots were killed and four times as many wounded. Among the Scottish wounded was a certain Captain Cullen, whose readiness to cut a throat in public or private found recognition in after years at Kirk o' Field. The English commander who reports the fight is silent on his own losses.

Where was Bothwell that day? Was it he who led the counter-attack at Swinton? Within a fortnight of the raid the Edinburgh authorities, remarking that their *Records of* city was "desolate of one superior of judgment, know-
Burgh of ledge and ability in the present appearance of wars and
Edinburgh, invasion of enemies," begged the Queen Regent to
9 May, 1558. appoint a nobleman "to have the cure and charge of the said town." The first name on the list was "my Lord Earl Bothwell."

Mary of Lorraine was impressed. In the early autumn she gave Bothwell the keeping of the castle of Hermitage. That lonely stronghold controlled Liddesdale and the restless families of Elliot and Armstrong; the keeper drew a monthly subsidy of twenty-three pounds. The Queen Regent felt she had found a natural Border leader.

Her French captains refused to be satisfied with this unprofessional way of fighting. Henri Clutin, commonly called the Sieur d'Oysel, wanted a properly conducted siege where all his art of war could be displayed.
Wm. Swynhoo Soon English spies reported his activity. "There came
to Lord yesterday to Home thirty score of cannon shot, carried
Shrewsbury, in creels on horseback, and eight puncheons of wine; as
Sept., 1557. I can learn, they intend to besiege Wark. There will be

a greater power than ever I saw of Scots together at one time."

To inspire the spirit of offensive, the Queen Regent moved to Home Castle, with its twenty-mile view of the Border. Troops, under the Duke of Chatelherault, late Governor of Scotland, concentrated at Maxwellheugh, across the Tweed from Kelso, and the French wasted no time bringing siege artillery over the river.

This display of energy did not suit a disloyal and petulant nobility. A delegation clanked to d'Oysel's tent. They were willing, they protested, to spend their lives in defence of their country, but any invasion of England or siege of Wark they refused to contemplate. It was irregular, they added, for the French General to start operations without orders from the Council of War.

D'Oysel exploded. He was known to be "choleric, hasty and too passionate" and the strictures of his allies left him, "not a little grieved, apprehending the majesty of his king to be somewhat touched in his person." But what was he to do? He had too few Frenchmen to start the "invasion" of England. The Scottish irregulars would not move without their feudal lords. Reluctantly he consented to abandon the offensive.

Mary of Lorraine shared his chagrin. Her adaptable mind grasped a remedy. What use was the obese Huntly, who had cut so lamentable a figure at Langton in the spring? Why not replace him by this youngster whose name was on every lip, who could fight and who knew what loyalty meant? Without his father's looks, he had inherited some of his charm. . . .

So it happened that, by the end of October, 1558, James Hepburn at the age of twenty-three was given the office of Lieutenant of the Border. His new post carried powers as great as could be enjoyed by a subject. He could ride upon disobedient persons, invade them with fire and sword, besiege and cast down houses held against him. He might direct letters in the sovereign's name and command assistance from neighbours under pain of death. *Accounts of the Lord High Treasurer, 29 Oct., 1558.*

He would have been less than human had he felt no

51

elation. Pride is betrayed in a letter that he prompted in later years: "Ye shall not omit his services," (Queen Mary's wifely pen dutifully traced the words,) "in the wars against England wherein he gave such proof of his valiance, courage and good counsel, notwithstanding he was then of very young age. Yet was he chosen out as most fit of the whole nobility to be our Lieutenant upon the Borders, having the whole charge as well to defend us as to assail. At which time he made many noble enterprises, not unknown to both the realms, by which he acquired a singular reputation in both."

Andrew Borde
(1547 A.D.)
Magniloquent perhaps, but Bothwell was a Borderer, with the virtues and defects of his kind. An English doctor who practised on the Border at this date does not impute modesty to his patients. "The people of the country," he said, "be hardy men and strong men, and well-favoured and good musicians. But of all nations they will face, crack and boost themselves, their friends and their country above reason."

Whether peace or war officially prevailed between the neighbouring countries, raids were at once the Borderer's means of livelihood, his substitute for modern *Fuller's*
Worthies 216. sport, and the cause of his misery. "They are like Job," remarked a critic, "not in patience and piety, but in sudden plenty and poverty; sometimes having flocks and herds in the morning, none at night, and perchance many again next day."

The laird lived in a stone peel tower that his enemies could not burn; his humbler neighbour in a hut that could quickly be rebuilt. He existed, the doctor records, "in much poverty and penury, having no houses but such as a man may build in three or four hours. He and his wife and horse stand all in one room."

The horse was an important member of the family— "a filthy thing they esteem it, and a very abject man they *Bishop*
Leslie;
de Origine. hold him, that goes upon his foot." To be well-mounted was essential for attack or escape. "Should they be forced out of their thickest woods, they betake them-

selves to rugged mountains. If they be driven from these, they fly to the banks of rivers and marshes," states a bishop.

Their pleasures, apart from raiding, were few. They drank no beer or wine, and subsisted on barley porridge, milk and meat, eating little bread. "They take great pleasure," certifies the bishop, "in their own music and in their rhythmical songs." An English captain speaks less kindly of this musical disposition and describes the nocturnal babel of their camps. "As we were then a-settling and the tents a-setting up, one thing *Patten. 75.* seemed to me an intolerable disorder, not unlike a masterless hound howling in a highway, some whooping, some whistling, and most with crying 'a Berwick! a Fenwick! a Bulmer!' as their captains' names were. It is a feat of war," opines the professional, "that might right well be left."

The Borderer liked his music, he needed "his nimble horse" and he wanted a few ornaments for his wife and himself. The ornaments, the same English captain complained after a disappointing experience in stripping the dead of Flodden, were not costly. "Their apparel so base and beggarly, the loon with the laird, all clad alike in jacks covered with white leather, doublets of the same or fustian, and most commonly all white hose. Not one with either chain, broach, ring or garment of silk, only chains of brass."

There was little outward sign of nationality. On raids crosses of St. Andrew or St. George were worn as a distinguishing mark, or rolled handkerchiefs and embroidered letters. Blood-feud, rather than race, bred feelings of hostility, and feuds were cherished as bitterly against fellow-countrymen as with the enemy. Where no vendetta existed, the Borderer was usually anxious to avoid bloodshed. "From shedding of blood," wrote the bishop, "they greatly abhor, believing that the goods of all men are by nature common, but that murder is prohibited by divine law."

So, for all the enduring state of war and the daily issues of death and destitution, there was little feeling of racial enmity. Raids had something of the nature of sporting fixtures, whose rules the opposite side was trusted to respect. What Froissart had written, still held good. "When they meet there is a hard fight without sparing. And when one party hath obtained the victory, they then glorify so in their deed of arms and are so joyful, that at their departing, courteously they will say 'God thank you!'"

This survival of chivalry is seen in the store the Borderer set on his promise. "Once having pledged their faith even to an enemy," wrote the bishop, "they are very strict in observing it;" while a less favourable critic admits that, "if they promise safely to conduct a traveller, they will perform it with the fidelity of a Turkish janizary." Such, indeed, was their respect for an oath that the innocence of criminals was sometimes established by the accused's asseveration. He was required to swear his guiltlessness by heaven above him, hell beneath him, his part of Paradise, by all that God made in six days and seven nights and by God himself.

In other ways religion meant little on the Marches. There was nothing to attract the visit of priest or preacher *Colville,* to lonely hillside or valley. "For lack of preaching and *Paranesis.* ministration of the sacraments" the inhabitants were in danger of becoming "either infidels or atheists." Sir Walter Scott has versified the moss-trooper's attitude to religion:

> "Prayer know I hardly one;
> For mass or prayer can I rarely tarry
> Save to patter an Ave Mary
> When I ride on a Border foray."

The Borderer had none of the interest in dogma of the Highland or Lowland Scot. Occasionally this indiffer- *Armstrong's* ence was carried to excess. A Liddesdale worthy, "Sym *Liddesdale* the Laird, that King James hangit," claimed to have *CXV.* "laid down" thirty parish churches in Scotland.[1]

[1] "Wanton Simmie Armstrong, officer of the law, part of Liddesdale," who was one of Bothwell's adherents, was a descendant of this *esprit fort.*

These peculiarities of the Border throw some light on the character and career of Bothwell. Indifference to dogma, cult of loyalty, distaste for bloodshed, recognition of feuds, faith in chivalry, reliance on force—all these marked his habit of mind. In themselves harmless or admirable traits, they account for his ill-success. He had the mischance to be born in a generation which, eager to discard an outmoded system of chivalry, threw overboard every rule of honourable conduct. Religion, was the excuse for bigotry, rapacity or political fraud; murder was the normal instrument of statecraft; cunning had replaced strength; and loyalty placed the loyalist at the mercy of the traitor. Hence qualities and principles which in some other centuries and countries might have earned an aura of fame, drew in his lifetime the limelight of failure and, after his death, kindled the phosphorescence of dishonour.

CHAPTER SIX

THE young Lieutenant lost no time. He explored means to co-ordinate the orthodoxy of France with the guerrilla genius of the Border. The finished scheme, designed to wipe out the memory of the Wark fiasco, had the merit of simplicity. He would lead a raid of Scottish irregulars to draw and contain all available enemy forces; meanwhile the French, keeping close to their base and employing their science of the siege, would take Norham Castle, outpost of the Percies.

Every detail was carefully worked out. Though Bothwell's successes were gained by exploiting an unexpected initiative, he did not despise a thorough preparation. As early as the 13th November, 1558, he began to collect forces for an operation timed for the last days of the year. The orders he issued for the concentration were intended to mislead: with local habits of intermarriage and fraternisation, he knew that plans were certain to leak out. He wanted the attack to be expected down the well-trodden route of Glendale, and he planted intelligence where it would reach Northumberland's ears.

The end of the year came with its merry-making. Bothwell had taken the season into account and its predictable effect on the movements of his opponent. The Earl of Northumberland went to his castle of Alnwick. This nobleman, who in later life earned the distinction of calling the Virgin Queen a bitch, enjoyed the character of an " affectionate and simple-minded man; a warm friend, a jovial and hospitable neighbour, a kind and generous master. Devoted to field sports and martial exercises, his nature was indolent and irresolute." Such a man would not let Christmas week[1] be spoilt by fear of Scots who had lately shown themselves indisposed to military action.

Any misgiving that crossed his mind was dismissed with the comfortable thought that Henry would look after everything. Sir Henry Percy shared Northumberland's reputation of a gallant soldier. If the younger brother's reserve and name for harshness made him less popular, his talents and judgment were universally respected. He had, moreover, a thousand horsemen under his orders in Wooler, a position chosen to repel any attack that might be made into Glendale.

On Wednesday after Christmas, at two in the morning, the jovial Earl was roused to puzzle an aching head over the message that a mud-caked horseman had brought. Trouble, Percy reported, might be anticipated in Glendale. With a curse, Northumberland pulled on his boots and shouted for every available man to follow him to Wooler.

Sir Henry's news had its foundation in fact. In the early December dusk, Bothwell had given his little body of eight hundred horse and as many foot the word to march. One of his rules was to employ the minimum force that would serve his needs. The rapier was his choice of weapons, not the battle-axe.

He rode at the head of his men. To their surprise he did not take the path leading to the ford that served the Glendale route into England. Ladykirk was his first objective and the ford hidden by an island from watchful eyes on Norham Tower.

A word to caution silence and the column breasted the stream. Each foot-soldier had a stirrup-leather to grip for help against the current that ran swift with the winter's rain. Once across, Bothwell led the way up the course of "the deep and sullen Till." Avoiding villages—

[1] Even in Lent the Percies kept a good table. At that season a previous Lord and Lady Northumberland had for their own supper (at which nine servants waited) "five manchetts (of bread), a bottle of beer, a bottle of wine. forty sprotts, two pieces of salt fish, a quarter of salt salmon, two sliced turbot, a dish of flounders, a turbot baken or a dish of fried smelts." Arnot, Hist. of Edinburgh 56.

Grindon, Duddo, Etal and Ford—he followed the valley for a dozen miles. Every man was wearing "a great kercher wrapped twice or thrice about his neck, not for cold but for cutting." Steel bonnets defended their heads, leather jacks their bodies. They carried long pikes, broadswords and bucklers; their leader, who believed in modern firearms, had ordered them to bring all the hagbuts and dags they could muster.

Presently the Till, which had been running turbulent between high banks, widened into swollen tranquillity. The jog-trot slackened. Bothwell was finding the position he had chosen on some secret reconnaissance. They reached Haltwellsweir,[1] a beech- and oak-clad slope, guarded on the flank by a swamp of sedge and willows. Sextus Julius, that specialist in stratagems and subtleties of war, could hardly have imagined a better site for an ambush.

While the Lieutenant was preparing his first important engagement, placing his infantry in the harsh bracken behind the leafless trees, he allowed a second warning to reach Wooler. It found Sir Henry ready to ride into Glendale. His frown deepened as he listened. The French were mustered on the Marches, intending to burn Norham.

Leaving urgent word for his brother to follow, Percy called out the last of the garrison and galloped to save his fortress from the French. His shortest route ran down the west bank of the Till to Heton, where was a ford by which he could cross and be quickly at Norham.

By now Bothwell's trap on the east bank of the river was set; it needed baiting. On the hill slope, southeast of Haltwellsweir, stood a couple of stacks where the villagers of Fenton Town had piled their wretched crops of hay. Thither, in the darkness, Bothwell had despatched a picked body of moss-troopers. As dawn

[1] Haltwellsweir has vanished from the largest map, but it is possible to identify the position of the ambush, interesting from the light it throws on Bothwell's methods. Lewis says it lay half a mile south of Broomridge, which Mackenzie places a mile south of Ford, where it is marked on early maps. Thus Haltwellsweir corresponds to the modern Kimmerston with its woods and bog. The meaning of "swyre" — "Watershed generally covered with bog" confirms this identification.

broke they saw Percy's horsemen cantering along the far bank of the Till. Blowing feverishly on the embers they carried, they thrust them into the hay.

Sir Henry was a quicker thinker than his brother, but the smoke and flame of destruction, not in Glendale or at Norham, but within striking distance of the depleted town of Wooler, puzzled and dismayed him. Attack seemed the only means of defence. He wheeled his company and cantered back to the crossing of the Till near Milfield.

He crossed the river within half a mile of the ambush. No sound came from the undergrowth.

The party by the blazing haystack had played their part. The flames revealed how small were their numbers. Obedient to orders, the decoys fell back on a second body of horse, stationed in the rear. Their flight lured Percy into incautious pursuit. Deliberately they led him past the swamp that screened the ambush.

As the English galloped by, Bothwell sprang the trap. He gave the word and every hagbut and dag was discharged. The noise echoed deafeningly in the little wood. Panic took the English. The horses, frightened by gunfire, bolted. The riders, confronted with an unknown and invisible enemy, raced madly north.

Bothwell halloed his moss-troopers in pursuit. His infantry he sent doubling along the river bank the shortest way to Ford. At no nearer point could the fugitives escape the encirclement of the Till.

> Tweed said to Till—
> What gars ye rin sae still?
> Till said to Tweed—
> Though ye rin wi' speed
> And I rin slaw,
> Where ye droon yin man, I droon twa.

Caught in the bend of the river between horse and foot, faced with death on the point of a pike or in the icy water, one hundred and twenty Englishmen sur-

59

rendered. The better-mounted, among whom Percy must be classed, reached Ford ahead of the footmen and escaped across the river. Bothwell followed their scattered flight, until he sighted a column riding hard from the south. It was Northumberland, with a hundred and thirty men from Alnwick and such reinforcement as he had been able to find in Wooler. Ignorant of their strength Bothwell called a halt. Collecting his stragglers, followed by a dejected group of prisoners, he led the way back to Scotland. Save for some dead horses and a few heaps that looked in the distance like untidy bundles of clothes or spilt sacks of corn, the fields were left to the occupation of melancholy curlews and screaming seagulls.

Of the French attack on Norham, nothing more is heard. Whether it failed, or whether lack of confidence in their Scottish allies caused its abandonment, is not on record. Bothwell had led a raid of classic proportions with plenty of prisoners, little bloodshed and notable moral effect. London, alarmed by the success of the new Lieutenant, promised to increase the manpower of the garrisons on the Border.

The reinforcements never came. The death of Mary Tudor dissolved the Anglo-Spanish combination that was waging war on France and Scotland, and the leaders of both nations lost no time opening negotiations. Sir Henry Percy met the Duke of Chatelherault at Norham and learnt that the Hamilton interest was ready for *State Papers* peace. Two days later he could add the assent of the *For. Ser.* Queen Regent and the French. The Laird of Grange, *1559/316.* ever *persona grata* with the English, paid a visit to discuss an armistice. Details had to be settled by the opposing leaders. If Northumberland would fix a day, Bothwell was ready to meet him.

A formal meeting of the recent opponents took place on the 23rd February, 1559. Captain Sarlebous represented the military might of France. Between the three a provisional armistice was arranged.

State Papers But the English were playing a double game. Already *For. Ser.* *24 May, 1559.* Percy had discussed with the Laird of Grange the attitude of the Queen of England towards the Lords of the Congregation. Under cover of armistice negotiations, the English promised the rebels a subsidy. Bothwell's talents lay in the field. Without inclination for intrigue, he had at first no suspicion of these perfidious manœuvres.

Peace, for what it was worth, was soon signed in the general Treaty of Cateau-Cambrésis, and the war between England, Scotland, France and Spain was officially ended. Tranquillity did not come lightly to the Borders. Early in April, Bothwell and Northumberland met again at Redden Burn. The Justice Clerk and the gentlemen borderers attended and with traditional ceremony a court was held to redress grievances that had arisen during the armistice period.

But the Justice Clerk fell ill, time was wasted and little had been accomplished when the meeting was postponed for a week.

Perhaps the delay was Bothwell's fault. His mind was not on Border routine. He had fallen violently in love with Janet Beton, whom tradition and Sir Walter Scott have made famous as the Wizard Lady of Branxholm.

CHAPTER SEVEN

THIS remarkable woman, first of several claimants to Bothwell's affections, was a niece of that Cardinal whose body had been hanged over the walls of St. Andrews to fulfil the prophecy of the martyred Wishart.

The family was catholic, of French extraction, in high favour at Court. Janet's younger sister, Margaret, was later selected as wet-nurse to the infant Prince James (who did little credit, judging by his youthful portraits, to her milk). Her lovely niece, Mary Beton, won fame in history and song as one of the Queen's Maries. Janet herself was a notable figure at the Courts of Mary of Lorraine and of her daughter, the Queen of Scots.

She was the daughter of John Beton, second Laird of Creich, from whom, (to draw from Sir Walter Scott's store of tradition) she inherited her interest in the occult:

> He learned the art, that none may name,
>   In Padua, far beyond the sea.
> Men said, he changed his mortal frame
>   By feats of magic mystery;
> For when in studious mood he paced
>   St. Andrews' cloistered hall,
> His form no darkening shadow traced
>   Upon the sunny wall.
> And of his skill, as bards avow,
>   He taught that lady fair,
> Till at her bidding she could bow
>   The viewless forms of air.

Two, possibly more valuable, secrets Janet's studies certainly discovered—the art of winning men's hearts and the magic of eternal youth. Four husbands and two recorded lovers did not exhaust her zest; patiently she entered the state of holy wedlock for a final experience at the age of sixty-one.

Her first legal husband died when she was not yet twenty-three; but she admitted that she had already taken another husband in the sight of God. Divorce released her next helpmate, Simon Preston of Craigmillar, a "man of very wicked life and no religion" whom Knox stigmatises as "a right Epicurean." So far she had borne two children, one to each marriage. *Liber Officialis Sanct. Andriae 86.*

Scot. Corre- spondence of Mary of Lorraine 370.

Her next venture was more prolific. The fruits of her union with Sir Walter Scott of Buccleugh were Walter and David, Grissel, Janet, Dorothea, and finally Margaret, the insipid ingenue of the "Lady of the Lake."

This married bliss came to an end in 1552, when Buccleugh met his hereditary enemies, the Kerrs, on the High Street of Edinburgh. They left him still breathing, in a merchant's booth, to be finished off by the daggers of their servants.

The guilty family, referring euphemistically to "the unhappy chance which happened to us in the sudden slaughter of the Laird of Buccleugh," implored the Regent's forgiveness. But justice was not to be baulked and the greater folk implicated were banished. The small fry complained of the punishment that overtook them— "We have no manner of thing to live upon, unless we steal to sustain us. Our wives and bairns dare not resort to friends, but lie in woods and fells." *Privy Council Register i. 133.*

Official retribution did not satisfy the widow. If her poetic descendant may be believed:

> O'er her warrior's bloody bier
> The lady dropped no flower or tear;
> Vengeance deep-brooding o'er the slain
> Had locked the source of softer woe.

At the head of two hundred of the surname of Scott she rode to the Kirk of the Lowes in Yarrow. There, she had learnt, the Laird of Cranstoun, a Kerr supporter, claimed sanctuary. (The Cranstoun crest was a crane dormant, with a motto that would grace a banker—"Thou shalt want ere I want.") The Laird had supplemented the right of sanctuary by barring and bolting the church door. The Lady of Branxholm took an axe and forced an entry to tear her victim from the altar.

Such was the character and record of the matron who, at the age of forty-three, mother of seven children, became the object of Bothwell's unchaste affections.

It is never easy to explain the heart's selections. Bothwell was twenty-four, head of the most important family on the Border; the most fortunate soldier in the country; holder of the highest office a subject could attain; his glance, it might be supposed, could flutter the feminine dovecots of Scotland. The success of Janet's mature appeal was attributed by the easy supernaturalism of her day to magic. If the young Earl really shared her interest in the subjects that dangerous word embraced,

> Her bower that was guarded by word and by spell
> Deadly to hear and deadly to tell,

may have stood open to the sympathetic amateur. It is more likely that a common bond was the enmity which a Hepburn shared against the Kerrs of Cessford.

Janet had been very beautiful, with the beauty of bone that defies time; she possessed a spirit independent of the years. The young Borderer had some quality of imagination which reached past tired eyes and fading colours. In the woman's maturity, this "glorious, rash and hazardous young man" found a sympathy that a girl of his own age could not give. From her high spirit he drew inspiration for his boldest moods, and in her unhackneyed intellect he discovered a challenge to his doubts.

The affair was too passionate to be kept secret. In April, 1559, a situation arose that a writer of farce might have created. Janet was cited to appear in a law-case which James, sheriff of her county, had to judge. No wonder if they laughed together over the new relationship. The joke evaporated when the plaintiff appeared in court. Judge and defendant, he alleged, had been "quietly married or handfast." Pressed to explain, he muttered darkly of "other causes of suspicion between them as is notoriously known." The hum of amused or disapproving comment can be imagined. In the silence that followed, the plaintiff protested against the sheriff's competence to judge the case. *Register of Acts and Decreets XIX. 346.*

The Session admitted the plea and a substitute was found for the impressionable sheriff.

That is all the evidence that Janet and James were quietly married, or handfast. Handfasting was a binding form of betrothal, where cohabitation took the place of a ceremony. The custom was recognised on the Border at least until the beginning of the eighteenth century. "In the upper part of Eskdale," relates a traveller of that date, "was held an annual fair, where multitudes of each sex repaired. The unmarried looked out for mates, made their engagements by joining hands, went off in pairs and cohabited till the next annual return of the fair, when, if each party remained constant, the handfasting was renewed for life. But if either party dissented, the engagement was void with the proviso that the inconstant was to take charge of the offspring." An echo of the custom lingers in the caution of *A Winter's Tale*— "If that shepherd be not in handfast, let him fly."

Guesses at the dawn of the custom are easy. A Scandinavian source is hinted by the Swedish word "handfaestinng"; and the practice was common in parts of Scotland most open to Viking invasion. An alternative origin might be found in the ancient Roman rite of marriage *ex usu*, by which a woman, who by consent of her parents lived with a man for a year without missing three nights, became his wife. The Roman Catholic church might tolerate the relics of this custom to supplement the rare visits of her priests to remote valleys. Recently America has revived handfasting with "companionate marriage." In judging Janet and James, we may remember that other usages than those of Anglican Church or Registry Office have prevailed in civilised countries.

Inequality in age condemned the romance to brief endurance, but its ending brought no unkindness. The couple stayed on friendly and generous terms. Janet, catalogued as Bothwell's "old friend and lover," was the first to be told of his next, disastrous amour. A year or two later, James, no longer the Queen's victorious Lieutenant, but her escaped prisoner, took refuge at the Hermitage. Then Janet hastened to show practical sympathy with gifts of "great victual for his house." There was nothing ugly in a love affair that could end so gracefully.

State Papers For. Ser. 31 May, 5 June, 1559.

The spring and summer that smiled on their romance were distracted by peace talks, as hollow and ineffective as any pacificism of twentieth century Geneva. Two commissions were in session. The first, in which Bothwell took no part, negotiated certain undecided aspects of the general peace of Cateau-Cambrésis. On the last day of May terms were signed at Ladykirk in the little grey stone church which a king of Scotland had dedicated to the Most Blessed Virgin of Upsettlington, in thankfulness for deliverance from the Tweed in sudden flood.

The same day saw a meeting of the Wardens of the Marches. Bothwell headed the Scottish side and did not treat the agenda—settlement of Border disputes, release of prisoners and establishment of peace on the Borders—with high seriousness. Had he begun to suspect the insincerity of the English? A certain levity is unmistakable. The English wanted to confer on the boulders in midstream; the Scots made them send their messengers to and fro so often that they were forced to cross to Scottish soil; "my Lord of Durham and all ancient Borderers thought they did us much wrong." The Bothwell technique may be detected and a malicious pleasure in baiting an elderly bishop.

Tempers did not improve and the irascible Sir Henry Percy complained to the Queen Regent that her officers went back on their promises. He asked for some "wise and discreet gentleman" to accompany the Scots at the next meeting. Mary of Lorraine replied that Bothwell and Home told a very different story. With little good feeling the next meeting (with an escort of forty horses on either side) was fixed.

Before the day important news reached Scotland. An accident at a Paris tournament had carried Mary Stuart to the throne of France. The young Lieutenant's formal appointment as Scottish delegate was confirmed by Francis the Second and Mary his Queen. "The probity, industry and loyalty of our chosen cousin" was favourably mentioned. An alteration, however, in the personnel of the commission suggests that the Secretary, William Maitland of Lethington ("by whom the weightiest affairs of Scotland be, in a manner, directed," and who tirelessly directed them with an Anglophile bias), had been busy. His father, Sir Richard Maitland, replaced the anti-English Lord Home, and added his support to Bothwell's hereditary enemy, Walter Kerr of Cessford, Warden of the Middle Marches.

Two letters that Bothwell wrote on the business of this commission may be quoted:—

"To the Earl of Northumberland and his colleagues, after our hearty commendations. Whereas it has pleased the Queen's Grace to give commission unto us to meet with you, as has been thought necessary for the entertainment of the peace as well by the Queen's Majesty your sovereign as the Queen's Highness our mistress, this present shall be to give you advertisement that we shall be ready to meet you at Our Lady Kirk the fifth day of September next to come, desiring you to send us warning with this bearer if you will keep tryste that day. At which time, God willing, you shall well perceive in us a good inclination to justice and combination of amity between the realms. Thus we commit you to the protection of God. Your loving friend in lawful manner."

The date suggested by Bothwell did not suit the English. They needed time for Sir Ralph Sadler's exer- *Teulet i. 345.*

67

tions to produce results. At the last minute the little knight with the pointed beard had been given a place on the commission, where his unrivalled talent for intrigue and corruption was finding scope. But even a *virtuoso* needed time to approach noblemen whose disloyalty was uncertain. So Bothwell had to write again. A gentle irony informs his letter:—

"We have received your writings making mention that you might not keep the first day appointed for certain causes contained in your last letter, which answer we accept in good part, howbeit we are somepart disappointed of our first meeting. Nevertheless we shall, God willing, meet you at Our Lady Kirk upon Monday next, the eleventh, at ten hours before noon or thereby, and there shall join with you in all matters conform to our commissions to the rest and quietness of both the realms and lieges thereof."

State Papers For. Ser. 1559/1123.
By now Bothwell knew what was going on. He had been the bearer of a message from the Queen Regent to Percy. She had felt safe in treating Borderers of either nation like gentlemen and she expressed her surprise that Sir Henry was in touch with her rebels. She took the chance to let the English know that her spies were not inactive and showed she knew of a secret mission of the rebels to Berwick.

After the delegates had passed the low nail-studded door of the church at Ladykirk and taken their seats under the vaulted ceiling, their work was short. On the 22nd September articles were agreed. Did any shadow of the future darken James Hepburn's mind as he put his signature to the last clause?

"It is complained that there are divers prisoners in either realm, some put in irons and fetters or cast into horrible pits or wild places against the order of charity among Christian men. Wherefore they agree that all prisoners shall be honestly treated in time coming."

SIR WILLIAM CECIL
(*By permission of the National Portrait Gallery*)

CHAPTER EIGHT

GREAT personages begin to crowd the story, three of the most famous in the history of Britain—Elizabeth, Cecil, Knox. Across their path with his broadsword and his motto of loyalty stands, like the giant-killer of a fairy story, the stubborn figure of Bothwell.

Elizabeth had recently come to the throne amid the shouts of her people. She was twenty-seven years old. Her face, the Venetian ambassador said, could be called pleasing rather than beautiful. She was tall and her figure good. Her complexion was sallow. She had fine eyes and beautiful hands, which she took care not to conceal. She had not yet fully developed that blend of ferocity, parsimony and indecision which by one of the paradoxes of history made her the greatest queen that England has known.

Her Scottish policy was settled from the start. An acute contemporary has summarised it : "Elizabeth began to secure her kingdom and her religion on so sure a foundation, she may claim to have effected more than all her royal predecessors. Her principal success was gained in the division of the French from the Scots. The power of a prince lies less in his might than in the weakness and ruin of his neighbours." *Castelnau (in Jebb ii. 452).*

In this melancholy theory Elizabeth had the able co-operation of Sir William Cecil. The person of that statesman "was always agreeable, although he was not remarkably tall nor eminently handsome; and became more so as he grew in years, when he preserved a fine and florid complexion." The little man (he noted down that he weighed nine stone five in his jacket) was a sincere protestant. "Prayers were read morning and evening at his house and he never failed to take rigid

account of such as neglected this important observance."
As practical in politics as in religion, "he often made use
of dissimulation, seldom of deceit; for he knew how to
conceal without counterfeiting the truth." He had
mastered the art of life until he could "preserve both
his interest and his conscience." Devotion to his country's
service raised a tireless energy and an unsurpassed attention to detail to a high level of statesmanship. Qualities
and defects made him a dangerous foe for Bothwell's
outmoded armoury.

James Hepburn's third great opponent was the
Reformer, John Knox. Though there was little personal
enmity between the two men, Knox's "demagogic genius"
drove him to assail everything the Borderer championed
—the monarchy, the old order, the old religion.

Estimates of the Reformer's character are various.
His admirers refer to him as "Heaven's Joy, Earth's
Praise, Scotland's Brightness." In Victorian judgment,
"he was beloved by children and a favourite in female
society. His correspondence with Mrs. Bowes, also with
Mrs. Lock, testifies to the gentleness of his heart." People
who differed from his theology were less charitable.

*David
Chalmers
" de Scotorum
Fortitudine"
276, 277.*

"Whenever he made a journey," one contemporary
records, "he took round with him a certain number of
women whom he used to satisfy his lust." The same
writer asperses the asceticism of his early life: "he
escaped by stealth from a monastery and, returning
to his father's house, while his father was living, had
intercourse with a nun." The story continues that young
John had to fly to England where he seduced three girls
under the promise of marriage. Little credence can be
put in the unsupported testimony of theologians, though
similar attacks are readily admitted where Bothwell is
the victim.[1]

Whatever the truth about the Reformer's early life
—he was renegade priest, notary, private tutor—in

[1] "And likewise did confess that he had taken away two ladies' daughters
out of Denmark into Scotland and made them both believe he would marry
them and did deflower them of their virginity." Testament of the Lord
Bothwell.

1559 at the age of fifty-four, he was back in Scotland, inciting the mob with sermon and text to smash altars and images, to sack chapels and monasteries and to burn abbeys and churches. By obliterating the beauty that past generations of pious and skilful men had created, he claimed to execute "God's just judgment" on the evil lives of the catholic clergy of the day. Both Elizabeth and Cecil disliked his views but found him an invaluable ally.

These were the forces that Bothwell had to face—the Queen of England, to whom intrigue was a second nature, her Secretary who had raised it to a science, and the Reformer, who used it along with any tool that came to hand in the service of his God. Behind the political scenes this trio jerked the puppets with whom Bothwell came directly in contact. The most important was Lord James Stewart, Queen Mary's illegitimate brother. This able and ambitious man had led the Protestant Lords into open revolt. The Queen Regent was resisting force by force and two armies rode about the country showing little disposition to put their demonstrations to the test of battle. Abortive parleys, grandiloquent proclamations and broken truces succeeded each other with tedious regularity.

England was watching her chance. "I doubt not," wrote Throckmorton, the ambassador in Paris, to Cecil, "but you consider how much it standeth the Queen to nourish and entertain the garboil in Scotland." Sir Nicholas added that he had been approached by a Scot "desirous to do the Queen of England service. His offer is to be employed on some part of the Border . . . I have not found any so meet to be used *and entertained* as James Melville." The aspirant was the author of the famous Memoirs, from which much of Bothwell's ill-fame derives. *State Papers For. Ser. 4, 27 July, 1559.*

Cecil had already chosen his tools. Sadler had *carte blanche* from Elizabeth "to practise with any manner of person of Scotland for the furtherance of her service; to reward any manner of person of Scotland with such

71

sums of money as he may think fit." Big business was afoot for the frugal Queen so wide to unloose the purse-strings.

Besides bribery, Cecil had an auxiliary strategy bequeathed by Elizabeth's tremendous father. The Hamilton claim to the throne of Scotland might not be undisputed, but that powerful family could at least provide a pretender. A civil war of succession could be waged to aggravate the civil war of religion.

Keith App. 23. Cecil has left a memorandum which outlines his tactics. Encourage the protestant rebellion to make common cause with the "next heir," before the French grow "too strong and insolent." Raise demands that no sovereign could grant. If the Queen of Scots—"as is likely"—does not accede, "then is it apparent that Almighty God is pleased to transfer from her the rule of the kingdom." The paper ends with an ingenuous caution against "the deceits and trumperies of the French!"

The next heir, the "mere Scotsman," whose advancement Cecil championed, was the Duke of Chatelherault. Unluckily, when Governor of Scotland, he had shown his disloyalty could not be counted upon. His eldest son, James, Earl of Arran, offered more promising material.

This unprepossessing young man, who was destined to play so unsettling a part in Bothwell's life, as a boy followed the French Court and saw active service before he came of age. Meeting Mary Stuart at Court, an attack of calf love was considered to have disturbed his mental balance; but there can be no doubt that a hereditary taint infected his blood. His youngest brother, Lord Claud, later went mad and tried to cut his wife's throat at table, while Lord David and Lord John "had a show of the same disease." The queens of Scotland and England were both wise to refuse at different times the Hamilton suit; Elizabeth's reasons were particularly practical: Arran was "too poor and not considered personally agreeable."

72

Unsuitable as a husband, his weak intellect and his rabid Calvinism made him the ideal pawn for Cecil's game. That adroit tactician could rate the moves that followed as equal to his most brilliant play.

Under his instigation Arran made an opportune escape from the French Court, where he had been performing the duties of Captain of the Scottish Archers. For a fortnight he lay hidden in a wood, living on fruit. The French authorities, acting on a hint from Mary of Lorraine, had the ports watched and portraits circularised. But Cecil had foreseen everything and under his instructions the fugitive made his way inland to Geneva. There he was granted an interview by John Calvin, who as a sufferer from eleven different diseases, must have found subjects in common with the afflicted Earl.

Sir William grudged him the time even for such edifying intercourse. He had given instructions to "devise the most secret and speedy way to convey the Earl to England or Scotland." A guide, "who had the High Dutch tongue very well," was engaged to smuggle him through Germany to the port of Antwerp.

Some days later the Queen of England granted an interview to the German Ambassador. When the diplomat hinted that he could guess the Hamilton's whereabouts, she replied with gravity that he must be mistaken; she had no information that Arran was in her territory. But, she added, "with an arch smile," she knew well that he was lately in a "*certain kingdom*."

Elizabeth did not need telling that Arran was hidden in Cecil's Westminster house, nor was she obliged to mention an interview at Hampton Court when she gave the traveller practical proof of her favour with a purse of five hundred crowns. (Unsatisfied by her bounty, the adventurer contrived to borrow a further two hundred crowns from Cecil, a loan which caused the Secretary no little anxiety.)

Meanwhile, a man of aliases, Thomas Randall or Randolph, whose wit has caused much to be forgiven

73

him, was chosen to escort Arran to Scotland. His passport was addressed to all mayors, sheriffs, bailiffs and constables. "Whereas this bearer *Thomas Barnaby*, gentleman, is appointed to accompany one *Monsieur de Beaufort*, a gentleman of our good brother the French King, sent into Scotland to our good sister the Queen Dowager, we command you not only to suffer them quietly to pass by you with their bags, baggage and necessaries but also to see them favourably used by the way." Randolph's ironic touch is visible in this document, which carried the Earl and the agent safely to Berwick.

One of the rules of the Cecil technique was to conceal the actions of the right hand from the left. With a refinement of indirectness, Sadler entertained at the same moment in the same building, unknown to each other, the Hamilton pretender and the representative of the Lords who were to back him. The ingenious Sir Ralph saw the advantage of making the rebels take the initiative. "Mr. Balnaves," he wrote to Cecil, "arrived here on Wednesday at midnight from the Lords of the Congregation. As soon as harvest is at good point they will assemble. The principal mark they shoot at is to make an alteration of the State and authority. They mean to bestow it on the Duke, or, if he refuses, his son. This is very secret. All the while the Earl of Arran was at the Castle, being arrived three hours after Balnaves."

State Papers For. Ser. 1559/1323.

But "with empty hand men should no hawkis lure," as Maitland of Lethington liked quoting. The price demanded by the Lords was a cool two thousand pounds deposited at Holy Island, whence it could be collected by sea "with much secrecy."

Finance was the revolutionary movement's weakest point. John Knox, a realist, wrote forcibly to the Marshal of Berwick: "unless some support be made to particular men they will not serve in this action. If any one says they can serve without support, they deceive you." But the "relief" that was given to Grange, Cockburn of

Ormiston, Sandy Whitlaw[1] and others did not produce the desired results. "The men of war (for the most part men without God or honesty,)" Knox records gloomily, "made a mutiny because they lacked a part of their wages. To pacify them a collection was devised. But because some were poor and some were niggards and avaricious, there could no sufficient sum be obtained." A move to melt down silver and plate was no more successful.

The Reformer sought solace in the bosom of his family. He had already written to Cecil asking free and ready passage through England for his wife, Marjorie, explaining that "his wicked carcass, now presently labouring in the fevers, needs her service." Under the *nom-de-guerre* of "John Sinclair," he next asked for a licence for his mother-in-law, Elizabeth Bowes, "to visit and remain with me for a season; the comfort of her conscience, which cannot be quiet without God's word truly preached and His sacraments rightly ministered, is the cause of her request and my care." This very proper explanation effectively disposes of the scandal spread by his antagonists.[2] *Knox to Cecil, 23 Aug., 1559. John Sinclair to Sir J. Crofts, 21 Sept., 1559.*

The day after "John Sinclair" had shown his concern for his mother-in-law's conscience, the Border settlement was signed at Ladykirk. Bothwell and Northumberland, two straightforward men, had been set to weave a rope of sand. The settlement they signed did not endure much longer than the time the ink took to dry.

The Scottish rebels, reinforced by Arran, his father and eight hundred Hamiltons, continued to manœuvre for position. They occupied Edinburgh, and the loyalists

[1] Sandy Whitlaw, "a very honest, sober and godly man and the most truly affectionate to England of any Scotsman, is very religious and therefore you must let him see as little sin in England as you may. The Queen's purse must be open, for fair words will not serve."

[2] "John Knox, your first apostle, was also a manifest adulterer, bringing forth of England both the mother and the daughter, whom he persuaded that it was lawful to leave her husband and adhere to him, making one flesh of himself, the mother and daughter." This irregularity was the charge of Nichol Burne, "Professor of philosophy in St. Leonards College in the city of St. Andrews, brought up from his tender age in the perverted sect of the Calvinists, and now by a special grace of God, member of the Holy and Catholic Church," in his *Disputation*. Paris, 1581.

withdrew to the fortified port of Leith. The air was dark with proclamations, manifestos, ultimata. In an appeal to the country the Lords dilated on the small support Mary of Lorraine could command: "two or three mean lords between Leith and Berwick; the Earl Bothwell and Lord Seton, the only two of all the nobility who keep company with her."

On 21st October, 1559 the Congregation met at the Tolbooth and formally deprived her of all authority and regiment. In public Knox was careful to point out that "her iniquity and disorder ought not to withdraw their hearts from the obedience due to the sovereign." He was more sincere in a letter to England, which explained that "the authority of the French King and Queen is yet received, and will be *in word* until they deny our most just requests, which ye shall, God willing, shortly hereafter understand." Cecil was fortunate in a collaborator, who adhered so loyally to his memorandum and could equal him in cynicism. "John Sinclair's" only failing was an insatiable appetite. Incessant demands for English money to pay the soldiers flowed from his pen. He was anxious Leith should be taken, but the Congregation forces daily diminished. Enlistment to the roll of the drum was tried, but the rewards offered were insufficient and "no will to hazard" was found. In his need Knox turned trustfully to Cecil. "The sending of a thousand (English) men can break no league with France. Ye may declare them rebels," he suggested ingeniously, "when ye be assured that they be in our company."

Keith App. 45.

Open intervention was not as yet on Sir William's programme. (Did not one of his patient memoranda start with an unusually candid admission? "1. It is against God's law to aid any subjects against their natural princes. 2. It is dangerous to do it.") Knox received a rap over the knuckles—"To be plain with you, you are so open in your doings as to make men half-afraid to deal with you." The adjective "open" does not seem to have carried its modern meaning.

But if English soldiers were for a time withheld,

English money could be obtained. Three thousand pounds had been brought in a portmanteau from London to the Border. The Queen's messenger had an anxious time. "Perceiving himself dogged by false varlets" he had to hire an escort. The money was mainly in French crowns, for Cecil, with his prodigious attention to detail and mastery of chicane, saw that their influx into Scotland would not be compromising.

Safe transport for the final stage of their journey was the next problem. The handling of the last subsidy by Mr. Henry Balnaves had given rise to criticism—"In times to come," he had been driven to complain, "I shall save myself from such blame with the grace of God. I think I deserve more thanks." An emissary was needed who would not lose the money on the way, or divert it on arrival. Various names were proposed and rejected. Choice fell on John Cockburn of Ormiston, who had recently joined the Congregation.

This "honourable and religious gentleman, very diligent and zealous for the work of the Reformation," was a distant connection of Bothwell's. It was at his house that the Fair Earl had arrested George Wishart. Cockburn had been in trouble for helping the English but Mary of Lorraine with her faculty for forgiveness had returned him his lands. In gratitude he had signed a bond pledging himself to serve her, about a year before he again deserted her cause.

In response to the rebels' urgent appeal, delivery of one thousand pounds to this honourable and religious gentleman was authorised. On Tuesday, 30th October, 1559, he arrived at Berwick and was taken to see Sir Ralph Sadler, recently promoted Deputy Warden of the Eastern Marches, in place of Northumberland who had been found too scrupulous for those eventful times. John Cockburn first received two hundred crowns "for his own relief" and to stimulate his zeal for the Reformation. Next, with elaborate mystification intended to preserve Queen Elizabeth's integrity, he was handed a bag, which Sadler and the Marshal of Berwick assured him

77

contained money "that they had shifted for and such as they could borrow of their friends." Besides 3,157 French crowns, value 6s. 4d. each and one silver crown, value 5s. 8d., John Cockburn was entrusted with a letter to his masters. There was also a promise of gunpowder and munitions.

He was wished Godspeed and conducted to the Border. Thenceforward he had to rely upon seven picked men he had brought and the secrecy that enshrouded his mission.

It was All Hallows' eve. Whatever his supernatural terrors, John Cockburn had no fear of human interference. Behind him was the might of England, reared on Cecil's genius. Ahead lay his own country and his own folk. Every yard he covered, the road became more and more familiar. He knew every short-cut blindfold. He let, it is recorded, the led horse straggle. He took off his steel bonnet and tied it at his knee. At last the dark bulk of Taprain told him he was only a few miles from the town of Haddington.

Suddenly, without a sound, shadowy forms blocked his path. An ominous figure gripped his bridle. His startled bodyguard did not know whether these were mortal men that loomed out of the darkness. John Cockburn drew his sword and slashed at the fingers fumbling with the precious burden strapped to his saddle. Why had he loosed the rein of the spare horse that might have carried him and his treasure to safety? Cursing, he spurred his tired mount and tried to break the circle of his assailants. A sword whistled through the air. Blood running over his face, Cockburn of Ormiston slid to the ground. . . .

A jingle as the heavy bag passed from hand to hand, a scrape of boot on stirrup iron, a clatter of hoofs in the darkness, and the incalculable Hepburn had struck another blow for his Queen.

The ambush had been shrewdly laid. Bothwell had obtained accurate information of Cockburn's plans by one Blackadder of a family ever loyal to his fortunes.

78

Posted in his opponent's moves, he had been studious to hide his own game. He was helped by the pressure the Lords were bringing to make him "swerve from his allegiance by promises of good deed." As a blind, he had sent Michael Balfour to Edinburgh for a safe-conduct to discuss the suggested treachery. Knox declares that Knox 1, 456. pending an answer Bothwell promised to refrain from offensive action; but the correspondence of the day gives no support to the charge.

As Cockburn rode from Berwick towards Edinburgh, his route lay through Hepburn lands, and Balfour's mission suggested that no detour was necessary. The Laird did not guess that Bothwell with twenty-four men —again the minimum force that would be effective—was waiting near Hailes Castle in country where every sheep track was familiar. The Borderer could pick a point where the calvacade was bound to pass. As the hours sped he reflected with satisfaction that neither Cockburn's hardihood nor Sadler's subtlety would deliver the French crowns at their rebel destination.

The plan worked without hitch. The suddenness of the attack, the sufficiency of Bothwell's force and the supernatural terrors of the night combined to minimise bloodshed. With the bag of money bumping at his saddle, Bothwell rode hard for Crichton.

Silence returned to the scene of the ambush. Cockburn's men lifted the body of their groaning laird and carried him to Ormiston, where his wounds were found to be slight.

Hue and cry followed. Too late Sadler tried to bar the stable door. Begging the protestant Lords to explain that the money was theirs (or, even more improbably, John Cockburn's) he hoped to save the Queen of England's face. Distractedly he wrote to Cecil, advising him "what mishap hath chanced, to our no little grief and displeasure. Surely we durst as well have committed our lives as the money to (Cockburn's) hands and would have thought the same to be in no danger, as he himself did warrant us most assuredly."

79

The pretence that the money did not come from England was unavailing. Word quickly went round. Soon the Spanish Ambassador in London was entertaining his master with the story and pointing out that the peace was now openly broken. D'Oysel wrote lamenting with mock chagrin that the money was too little "if it was to fall into such good hands," and suggesting that the French Ambassador should tax Elizabeth. She would deny all knowledge, the French general was sure, but a straight look might be rewarded with a blush.

With one stroke Bothwell had deprived the rebels of the help they sorely needed, and had stripped the English of their pretence of neutrality. But the consequences of his *coup* were not yet exhausted.

The Lords were determined not only to recover the treasure but to punish the man who had outwitted them. News of his exploit had reached Edinburgh a little sooner than he had counted. Lord James Stewart and the Earl of Arran collected a punitive expedition whose strength was estimated as high as two thousand men and a couple of guns.

But Bothwell understood the value of mobility. Trusting to his wits, a quarter of an hour before the avengers arrived at Crichton Castle, he "departed suddenly upon a horse without saddle, boots or spurs"—but clasping the bag of crowns. Details of the hazardous ride have not been preserved. A family tradition records that the Earl doubled back to Haddington. There he was warned that the pursuit was entering the west gate. Abandoning his horse, he ran down a lane called the Goul to the Tyne, and hearing, no doubt, the bay of hounds, ran down the bed of the shallow stream for one hundred and fifty yards. Cockburn of Sandybed's back door gave on the river. In the kitchen a girl was turning the spit. Disarmed by the young fugitive's appeal, she consented to change clothes. Laughter repaid her, if no more substantial coin, when the Earl was forced to perform her duties for several days, until the coast was clear.

Bothwell's gratitude settled a yearly grant of four bolls of wheat, barley and oats on Sandybed and his heirs, which was duly paid for the next two hundred years.

Once the Earl had made good his escape, there was no attempt to defend the castle. Its captain, John Somerville, threw wide the gates and surrendered to the besiegers. He was sent after his vanished master with an ultimatum: unless the subsidy was restored and the wrong to John Cockburn redressed, Crichton would be spoiled and burnt, its owner's property confiscated and himself declared the enemy of the Congregation. To prove that these threats were not empty, Captain Forbes and fifty hagbutters were put in charge of the castle. After spending the night there, Lord James and Arran withdrew with the rest of their force to Edinburgh.

On arrival they were met by fresh repercussions of Bothwell's exploit. Their absence had been noticed in Leith; the leaders they had left behind were devoutly occupied, listening to Knox's sermon. D'Oysel seized the moment to order a sortie. Five hundred foot and a company of horse poured out of Leith. Their objective was a two-gun battery from Dundee that had been brought into action against the walls of the beleaguered port. Meeting no resistance, they stormed the position. Part of the gun crews they slaughtered and, burning and looting, drove the rest before them to the walls of Edinburgh.

This engagement, which cost the Congregation thirty lives, forty prisoners and two good guns, did little to soften their hearts towards Bothwell. On the third of November, Arran and the future Lord Herries rode at the head of three hundred horse to Crichton. Its owner by now had taken shelter with a neighbour at Borthwick Castle. Stoutly refusing to return the subsidy or to comply with the Congregation's terms, he watched while his castle was sacked and its contents, including his charter chest, carried to Edinburgh. Eight years later the memory rankled as he read an account of how he "was content to suffer his principal house and rich movables to be sacked, to have his whole living destroyed, before he would swerve from his obedience."

Shortage of funds and defeat in the field had damped the ardour of the Congregation; numbers were falling fast. Success had the opposite effect on the French. They staged another sally, this time to cut their besiegers' food supply. Thirteen hundred infantry and a company of cavalry rode through the gates of Leith. Lord James and Arran tried to stem the rush. In a hand-to-hand encounter, the two leaders narrowly escaped capture when the protestant ranks broke. The French estimated their enemies' losses at three hundred killed and two hundred taken prisoner.

This was the end of the occupation of Edinburgh and the first siege of Leith. Desertion became wholesale and "with the sword of dolour passed through their hearts," midnight evacuation of the city was decided.

Challoner to Cecil, 1 Dec., 1559.

The retreat to Stirling was "next door to a flight." Something more than Mr. Knox's "comfortable sermon" was needed to restore morale. Thomas Randolph, the English agent in the Lords' camp, dated the collapse from the fatal All Hallows' eve. Pathetically he laments "the worst success in a matter that I hoped so well of, that ever I should see." He never forgave the defeat of the English designs. His witty and vindictive tongue never ceased to assail his enemy "and that unhonourable and thievish act that ventured the loss of the chief nobility of this realm." Much of the abuse which has been showered on Bothwell dates from this exploit, since no bitterness can equal that of the dishonest man who has been outmanœuvred and deprived of the fruits of his dishonour; while no one has appreciated a last sword-cut of chivalry that checked a revolution, and confounded the policies of two nations.

Randolph to Sadler, 11 Nov., 1559.

82

CHAPTER NINE

WITH, we must hope, a hearty feeling of gratitude to Bothwell, the Queen Regent marched out of Leith and back to Edinburgh. Her army consisted of three thousand French with a sprinkling of Scots and even a few English mercenaries like Hector Wentworth, "a proper man with an auburn beard." Besides Bothwell and his Hepburns, she had the feudal support of Lord Borthwick, Lord Sempill and Lord Seton, "a man without God," said the protestants, "without honesty and oftentimes without reason." These and the bishops she could trust. The rest of the nobility who had not openly espoused the cause of the revolt, preserved a dubious and uncertain neutrality. As a bewildered Frenchman remarked: "You cannot tell friend from enemy, and he *Teulet i 311* that is with us in the morning is on the other side after dinner."

Bothwell's unswerving loyalty and his audacious ingenuity made him the Queen Mother's most valuable servant. But he had the limitations of an honest man. He had just beaten Cecil and Knox on the Border by Border methods. Had he been a statesman of their calibre he could have fought them in a larger and a more slippery ring. There was trouble to be raised for England on the Continent; mischief to be made between Cecil and Elizabeth; distrust to be sown between Knox and the Lords. Bothwell's brain directed his sword-arm; it did not conceive politics as anything but a series of isolated and honourable thrusts. The treasure raid of Taprain was a lesson to Cecil. He stopped secret subsidies and turned to direct intervention. The man who gave the lesson was not himself disposed to learn.

Bothwell's allegiance was to the past. He turned a contemptuous back on a modern world of expediency

83

and intrigue. He had just defeated that world by the use
of his natural, old-fashioned weapons. His next move
was equally natural to him and equally out of date.
Following the rules of chivalry, he proclaimed the Earl
of Arran a traitor by sound of trumpet and challenged
him to "singular combat according to the law of arms."

The Hepburns were given, as has been noticed, to the
bloodless sport of issuing challenges, a habit as innocuous
as a modern duel. Trial by combat, a relic of the
touching mediæval belief in Heaven's intervention on
the side of the innocent, still lingered in legal theory.
The sack of Crichton and the Queen Regent's grievance
against the Hamilton pretender provided an excuse to
test the theory.

Bothwell's cartel was an imposing document. It
started with his resentment at Arran's threats to expel
him and his helpers, "true subjects to the authority,"
from their native realm of Scotland. It alluded to the
looting of his house and goods. "Having respect to my
honour," it continued, "I am compelled to seek remedy
and on a convenient day, in a competent place, I am
content to defend the said quarrel before French and
Scottish, armed as you please, on horse or foot unto the
death. When, God willing, I shall offer to prove that you
have not done your duty to authority as a nobleman
ought, nor yet to me."

Arran's answer, issued from the safe distance of
Stirling, was not calculated to turn away wrath. He
had never, he retorted, threatened any true subjects,
adding unkindly: "Of that number, I neither esteem
you, Earl of Bothwell, nor your assisters. As to that
thing I have done unto yourself or house, it is much
less than the injury done by you to my friend. You have
no place to seek the combat of any man of honour, for
it is the deed of a thief to beset a gentleman's road and
rob him of his goods. As to revenge, if you think it not
sufficiently revenged already, be assured the next time I
come that way, the thing left undone shall be achieved.
When you may recover the name of an honest man, I

shall answer you as I ought, but not before French, for there is no Frenchman in this realm with whose judgment I will have to do."

The honour of both sides being satisfied by this dignified interchange, the matter was allowed to drop. Bothwell's indignation did not extend to the Laird of Ormiston, whose misadventure had been the direct cause of the quarrel with Arran. His name had been published on a list of traitors and confiscation of his goods decreed when he received a surprise visit from the man who had lately outwitted him. The Laird was a connection by marriage; he was recovering from a painful wound; but neither kinship nor commiseration prompted the call. John Cockburn was the most resolute of the lairds of Lothian, who had for the most part followed his lead and joined the Congregation. Bothwell knew their fickleness and saw a way to re-enlist their loyalty. He hinted to the convalescent that if he would return to his allegiance, the past could be profitably forgotten. *John Wood to Randolph, 30 Nov., 1559.*

But the Laird was too far committed. He put his visitor off with fair words, and without making any promise, "drove time honestly."

One of his neighbours was more amenable. The Laird of Halton had married John Cockburn's daughter. His disloyalty too was in danger of punishment. French soldiers were out to arrest him, when Bothwell appeared in the rôle of guardian angel and secured their return to camp. Halton was more grateful than his father-in-law and he signed a bond of friendship with his benefactor. *State Papers For. Ser. 1559/397. Noailles to d'Oysel, 22 Dec., 1559. Bannatyne Misc. iii. 306.*

Bothwell was aware how desperate was the Regent's need of supporters, however irresolute. Elizabeth and Cecil, warned by the quick collapse of the rebels, saw that the revolution would not succeed without active help from across the Border. Six weeks after Bothwell's *coup*, Sadler had instructions from London. A fleet was to be sent and an army levied to drive out the French and set the crown on Arran's bewildered brow. The fleet, which was to consist of fourteen ships, would block the Firth of

Forth and stop reinforcements reaching the French from oversea. The land attack was to be led by Lord Grey de Wilton and launched by four thousand infantry and two thousand horse.

A glimpse at Bothwell's intelligence system is preserved in a letter that his satellite, the notorious Black Ormiston, had written from his home, the Moss Tower in Teviotdale, to various members of the English family of Forster. Addressing his "very assured friends and worshipful men," he asked for advice. He was bailiff to Lord Bothwell against whom (and against the Queen) a force of English was coming to Scotland. The Forsters knew that their correspondent's neighbours "had him in envy and malice, and misreport[1] him all they could to cause him and his poor men to be harried." Accordingly a hint would be acceptable—ought he not to thresh his corn and hide his belongings? The overture throws a curious light on the neighbourliness that prevailed on the Border between men ready any night to drive each others' cattle.

When Mary of Lorraine was convinced that invasion was inevitable, she took steps to ensure the safe arrival of reinforcements from France. A winter offensive into Fife she saw would serve two purposes. The rebellious Lords who had retreated thither might be put out of action before English help arrived; and if St. Andrews and both coasts of the Firth of Forth were held, safe landing would be secured for French transports.

Sadler to Cecil, 28 Dec., 1559.

On Christmas Eve, while Jack and John Daw and William Hog were doing their best to keep the Court cheerful with the music of their viols, a joint force of eighteen hundred French and Scots marched out of Edinburgh. Their immediate objective was Stirling. Their leader, so the spies of England reported, was the

---

[1] Black Ormiston was subject to misrepresentation all his life. Thirteen years before this letter, he had been summoned "for deforcing a messenger-at-arms and seizing and tearing his letters." Fifteen years later he was hanged. The last of his name is said to have sunk to the office of common hangman. The family arms, "three pelicans in piety gules," seem inappropriate.

Earl of Bothwell. On the way the army planned to loot the Hamilton castle of Keneil, near Linlithgow. So far the influence of the owner of Crichton may be felt.

But from that moment, for the month the Fife offensive lasted, the Earl gives no further sign. Sarlebous is found in command of the advance guard, and d'Oysel of the main body at Stirling. A flank attack crossed the Forth to connect with the advance guard in Fife, but Bothwell did not lead it. Commissariat arrangements were made and the Stirling authorities charged to cause provision, "such as bread, drink, flesh, and fish," to follow the army. But it is the redoubtable Captain Cullen, as much at home on the ocean wave as on the battlefield, who organises a transport service, and presses the fishing boats of Musselburgh to carry supplies across the Forth. *Randolph to Sadler, 31 Dec., 1559.* *Teulet i. 404* *Accounts of Lord High Treasurer.*

Bothwell's name is never mentioned. Perhaps an explanation of his temporary disappearance may be found in a sinister little note scribbled by the egregious Randolph. "What shall be done," he wonders innocently, "said or written to the Earl of Bothwell?" *Randolph's Memorial, 12 Dec., 1559.*

The answer to the significant question is extant in Cecil's own handwriting. When "preserving both his interest and his conscience," he did not employ a secretary.

"If he cannot be won from the French," he wrote pointedly, "*practise the taking of him.*"

It is possible that some word of the kidnap plot reached the ears of the intended victim or his ruler. Bothwell was too valuable a servant of royalty to risk losing—did not the French Ambassador estimate the damage he had done to the Queen of England at £14,000? The Queen Regent knew he would be safe among his own people. So "strong arm" methods were thwarted, and Cecil had to bide his time.

Towards the end of January, 1560, Randolph records Bothwell's short period of leave and a scandal about his sister, which he was too modest to commit to paper. "Because you will judge it to be but a merry matter," he assured Sir Ralph, "I will leave it to a further time, though it is worth the reporting." "Merry" on Elizabethan lips generally carried a ribald inflection, but the details of Lady Janet's indiscretion remain tantalisingly locked in Randolph's appreciative bosom.

Further evidence that Bothwell took no part in the invasion of Fife may be deduced from the conduct of the French. His humane temper could have restrained their exuberance, released after weeks of siege. Stirling was pillaged; Kinghorn was captured and "two that professed Jesus Christ, a Dutchman and a French boy, fervent in religion and clean of life," were hanged from the steeple of the parish church. It was suspected that wives and daughters of the loyal lairds of Fife "got favour of the French." Grange's house was blown up with gunpowder and its owner was shot "right under the left pap, through the jack, doublet and sark till the bullet did stick in one of his ribs." The patient may be excused his irritable announcement that he meant to discontinue saving French prisoners from having their throats cut. Knox tried to revive flagging spirits with another comfortable sermon at Coupar, in which Arran was unfavourably compared with Jehoshaphat, "who kept not himself in his chamber, but frequented the multitude and rejoiced them with his presence and godly comfort."

If the unfortunate Hamilton, whose malady was gaining ground, was considered to keep himself too "close and solitary," he and Lord James, with a company reduced from eight to two hundred men, put up a gallant fight. For twenty-one days they slept in their clothes, without taking off their boots. But the Congregation forces were fighting a losing battle. All they could do was to play for time until English succour could arrive. Driven out of Dysart, they fell back on St. Andrews. Their communications threatened, they retired to Coupar. The French, burning and looting, advanced to within six miles of their objective. With St. Andrews in their hands reinforcements could flow in from the Continent.

The stars had fought against their safe arrival. A force had been embarked at Dieppe only to come to grief on the coast of Holland. Four vessels foundered and a thousand infantry perished. The wreckage of the disaster washed up on the coasts of Norfolk. The remainder of the flotilla had put back to port, "compelled to confess that God fought for the defence of Scotland."

Challoner to Cecil, 13 Jan., 1560.

Quadra to Duchess of Parma, 21 Jan., 1560.

But the King of France, under the tutelage of the Guises, still pursued his efforts to preserve his bride's inheritance. Munitions were safely delivered by twenty small ships under Captain Martigues. Troopships were daily expected. When a sail was sighted on the horizon the joy of the French advance guard marching through the snow can be pictured. With Gallic enthusiasm they fired a salvo of welcome in the air.

As the galleys sailed majestically into the Forth, delight changed to bewilderment. The fleet was seen to intercept Captain Cullen's convoy. Amid, says Knox, "pulling of beards for anger," the truth was realised. Sir William Wynter's fourteen English ships had dropped anchor in time to save the protestant cause in Scotland.

The supply service from Leith was cut, and the Fife offensive had to be hurriedly abandoned.

The French retired once more to the port of Leith, which they looked on as "one of the most evil places in the world," with no fortification but trenches. The Queen Regent despite Elizabeth's protestations of friendship, knew that war was inevitable. She took every measure to order the country in a state of defence. She summoned all and sundry, doubtful supporters as well as confirmed loyalists, to resist the invader. She had no need to send for Bothwell; when, *pour encourager les autres*, proceedings were started against Arran for his rebellion, the Hepburn was eager to give evidence.

Pollen cxxxvii.

He was at her side the day she sat in state to hear the Chester Herald deliver the formal declaration of war. D'Oysel represented France; the Archbishop of St. Andrews, the Church; and Bothwell, Seton and Sempill, the loyal nobility.

The devoted Borderer must have noticed with dismay signs of her failing health—indeed, as a French bishop remarked, she stood in need of everything but greatness of spirit. Was it at Bothwell's suggestion that she finally consented to nurse her strength within the walls of Edinburgh Castle? The fortress was held by the neutral Lord Erskine, but Mary of Lorraine's partisans victualled it to resist a lengthy siege. Provision was made of flour, meal, oats, peas, beef, butter, cheese, salt, figs, raisins, ale, wine, beer, vinegar, dried ling, salmon, skate, herrings, candles, coal and hay. Bothwell's efforts to distract the sick woman may excite a smile. He was Admiral of Scotland and William Harlaw, sailor, was allowed to offer his ruler "ane skin of ane monstrous fishe of the sea" that he had caught. The invalid laughed and gave the man a present of money.

Simancas 92.

The invasion was awaited with stoicism. Thomas, fourth Duke of Norfolk (said to be unfit to command a platoon), was drilling an army of eight thousand men at Newcastle. At Berwick he signed a treaty with the Scottish rebels, securing their co-operation. An army crossed the Border on Saturday, the 30th March. Lord Grey de Wilton was in command, with Arran and Lord James again to lead the Congregation forces. These took the field with provisions for twenty days. After that time they were liable to evaporate, and the wary

Keith Ap. 27.

recognised that the way to beat them was to "prolong time and not to fight with them, but stand at defence."

Accordingly the invader at first met no resistance. A screen of light cavalry, commanded by Sir Henry Percy, secured the baggage train from molestation by the French garrison in Dunbar. Restalrig, a mile from Leith, was reached without opposition; there the horsemen bivouacked. The more military of the Scots camped with them, but the Duke of Chatelherault settled himself at Holyrood House, whither his son was shortly fain to retire. Arran was "ill at ease, rather from care of mind than pain he feels in his body." Leith was blockaded by sea and land but actual fighting did not begin till the eve of Palm Sunday, when a thousand French made an unsuccessful sortie. Throughout Holy Week an artillery duel raged. During its progress the English infantry grew careless, "some of the captains going into Edinburgh and the common soldiers falling to play at dice and cards."

This was the kind of opportunity Bothwell never missed. On Easter Monday, with George Seton, he led a sally out of the beleaguered port. Again his forces were small—fifty horse and five hundred hagbutters, but again his objective was reached and three of the guns bombarding the town were spiked.

Bothwell, ever quick to recognise the key to a position, selected the English general for his personal attack. Lord Grey de Wilton was the one capable leader the English could boast and his elimination would have been a grievous blow. Charging hotly, Bothwell "overthrew" and wounded him. He also wounded his son, Arthur Grey, in the shoulder. Rumour ran that his old antagonist Percy was killed, but Sir Henry was destined to survive and meet a darker fate many years later in the Tower of London. People who saw the skirmish described it as the hottest they had ever witnessed. Nearly half of Bothwell's men were killed, but the losses they inflicted were more than double. Randolph's brother (who supplemented his income as Governor of Dover Castle by drawing a pension from Spain) admitted that the English received "a good trouncing." *State Papers For. Ser. 1560. 1082.*

Bothwell's ordinary duties during the siege, if less spectacular, were no less valuable. Slipping out of Leith under cover of darkness, his irregular horse harassed the columns bringing supplies from Berwick. Operating in the country between Dunbar and Edinburgh, his mosstroopers exploited their knowledge of the terrain and their flair for plunder. *Jebb i. 244.*

In the bloody repulse of the general assault that de Wilton launched on the 7th May, the Hepburn share is not particularised. The English infantry ran up to the walls carrying twenty-two scaling ladders that (typical of war) were four feet too short:

For this assault lewd ladders vile and naught
The soldiers had, which were too short, God wot;
The proof thereof with blood the poor men bought,

wrote a humble poet who fought in the engagement.

A few of the party succeeded in climbing the walls—
only to be killed inside by gunfire. Those at the foot of
the ladders were mown down by the volleys of two
thousand hagbutters. The ladies of the garrison played
their part. "The Frenchmen's harlots, of whom the most
part were Scots whores," John Knox relates emphatically,
"did not less cruelty than the soldiers. For besides that
they charged their pieces, some continually cast stones,
some carried chimneys of burning fire, some brought
timber which with great violence they threw over the
wall upon our men."

Choosing their moment, two hundred French men-at-
arms and five hundred horse (the Bothwell touch may be
detected), made a sortie and cleared the English trenches.
All this time the Scottish rebel army, through misunder-
standing or ill-will, watched the massacre of their allies
without attempting to relieve them.

This heavy reverse proved to the satisfaction of
besiegers and besieged that Leith could not be taken by
assault. Starvation was another matter. Until long-
awaited reinforcements could arrive, the fewer mouths
the beleaguered town had to feed, the greater its
resistance to famine. Here Bothwell could be doubly
useful. He and his men knew the way past the enemy
outposts. Once clear of the town, his services could be
employed in the delicate work of securing support from
overseas.

A week after the repulse of the general assault, Bothwell had made his way to Crichton and was writing
Mary of Lorraine one of the last letters she was fated to
receive.

*Chalmers:
Life of
Queen Mary
ii. 217.*

"For the Queen's Grace. Please your Highness be
remembered I wrote unto your Grace before, concerning
my departing towards our sovereigns in France, which

your Grace thought good. Wherefore I have lately prepared me for the same and have been in readiness this four or five days past—like as I am yet, waiting on your Grace's despatch only. For I have made the greater haste, to the effect I may return again with the army, and have some charge therein by your Grace's writings, such as our said sovereigns and your Highness thinks me most able for, that I may be always in the room when service occurs. But I have not the commodity thereto at this present nor hasty appearance thereof without the same, desiring your Grace most humbly therefore to further the same writings for the cause aforesaid. And if there be any other thing it will please your Grace to command, I shall do my diligence to perform the same. My most humble commendation of service being made unto your Highness, commits your Grace to the keeping of Almighty God, your Grace's most humble and obedient servitor—Bothuille."

The letter reflects the Borderer's devotion to the ruler he served so well. His anxiety to continue in her service even when his own resources were exhausted, and his eagerness to fight under the banner of the army he was commissioned to summon, must have touched the dying woman. How effectively his loyalty had emptied his purse is shown by two deeds of this date. In March he sold land to James Barron and in April to Adam Hepburn of Smeaton. All through his life his fidelity to the Crown put a strain on an estate already impoverished.

Mary of Lorraine's last words to her young "servitor" have not been preserved. She did not keep him waiting for the letter he wanted to her daughter, Queen of France and Scotland. Two days later he was off. To his mission at Queen Mary's Court had been added a more difficult and exacting embassy. *Mary of Lorraine to d'Oysel, 17 May, 1560.*

Even if he succeeded in extracting prompt and adequate reinforcements from France, their arrival was not secured. Transports must run the gauntlet of the English navy and force, or evade, the blockade in the Forth. Bothwell had orders to make his secret way to the Court of

Denmark and in his capacity of Lord High Admiral of Scotland to persuade Frederick II to lend his fleet.

At this time Denmark was perhaps the foremost naval power in Europe. The glory of the Hanseatic League was passing; Spain's vigour was sapped by the struggle in the Netherlands and by English privateering enterprise in the Spanish Main; the future hid the growth of the English and Dutch navies. The Danish fleet numbered some thirty sail and was the private property of King Frederick II, whose German extraction and orientation gave him a semi-independent position. If his help could be won for the Queen Mother, Bothwell would do her notable service.

The ground had been well prepared. Six months earlier there had been rumours that the Rhinegrave was to enlist five thousand German mercenaries for service under

Keith App. 28. Mary of Lorraine. The help of Frederick's ships to transport and convoy them was said to have been bought by the Duchess of Lorraine's surrender of her claim to the Danish crown.

Quadra to Philip II., 13 Dec., 1559. Quadra to Duchess of Parma, 21 Jan., 1560. The story reached Cecil's ears. They heard too that Frederick's brother, Duke Adolph of Holstein, was raising troops to embark for Scotland at Danish ports. Believing that every man has his price, Elizabeth tried to buy off the Duke with a pension. Her cynicism was justified, for Adolph already drew one from Spain.

Quadra to Philip, 19 Feb., 1560. It did not stop the preparations. Letters from the Rhinegrave to a colonel in the Danish service fell into Elizabeth's acquisitive hands. The colonel was to equip

Giovanni Michel to the Doge, 20 April, 1560. forty troopships in Hamburg for Scotland. The story of a secret understanding between Denmark, Germany and Scotland reached diplomatic ears in Venice.

Cecil had his listening posts in every capital. In the middle of May, just before Bothwell started North, the

Johannes Spithovius to Cecil, 15 May, 1560. sleepless Secretary was warned by an agent in Copenhagen that the King was coming to review his fleet. Where it was going was kept secret, but the ships were so well furnished, their companies so complete, that some important expedition was suspected.

FREDERICK II. IN 1578
(By Van der Schardt)

Bothwell's mission was well timed. Here was a chance to meet Cecil at his own game. If Frederick could be persuaded to throw the Danish fleet into the scale, the English blockade might be smashed and English intervention in Scottish affairs receive its death-blow.

As usual Bothwell hid his play. From Crichton he rode north with a small train. Covering his tracks, he visited the Earl of Atholl and other gentlemen of the Highlands, "making no long stay and giving no notice of his coming." No doubt one of his minor duties was to weigh their loyalty.

On the 20th June Cecil's Copenhagen agent sent off a second report. The French Ambassador was pressing Frederick to lend his fleet for service in Scottish waters. Bothwell had no doubt arrived and the despatch he carried had stimulated the Ambassador to exert his full powers of persuasion. The Lord High Admiral of Scotland was graciously received by Frederick II. He found that monarch, who was later to play so devastating a part in his fortunes, a man of his own age with small hands and heavy buttocks. A long head, long face, long nose suggested a cold and capable nature. Experience of life had not yet soured the disappointed mouth or dulled the baffled eyes. When the full lips under the formidable moustache opened, the German language that proceeded occasioned no surprise. Bothwell could find two subjects that no linguistic difficulties could bar—field sports and wine. On Frederick's tomb his dog is commemorated with the epitaph: "Trew ist Wildpret." His wine-glass, to hold three litres, may still be seen in evidence of his capacity. Throckmorton thought him "a dissolute and impudent Prince," adding with disillusionment, "though he be a protestant." Less severe critics give him credit for being "ever the most gracious and amiable of hosts, who could always carry off a carouse with ease and dignity." His people loved him, for the debaucheries of monarchs, provided they are not tyrannic, seem to give their subjects matter for pride.

Bothwell created a good impression. When Frederick

Spithovius to Cecil, 20 June, 1560.

Resen's Annals of Frederick II. Fol. s 42.

95

and his brother had listened to what he had to say, they did him the honour of escorting him in their own royal persons from Copenhagen across the sea to Jutland, and through the Duchy of Holstein to Germany. The answer to his embassy is not on record, but if the King took the trouble to escort the envoy on his way to bargain with the Rhinegrave for the five thousand mercenaries, it cannot have been unfavourable.

At that moment fell the first of the strokes of bad luck that followed James Hepburn throughout his career. Just as the first part of his embassy had been brought to an apparently successful close, news arrived of the death of the Queen Mother. The blow was doubly severe. In Mary of Lorraine the young man had lost a patroness who trusted him and understood him, who guided and inspired his natural audacity. Moreover, by her death, he lost the best chance he ever had to smash the power of the combination that was fated in the end to destroy him. However faithfully he might serve her daughter, he was never to receive the backing he needed to put him on equal terms with his enemies.

When Bothwell left Scotland the Queen Mother was dying of an ascitic dropsy, or, as Knox preferred to put it, "her belly and loathsome legs began to swell, till that God in His wisdom took her away from this world."[1] Knowing she could not recover, she worked to lighten her daughter's task, drafting a list of important people in Scotland with notes on their characters. On the paper she marked who could be trusted and who could not. It is easy to guess the mark against Bothwell's name.

She must have regretted his absence when she called the leaders of both sides to her room in the castle to hear her dying words. "They found her to their judgment worse, her lips, hands and legs very cold, her tongue and wits failed very greatly, and she herself without hope of

---

[1] The Reformer, as the civilised eighteenth century "saw, treated this queen in language too much below either a gentleman or a divine to utter . . . what enthusiasm, venom, scurrility, and indecency!" (Keith).

life." She roused herself to make a despairing appeal to the group of grim, self-interested nobles, "to whom she expressed her grief for the troubles of the realm, commending earnestly the study of peace, advising them to send away both French and English out of the country. Bursting forth in tears she asked pardon of all whom in any way she had offended; professing she did forgive those who had injured her and embracing all the nobles one by one, she took her farewell."

She had been the inspiration of other brave men than Bothwell—"many gentlemen," wrote one who *Teulet i. 559.* fought for her, "have told me, that were it not for love of her, they would have done nothing."

Her life was guided by a great compassion. "Do justice," she wrote, "to this poor woman, for they have done her great wrong. The little flies are taken in the net, and the larger pass through." She was helpful to the poor, especially to those whom she knew to be ashamed to beg. Women in travail she visited and helped, both with skill and counsel. Her failure to bring peace to the country of her adoption must be charged to the irreconcilable hearts of her opponents and, it must be admited, to her own bias in favour of the country of her birth. Even in small things she followed French fashions. Her shoes were made in France, whence were sent fruit and vegetables for her table—green peas, white peas, pears and medlars.

Her will made provision for her humblest servants, little Anne, big Anne, little Jock in the pantry, little Janet. She had wanted to be buried in the Benedictine Abbey at Rheims where her sister was abbess, so a pewterer was set to supply "ane wobe of lead to be ane sepulture to incluse the Queen's Grace."

Her death was followed by the peace that her life had failed to ensure. Within three days negotiations were on foot. With the common man's readiness to be friends with his enemy, the soldiers of both armies met and fraternised on the sands of Leith. The English brought beef, bacon, capons, chickens, wine and beer. The beleaguered French produced a cold capon roast, a pasty of baked horse and six rats well roasted.

Bothwell was on his way to Germany when the news came. However ready he may have been to pursue the diplomatic struggle with Cecil, negotiations for peace cut the ground from under him. With France and Scotland ready to sign a treaty, neither the Rhinegrave nor Frederick could be expected to take measures hostile to England. Did duty seem to recall the envoy to the internecine struggle in Scotland, or beckon him to the elegant Court of the young Queen of France? The Regent's death had ended a chapter of his life and he was young enough to believe that the future lay in his own hands.

CHAPTER TEN

ANNA was the daughter of a retired admiral. Christopher Throndsen, member of the Rustung family, had distinguised himself in the naval service of King Frederick's father. A Norwegian nobleman, he had recently promised to spend his days in Denmark, with a grant of land to compensate his expatriation. He had a home in Copenhagen where Anna was living when she met Bothwell. Anna had been helping her father with his business affairs for some little time and seems to have done very much as she liked. Her mother—Karine, child of Knud Pedersen Skanke, deacon in the chapter in Throndhjem—had a large family and could not be expected to watch them all. A son, Enno, and seven daughters—Anna, Maren, Magdala, Margaret, Else, Dorothy and Christina—all made their demands on her time and attention. It was no easy matter to find husbands for all the girls. Else, the third daughter, was attractive. She married thrice, the last time to a Scot settled in Norway. His name was Andrew Mowat, a widower. It was not a very good match, and on his death he could leave her and her four children only five hundred dollars. Dorothy, her eldest sister, married another Scot, John Stewart, who lived in Shetland. The family felt at home with men of that nation, and when the young Scottish Admiral, who had recently come to Copenhagen, showed an interest in Anna, ideas of a marriage into the nobility of the Lowlands took shape.

Anna was dark. She flattered herself she looked Latin. There is an account of her at a fashionable wedding, "decked out as a Spaniard, that is she had a gold chain round her forehead, besides a necklace full of precious stones and a wreath of pearls with a feather of pearls in it, and a red damask tunic."

Proc. of Scottish Soc. of Antiquaries 1892/93. Gilbert Gouldie. Schiern 54 ss.

Anna Throndsen to Frederick II., 11 Mar., 1559. (Hansborg xxxix 28a).

Reg. of P.C. XIV. cxi.

Absalon Pedersen's Dagbog 107.

When Bothwell remembered his diminished lands his eye may be forgiven for pausing on the jewellery. It seemed to excuse a rather tiresome pose. He had, besides, a weakness for unusual looks. Janet Beton had been no domestic type. Exotic femininity had an appeal for him, and he nursed the man of action's pathetic respect for intellect in women.

To Anna the Admiral of Scotland looked a brilliant match. His birth, his position, the mission he came on, his youth and the future which lay at his feet alike commended him. She was, it has been mentioned, a good woman of business; did she see her chance in the empty Hepburn coffers? Many of James's problems would be solved by a rich marriage. Some one—was it Anna or her parents?—mentioned a dowry of forty thousand silver dollars (that was the figure that Bothwell or some one in his train passed on in a letter to Janet Beton) and the young Earl was caught. "With hand, mouth and letters," he offered both Anna and her parents, "to hold her as his lawful wife."

Randolph to Cecil, 23 Sept., 1560.

Absalon Pedersen's Dagbog 148.

de Thou xl. 819.

Anna was no prude, and intimacy, in the law court sense, anticipated any formal union; but the mirage of the silver dollars receded. The news of the Queen Regent's death and the Treaty of Edinburgh ended Bothwell's official duties in the North without freeing him from his new obligations. His solution has occurred to other entangled males. Temporary absence might merge into permanent separation. And had not the Earl Bothwell a duty to pay his respects to the young Queen at Fontainebleau?

But by now Anna was desperately in love. She announced her intention of accompanying her lover to France. There is no record that her family made any attempt to stop her. An explanation of their indifference will be suggested in the following pages and her condition may have made them reluctant to detain her. Faced with arguments that he could not resist, Bothwell accepted her company with a sinking heart.

'HAFNIA vulgo ᚲᛟᛈᛖᚾᚺᛁᚹᛖᚾ Vrbs Daniæ primaria quā se terra marique conspiciendam exhibet   Anno Salutis M. D. LXXXVII.

COPENHAGEN, 1587

(By courtesy of the Royal Library, Copenhagen)

Particulars of their journey are lost. Accidents and adventures befell them. Towards the end of August no news of Bothwell's whereabouts was to be had and he was stated to have perished. By 12th September he had reached Flanders. There he decided Anna must stay for the time being. *Throckmorton to Cecil, 22 Aug., 1560.*
Throckmorton to Cecil, 12 Sept., 1560.
Frederick II. to Augustus of Saxony, 22 June, 1568.

It has sometimes been incorrectly stated that he deserted her. No better witness can be called than Anna herself. In later days, in the time of his adversity, she sued her lover in a Norwegian court of law. On that depressing occasion she stated that the young Earl had taken her "from her fatherland and from her ancestral roof away from her parents to a foreign country under colour of marriage." Anna, who knew the truth, makes no charge of desertion. Bothwell did not deny that "she had spent and pledged clothes, precious objects and other articles in foreign countries at his request to supply the needs of his people," and promised the Court to compensate her. Neither side hinted at a desertion and there can be no doubt that the separation in Flanders was a temporary expedient, and that after some three months pushing his fortunes at the French Court, he returned to Flanders, collected the love-sick girl and took her to Scotland. *Absalon Pedersen's Dagbog 148.*
Teulet Lettres 142.

The reason for the parting is not hard to find. Bothwell left Scotland a poor man. He spent all the money he had with him executing the commissions of his ruler at various Courts, maintaining the appearance proper to a queen's envoy. The journey with Anna to Flanders took his last penny and he was obliged to let his mistress sell her valuables to support the small train he had brought with him from Scotland.

For his financial embarrassment there was one remedy. Could he not recover at the French Court the money he had spent in Scotland and in Scandinavia on behalf of his Queen? But what chance did he stand of winning her favour, if he arrived at Court with a foreign mistress in tow? A temporary separation looked doubly advisable. Apart from her irregular position, Anna's accomplishments were not likely to help at the highly civilised Court of France, where the unfortunate Norwegian would be quickly recognised as a bogus intellectual of the most distressing order. This harsh judgment is supported by some bad poetry and an egregious love-letter which the writer of this book believes to have been written by Anna, though both compositions are generally ascribed to a more illustrious pen.

A long dispute has raged round the problems of the reign of Mary Stuart; "there is scarce any part of history," declared the eighteenth century, "wherein authors have more differed and contradicted one another with greater warmth and spite." Contradiction reaches its climax over the so-called Casket Letters. These documents take their name from the silver casket in which they were alleged to have been found after Bothwell's defeat at Carberry Hill. They were held by the Queen's enemies to prove her adultery with that nobleman and her complicity in her husband's death. Consideration of a part of their contents must here briefly interrupt the story of James and Anna.

It was Cardinal Richelieu who remarked with the emphasis of experience, "Give me two lines of a man's handwriting and I will hang him!" Unfortunately for those who would base any conclusion on the Casket Letters, the Queen's handwriting is conspicuously absent. Three hundred and fifty years ago, as soon as their purpose was served, the alleged originals disappeared. All that exists to-day is a collection of copies and translations which do not agree with the descriptions of contemporaries who claimed acquaintance with the originals.

It is true that before they conveniently vanished, an investigation was held into their charges against the Queen; but the procedure followed would satisfy no modern court. Every shift was adopted to avoid producing the originals. At last they were read in the absence of any representative of the Queen. On another occasion they were laid on a table to be hastily compared with admitted specimens of her hand. They were hurriedly withdrawn and neither the Queen nor any partisan of hers was ever allowed to see them. No witness was examined to confirm any of the statements contained in the letters.

But though the conduct of the case reeks with fraud, it is difficult to believe that in the time available to the captors of the Casket, such a bulk of evidence could be manufactured. The supposed forger must be credited with abnormal energy and ability if he sat down before a blank sheet of paper to produce in an imitation of the Queen's hand a document as circumstantial as the "Long Glasgow Letter." At the same time he must be convicted of excessive flippancy if he wasted his time inventing anything as futile as the "Margaret Carwood Letter."

A far simpler method could be trusted to give better results. After Mary's capture, her enemies had access to her papers; Bothwell's private correspondence no doubt also fell into their hands. Those rugged consciences made no difficulty of inserting into a chance love-letter received by the gallant Earl, an extract from one of Mary's papers that would attribute the concoction to her. In other cases into one of Mary's genuine memoranda could be imported some lurid patch from the Bothwell collection. The services of an expert forger could then be called in—and at that date plenty of amateurs or professionals were easily found[1]—to copy the compound into a reasonable imitation of Mary's large Italian hand. The result would not stand up to careful examination, as the reluctance to exhibit the Casket Letters, their brief appearances and their final disappearance indicate.

If the forgeries are closely examined, it is not impos-

[1] An admitted forgery of Mary's signature may be seen on what is known as the "First Marriage Contract." Mr. Ainsworth Mitchell, Secretary of the Society of Public Analysts, has examined it along with specimens of Maitland's handwriting. He states that the letters of the forgery show the same method of formation and also the same method of holding the pen and applying pressure. In this scrutiny photographic enlargement and the methods of modern crime-detection were employed. ("Discovery," June, 1925, "The Evidence of the Casket Letters," 1927.) Failing Maitland, there were plenty of competent forgers. There was Archibald Douglas, who forged the letters of the Bishop of Ross to the Earl of Lennox. There were more obscure practitioners like William Wharton, whose offer to "counterfeit" Queen Mary's hand has been preserved. (Hosack ii. 218 ss, Boyd's Calendar iv. 655, 559.)

sible to resolve them into their component parts and even to assign the bits to the original writers. A feeling for style and some knowledge of the circumstances of possible authors helps analysis. To shorten the present digression from the story of Bothwell's life on the Continent, only the Eighth Letter and parts of the Sonnets need be taken, compositions which sameness of psychology and wording prove to have proceeded from one brain and one pen[1]— not the same pen, any impartial reader will agree, that wrote the numerous letters of Mary Stuart over which no controversy rages. The Queen's ordinary style was clear, disfigured by none of the tropes and affectations of the Eighth Letter. On the manner of the Sonnets we have the verdict of two great masters of literature, men moreover who knew the Queen personally and how she wrote. Ronsard agreed with Brantôme that the verses were: "too clumsy and unpolished to come from her workshop." It does not need the taste of these giants to see that.

Suppose it was not a queen whose mother tongue was French but a love-sick foreigner who wrote this inexpert rubbish? The daughter of a Norwegian admiral might know enough French to charm a Scottish lover, might even have originally attracted his notice by acting as interpreter in the negotiations for the loan of the Danish fleet; could she be blamed because she could not write reasonably good love-letters and poetry in a foreign tongue? But, if Anna's clumsy efforts fell ultimately into the hands of the men who were

---

[1] Thus both in the Eighth Letter and the Sonnets the writer uses the phrase "seul soutien de ma vie." In both documents she addresses the object of her affections as "mon seul bien" and "mon cœur." In the Sonnets she states that he is "en possession du cœur," while in the Letter she calls him "possesseur du cœur." She alludes to her "âme assujettie" in the poetry and to her "pensées assujetties" in the prose. The phrase "loyale femme et seule amie" may be compared with the words "chère amie . . . et loyaument aimer." If it be objected that such phrases are the commonplaces of amatory expression, these similarities of words are further supported by coincidence of tone. The desire for self-perfection to become worthy of the beloved and the almost masochistic abasement are identical in both effusions. The Glasgow Letters, the "Medea" Letter and the "Abduction" Letters breathe quite different tones and in the opinion of the present writer were by different hands.

preparing a case against Mary Stuart, many difficulties vanish.

Evidence must be brought to support this theory. The convenient disappearance of the originals of the Casket series rules out any comparison of handwriting, though Anna's firm, round, disjointed script is preserved *Hansborg* in the Copenhagen Archives. Only tests based on internal *xxxix. 28a.* evidence can be applied. Which of the two women do the circumstances described in the documents under review fit? At first sight two words in the Sonnets seem to point unmistakably to the Queen. Into her lover's hands, declares the authoress, "and into his full power, I place my son, my honour and my life, my country, *my subjects*, my subject soul . . ." Anna, of course, had no subjects to sacrifice and it is impossible that she wrote those two words. An examination of the metre suggests, however, that the three syllables, which spoil the deca-syllabic scansion, have been interpolated by the forger. If from the line "*mon pais, mes sujets, mon âme assujettie*" the third and fourth words are omitted, the residue con-forms to the standard length of every other third line of the twelve Sonnets. At the same time, the awkward juxtaposition of "sujets"—"assujettie" is avoided and the one conclusive identification of Mary Stuart as the authoress of the Sonnets disappears. The remaining items on the list of sacrifices to passion fit Anna better than Mary. Would a queen who regarded herself as a Frenchwoman talk of Scotland as her "pais" and not rather as her "royaume"? When did she put her son in Bothwell's power, or indeed her life? It may be objected that no record exists of any child of Anna's. But Bothwell had one natural son, William. That he was called after *Bannatyne* a favourite cousin and that his grandmother, the Lady *Misc. iii.* of Morham, continued to see him to the end of her *304, 423.* life, when she left him "her whole goods," suggests that the unmarried mother had some standing in the eyes of the family. It does not require a sustained flight of imagination to suppose that when Anna went back to Norway, her lover consigned her child to his mother's care and might be said to hold the boy "*en son plein pouvoir*."

The main autobiographical detail of the Sonnets will be examined later in this book, but it is desirable to cite here a couple of passages that describe the early stages of the liaison and the elopement.

"Alas!" the victim of Bothwell's love-making laments, "is he not already in possession of the body and the heart that shuns no pain or dishonour, slight to relations or worse affliction? For him I count all my friends as less than nothing . . ." This is natural language for a girl who has run away with a foreigner from her family, home and friends. The words are a grotesque understatement if they are twisted into an allusion to the horrors of Kirk o' Field haunting the conscience of a supposed murderess!

Bothwell, writes Anna again, has cost her many a tear, "first when he made himself possessor of a body whose heart he had not won." Surely an admiral's daughter would be more exposed to a cave-man courtship of this sort than a queen with courtiers, guards and ladies always within call. But the poetess affixes her signature most patently when she lists her sacrifices. "For him," she laments, "I have set at naught honour, which alone can bring us happiness, for him I have risked position and good conscience, *for him I have left my family and friends* . . ." As clearly as poetic diction allows, Anna is describing the straits to which elopement led her and the sacrifices that passion imposed. By what stretch of imagination could the words, "*pour lui tous mes parents j'ai quitté et amis*," be put into the mouth of the Queen?

The love letter remains. Its affectations almost provide Bothwell with an excuse for neglecting its authoress. It can hardly be put into straightforward English.

"Sir," it begins plaintively, "I leave you to judge if weariness produced by your absence and by your forgetfulness, or fear of danger which every one predicts to your beloved person can console me, in view of the unhappiness my cruel lot and continued misery threatens, following the misadventures and fears, both recent and further past, of which you are aware."

Anna in this rambling sentence expresses her fear of the danger that would threaten her lover riding through a France where no isolated protestant, so soon after the Tumult of Amboise, would be safe. Her personal misfortunes refer, if not to the existence of an unborn child, to the hardships of the journey from Copenhagen.

"But for all that, I do not complain of your scant remembrance and scant care, still less of your broken promise and cold letters, since I have made myself so much yours, that your will is agreeable to me." Stock reproaches of a lonely girl, betrayed under promise of marriage, natural on poor Anna's lips, but less appropriate to a queen.

"My thoughts so willingly submit to yours that I want to suppose that all your actions proceed from none of the above-mentioned causes, but from just and reasonable grounds which meet my own desires. By that I mean the arrangement which you have promised to make definitely for the security and honourable treatment of the sole support of my life. I have no other reason to wish to stay alive and, but for it, want only speedy death." Her lover, Anna hopes, is at last taking steps to provide for the unborn child for whose sake alone she values her life.

"To prove how humbly I submit to your commands, I send you by the hand of Paris, as a token of my homage the ornament of my head, which directs the other members, signifying that if you are invested with the spoil of the chief member, the rest of the body is your subject, with the heart's consent." This purple patch indicates the despatch of a bit of her hair by the hand of her lover's page, Nicholas Hubert, alias French Paris. (In 1567 Paris *Teulet* claimed to have been in Bothwell's service for five or *Lettres, 82.* six years, no doubt from the date of this stay on the Continent.)

"In place of the heart which is already yours, I send

107

you a sepulchre of hard stone, coloured black, sown with tears and bones. I compare it with my heart which is likewise fashioned into a secure tomb or repository for your commands, and especially for your name and memory, which are therein contained, as the hair in the ring." Anna sends the lock of hair in the recess of a mourning ring made of onyx or black enamel with a symbolic setting of tears and bones, no doubt represented by pearls. The believers in the Queen's authorship of this letter try to identify this ring with the "*table de diamant emaillé de noir*," later bequeathed to Bothwell by Mary. Even if it were likely that a "table-cut diamond" should be enamelled over until it could be described as a "hard stone coloured black" where is the mention of the unmistakable ornament of rococo bones and tears, which Anna so tediously describes?

"Never shall your memory issue, until Death gives you my bones for a trophy, just as the ring is covered with them—a sign that you have made a complete conquest of me and my heart, to the point of leaving you my bones in memory of your victory and of my happy, willing loss wherein I was better employed than I deserved." In this account of her seduction, Anna seems to have met her lover at least half-way.

"The enamel round the ring is black to symbolise the resolution of her who sends it. The tears are innumerable, like my fears to displease you and my tears for your absence and for regret that I cannot be yours in outward appearance as I am unfeignedly in heart and soul. I should have good right to that (public recognition), were my merits greater than the most perfect woman in history, which is what I want to be." Anna was crying, she says, for her lover's absence. He was in France while she was in Flanders. That gave some point to the heraldic significance of the colour of the ring— black for constancy. Why should Mary weep for the absence of a subject who was never away, during the period of the alleged adultery, for more than a few days, and whom her will could recall at any moment? The

108

writer of the letter regards her own unworthiness as the obstacle to marriage with the object of her passion. Bothwell may well have encouraged Anna to feel that inferiority, since at the beginning of the liaison he was a free man and could easily have married her, had he wished. In the supposed case of Mary and Bothwell a much more solid obstacle intervened—the existence of another husband and another wife.

"Receive then this ring, O my only possession, in as good part as my joyful acceptance of your wedding (ring). It shall never leave my bosom until our bodies are publicly joined and is a token of all I hope for and desire of happiness in the world." With this hint of a concrete proof of his promise, Anna gives the imprudent lover a sight of the whip she was to wield at the law suit which ended the romance seven years later. Then "she caused letters to be read before him" in which "he had promised to hold her as his lawful wife." His answer to this effusion may have figured among them. *Diary of Absalon Pedersen, 17 Sept., 1567.*

The letter ends with an involved peroration, in which Anna styles herself his "humble, obedient, loyal wife and only love," but which throws no further light on the circumstances of the couple. Compassion must be felt for the lot of the seduced intellectual, however enthusiastically she may have invited her fate. A little sympathy may be kept for the seducer whom she must have bored profoundly.

CHAPTER ELEVEN

BOTHWELL rode off with empty pockets and a light heart. Behind him a lachrymose Anna fluttered a damp handkerchief. Before him lay adventure and beauty at the most cultivated Court in Europe. A hundred questions filled his brain. Would the Queen of Scots like him as well as her mother had done? Would her Guise uncles be friendly? Had he stayed too long in the North? Would it have been wiser to return home to raise money for more lavish display?

Several considerations gave an answer. The death of Mary of Lorraine had removed his only powerful friend in Scotland. True, a clause guaranteeing oblivion of past differences was included in the Treaty of Edinburgh, but the protestant Lords who had now the upper hand showed *de Randau's* no intention of observing it. Sempill, with a much *protest to* shorter score against him, had been obliged to take *Throckmorton,* refuge inside the walls of Dunbar. *17 Sept., 1560.*

The French countryside, through which Bothwell rode, showed fewer outward signs of the Reformation than his own land. Here were no blackened ruins of abbeys and churches. Here the old religion held its own and had handled the reformers savagely at the unlucky rising known as the Tumult of Amboise. The hearts of the huguenots smouldered with resentment. Anxiously the boy king had summoned an extraordinary assembly at Fontainebleau in August to discuss the religious question. In a fiery speech Coligny demanded toleration for his co-religionists and swore that fifty thousand men would support his claim. The matter was adjourned to the meeting of the States General, fixed for the autumn at Orleans. But conspiracy was brewing against the Guise domination. The fervour of Calvin and Bèze fanned dissatisfaction in the South.

The young adventurer thought less of these grave matters than of the reception awaiting him at the hands of his queen—"such a queen", declared Doctor Johnson, a man not given to promiscuous enthusiasm, "as any man of any gallantry of spirit would have sacrificed his life for."

Mary Stuart was eighteen when Bothwell reached her Court. He saw her beauty in a light denied to later generations that have only a few indifferent portraits and many unauthentic pictures to go by. The verses of her poets preserve something that Bothwell was privileged to see—an evanescent charm difficult for paint-brush or pen to capture.

> Tout ce qui de beau ne se garde longtemps,
> Les roses et les lis ne regnent qu'un printemps;
> Ainsi votre beauté, seulement apparue
> Quinze ans en notre France, est soudain disparu,

wrote Ronsard with the poet's consciousness of the transience of beauty. Her vanished loveliness lingers in his memory of her hand, "*longue, gresle et delicate*"; in Brantôme's worship of her hair, "*si beaux, si blondes et cendrés.*"

Bothwell looked with delight on a luminous, transparent complexion, eyes that changed their lights from chestnut to hazel and shot a narrow, shy look from under heavy lids, eyebrows well marked and arched on a wide forehead, and a carriage and manner that proclaimed pride of race.

Much was to happen to the girl in the next seven years—much that has made her story "among such things as are taught to children from the cradle to make them fall in love with reading." To see her with Bothwell's eyes at their first meeting, her later life must be forgotten with the conjectures, slander or advocacy of the historians. He did not expect to find the budding Messalina that her enemies have painted, corrupted from her earliest youth by contact with the licentious Court of

Francis I, for he knew that casual monarch had died a year before the child of five-and-a-half arrived in France. The Court of Henry II, which Mary sometimes visited as a girl, was decorous as Courts then went. Mary was not exposed to the treatment her cousin Elizabeth suffered at the hands of the High Admiral of England, who had married her father's widow. "He would come into the Lady Elizabeth's chamber before she was ready and sometimes before she did rise, and he would ask her how she did and strike her on the back or on the buttocks familiarly; and if she was in bed, he would open the curtains and make as though he would come at her. And one morning he strove to have kissed her in bed and this examinate bade him go away for shame. He did use to come up every morning in his night-gown bared-legged in his slippers. This witness told my lord it was an unseemly sight to come bare-legged to a maiden's chamber . . ." Possibly mere instances of the exuberance to which sailors are only too prone, but a confession like Catherine Ashley's would not be slurred over in a life of Mary Stuart.

Haynes State Papers 99, 100.

If Bothwell was not ogled by the precocious voluptuary her enemies like to depict, neither was he dazzled by the paragon of learning and girlish wisdom that her panegyrists have imagined. Mary received the elaborate education the Renaissance gave to well-born girls, without attaining any blue-stockinged pre-eminence. Her French, Bothwell recognised, was graceful, but as she had spoken it from a child, that did not surprise him. A greeting in Scots was not beyond her[1] in compliment to the Borderer. Of Spanish and Italian "she had a useful knowledge rather than a pretentious fluency"—in less courtly language, a smattering. She read Latin more easily than she spoke it. Her singing voice was natural, not trained. She played the cittern, harp, virginals and danced gracefully. She was fond of riding, travelling

Conn (in Jebb ii. 15).

---

[1] The vexed question of whether Mary talked Scots is surely settled by Gouda's statement that "*Scotice respondere coepit*," when Master John Rivat was present to translate her French to Father Edmund Hay. (Pollen 17.)

long distances on horseback, and showed all the Stewart love of hunting and hawking. More showy horsemanship she left to the other sex. Her needlework was her strongest suit. Had Bothwell been a churchgoer, he could have seen several tapestries from her needle on the altars of France, the country that had brought weaving and embroidery to its highest perfection.

In matters of religion the young Earl found in his queen something of a kindred spirit. The martyr of the Holy Catholic Faith had not yet been created by adversity and political interest. Her youth was informed by a spirit of toleration that found no place in official formulæ. "For my part," she said about this time, "I am none of these that will change my religion every year, and I mean to constrain none of my subjects, but would wish they were all as I am." Even that good protestant Cecil *Cecil to* considered that she was "no more devout towards Rome *Challoner,* *8 June, 1562.* than for the contentation of her uncles."

Bothwell had to wait for an audience. When he reached St. Germain-en-Laye, Mary was indisposed and the whisper ran, as is the habit when young queens keep their beds, that the country was to be blessed with an heir. There was no truth in the rumour; her health was always poor. Her stock was not robust for her father had died at the age of thirty-one and her mother at forty-four. In Mary's eighteenth year she was not expected to have *Mason to* long to live. Consumption and anæmia were diagnosed; *Cecil, March,* she was subject to fainting fits. All her life she suffered *1559.* from a pain in her side, especially in the late autumn. Medical science had not advanced far enough to recognise indigestion arising from a gastric or duodenal ulcer. *Sir George* *Turner 46.*

To her bad health must be attributed her fatal reliance on the stronger wills of others. Often she felt too ill to take a line of her own choosing. The subject of her uncles' influence was a commonplace at Court—how the young Queen and her boy husband did nothing that did not serve the Guise interest. Bothwell must have wondered anxiously who was destined to dominate in Scotland. As he wondered and waited, he had to be content with the courtiers' estimates of his new sovereign. Sir James Melville, who shortly after made his way to Court at Orleans, may speak for them. "She was so affable, so gracious and discreet that she won the hearts of many both in England and Scotland, so that I thought her more worthy to be served for little profit than any other prince for great commodity. Then she was naturally liberal more than she had moyen. She was of quick spirit and would sometimes be sad when she was solitary, and glad of the company of them that had travelled in other parts."

Others talked of the Queen's contempt for ceremony, of her ready wit and vivacious sallies, of her love of poetry and literature, and her taste for pleasure—masques and dancing, cards and music. How fond she was of little dogs and how much thought she gave to clothes. The critical whispered her failings. Her temper was hot; under provocation an imprudent jest or a threat would flash out; she resented passionately any infringement of her royal dignity. At this date not even the wildest tongues hinted at the faintest scandal.

At St. Germain James Hepburn found several familiar faces. Lord Seton was there, and Captain Martigues and the Sieur d'Oysel. As they exchanged anecdotes of the siege of Leith, each warrior wondered if his visit to Court would earn the reward his merit deserved.

The golden shower did not flow very freely. There was some talk of giving d'Oysel the Order of France, but his comrade-in-arms, Captain Martigues, turned the royal pair against him and in the end d'Oysel "found so much favour that he had leave to retire himself to his own house."

Seton started better. At first his hopes were "something countenanced." But nothing definite was done and ere long he became "so evil satisfied that he desired to return into his own country." He regretted openly the ten thousand francs he had spent on the defence of Leith and the plate he had sold. But in the long run his promise to stand by the late Regent during her life met its material

114

reward with the post of Gentleman of the King's Chamber, a salary of eight hundred francs, an assignat for the money he had spent in the Queen's service and an abbey in the north of Scotland.

As long as the Court stayed at St. Germain, Bothwell, whether from delicacy or policy, did not press his claims. He had been penniless in Flanders, how he kept up appearances at the luxurious Court is a mystery. Every one was busy with the Festival of the Knights of St. Michael, but protestant scruples offered an excuse for absence. Sir Nicholas Throckmorton, the English ambassador, asserted his religious independence by refusing to kneel at the Elevation of the Host. Next day there was a Requiem and Dirge for the dead members of the Order and King Francis gave the conscientious ambassador a hint that he had better stay away if he felt so strongly. After that Sir Nicholas was surprised to find "some alteration in his entertainment." He had to wait in the room of the Captain of the Guard which, he remarked, was more like a prison than a place for receiving a prince's minister.

The latest news from England caused Elizabeth's representative some embarrassment. Lady Dudley, better known by her maiden name of Amy Robsart, had been found dead at the foot of a staircase in Cumnor Hall. The official explanation of "accidental causes" met a barely veiled incredulity, and Court gossips whispered that an inconvenient wife of a queen's favourite had "had her *Throckmorton* neck broken with other appurtenances." But soon the *to Cecil, 10* moment came for the move to Orleans, where the States *Oct., 1560.* General had been convoked. The King, on the advice of *Giovanni* his wife's uncles, summoned the notables of Paris—coun- *Michel, 11* cillors and presidents, deputies and doctors—to the great *October.* hall of the Louvre. He explained that religious disorder was the cause of his journey. For his own defence and "for his hearers' safety" he was compelled to avail himself of a loan of 400,000 francs, which from the love they bore him they would, he knew, be glad to contribute.

The royal couple—they were little more than children

—started for Orleans. The air was full of rumours of a rising in the South and ample precautions were taken for their safety. Horse and foot guards were heavily armed and reinforced by three companies of veteran infantry. Bothwell had opportunity to admire the French man-at-arms, whom he had seen in action, on ceremonial duty.

Les Ordres tenuz à la reception du roy. (Paris 1560).

The huguenot city of Orleans was making nervous preparations to receive its sovereigns. Word had gone round of the 400,000 francs demanded at the Louvre. Early on the morning of the 18th October the royal cavalcade appeared on the Paris road. A stand, erected outside the city gates, had been decorated with tapestry and coats of arms.

A procession formed up at nine in the morning. Eyes, accustomed to the simplicity and poverty of Scotland, were dazzled by the splendour of the spectacle. In the lead, helmet on head, came four hundred hagbutters in black, with violet and yellow scarves. The town bands followed on horse and on foot—watermen of the Loire, wine-growers of the valley, and merchants and tradesmen of the town. Each company had its banner, drums and fifes, halberds and pikes.

Commerce was followed by Law. Archers in parti-coloured red and yellow and mounted crossbowmen, two and two, came first. One hundred and twenty-six police officials marched by in velvet and grey satin. Night-watchmen, fully armed, preceded a band of notaries, lawyers and councillors escorting the Bailiff and Provost. The two officers halted at the royal stand long enough to deliver a speech of welcome.

After Law, Learning. The University of Orleans provided, in the opinion of spectators, the finest part of the procession. Four "nations"[1] of scholars marched bravely by. Eight beadles brought up the rear and made way for the masters of the schools, eight doctors and the rector, all in their scarlet robes. The rector led his learned

---

[1] The Normans, Picards, Germans and French. The former Scottish " nation " had been merged with the Norman.

ORLEANS IN THE REIGN OF CHARLES IX.

(*By courtesy of the British Museum*)

colleagues to the presence and inflicted another oration.

Prancing behind Wisdom came Youth—the young men of Orleans on good horses, gay in purpoints of yellow satin, lined with violet taffetas and trimmed with gold. Their collars were black velvet.

More archers in red and yellow preceded a procession representing Authority, in which the notable inhabitants were followed by the Governor, twelve magistrates and two councillors in scarlet. The keys of the city were presented with the inevitable speeches. King Francis felt his turn was due. He was not there to miss the moral. Loyalty and obedience to God and to himself were his recommendations. With those provisos he assured his subjects that they could count on being well governed.

However interesting the display had been to foreigners who watched its magnificence for the first time, young Francis must have welcomed the signal to leave his chair and ride his horse through the city gate. Noblemen, courtiers, archers, Swiss guards, men-at-arms wound their imposing way through the narrow, decorated streets. Drums, trumpets and cannon sounded.

Stands were packed with the poor children of the town. Spectators gathered at the street crossings and shouted *Vive le Roi!* as their monarch passed. On every side Latin inscriptions, triumphal arches, obelisks and columns met the King's indifferent glance.

The Bishop was waiting at the great church, ready to add another speech to the rigours of this exhausting day. At last the weary boy could retire to the house that had been prepared for him, and the horsemen of the procession went to fetch the Queen.

Her ladies rode with her, each with a lord by her side. Which of those charmers fell to Bothwell's share is not recorded, nor whether the image of poor Anna obtruded. It was a far cry from the glories of a state entry in Queen Mary's train to the lonely lodging in Flanders.

All the magnificence failed its purpose. A tax of ten thousand francs was laid on the city of Orleans and a further exaction of a hundred thousand threatened. To *Francis Edwards to Cecil, 18 Nov., 1560.*

117

keep the veteran infantry who filled the town cost money, but the Guises felt the latent disaffection demanded their presence. Burghers had to hand over their weapons, even their knives. Suspects were fined or thrown into prison; when there was no longer room in the ordinary gaols, church steeples served. Some victims met, it was whispered, a darker fate, "despatched by night and sent by water in sacks to seek God."

Bothwell was not the man to waste much sympathy on the sufferings of his co-religionists. He knew from experience the treatment the weaker side had to expect. He had been kindly received by the royal pair and he was enjoying the glittering parade of Court life. His immediate necessities had been relieved. In his own words: "the Queen recompensed me much more liberally and honourably than I had deserved." Less loyal natures might not have called the reward excessive. He was given a present of six hundred crowns and the post of Gentleman of the King's Chamber with the salary it carried. There was some talk of granting him the abbeys of Melrose and Haddington. Melrose had come into the hands of the Cardinal of Lorraine, but Michael Balfour and Lord Arran both had claims which they were prepared to press. Haddington Abbey was already in the gift of Bothwell's family and his father had nominated Elizabeth Hepburn to be its abbess. Bothwell's gratitude was expressed for rather nebulous benefits.

Les Affaires du Comte de Boduel, p. 7. State Papers For. Ser. 1560/619, 621.

His opinion on Scottish problems could not fail to be valuable to Mary. The death of the Queen Mother had left the country without an acting ruler. There was as yet no question of the Queen of Scots undertaking in person the ungrateful task of government. Had she been willing to exchange the civilisation of France for the discomfort and danger of her native land, her duty to her husband and to her adopted country prevented the sacrifice.

Bothwell brought first-hand knowledge of the personalities of her northern kingdom. Who was better qualified to express an opinion on the aspirations of Arran? (Even the outspoken Borderer would have tact enough to suppress the Hamilton dictum that there was but "a skittering lass" between that family and the throne.) He had to be more careful in what he said of James Stewart. If Cecil had recently made the significant remark that Lord James "was not unlike either in person or qualities to be a king" Bothwell had to remember a brother's hold over his half-sister's affections.

There was no harm, however, in giving a candid opinion on the proposals which "that ancient and honourable father," James Sandilands of Calder, had brought. He had just presented his credentials from the protestant Lords together with a copy of the Acts that a parliament of doubtful legality had passed since the Regent's death. To give good measure, he added a list of twenty-four names from which, it was suggested, a governing body should be chosen. By the Treaty of Edinburgh five members were to be selected by the Congregation, seven by the Queen. It did not need Bothwell's knowledge of Scottish politics to tell Mary that the Lords' nominees would work against her. It was less easy to recommend a group that could be trusted to serve her interests. Over the first name on the list Bothwell would make no difficulty (though perhaps some show of modesty). After himself could come the Primate of Scotland who, though a Hamilton, was bound to the Queen by religious self-interest. Bothwell, during his visits to the north of Scotland, had tested the loyalty of Atholl, and Huntly, as a strong catholic, could be trusted. On the other side of the fence, there was Argyll, who might be induced to turn his coat once again, Chatelherault who could not be left out, and Lord James Stewart. Bothwell disliked and mistrusted "the bastard of Scotland," but he was capable and powerful and his Stewart blood might keep him loyal.

The prospects of a workable coalition were not bright, but the young adventurer was an optimist. If Queen Mary would give him leave to start, he vowed he would live in Scotland "despite of all men." More than that, he promised to accomplish great things for his Queen. She smiled on his enthusiasm and gave a gracious consent.

It was the first bitter day of a mild autumn. To avoid witnessing the execution of Condé, she and Francis were on the point of leaving Orleans for the Chateau of Chenonceau with its honeymoon memories. The Balliage, the house they had occupied at Orleans, was already dismantled. The royal beds, coffers and tapestry, which by the custom of the time accompanied the Court, had been sent ahead down the Loire. Francis's boots were on, the Royal Barge was ready, when he complained of a pain in his head and in his right ear. The pain became acute. Orders were countermanded, Bothwell was told to postpone his departure, and the journey to Chenonceau was abandoned.

The King grew rapidly worse. Shivering with fever, he was taken into the empty house and put to bed on a mattress, until a canopy could be set over him. His ear began to discharge—"besides this he was loose of his body, which within ten or twelve days brought him extremely weak." When the discharge stopped, he suffered agony in his teeth and jaw, and from an inflammation behind his ear, "like a large nut"—which increased and diminished. Ambroise Paré, his doctor, gave him a purge of rhubarb, which made him vomit. For a fortnight the boy endured violent headaches, fever and sickness.

Towards the end he became delirious. The gates of the Court were closed and no one was allowed in his room but the Guises, his mother, Catherine de Medicis, and his distracted wife. On Monday, 3rd December, he was dying. All Tuesday the Court spent on its knees in prayer, and processions were formed in the churches. Catherine's anxiety was aggravated by the predictions of the astrologers. Her daughter-in-law's sorrow took the more practical turn of "long watching and painful diligence."

By now the King was speechless, "saving a soft hollow rattling sound." At eleven on the night of Thursday, 5th December, he died.

At an autopsy, his brain was found to be diseased.

Opposition theologians took great pleasure in this; John Knox wrote that he had "suddenly perished of a rotten ear—that deaf ear that would never hear the truth of God." Calvin gave the Deity double credit—"suddenly God appeared from Heaven and He who had pierced the eye of the father smote the ear of the son." In later years Mary's libellers accused her of poisoning the boy, forgetting that she stood to lose everything by his death and ignorant that future science would have no difficulty in diagnosing a cerebral abscess and septic meningitis that followed a disease of the middle ear. *Corpus Reformatorum xiv. 270. Murdin's State Papers 57.*

After a suitable pause, the Court left Orleans—"and so by degrees," prophesied a shrewd Italian, "will every one forget the late king except the young queen."

She wrote some touching verses on her loss that were approved by Ronsard. Their simplicity makes a notable contrast with the affectation of Anna's Sonnets.

> . . ."Si en quelque séjour
> Soit en bois ou en prée;
> Soit sur l'aube du jour,
> Ou soit sur la Vesprée,
> Sans cesse mon cœur sent
> Le regret d'un absent . . .
>
> "Si je suis en repos
> Sommeillant sur ma couche,
> J'oy qu'il me tient propos
> Je le sens qui me touche;
> En labeur et requoy
> Tousjours est prèz de moy . . .
>
> "Mets chanson ici fin
> A si triste complainte
> Dont sera le refrin
> Amour vraye et non feinte,
> Pour la separation
> N'aura diminution."

CHAPTER TWELVE

*Throckmorton
to Elizabeth,
28 Nov., 1560.*

BEFORE Francis was dead, Bothwell had left Court. His sudden departure "to return into Scotland by Flanders" puzzled the English ambassador. Sir Nicholas suspected some political *coup* and warned his correspondent in London against the Earl's character and intentions. He was in the eyes of the diplomat "a glorious,[1] rash and hazardous young man—and therefore it were meet his adversaries should both have an eye to him and also keep him short." His adversaries did not know that he was hurrying to Flanders to share with a lonely mistress the rewards he had won. Or did another letter, not preserved in the Casket, contain an urgent summons dictated by Anna's interesting condition? It is enough to suppose that Bothwell had left her with a promise to return as soon as his fortunes were retrieved.

*State Papers
For. Ser.
1561/16.*

*P.C. Reg.
xiv. 211.*

It is certain that he quitted Court for Flanders soon after the 17th November and did not reach Scotland till the end of the following February. It is also certain that Anna crossed to Scotland and lived there in considerable comfort, since her passport to return from Scotland to Norway is dated 17th February, 1563, and contains allusion to "all her goods movable and immovable." Of how the lovers passed the three months in Flanders there is no record. If Anna was enceinte and Bothwell impatient for instructions their sojourn may not have been very happy.

A meeting of neighbours on whom he had been counting to "do great things" was held at Dunbar about the beginning of December. In Bothwell's absence little was effected, though sentiments of loyalty to the Queen were expressed. Besides various Humes and Kerrs, Bothwell's cousin, the Laird of Langton, and his bailiff,

---

[1] Glorious in the sense of Plautus's "miles gloriosus" = vainglorious.

James Ormiston of Ormiston, attended to represent his views.

Black Ormiston was not free from anxieties on his own account. Once again the neighbours were "misreporting him." He was accused of receiving oxen stolen in England. True to his lord's tradition, he challenged the accuser and threw his glove in his face. No combat, of course, ensued and the dispute was carried before a Border Court which Arran was holding at Jedburgh. Seizing an opportunity to settle accounts, the Hamilton sentenced Ormiston to a term of imprisonment, in which punishment an uneasy sense of impartiality included the accuser, John Rutherford of the Knowe.

There were other signs of activity on the Border. The English Warden, Sir John Forster, was disturbed by the raids of the men of Liddesdale. He sent his sergeant to the Hermitage with twenty-three complaints addressed to Lord Borthwick. The Castle garrison refused to accept the list and protested that they held the place for the Earl of Bothwell. To make themselves clear, they took the sergeant prisoner and stole his horse and gear. These high spirits Sir John attributed to their lord's return to Scotland.

For Bothwell was back. He had hurried to Scotland in time to receive Queen Mary's charge to convoke a Parliament. This commission had been despatched by the hands of four loyal lairds and addressed to Bothwell and the other noblemen nominated by the Queen to represent her in the Coalition prescribed by the Treaty of Edinburgh. The lairds also brought three hundred letters to be presented to her principal supporters with formal notification of the death of the King of France.

But the idea of a Coalition Government was never put to the test. The protestant Lords saw that Bothwell and his associates had the authority and the strength to resist a *coup d'état*. They took the ingenious step of sending their leader, Lord James Stewart, to France to invite the widowed Queen to return to her realm and govern it herself. Lord James knew that she would always

123

depend on the guidance of a stronger will; he was determined that the claims of blood and administrative ability should compel his choice as mentor. The invitation to Scotland, which appeared to demonstrate the loyalty of the Lords, bore the hall-mark of the Secretary's ingenuity, for Maitland of Lethington was Lord James's ally and the cleverest man in the country. The only countermove open to the loyalists was to hurry off their own representative with a similar invitation. They chose John Leslie, who succeeded in due course to the Bishopric of Ross.

The two deputations, separated by a day, intercepted the Queen of Scots on a round of visits to Guise relations. The bad terms she was on with Catherine de Medicis, now the dominating figure in France, disposed her to listen to the proposal of a return to Scotland. Family ties and a natural amiability inclined her to reconciliation with her half-brother. His character seemed to combine the uncomfortable virtues that public life demands. "He dealeth," said Randolph, "according to his nature—rudely, homely and bluntly." (His sufferings from dyspepsia may account for part of his bluntness.) "His house is more like a church than a Court." His admirers searched history, sacred and profane, for his equal.

"*Ane Tragedie*" (*1570 A.D.*)

He had likewise the justice of Jethro
And also the chastity of Scipio;
He had of David the benignity
And of Titus the liberality.

Throckmorton to Cecil, 9 Nov., 1561.

Unfortunately for the Queen, she was to find that two devouring passions—ambition and avarice—took precedence of more amiable traits. Of the second failing, she had some warning. Recently Lord James, hoping his part in the last war had been forgotten, had applied for the arrears of a pension once paid him by the French crown, and had tried to secure its continuance. He failed to mention a simultaneous allowance from England. It was some months since Cecil had written his name on the list of corruptible material. "The Earl of Glencairn is *Cecil to Throckmorton, 27 Mar., 1560.* poor, honest, constant and wise;[1] Maxwell is very wise and religious; Home would be caught with a hook of a few ducats; Lethington is a rare man for all good qualities; *the Lord James would be gratified*; Kirkaldy has need and reason to be remembered."

James Stewart quickly proved the money pressed into his palm a good investment. He sought the English Ambassador at his lodging and "declared to him at good *Tytler v. 179.* length all that had passed between the Queen, his sister, and him." Sir Nicholas was impressed by the use that could be made of so well-informed an ally and urged his sovereign to continue her liberality—"since his being here, he hath dealt so frankly with me, that I must believe he will so continue after his return home. And *Throckmorton to Elizabeth, 23 June, 1561.* in case your Majesty would now in time liberally consider him with some good means to make him the more beholden to your Majesty, it would in my simple judgment serve to great purpose."

Mary, ignorant of this double-dealing, naturally accepted at face value her half-brother's offers of loyalty, but the reputation for duplicity which Maitland of Lethington enjoyed was common property. "What sort of man is Lethington?" once asked an ambassador. "A sort of Scottish Cecil!" was the comprehensive reply. Another foreign diplomat, versed in the artifices of the Holy City, paid him the compliment of calling him the most crafty of men. Fascinated by the charm of his intelligence, Queen Mary sought to attach the Chameleon, as Buchanan nicknamed him, to her service. Pathetically she sought to disarm his treachery with frankness. After mentioning that she was aware that nothing passed among her nobility without his knowledge and advice, she assured him that if he gave proof of the good will he promised, he need fear no calumniators, "for such have *Mary to Lethington, 29 June, 1561.* no part with me. I look to results before believing all that is told me. For the scruple that may arise from your

---

[1] The words "honest" and "wise" are used in the Elizabethan slang sense of "pursuing the same religion and the politics as the speaker."

acquaintance with England, it will cease with your intelligence there." Proof of the coin which repaid this confidence, is the presence of a copy of this letter in Cecil's files. Queen Mary's tragedy was due to the faith she placed in the unfaithful. When she encountered loyalty, like Bothwell's, she was apt to throw it away.

That "hazardous young man," ever fatally indifferent to intrigue, was taking no steps to checkmate his enemies' activity. He was busy with his own affairs—Anna Throndsen, a match with Lord Ruthven, (who sent to England for his geldings) an abortive attempt to reconcile his enemies, a move to consolidate the promises made him at the French Court. He came to terms with one of the *Bannatyne* claimants to Melrose Abbey. Michael Balfour (it was *Misc., iii. 305.* waste of time approaching Arran) agreed to sign an obligation to give the whole lands in fee to Bothwell and his heirs. The occupants of the abbey were less amenable and Bothwell had to employ all his powers of persuasion.

"Us brothers of the Abbey of Melrose," reads a statement signed at a later date by the dean and another monk, "having respect to God and good conscience and for the very zeal and love that either of us bears to the Eternal Truth and for the exoneration of our consciences, affirm that the fee we subscribed to James, Earl of Bothwell, was subscribed for very dread and fear of our lives. Who said in presence of diverse honourable men that he should exile us from the place of Melrose, take away the keys of our chambers, and shortly burn and mark us with hot keys on our cheeks, with many other injurious words. And therefore, as we shall answer before the Eternal our God, whatever we did in his favour, we did the same for very fear of our lives, not having respect to God or good conscience, common weal of the country, nor yet our own wills."

If the Earl had a firm hand with monks, the Abbey was accustomed to a certain emphasis. A little earlier Walter Chisholm had threatened to "stew the luggis" (ears) of the Prior. The faults may not have been all on

SIR NICHOLAS THROCKMORTON
(*By permission of the National Portrait Gallery*)

one side. An ambiguous reputation attached to the corporation.

> The Monks of Melrose made good kale
> On Fridays when they fasted,
> They wanted neither beef nor ale
> As long as their neighbours' lasted.

While Bothwell was thus engaged, he had no suspicion that his enemies were winning the Queen's ear. On the surface his favour ran high. Mary made a provisional order that when the French garrison evacuated Dunbar, Bothwell should occupy it in her name. His position looked secure to the outside world. The Countess of Lennox, in England, sent to inquire his feelings about her son's alliance with the Queen. Bothwell's answer to this first hint of the Darnley marriage has not been preserved. *State Papers For. Ser. 1561. 26.*

If the Queen was giving her confidence to his ill-wishers, she was quick to call him in when she needed a man of action. The decision to return to Scotland was easier to take than to fulfil. Queen Elizabeth refused a safe conduct through England. The pretext was Scottish delay in signing the Treaty of Edinburgh; the real reason a belief that Queen Mary was better kept out of the British Isles. *Cecil to Throckmorton, 14 July, 1561.*

In an indignant interview with the English Ambassador Mary Stuart's quick temper flamed. In her childhood, she reminded him, England had tried to stop her passage to France. If she cared to employ her friends, she had as good means to help her home.

The Admiral of Scotland was the "friend" in her mind. Already he had received his summons. His arrival post-haste in Paris was predicted by the Venetian Ambassador for the 3rd July and recorded by the English Ambassador on the 5th. Little escaped Throckmorton's shrewd eyes and his mention of Bothwell's movements in connection with preparations for the sea voyage shows *Throckmorton, 5 July, 1561.*

that he understood why the Admiral was wanted. John Leslie, in a list of arrivals, brackets Bothwell's name with the Bishop of Orkney and Lord Eglinton. The association is significant, for the Bishop's seamanship was proved in after years at Bothwell's expense, while Eglinton was "vehemently suspected of Piracy." The business of the trio was clearly nautical and a contemporary diarist was not far wrong when he stated cryptically that the Queen was "stolen out of France by certain Lords." The details of this characteristic stroke have been so far lost that historians have even queried Bothwell's presence in France.[1]

Leslie's History 284.

Hardwick's State Papers i. 176.

Birrel's Diary 4.

His efforts were hindered by the Queen's indifferent health. On his arrival she was confined to her bed with a tertian fever. When she was better she sent for Throckmorton, and, inspired no doubt by Bothwell's intrepidity, told the Ambassador that "she was determined to adventure the matter, whatsoever came of it." Sir Nicholas accepted with becoming gravity her assurance that no Scot had come to Court since her husband's death "but such as are either come for their private business or such as dare not tarry in Scotland." Bothwell's name might be placed, by any one less acute than Sir Nicholas, in either category.

Keith 173.

On the 25th July, 1561, the Queen of Scots took her leave for ever of the French Court and on the 14th August embarked at Calais on an adventure her instinct mistrusted. The sight in harbour of a fishing boat foundering with all hands did not dispel presentiment. Mary's heart was tender. To Brantôme's surprise she would not allow "a single galley slave to be beaten, however lightly!"

Bothwell was not on the galley that had been chosen for her accommodation. The company was ornamental —the Queen's four Maries and three of her uncles, the Marquis of Elbœuf, the Duke of Aumale and Francis of Lorraine, who, as General of the Galleys, was in formal charge of the expedition. The naval manœuvres are hidden in a fog, atmospheric as well as metaphoric,

[1] See Hay Fleming pp. 37, 236.

but it seems clear that Elizabeth, prompted by Lord James, sent an English squadron to intercept her cousin or at least to prevent her landing on English shores. From Yorkshire comes a picturesque glimpse. Off Flamborough, two great galleys loomed out of the mist within a furlong of the pier. The larger was all white; the second was red flying a blue pennant with the arms of France and a white flag that glistened like silver at the stern. Both vessels cast anchor and put out two men stripped to swim and boats to take soundings. The mist lifted and revealed thirty-two "tall ships" farther out to sea and on the horizon twenty more. Had Bothwell's boast been vain and was the Queen of Scots already fated to fall into her cousin's relentless hands? It must be admitted that neither the Admiral's precautions nor the efficiency of the French fleet saved her. Mist descended to prevent an engagement. The only capture was Lord Eglinton's vessel and two ships transporting the royal stud. The galleys that bore the Queen and her train anchored at Leith at nine o'clock in the morning of the 19th August in a thick Edinburgh "haar."

CHAPTER THIRTEEN

THE capital, to which Bothwell followed his Queen, looked pleasant enough on a sunny day. Edinburgh was small, compared with the Paris or Orleans he had lately visited—an Italian mile, the description runs, in length, and half that distance in breadth. Inside the area lived some thirty to forty thousand souls. The walls of the houses were of squared freestone, the roofs of slate or red tile. Thatch had been made illegal but could still be seen.

Two streets, the High Street and the Cowgate, ran down the steep spine of rock that joined the Castle to the Abbey of Holyrood. The High Street was well paved with square boulder stones and drained by channels on either side. It was kept clean and excited the admiration of foreigners. There were no pavements and wayfarers walked down the middle of the street between good, hewn-stone houses from whose façades projected wooden galleries.

The top of the High Street was separated from the Lawnmarket by the Luckenbooths and the Old Tolbooth, a building used as a prison, Supreme Court and some-times the seat of Privy Council and Parliament. At the foot of the street the turreted Netherbow Port opened on the Canongate.

The Canongate was the Court suburb and ran on down hill to Holyrood. Along it were set the houses of the nobles; behind them spread gardens and fields. Parallel to the High Street lay the Cowgate, which was bordered by the orchards and gardens of the ruined Black-friars Monastery. Here, too, could be found genteel residences, and in Blackfriars' Wynd.

At right angles to the two main streets, pitching off the ridge, ran the wynds. No attempt was made to keep them clean. They were blocked with middens (cleared, in theory, once a week), tar barrels, stacks of heather, broom or peat. Low arches spanned crooked passages; narrow doors opened through walls built at irregular angles. Roofs that almost touched were constructed on every level and of any shape—gables, domes or cones.

Among the wynds the wayfarer came on courts or gardens enclosed by dilapidated dykes. A little corn or some cabbages grew there, and a few bee skeps stood in the shade of a tree.

Each trade kept its own quarter. Goldsmiths plied their art near the Mint at the foot of Elphinstone's Court; linen-merchants drove their bargains in the Lawnmarket; braziers and tinsmiths made the West Bow noisy and the meat market tainted the air of the Canongate, just below the Netherbow. In their booths the merchants kept an axe or a pike to seize when the common bell summoned them to intervene in feud or killing. Each booth was bound by law to show a lantern after dark.

At the Tron in the central market place, where produce was weighed, gathered the kail wives. Here stood the stocks for the accommodation of minor criminals. The ladies of the town haunted the Market Cross, where proclamations were read and where more serious offenders expiated their crimes on gallows or pillory. Bankrupts, too, were exposed, wearing a yellow hat.

On the south side of the town reforming zeal and foreign invasion had reduced the monasteries of Blackfriars and Greyfriars to heaps of stone, useful when a dyke or a wall needed mending. Between these sites, on rising open ground, stood the tall, ruined tower of Kirk o' Field, whose precincts were destined to play so baleful a part in Bothwell's life. Beyond ran the city wall that had been hurriedly thrown round the town after the battle of Flodden and stood always in need of repair. Outside the wall lay meadows and woods, with burns and lakes full of fish.

The town was packed with nobles, their retainers,

their kinsmen; burghers, merchants, craftsmen, traders; servants, artisans and apprentices; their wives and children. The eyes of all were fixed on their sovereign. Most felt the spell of her youth and beauty. Every heart throbbed with patriotism, admiration, loyalty, self-interest, jealousy, bigotry, hope or cupidity. The Queen of Scots had the chance to guide and mould these passions to the service of herself and her country; to inspire the mean-minded and to control the high-spirited. The graceful, delicate girl who was given this opportunity did not know how to use it. On her arrival at Holyrood Mary went to bed and stayed there a fortnight.

Castelnau (in Jebb ii. 455).

So there was time for hopes to fade, enthusiasms to wane, quarrels to explode, rumours to circulate. Mary had missed her chance of becoming a national heroine. Her loyal supporters suffered. Bothwell watched the command at Dunbar, which had been promised him, pass into the hands of one of her half-brothers; the Lieutenancy of the Border, which he had enjoyed, fall to another—the formidable Lord James. As a final blow, on the pretext of avoiding friction with Arran, he was temporarily forbidden the Court.

Randolph to Throckmorton, 26 Aug., 1561.

The excuse was not even plausible, for the guilty consciences of the Hamiltons kept them away from Edinburgh. Arran, with Knox, had become the inspiration of the extreme protestants, who with shouts of "Death to the Idolater!" tried to stop the celebration of the Mass in the Queen's private chapel.

Bothwell escaped the spectacle of this malignity. On the Border he found plenty to do. His achievement is summarised in a memorandum which Queen Mary signed in later years. "After our returning into Scotland," she stated, "he gave his whole study to the forth-setting of our authority and to employ his person to suppress the insolence of the rebellious subjects inhabiting the countries lying west the Marches of England, and within a short time brought them to a perfect quietness." She adds that her intention had been to employ him on similar work in other parts of her realm, had not Fate

132

ordered otherwise. She had the perspicacity to recognise his value. The Borders, says a report intended for foreign consumption, were reduced to a state of incredible peace and the robbers infesting them were subdued by drastic and impartial measures. But Bothwell's administration, however beneficial to the peace of Scotland, was harmful to his prospects, since his necessary absences from Court (his banishment was forgotten as soon as Mary left her bedroom) exposed him to the innuendos of his enemies, which she lacked strength of mind to ignore. *Pollen 95 (2).*

She did him, however, the justice to include his name on the list of Privy Councillors issued three weeks after her return. Of the dozen Councillors, at least six had to "make continual residence with the Queen" and needed her licence to depart to their own dwelling-houses. The margin allowed Bothwell to continue his more congenial work on the Border. On the occasions when he attended a Council, he found that meetings were held in the Council Chamber from eight in the morning until ten and from one in the afternoon until three. Silence was imposed once the Councillors had taken their seats and no one was allowed to speak or "round with his marrow," until invited by the Chancellor. At his request any two members would "reason upon a matter, and after them another two as shall be thought good." When discussion was deemed sufficient, the Chancellor took a vote. *Keith 187.*

Bothwell's colleagues represented many degrees of religious and political opinion. Men of such widely different convictions and interest can rarely have agreed on any contentious subject. Personal quarrels, no less than variety of views, divided them. Among the Councillors, Bothwell had to reckon several bitter enemies.

The Duke of Chatelherault had been the Fair Earl's foe and the quarrel with Arran had transferred his hostility to James Hepburn. His age, however, and his irresolute disposition made him a less dangerous enemy than his heir, whose disordered fanaticism also found a place at the Council table. With the vehement Earl of

Glencairn and the unstable Earl of Argyll, the extreme protestant faction was numerically powerful.

The less rigid section of Reformed opinion was ably represented by the discretion of Lord James and the moderation of the Earl Marischal. The subtlety of Maitland, Secretary of the Council, completed a formidable unit, which saw in Bothwell the most serious obstacle to its ambitions.

From the catholic Lords Bothwell was estranged by religion, but loosely connected by Francophile policy. Their influence on the Council was diminished by the family feuds which divided them. The Earl of Atholl, whose courage exceeded his discretion, and the colourless Earl of Errol both cherished a hereditary enmity against the least incapable of their religion, Huntly, the Cock o' the North.

Two "dark horses" could not at this date be classified —Erskine, whose chief interest lay in the pleasures of the table, and Morton "steeped in lust and guilt," whose character was late to develop.

Of the officials of the Council far the most important was the Secretary, William Maitland of Lethington. James Macgill, Clerk of the Register, a recent convert to the Reformed Faith, and the Treasurer, Robert Richardson, were later more vigorously than kindly described as "crafty perjured foxes, heirs to Judas, sons to Satan and of the progeny of cruel Cain." The Justice Clerk, Sir John Bellenden,[1] "not least among the flatterers of the Court," was always ready to join the stronger side.

It is understandable that Bothwell found the air of the Border preferable to the atmosphere of the Council Chamber. His duties occupied him all autumn though messengers kept him in constant communication with the Queen and her Council.

But Mary was impelled by temperament and policy to try to heal the quarrels that divided her nobility.

[1] His son, Lewis, succeeded him in the office. The younger Bellenden "by curiosity dealt with a warlock called Richard Graham to raise the devil. Who having raised him in his own yard in the Canongate, he was thereby so terrified, that he took sickness and died."

Her gentle mind did not understand the Scottish capacity for hatred. Unwittingly she had inflamed the Bothwell-Arran dispute with the rash promise of Melrose. Arran Randolph to Cecil, 24 Sept., 1561. drafted some infantry to hold the Abbey against the claimant and the two sides set about "taking up their tithes, both well armed and horsed." The views of the farmers, who had to pay twice over, are not recorded.

Before tackling this dangerous feud the Queen demanded the reconciliation of her half-brother with Bothwell. Ingeniously she tried to soften their mutual dislike by associating them in congenial occupations. To this end she organised a friendly visit to Berwick, hoping at one stroke to improve relations with a foreign power and between her subjects.

Bothwell found various friends in a party which numbered some three hundred guests. The Frenchmen who had accompanied the Queen from Calais were there. So were Lord Robert and Lord John, the more amiable of her half-brothers. Morton, Borthwick and Home were invited as buffers between the hostility of Bothwell and Lord James.

The start was early but the Queen was determined to spare no effort to make the day a success. She got up early on purpose to see the party off. When they had ridden out of sight, she went back to bed, but to preserve amenities she sent her four Maries as far as Seton House. Quarrels could hardly explode in such gracious company!

Bothwell and Lord James were on their best behaviour and the midday meal at Seton was eaten without incident. When the expedition reached Dunbar Castle, so lately promised to Bothwell, a sigh of relief greeted Bothwell's unflagging urbanity. There the night was passed, not without festivity, for the Earl of Huntly "with a fall did put his arm out of joint." Randolph, failing to enter into the prevailing geniality, adds that "some are so uncharitable that they wish it had been his neck."

Next day the cavalcade was met on the Border by the Berwick officials. Lord James made a little speech, whose patronising tone Bothwell had to stomach, asking that "no token of unkindness might be used towards Lord Bothwell or Lord Home, because he purported to convey them as near the walls as he might." After international compliments of average insincerity, the two parties halted within crossbow shot of the town. "The Scots never offered to depart till they had heard all the artillery shot off. It liked all men so well that Lord James swore by his honour he never heard thing more royal." With determined amiability, Henri de Damville, the French marshal, was loud in his admiration of the English hagbutters.

Relations between individuals were as smooth as between nationalities. The Scots were taken to the lodging of Valentine Browne, the Treasurer, given supper and, next morning, breakfast, so that "not one departed without his bellyful of good cheer." As a final compliment each nobleman was presented with a gelding, better, says the English reporter complacently, than any they had brought out of Scotland.

On the way back to Edinburgh, the Scots slept at Coldingham. Bothwell was hoping that the partiality its Commendator, Lord John Stewart, showed for his sister, Lady Janet Hepburn, might ripen into something more decisive. A marriage would help his standing with the Queen and improve his relations with Lord James. He liked the Commendator, ("a man of mild disposition, who cultivated the greatest familiarity with all the nobles of the country,") and sympathised with his recipe against the virulence of the godly. "Do I see the Queen's Majesty so troubled with the railing of these knaves?" the Commendator had muttered. "I shall leave the best of them stikkit in his pulpit." Lord John's threats reached Knox's ears until the prophet vowed that "modesty" would not suffer him to write "what further villainy came forth of his stinking throat and mouth."

Sympathy between Lord John and the Hepburn brother and sister, and the guarded civilities exchanged on the Berwick picnic, built a precarious bridge between

136

Bothwell and Lord James. Bothwell trusted himself to its support long enough to attend four meetings of the Privy Council during the middle part of October. His presence was valuable with Border affairs on the agenda. He took a step towards the settlement of outstanding disputes by transferring his claim to Melrose Abbey to the third of the Stewart brothers, Lord Robert, Abbot of Holyrood.

Randolph to Cecil, 24 Oct., 1561.

The way was paved to a formal truce. On the 11th November, 1561, in the presence of the Queen and at her express command, appeared James Bothwell and George Seton and agreed on behalf of their family, friends, tenants and servants that their opponents should be unharmed, unvexed, unmolested and "undistrublit" until the following first of February. Lord James and John Cockburn of Ormiston entered a similar undertaking. The limited period of the truce testifies to the parties' real feelings.

The reconciliation lasted long enough for Bothwell to ride with Lord James and the Earl of Morton to Jedburgh. There Lord James in his capacity of Lieutenant was to hold a Court of Justice. For a fortnight the Raid of Jedburgh pursued its relentless course. Lord James burned many houses, hanged a score of law-breakers and carried another forty or fifty to Edinburgh for more considered punishment. Neither bribes nor prayers availed, though Bothwell's clemency obtained remission for the Liddesdale clans. Lord James did not believe in half measures. One Peter Turnbull, alias the Monk, was wounded resisting capture. His cure at the hands of Robert Henderson cost the country five pounds. As soon as he was well, he was turned over to the hangman.

This Robert Henderson was a remarkable surgeon. A few years later he is heard of treating "a dead woman, raised forth of the grave, after she had lain two days in the same, alleged to have been strangled."

CHAPTER FOURTEEN

LORD JAMES had a rough-and-ready rule for the minor law-breaker—a rope for his neck and a torch for his thatch. The peace of Scotland would have been more secure if his sister had not tried to remedy the lawlessness of her major criminals by methods of forgiveness and conciliation. A touch of Tudor ferocity, occasional resort to the axe and the scaffold, would have served her better.

The Hamiltons avoided Edinburgh until they were sure of their ground. The Duke stayed at Keneil, while Arran sulked at St. Andrews. His inaction was ascribed by his friend Randolph to three causes—dislike of the Roman rites practised in the Chapel Royal; lack of means to make a show at Court (which "manifests to the world the beastliness of his father, that hath more money than either Faith or God"), and anxiety to avoid Bothwell (which "argueth less courage than many men thought.").

Three months passed and the family saw there was nothing to fear from the Queen. In the middle of October James Hamilton, Primate of Scotland, rode up the High Street with eighty horsemen at his back. He was joined by Gavin Hamilton, Abbot of Kilwinning. A fortnight later the Duke of Chatelherault presented himself at Court and was kindly received by the Queen. Arran's movements were more sensational.

It was Sunday night. The men of action, Lord James and Lord Bothwell, were hanging thieves at Jedburgh. The courtiers were about to take their leave and the Queen was thinking of bed, when whispers of impending peril began to pass from mouth to mouth. No one knew what threatened. No one knew what steps would meet a danger that no one could define. Concern, alarm, panic seized the elegant company.

Lord John and Lord Robert Stewart rose to the occasion. They set a guard over the Queen's person, they called armed burghers from the town, they stationed pickets round the palace. The night passed without incident.

In the morning an explanation of the night's alarms was on every lip. Arran had crossed the Forth with horse and foot. He was going to kidnap the Queen. All the Hamiltons in Edinburgh were waiting to join him.

The Queen's friends rallied. They made permanent the extemporised guard; they allotted every nobleman, lodged in the precincts, his turn of duty; they set builders to block access to the royal apartments. The Duke's hurried appearance at Court made their precautions a little ridiculous. It was true, he admitted, that his son had crossed the Forth. But his destination had been Keneil—and all his company two men and a page! Queen Mary accepted Chatelherault's assurances and gave orders to disband the guard. She took, however, the reasonable precaution of doubling her bodyguard of twelve halberdiers, commanded by Captain James Stewart, a step which gave the fanatics excuse to raise a cry of tyranny.

The grounds for this midnight alarm that evaporated in comedy, lay in the crazy talk of the Earl of Arran, whose disordered mind, obsessed by Mary's beauty, toyed with dangerous fancies. Shortly before his unexpected journey to Keneil, he remarked on the ease with which a Queen could be kidnapped at Holyrood. A plot that had once been hatched against the Queen Mother he hinted might succeed with her daughter. His sudden move and the orders he left for Forbes, his aide-de-camp, to follow, convinced an indiscreet confidant that a warning, necessarily vague, had better be conveyed to Holyrood. *Randolph to Cecil, 2 Jan., 1562.*

In a few days the panic was forgotten and the Court resumed its normal occupation of amusing itself. Elizabeth's agent found some compensation for his exile. He found the ladies of Edinburgh "merry, louping and dancing, lusty and fair." Some attempt was being made to introduce a little Gallic lightheartedness to the solemnity of the North. On a Sunday in November the sands of Leith were enlivened by the spectacle of six gentlemen, led by the Queen's uncle, in the dress of foreign knights. They were running at the ring against six other aristocrats in female disguise. Their thanks was the comment of the godly: "fain would fools ape France."

Bothwell, kept by duty at Jedburgh, missed the entertainment. He returned to show his uncourtierlike quality at the next function. The anniversary of Francis's death demanded solemn Requiem and the depressing offering by his widow of a great wax candle trimmed with black velvet. Bothwell's protestant prejudices kept him away. He even refused to ingratiate himself with the Queen by wearing mourning. It is difficult to guess the reason of his *intransigeance*, since in more important matters he showed himself readily obedient to her wishes. His eagerness to obey her laid him open to a snub. When the Duke of Chatelherault announced his intention of attending the Church Assembly, Bothwell, conscious of Mary's desire for peace, sent him an assurance of good will and a guarantee of safety. The Duke's ungracious answer was to express surprise that such offers should be made by an inferior in rank.

Forgiveness of injuries was not in fashion on the Border. The reception of his overture roused Bothwell's bitter humour. Arran, for all his rigid principles, had his weaknesses. One of them was for "a good handsome wench, a merchant's daughter," called Alison Craig. Arran had formed the habit of visiting her secretly at the house of her father-in-law. By a coincidence convenient to Bothwell, that accommodating relative was Cuthbert Ramsay, whom Bothwell's grandmother had married *en quatrièmes noces*. What could be more amusing, thought Bothwell, than to expose the lapses of his hypocritical adversary at the house of his avaricious connection?

Anxious to share his joke, the Earl invited the company

140

of Lord John Stewart and the Marquis of Elbœuf. Christ-
mastide gave an excuse for masks. The disguise gained
the revellers admission to Cuthbert's easy-going establishment in St. Mary's Wynd. But their information was
at fault and they found no trace of the Calvinist Lothario.
The scent, however, was fresh, for next night saw them
once more at Ramsay's door.

This time the gates were bolted in their faces. Guessing
this meant their quarry was there, they smashed the doors
and forced their way into the house. Again they were
disappointed; Arran had made his escape.

"The horror of these facts commoved all godly
hearts," and the Church Assembly presented the Queen a
petition "to crave upright and true judgment against
such persons as have done what in them lies to kindle
God's wrath against this whole realm. The impiety
committed is so heinous and so horrible that we should
think ourselves guilty if we pass it over in silence." The
Queen's sense of proportion led her to reply that the
Marquis was a foreigner, and his companions had the
excuse of youth (Lord John was under twenty). She
promised to "put such order into them" that the injured
parties would have no cause to complain.

She fulfilled her pledge and, as Randolph admits, "in
words sharp enough" reproved the rioters. His statement
that Bothwell and Lord John defied the Queen and
threatened to repeat the offence is less credible. Bothwell
was Randolph's *bête noir* and the law of libel did not run.
This stage in the Alison Craig affair is more convincingly *Quadra to*
described by King Philip's Ambassador in London. The *Philip, 17*
story came from Mary's equerry, who was in Edinburgh *Jan., 1562.*
when "the horrible fact and impiety" occured.

The Hamiltons, it appears, felt that the exposure of
Arran's gallantries invited savage reprisal. One of the
clan—Gavin Hamilton is indicated—took three hundred
armed men to waylay Bothwell and his friends on their
return from a Christmas Eve supper.

No secret, however sanguinary, could be kept in that
city of divided loyalty. Without waiting for supper,

Bothwell slipped away to his quarters. Discovering a tenderness for Court etiquette, he sent a messenger to the Queen apologising for his absence, but taking care that its reason should appear. Then, in the best tradition of gang warfare, he set out to collect a stronger force than the Hamiltons had been able to muster. Counting the Marquis's men and Lord John's, four or five hundred answered his call.

This version of events is confirmed by John Knox, who admits that Gavin Hamilton "was the principal man at the beginning, and to him (though he was a papist) repaired many of the faithful"; Bothwell, he implies, did not take action until word was brought that the Hamiltons "were on the street."

With Hepburns massing at Bothwell's house and Hamiltons sharpening their spears in the market-place, nine o'clock on Christmas Eve saw a conflict imminent. The common bell was rung and the burghers called out to keep the peace with pike and axe. No ingredient was lacking for a first-class fracas.

Bothwell's message to Court saved the situation. It brought an armed force running up the hill with the protestant Lord James and the catholic Earl of Huntly in command. Their joint arguments were supplemented by orders to clear the streets under pain of death; "within half an hour there was never a man to be seen."

(Confronted with violence of this sort, the twentieth century need assume no complacent air of superiority. Belfast on a day of Orange Procession, Chicago during a night of gang warfare can only boast the progress that sub-machine gun and tear-gas have asserted over jack and spear.)

Next day, the anniversary of the birth of the Prince of Peace, Bothwell and the Duke were called to the Queen's presence. Deputations of the rival sects accompanied the protagonists. With the protestant Bothwell heading catholics, and Gavin, a papist, championing protestants, it must have been difficult to know which procession to join. Arran appeared and made the unlikely excuse that

142

neither he nor his father had any knowledge of the attack on Bothwell, which had been organised by a young kinsman. The Queen pretended to believe him and worked to compose this unprofitable quarrel. The Hamilton was adamant. He refused the Queen's arbitration unless Bothwell should publicly deny his charges with sound of trumpet at the Market Cross. In despair the Queen "concluded for the avoiding of cumber that Bothwell should leave the town."

Randolph to Elizabeth, 6 April, 1562.

It was Mary's habit to choose the easiest way out of a difficulty. Bothwell, she knew, would obey, while Arran's allegiance was more doubtful. The Borderer, in any case, was on the point of leaving Edinburgh. There was much to be done at Crichton. In a fortnight's time Lady Janet was to be married there to Lord John ("a sufficient woman for such a man" was John Knox's tart comment), and the Queen had signified her will to stay the night at the Castle.

In the sixteenth century Crichton was probably less lovely than are its ruins to-day.

> The Castle rises on the steep
> Of the green vale of Tyne,
> And far beneath, where slow they creep
> From pool to eddy dark and deep,
> Where alders moist and willows weep,
> You hear her streams repine.

The lovely Venetian arcade, the grand staircase and the eastern gallery were not yet built. It was Francis, last Earl of Bothwell, the child with whom this Sunday's union was doubtfully blessed, who added that time-defying beauty.

> Nor wholly yet hath time defaced
> Thy lordly gallery fair;
> Nor yet the stony cord unbraced
> Whose twisted knots with roses laced
> Adorn thy ruined stair.

143

> Still rises unimpaired below
> The courtyard's graceful portico . . .
> Though there but houseless cattle go
> To shield them from the storm.

James Hepburn lived in the South wing, with large rooms one above the other, wide fireplaces and tiled floors. The Keep, the earliest part of the Castle, was occupied by retainers, and the servants had cottages and a bothy to the west of the main building.

Finances were at a low ebb, (for feuds cost money and more land had had to go) but Bothwell was resolved to give his sister a wedding worthy of the Queen's presence and the semi-royal blood of the bridegroom. It was also an opportunity to impress his enemy, Lord James, who rather unwillingly accompanied Queen Mary. She was at her most gracious—if only to compensate for her brother's lowering looks. She even attended the religious ceremony, though it was celebrated with protestant rites.

At the banquet which followed, the Marquis of Elbœuf lived up to his country's reputation for tact and vowed he had never seen such a bridal in France. He may not have exaggerated, for Bothwell's Borderers had been busy. "There were of wild does and roes eighteen hundred, and as for rabbit, partridges, plovers, moor fowl, wild geese, wild duck and drake and other kind of delicate wild beasts—they could not be counted."

After the feast there was "much good sport and pastimes." That is all that Randolph can record of a wedding he had not been invited to attend. Tradition assigns the bracken-clad haugh below the Castle, where in summer fireflies played, as the scene of the sports. The Marquis, Lord John (with his "leaping and dancing") his bride and her brother could be counted on to prevent the party flagging. When at length the long day's merriment was over, the Queen withdrew, tired out, to the room that had been prepared for her.

Next morning, as Bothwell watched her train ride

after her across the valley to Borthwick Castle, he could heave a sigh of relief and congratulate himself and his helpers on a successful entertainment.

He had reason to be satisfied. Half a dozen years had passed since he had succeeded to an impoverished estate and a discredited name. If the estate was still embarrassed, his name ranked with any in the land. Hardly more than a boy, he had been called to play the highest rôle that could be confided to a subject. He had taken a distinguised part in the wars and councils of Mary of Lorraine. He had been chosen for an important embassy. He had placed the steady loyalty that had served the mother at the daughter's disposal. After some hesitation she had chosen to give her confidence to his enemies. Refusing to be intimidated, but rejecting no reasonable accommodation, he had arrived at a suspension of hostilities with his most dangerous foes, Lord James and Lethington. He could discount the more noisy, but less deadly, enmity of Arran for he had planted a wholesome fear in Hamilton hearts. The Queen's good will was sealed by Janet's marriage, and the honour paid to his roof seemed to crown the edifice he had patiently raised.

The sky looked cloudless. Bothwell was twenty-seven and the world lay at his feet. With considerable self-restraint he decided to play a safe and meritorious game. For the next three months he scrupulously followed the wishes of his queen, the counsels of his religious superior, the teachings of Christianity. The results, it will be granted, were disappointing.

CHAPTER FIFTEEN

QUEEN MARY had a bent for match-making. During the six active years of her reign, her Court saw a series of brilliant marriages. The next bridegroom was Lord James. His bride was Lady Agnes Keith, daughter of the Earl Marischal, and the magnificence of the entertainment "offended many of the godly." He asked among many others the Earl of Arran, but probably regretted his invitation. His hospitality was too much for his guest, who, the day after the feast, had one of his vague attacks, "as much of misliking as of any other disease." The Earl was "so drowned in dreams and so feedeth himself with fantasies, that either men fear that he will fall into some dangerous and incurable sickness, or play one day some mad part that will bring him into mischief." One of the fantasies was a project to retire to France and resume his duties as Captain of the Scottish Guard.

Randolph to Cecil, 28 Feb., 1562.

The Queen guessed that this craze showed the effect of the quarrel on overwrought nerves. She knew that James Hepburn only sought "to have a better and quieter life at Court," and was even advised by well-meaning friends "to own his fail to Arran as far as a man can do with honour." Judging the moment ripe for another effort to liquidate the feud, she summoned Arran from his sick-bed to appear before the Privy Council and undertake to observe the oblivion clause of the Treaty of Edinburgh. She listened unimpressed to the Earl's vehement protests that the clause did not cover his case and insisted that he should accept her ruling. She was not content until a formal pacification had been signed between the two enemies and the signatures of John Cockburn of Ormiston and Lord James had been appended.

Randolph to Cecil, 27 Dec., 1561.

Randolph to Cecil, 2 Jan., 1562.

Register of P.C., 20 Feb. 1562. Randolph to Cecil, 21 Feb., 1562.

Queen Mary, enjoying perhaps a spell of better health,

had put her foot down. Whenever she did, she surprised and defeated those who sought to impose on her. Bothwell co-operated. As a realist, he had little faith in formal bonds which were rarely worth the parchment they were written on. He saw that only a personal reconciliation could attain the end desired. He decided to invite the mediation of the religious head of Arran's party.

Guessing that his name would not afford the best introduction to Knox, Bothwell enlisted the services of a common friend. He chose James Barron, a wealthy merchant whose name headed his list of creditors and who might well be anxious for the feud to end, before complete insolvency overtook his debtor. As Barron was an active member of the party of reform he had no difficulty in arranging a meeting with its leader.

A first interview took place at the manse in secret, by night. It was amicable enough to call for a second encounter in Knox's study. These were the first times that Borderer and Prophet, protagonists of factions that sought each other's destruction, met. Two men "who never feared or flattered any flesh," stood face to face, each trying to probe the other's thoughts.

Bothwell broke the silence with a comment on the inevitable difference in their points of view. The attack on John Cockburn, which had started all the trouble, he explained as a military necessity not marked by personal animosity. He showed how Cockburn's cause had been taken up by Arran, "whose favour," he insisted, "he was most willing to redeem."

If Knox waited for any exemplary sentiments on man's duty to live at peace with his neighbour, he was disappointed.

"If I could have my Lord Arran's favour," the practical Scot explained, "I could wait upon the Court with a page and few servants, to spare my expense."

He glanced at his principal creditor, sitting motionless in the shadows.

"Whereas," he went on, "I am now compelled to keep for my own safety a number of wicked and unprofitable men to the utter destruction of my estate that is left."

Knox had a sense of humour. Moreover he appreciated, without always practising, straight dealing.

"My Lord," he began courteously, "would to God, that in me were counsel and judgment that might comfort and relieve you!"

He stroked his straggling beard and expressed a more human sentiment than his visitor had expected.

"I have borne a good mind to your house and have been sorry at my heart of the trouble that I have heard you to be involved in."

A gesture of acknowledgment may have passed unnoticed. Knox's mind was on the past.

"My great-grandfather and father," he mused, "have served your Lordship's predecessors. Some of them have died under their standards. This is a part of the obligation of our Scots kindness."

The two men, who from different points of view understood loyalty, were silent. Then the Reformer resumed in his professional voice.

"God," he stated, "has made me His public messenger of glad tidings. I am sorry you have given men occasion to be offended with you. I am more sorrowful that you have offended the majesty of God. Therefore my counsel is that you begin at God. I doubt not that He shall bow the hearts of men to forget all other offences."

An impatient shrug, a half-turn towards the door, made the preacher hasten to hold out more immediate hopes.

"As for me, if you will continue in godliness, your Lordship shall command me as boldly as any that serves your Lordship," he added quickly.

Bothwell saw that his point was gained. Without preliminaries, he asked his host to discover whether Arran was ready to make up the quarrel. Then, with due precautions to preserve his incognito, he withdrew.

He could not wait in Edinburgh to see results.

He was wanted on the Border, where a meeting had been fixed at Berwick to settle a dispute between the Marshal of that town and the Scottish Warden of the Western Marches. On the way to Berwick the fatality which dogged Bothwell's path nearly spoiled everything. *Queen Mary to Sir Thomas Dacre, 28 Feb., 1562.*

A bodyguard of eight rode with him, as much to impress the English as for protection. His route through Haddington and Dunbar passed Ormiston and his ill-luck brought the laird, his wife and his twenty-three year old son riding into the fields looking for game. Since the affair of the subsidy, John Cockburn's nerve or his conscience was bad. Sighting the distant flash of a spear, he cantered with his lady to the hamlet of Ormiston and sent his son to reconnoitre. *Randolph to Cecil, 21 March, 1562. Knox ii. 324.*

Alexander Cockburn, a pupil of Knox, had been taught the value of the offensive. Riding up to the group he recognised his father's enemy. The opportunity was too good to miss. He levelled his pistol and fired, thinking "being well mounted, to have avoided the danger." Two errors invalidated Alexander's calculations. He missed his aim; he had forgotten the Earl's horse might be a match for his. Whether time pressed, or whether a hostage looked useful so near his enemy's home, young Cockburn was obliged to ride the rest of the road to Berwick. From there he was "courteously enough sent back."[1]

A distorted account reached Knox, who was "so greatly displeased that he almost gave over further travailing for amity." It did not strike him, or the writers who follow Randolph's prejudiced stories, that Bothwell, who had not provoked the pistol shot fired in his face, had acted with commendable restraint.

The Reformer, however, did not give up his peace-making and eventually induced John Cockburn to submit his grievances to the verdict of the Earls of Arran and Moray. He obtained a written statement

---

[1] Alexander Cockburn died young and was accorded by Buchanan the epitaph : *Excoluit virtus animum, ingeniumque Camenae.* Virtue informed his heart, his wit the Muses.

from Bothwell that he would accept this far from impartial jury.

On Tuesday, 24th March, 1562, a group of men could have been seen walking doggedly down the Blackfriars' Wynd. Bothwell and his friends were on their way to pay a peaceful visit to the Hamilton house that stood to the north of Kirk o' Field. An embarrassed group waited indoors to receive them. Arran struggled to control his nerves. The impetuous Gavin Hamilton, chosen to act as his cousin's second, fidgeted in sympathy. The black-robed prophet hovered ready to "bear witness and testification of the end of the agreement."

Bothwell, as he climbed the stairs, needed all his magnanimity and the prudence of his second, the Laird of Riccarton, to proceed with this public reconciliation. His task proved easier than he could have hoped.

"As the Earl of Bothwell entered the chamber and would have done the honours that those friends had appointed, the Earl of Arran gently passed unto him, embraced him and said: 'If the hearts be upright, few ceremonies will serve!'"

The Reformer did not propose to miss the chance of calling attention to his part in advancing the millennium.

"Now, my Lords," he began, "God hath brought you together by the labour of a simple man. I know my labours are already taken in evil part, but because I have the testimony of a good conscience, I the more patiently bear the misreports and wrongful judgments of men."

He glanced from Bothwell's lean, saturnine features to Arran's narrow, pasty face that stared out between two long locks of hair. The latter's words and actions were unexpectedly generous. Why were his eyes so strained? Knox could not repress a twinge of uneasiness.

"Whatsoever I have done," he reassured himself, "it is in God's fear, for the profit of you both, for the hurt of none, and for the tranquillity of this realm."

He took his leave as the seconds embraced and the two Earls crossed to the window. They stood a little time in

150

talk, until after a suitable interval Bothwell followed Knox from the room.

The Hepburn left nothing to chance. Next morning he was back with all the protestant friends he could collect. He insisted that he could not rest until he had accompanied his new friend to hear the sermon. Together they worshipped, together they took their midday dinner, together they went hunting, together they rode, with Gavin in their company, to visit the Duke at Keneil.

News that the two Earls had made up their quarrel spread fast. "All Edinburgh and most of Scotland spoke of their sudden familiarity." Some spoke too loud. "Loving to God!" exclaimed Ninian McCrechane, cook *Records of* to Timothy Bancour, in the High Street. "My Lord *the Burgh of* *Edinburgh, 8* Arran and my Lord Bothwell are agreed. Knox's quarter *April, 1562.* is run. He is scourged through the town."

Here was the misreport the Reformer anticipated, but the patience with which he promised to bear it was less manifest. The indiscreet cook "was ordained to be scourged within the Tolbooth and thereafter to be brankit."[1]

If the fruits of the pacification were painful to Ninian, they were deadly to the prime mover in that conscientious settlement. The biographer, from his observation post on the vantage ground of posterity, likes nicely to detect the operation of cause and effect that lets him smugly allot the rewards of prudence, enterprise or policy, and apportion the penalties of imbecility, inertia or improvidence. Reluctantly he must here admit that he can discover no other cause for the impending catastrophe than the practice of the virtue which proverbially meets a disappointing return. Had Bothwell disloyally denied the Queen's wish, had he unchristianly rejected the Reformer's advice, had he ungraciously refused the Hamilton olive branch, he would have escaped the ruin that was to be his reward. Three days after that brotherly embrace Arran's reason underwent complete eclipse. Ridden by the mania of persecution, he accused his new friend of an attempt to involve him in fantastic treason.

[1] The branks were the pillory or the scold's bridle.

151

Knox ii. 325.
Randolph to
Cecil, 31
March, 1562.

Among the first to hear the crazy story was John Knox, as he sat dictating letters in his study after the sermon of the day had been preached.

"I am treasonably betrayed," wailed Arran with tears in his eyes.

Knox asked the name of the traitor.

"One Judas or another," was the incoherent reply. "I know it is only my life that is sought. I regard it not."

Knox pressed for details and elicited an incredible story of a Hepburn plot to murder Lord James and Lethington, to kidnap the Queen, hand her over to Arran at Dumbarton Castle and establish a joint dictatorship.

"And so shall he and I rule all," finished the paranoiac. "But I know this is devised to accuse me of treason. I know he will inform the Queen. I take you to witness that I open it here to you. I will pass incontinent and write to the Queen's Majesty."

Knox tried to soothe his frantic visitor. As he had not consented, he could not be held guilty. Arran shook his distracted head.

"You do not understand what craft is used," he objected dismally. "It is treason to conceal treason."

The Reformer advised him to keep his fancies to himself. Arran wrung his hands.

"He will offer me the combat!" he forecasted correctly. "That would not be suffered in France."

Abruptly he dashed out of the room and from his lodging despatched to the Queen and Lord James, who were hawking at Falkland Palace, a full account of the imaginary plot.

Summons of
Treason
against
Bothwell, 23
March, 1565.

Bothwell, he alleged, had hinted that enemies were thwarting Arran's pretensions to the Queen's hand, and plotting the ruin of the house of Hamilton. To defeat their machinations, why not capture the Queen, when she came south of the Forth after Easter? An opportunity would offer when she was out hunting "or otherwise passing her time merrily." Hack to pieces anybody who resisted, carry Mary to Dumbarton Castle, and "there keep her surely, or otherwise demean her person!" Should Arran feel any scruple, he need only watch while Bothwell "put all things into execution."

The madman's pen revealed the suppressed desires that filled his imagination. He sent off his letter, mounted his horse and rode to Keneil. From previous experience his symptoms were recognised by the Duke and the invalid was locked in his bedroom. In spite of every precaution, he contrived to smuggle out a second letter. This time he wrote in cypher for Randolph to decode and hand to Lord James. In it son accused father of complicity in the mythical plot.

The next night the lunatic escaped from the tower where he was confined. Clad only in doublet and hose, he lowered himself from a window by a rope made of his sheets and blankets. As the descent, according to Randolph, covered one hundred and eighty feet, a considerable quantity of bedding is indicated. Satisfied with a good night's work, he disappeared.

His Edinburgh letter had already reached the Queen and her brother; the cypher letter found them out hunting.[1] It was hardly read before Gavin Hamilton rode up with the news of his demented kinsman's escape. "He desired her Majesty not to give credit to anything that Arran had written or should report, for it was all false, both of his father and of the Earl of Bothwell." If any testimony to Bothwell's innocence need be added to the assurance of the man who a few months before had sought his life in the streets of Edinburgh, letters from John Knox supply it. In them the Reformer stated that he *Knox ii. 328.* "did plainly forewarn (Lord James) that he espied the Earl of Arran to be stricken with frenzy and therefore willed not over-great credit to be given to his inventions."

A little later in the day Bothwell himself, ignorant of his danger, rode to Falkland. His innocence and his protests were disregarded. Lord James had taken charge,

---

[1] The suspicious eye may look askance at this letter. Why was cypher employed? The decode would give Randolph the chance of including a few damning details for which Arran's handwriting would not be needed. It is a little odd that Randolph had the key to the cypher out hunting.

"a man of a deep reach in wit," a master at exploiting the misfortune of his opponents. Bothwell and Gavin Hamilton were both committed to safe custody.

Arran was still at large. He made his way in disguise to Stirling and thence, late at night, to the house of his friend, Kirkaldy of Grange. His privations brought a change for the worse and "he began to rave and speak strange purposes, as devils and witches and such like, fearing all men that they came to kill him."

Grange reported his guest's arrival and condition. His news brought Lord James hot-foot to discover what use could be made of the maniac's ravings. But Arran was too mad to be of much use. He gave "many tokens of an unquiet mind, both in his talk and his doings." Among his delusions was the conviction that he was the Queen's husband and in her bed. He was taken to a house in St. Andrews, where he was "well kept and used as a man ought to be in that case."

A more stringent confinement in the Castle of St. Andrews was prepared for Bothwell and Gavin Hamilton. At a rigorous examination they confessed nothing. Even Randolph, who talked gleefully of Herod and Pilate falling into the pit they had digged, had to admit that *Randolph to* "on examination there appeared very little of any such *Cecil, 25* attemptate." But he continued to hope for the best *April, 1562.* and hinted at the violent end awaiting his enemy, while "as for the Abbot, his flocks shall be never the worse fed, though his head were from his shoulders."

At last the invalid got some sleep, to wake apparently lucid. He was paid a visit by the Queen, who without much imagination told him that he must either justify his letters or confess their malicious falsehood. At her request, Randolph went to see him. As is sometimes the case with lunatics, on ordinary topics "good and resolute answers were given." Mention of the cypher letter drew the reply that "all those things were but fantasies."

"I know not," he added wearily, "how God has suffered me to be deluded with devils and witches."

"What witches?" asked the practical agent. "Lord

154

James's mother!" whispered Arran unexpectedly. In the presence of Argyll, his delusions returned and he repeated his story of the kidnapping.

"What," asked the Campbell fatuously, "would you have done with me?"

"You should have gone with your marrows!"[1] was the disconcerting reply.

Intervals of sanity intervened when the patient "utterly denied what he had written to the Queen and others as well of the Earl of Bothwell as of his father." The Duke stayed at Keneil, overwhelmed by the disaster to his house.

"Twice before," he admitted, "he was in the same case. He takes it of his mother."

The unhappy father wrote vainly to the Queen, begging her to release all three prisoners and offering bail. But by now Lord James was firmly in the saddle.

He confronted the two Earls in the presence of the Queen and her Council. Arran, in the grip of his delusions, charged Bothwell with treason. Bothwell had had no chance to study his accuser's condition, and at first could devise no better test than the inevitable trial by combat. Perceiving, however, that Arran was in no condition to fight, he suggested as an alternative a Court of Law. Impartial investigation was the last thing James Stewart wanted. After some mutual contradiction ("the one as constantly denied, as the other affirmed") Bothwell was led back to his cell, and Arran was taken to Lord James's house. After some days of coaching and "reasonable liberty," he confirmed his charges against Bothwell, but exonerated his father. A further examination by the Council produced no new facts, and before he could again withdraw his accusation, he was hurried to the Castle of St. Andrews.

In the grip of his malady, Arran disappears from this story. He stayed some months at St. Andrews, and "James Stewart of Cardenhall, called Captain James, was evil bruited for the rigorous entertainment he showed him

[1] Fellows.

155

in his sickness." A hint at his treatment is given by a treasury entry of thirty shillings and eightpence paid "to certain smiths in St. Andrews for locks, keys and bands," on an account rendered by Captain Stewart.

Accounts of Lord High Treasurer, 25 April, 1562.

From St. Andrews the lunatic was moved to Edinburgh Castle where he attacked his attendant. In January, 1564, his symptoms are recorded. "He desires solitariness and dark rooms, is suspicious of all men and his whole body is infected with the yellow ganders (jaundice). The order of his life is to lie long abed and eat little, without any sound sleep." The next year he attempted suicide. His body had become bloated and dropsical. A little later he lost his speech. Various noblemen, induced by pity, went surety for him to the figure of twelve thousand pounds Scots and secured his release. He who had been claimant to the crown of Scotland and suitor to two Queens, lived out his days in dim-witted retirement. He died in 1609.

Randolph to Cecil, 15 Jan., 1564.

de Foix, 18 Sept., 1565.

Randolph to Cecil, 2 May, 1566.

The head of his house met easier treatment. Chatelherault's infirmity of age and purpose did not threaten the royal bastard's designs, though the end of the Hamilton occupation of Dumbarton Castle was demanded. The Duke threw himself at Mary's feet, "declaring his grief that she suspected him. The Queen was not a little moved to see the old man's tears trickling from his cheeks, as it had been a child beaten," but she insisted, "in friendly fashion," on the surrender of Dumbarton.

This clemency to a nobleman, who had been consistently disloyal, may be contrasted with the treatment meted out to Bothwell. The evidence was the same—the unsupported word of a maniac whose hereditary lunacy was not in doubt. But Bothwell was kept in close confinement in St. Andrews, and his daily petitions to have his innocence tried went unanswered.

The Queen of Scots is credited by friend and foe with generosity to her servants. This treatment of a loyal supporter can hardly be excused, though it can readily be explained. As ever, she was under the guidance of a stronger will. Lord James and his ally, the Secretary, produced excellent reasons why Bothwell's case could not be tried. If he were acquitted, the law of the land would automatically convict Arran of false accusation and would inflict on him the punishment he had claimed for his victim. To bring "the next heir" to the scaffold might provoke dangerous repercussions.

When they had found this excuse for injustice, their next care was to undermine the Queen's natural clemency. To exploit her feminine weakness they obtained a letter from her cousin of England, pleading Bothwell's cause and urging moderation. The patronising tone of Elizabeth's letter and the suggestion that the prisoner had been influenced by English intrigue played their calculated part. Queen Mary "showed herself not a little offended with the Earl of Bothwell to whom she had been so good." She quoted a passage from Livy, whose works she was reading daily after luncheon with "a learned man Mr. George Buchanan." The Roman historian had thrown off the epigram that not to try a criminal was better policy than to acquit him—" *hominem improbum non accusari tutius est, quam absolvi,*" but we may guess that Mary had not found the maxim without Mr. George's help. Randolph, who played his part in the campaign, was delighted. "The Queen," he testified cynically, "in this case both honourably and stoutly behaves herself, determined not so reasonably to deal as may be against her reputation."

So Lord James won the trick. With relentless efficiency he had followed up his opportunity. Arran's delirium provided an instrument to ruin the strongest family in Scotland, to strip the senile father of his fortress, to imprison the demented son and the active kinsman. The same tactics divested the Queen of her only loyal and powerful supporter, denied him a trial, and kept him in prison, disgraced and friendless.

Queen Mary's own graceful account of her servant's downfall was written later. "As envy ever follows virtue and this country is somewhat subject to factions, others by reports and misconstruing of his doings went about to put him out of our good grace. At length,

Quadra to a Lady: 30 April, 1562.

157

upon colours invented by his evil-willers, for satisfying them that would not abide his advancement, and avoiding of further contention which might have brought the whole realm into trouble, we were compelled to put him in ward."

In ward he stayed. From St. Andrews he was taken to Edinburgh Castle, under escort of a troop of horse. In that prison his bitter sense of humour may have been tickled to meet on the democratic footing of misfortune Sym Scott, Patrick and Robert Turnbull, whom he had last seen from the judgment seat at Jedburgh.

CHAPTER SIXTEEN

FOR four months Bothwell watched the rain fall outside the bars of his window. It was "an incredibly bad season; neither sun nor moon have performed their appropriate offices. It has rained so abundantly and almost without intermission." Nor could the prisoner take comfort from such news as was allowed to reach him. In the belief that "the thieves of Teviotdale and Liddesdale, besides being enemies to all virtue and policy, are those in whom Bothwell trusts if he gets his liberty," Lord James paid a surprise visit to Hawick and arrested fifty-three of them on a fair day. Twenty-two "for lack of trees and halters," he drowned, others he executed at Jedburgh and the remainder he brought to the capital to suffer "according to their merits" on the Boroughmuir. His exertions met a disappointing reception from the sensitive little Queen, who was "no wit content with the good success that God gave him."

Teviotdale was Bothwell's at heart, except for the Cessford Kerrs, who were busy quarrelling with Black Ormiston about the house of Ancrum. The case reached the Privy Council and the Kerrs had to promise not to enter the lands or rooms of Ancrum nor to make molestation, stop, trouble or impediment to the Earl of Bothwell, his tenants or servants. James Ormiston came little better out of the dispute. He was told to remove, desist and rid him, his family and servants, leaving only one ploughman to labour the ground.

Reg. of P.C.
I. 206.

Bothwell had friends in other parts of Scotland who did not forget his adversity. Great-uncle Patrick, for instance, did his best from the episcopal throne of Spynie. "Young Lord Hugh of Lovat," a Fraser descendant recorded, "designed to go South and take a view of the Court for his further accomplishment, encouraged by

Fraser's
Polichronicon
(1666).

the Bishop of Moray, an ambitious man and a politic, who was labouring to make a party in the North for his brother (*sic*) Bothwell now under a cloud and imprisoned at Edinburgh."

The North of Scotland was in a state of nervous anticipation. The Highland nobles, of whom the Earl of Huntly was the most powerful, had watched Hamiltons and Hepburns crushed in the Lowlands. Was the family of Gordon the next to make way for Lord James's insatiable ambition? What was the object of the progress through the Highlands which the Queen undertook early in August? An enlightening comment was made by the Primate who, "be he never so close, could not altogether hide his mind, but at his own table said: 'The Queen is gone into the North, belike to seek disobedience; she may perchance find the thing she seeks.'" The Archbishop, a shrewd observer of a delicate situation, guessed that Huntly felt secure in the catholicism that he shared with the Queen and in his feudal strength. The Cock o' the North had not learnt the lesson of Bothwell's fall—that not Mary's humanity or her inclinations, but her brother's ambition, directed policy. The miscalculation led to the fatal field of Corrichie, Huntly's mysterious death and the eclipse of the Gordons as a political force. Guided by Lord James, Queen Mary was induced to eliminate her most powerful catholic supporter.

Knox ii. 347.

Bothwell did not await the disastrous end of the rising. In his cell he debated how to discover the Queen's real feelings. The furtive channels of communication, which, for all a gaoler's care, prisoners maintain with the outside world, carried a message to Mary. Was it Bishop Patrick who probed her mind? Or did Mary Fleming, soon to prove herself a friend to Bothwell, whisper in the royal ear? By one means or another the answer was smuggled back to the Castle that the Queen was aware he was the victim of injustice. She had, however, no authority and for the time being could give no help. The message ended with the hint that the Earl "should do the best he could."

Les Affaires du Comte de Boduel 8.

Bothwell's best was apt to be remarkable. "The Queen's answer," he relates casually, "was the reason I set myself to leave prison." On the night of the 28th August, 1562, he broke one of the stanchions of his window and, squeezing himself through the gap, swung down the face of the Castle rock. In the dark that precipice might daunt an experienced Alpinist. True, Bothwell had the help of James Porterfield, servant to the Captain of the Castle. The Turnbulls, his fellow prisoners, may have lent a hand, for when the fugitive reached Hawick, the first to join him were "the Trumbles of Liddesdale." *Dacre to Cecil, 7 Sept., 1562.*

Knox, seeking to implicate the Queen, tried to spoil a good escape with the innuendo that Bothwell "got easy passage by the gate." The fugitive's own version is more credible—that he had her good wishes and none of her help. Some six months later he offered to be tried by his peers for escaping from the royal prison, and it is clear that he regarded himself technically as a law-breaker. Knox himself urged him to keep the peace, "that his *crime* of breaking the ward would be the more easily pardoned." Even a theologian cannot have it the two ways that Mary both arranged the escape and held it a crime! *Percy to Cecil, 13 Feb., 1563.* *Knox ii. 351.*

Once clear of the Castle, the Earl "showed himself not very much afraid." He assumed there would be no great zeal to renew an illegal confinement. For a week he lingered in the neighbourhood of Edinburgh. His mother's house at Morham received him and Crichton Castle. His troubles had emptied his purse. Mortgages had to supply his immediate needs.

As soon as the necessary documents were signed, the leisurely fugitive left Lothian for the Hermitage. In this time of need he received the gift of provisions from his neighbour and ex-mistress, Janet Beton. If he took the advice of some of his counsellors to defy authority and face a siege, the castle needed not only provisioning, but work on the fabric. An English secret service report gives an unflattering picture: "It is an oulde house, not strong, but evil to wyn by reason of the strate ground *Armstrong cxvi.*

Teulet i. 374.

aboute the same." Spaciously constructed, it held more
than six hundred men, horse and foot, within its walls;
nearly fifteen hundred moss-troopers could be raised
in the vicinity. Its reputation was not savoury. Nicholas
de Soulis, whose family had built it some two hundred
and fifty years before, was said to keep a familiar spirit
in one of the dungeons. The creature's innocent name
was Redcap, but the colour of its headgear had to be
maintained with infant blood. It was the Bad Lord's
importunities, and not his sorcery that brought him to
a lamentable end. "Oh, *boil* him!" cried the King of
Scotland, "but let me be plagued no more." His literal-
minded auditors seized de Soulis,

> They rolled him up in a sheet of lead,
> A sheet of lead for a funeral pall;
> They plunged him in the cauldron red
> And melted him—lead, bones and all.

Even after his demise, unholy forces did not desert
the dungeon, "a willow inserted in the chinks of the
door," was claimed to be found, "peeled when withdrawn."
Unearthly sentinels were remarked on the battlements—

> They pace their round with lifeless smile
> And shake with restless foot the guilty pile.

During the last year or two they have been mistaken for
employees of the Board of Works.

In Bothwell's day the sentries were real, and the
square, windowless building of unfriendly grey stone
hummed with activity. Through its high, arched entrance
and across the stone flags of the hall, tramped a string
of messengers. Lord Gordon, Huntly's eldest son, was
South, trying to whip up support for his father's desperate
adventure. He tampered with the uncertain fidelity of
Knox ii. 347.
*Acts of the
Parl: of
Scotland ii.
577.*
the Duke of Chatelherault and explored the less variable
loyalty of the Earl of Bothwell. People were saying that
he paid the Hermitage a personal visit, begging its keeper
to raise men and horses for the Gordon cause. But James

Hepburn, whatever his wrongs, was not to be lured into rebellion. Apart from his natural instinct for loyalty, he did not want to back the losing side. It did not need a letter from the Warden of the Western Marches, prompted by Knox, to make him rebuff the tempter. "Behave," wrote the future Lord Herries, "as it becomes *Knox ii. 351.* a faithful subject and keep good quietness in the places committed to your charge." Before Bothwell had been at liberty three weeks he had chosen his path and was urging all his friends "to keep good quiet." Five weeks before *Forster to* the ruin of Gordon hopes at Corrichie, he wrote to the *Cecil, 17 Sept., 1582.* Queen submitting to her orders and making offer of *Randolph to* "good service." His great-uncle had recently been her *Cecil, 23* host at Spynie and the conciliatory note bears the *Sept., 1562.* stamp of his counsel, which may also have prompted the letters Bothwell wrote to Maitland and Lord James. Do what he could, his overtures met everywhere a cool reception, and, reduced once more to seek James Barron's financial aid, he paid a flying visit under strong escort to Edinburgh and Leith, at which port he could make arrangements for the journey abroad that was beginning to look inevitable.

By the 22nd November, the collapse of the Gordons had let Mary return to Holyrood House. Her health played its usual unlucky part in Bothwell's fortunes and she took to her bed, sick of the "new acquaintance," a then unfamiliar disease whose symptoms were a pain in the head, a soreness in the stomach and a great cough. Our centuries of progress have found a different name for the malady, if no remedy. During his sister's disappearance, James Stewart—he had started for the Highlands the Earl of Mar to return the Earl of Moray —resisted the influenza epidemic long enough to issue an order for Lord Bothwell under pain of treason to return to his prison.

The fugitive knew that resistance was hopeless. The Gordon collapse had left his enemies stronger than ever. Submission meant a life-long captivity in the Castle and life there did not necessarily last long. Flight was the only alternative and Bothwell felt it was time to profit by the inquiries he had made at Leith.

Towards the end of December, the Lord High Admiral of Scotland gave a quick glance over his shoulder and slipped on board a merchant vessel that was lading a cargo for France. The ten traders who had chartered her to carry their goods and their persons were unaware of the presence of the distinguished stowaway. Anchor was weighed and the sails were set for France. There was a heavy sea and the wind was rising.

Word of the unobtrusive departure did not take long to reach the authorities. A sergeant-at-arms was sent to summon the Hermitage to surrender and the Warden of the Marches had orders to look out for trouble. "The Liddesdale men," it was feared, "will ride safe now that the Earl Bothwell is away, for whose sake they abstained before." Queen Mary heaved a sign of relief. Her resourceful subject had spared her the distress of punishing him further. If he reached France and the Duke of Guise, her uncle's generosity might make up for the treatment loyalty had received at her hands. Convalescent at last, she rode to Dunbar "to be merry with my Lord John of Coldingham." As the Commendator had married Bothwell's sister, the subject of their mirth may be guessed.

The scene changes to Holy Island, twenty miles down the coast on the English side of the Border. A survey, which Queen Elizabeth's officials had made the year before, gives a picture of some desolation. "The Holy Island is situate within the sea and yet at every tide of low water men may pass into the same on horseback or foot, and it is in compass about three miles and hath a little borough town, all set with fishers very poor and is a market town on the Saturday, howbeit it is little used. And there was in the same Island one cell of Monks, which mansion house was built in four-square of two courts and now is the Queen's Majesty's storehouse, and also another house in the town called the Palace, which is the new brewhouse and bakehouse. And in the same

Island is also one fort, which serveth very well for the defence and safeguard of the haven, the which haven is a very good and apt haven . . . ."

On Monday, the 28th December, 1562, a storm-tossed ship ran before the gale into that harbour. Beblowe, the fort that guarded it, was only a rock "vanmured with a few turfs many years since, which is now decayed. The gunners cannot occupy it, nor the soldiers, which are few in number, place themselves for defence, as the fort is rotten."[1] One of the storm-bound travellers did not want to meet even a few English soldiers. Fearful for his freedom, exhausted by the sea-sickness to which he was ever disposed, the hereditary Admiral lowered himself wearily over the side of the battered vessel. Without a glance at St. Cuthbert's once-famous shrine, "now the Queen's Majesty's storehouse," followed by a single servant, he made his way along the street of the little fishing village, "the more part" of which was "decayed in houses." Out of its fifty inhabitants, "most of them aged," a dozen were Scots. A compatriot in distress was unlucky if he could not procure a guide to take him across the wet sands to some place of comparative safety on the mainland. To borrow or buy a horse would attract attention; the Earl with his single retainer "departed on foot into Scotland" to disappear for six days.

(Coldinghame was near, James was in touch with his sister—did he not shortly repay her two thousand crowns he had borrowed?—and just two days after the stowaway landed at Holy Island, the Queen had gone to be merry with the Commendator! The Dramatic Muse would enjoy a surprise visit with royalty occupying the spare room; a scene of sisterly embarrassment, brotherly aplomb, regal condescension and laughter over the fugitive's story; but Clio only purses her lips.)

When the tantalising six days are up Willie Tatt

[1] The author of this pessimistic report, Sir William Read, captain of Holy Island, lies buried there in the parish church of St. Mary. Over his dust an epitaph proclaims the indubitable truth:
> " *Contra vim mortis*
> *Non est medicamen in hortis.*"

of Tynedale, servant to the Earl of Bothwell, is seen riding with an Englishman from the direction of Scotland down the village street of Berrington. The horsemen knock at the door of John Rively, a friend of the Forster family, with whom Black Ormiston, it may be remembered, was on writing terms. Rively opens the door—it is a Sunday afternoon—and hears that Tatt has come "in a trodd of sheep" and wants help in tracking them. He invites Willie to stable his horse and learns how his master is in displeasure with the Queen and Court of Scotland. By roundabout ways Tatt reaches the point. Will Rively let the Earl "be in his house for two or three days to prepare himself?" The nature of the preparation is not divulged, but the North Sea can be seen from Berrington, and Holy Island harbour is only hidden by a ridge of purple heather.

Next day, guided by Tatt, Bothwell himself and David Chalmers, a lawyer bred for the church, arrive at Berrington. There they are joined by James Porterfield who, since the escape down the Castle Rock, has joined his fortunes to the fugitive's. Rively hides the party, horses and all, in some sort of a quarry or vault provided with a door that locks.

All next day the Scots lie low. On Wednesday morning David Chalmers wants a guide to the Island to see if there are any ships. Rively deputes his nephew and hints that a bottle of wine would not come amiss. Young John takes Chalmers to the edge of the fishing village and is sent off to see about the wine.

Here the influence of trifles intrudes. Had the lawyer been content to wait one more day, had the farmer not felt thirsty, Bothwell's after-life would have been different. For back in Edinburgh Randolph had learnt that the ship which was carrying his enemy had called at Holy Island. A letter to Berwick had her detained and searched. Captain Carew, in charge of the search-party, found nothing of interest in the ship but, painstaking officer that he was, he extended the search to the village. He noticed young John Rively buying a bottle of wine, put two and two together, and deduced that there were guests at Berrington.

David Chalmers started back with the wine; Captain Carew hurried to Berwick to report.

After supper, when the bottle had loosened Rively's Northumbrian tongue, Bothwell conceived some doubts of his reliability. In French he made "his man" party to his suspicions. (Was "French Paris," the page, his confidant, or was it David Chalmers, who wrote a history of the kings of England, France and Scotland, not to mention the Popes and Emperors, in the French language?) Rively misliked what he could not understand and, breaking up the party, "mused thereon in bed." Bothwell went to bed in the vault but, as a precaution against treachery, told two of his men to keep their clothes on and their weapons handy. He also had the horses saddled. It was a pity he did not act on his premonition.

About four in the morning a party arrived from Berwick to test Captain Carew's guess. There was the Master of Ordnance, the Under Marshal, and Captain Cornwall with some of the garrison. Rively went to the door in his shirt. He made no attempt to shield his guests and guided the soldiers to the vault. The door was locked, but he succeeded in convincing the Scots that there were friends outside. The door was opened and the Earl was taken in his bed.

They hurried him to Berwick. Rively they arrested for harbouring suspects, despite his protests that he had intended to give them up. "Being well allied in this part of the country," he was released under heavy bail and, furnished with a letter from his influential connection, went to London to see Cecil. Sir William, who knew so well "how to conceal without counterfeiting the truth," secured his pardon. In the Northumbrian he had found a useful tool.

So at least thought Bothwell who afterwards remarked *Bedford to* genially that "he meant not to kill any in England so *Cecil, 25* soon as Cecil, and one Rively." *March, 1565.*

CHAPTER SEVENTEEN

THE Fates, employing such questionable devices as a North Sea squall and an untimely purchase of a bottle of wine, had returned Bothwell to his enemies' power. The task of exploiting the advantage lay in the capable hands of Sir William Cecil, who had not forgiven "the unhonourable and thievish act" of All Hallows' Eve four years before. Some subtlety was needed. The Earl might be a prisoner, but he had been taken from an innocent bed by the officers of a friendly Queen in time of high peace. No charge, criminal, civil or political, had been preferred. As soon as he reached Berwick, Bothwell in full flush of innocence, demanded paper and ink. Briefly and effectively he put his case before the most powerful Englishman he knew. That the acquaintance had been struck up by the light of burning haystacks was no disadvantage. The Earl of Northumberland, at the moment following the Court in London, was well situated to help a fellow Borderer.

"Being deliberate," wrote Bothwell in his well-shaped Italian hand, "to go into France to the Queen's uncles by sea, I have been driven by storm in at the island beside Berwick, in which town I am kept by Sir Thomas Dacre, Knight. Having some little acquaintance with your Lordship" (by the rules of chivalry there could be no better introduction than the Till Raid), "and being afraid lest my unfriends may labour to get me delivered into Scotland to my utter ruin and displeasure, I pray you to solicit the Queen's Highness, your Mistress, in my name, to retain me under her protection, and I would rathest have the commodity to offer her my humble service personally. Excuse my homely writing. Your Lordship's 'luffing frend leffully, Birthvill.'"

News of his capture did not take long to reach the *Randolph to Cecil, 22 Jan., 28 Feb., 1563.*
Court of Scotland. To Randolph, who boasted openly
that he was Bothwell's enemy "as well in tongue as in
body," who never ceased advocating "what others have
mortally intended," fell the agreeable duty of enlightening Mary. She was just leaving Edinburgh to attend
the marriage of Margaret Campbell, sister of the Earl of
Argyll. She heard the agent in silence.

"I stood long in doubt," was his sarcastic comment,
"whether she did con me any thank for my news
or not."

He hastened to assure her that the arrest had been
made "for goodwill borne her," since every one knew
that Bothwell had broken her laws. Still there was
silence. At last she broke it to murmur that she would *Inventories lxxxii.*
have to consult her Council. Then she had to hurry off
to watch a wedding masque that represented a country
where shepherds played lutes and wore pouches of white
damask.

Randolph turned with a smile to Bothwell's implacable
enemies—Moray, formidable "for his credit with the
Queen," and Lethington, whose hostility was the more
dangerous because it was hidden. The agent reported
the Queen's reception of his news. The allies agreed that
it proved her more favourable to Bothwell "than there
was good cause." Nevertheless, urged Randolph, if they
could secure his extradition, Moray had influence enough
"to dispose of him as they would."

The Bastard's fingers caressed his sparse black beard.

"The Queen," he admitted regretfully, "is persuaded
that whatsoever we say against him is rather of hate to
his person, than that he has deserved."

Maitland nodded. Bring Bothwell back to Scotland
and the utmost they could hope to get him was a term
of imprisonment. Even were he securely lodged in the
Castle, "any mischief that any occasion may move the
Queen to use him in," would procure his release. Moray
joined in urging a letter to Cecil, begging him keep the
fugitive under arrest in England. Queen Mary might

press for his return, but her wishes could be safely ignored. Reluctantly Randolph gave in.

He had to observe the form of consulting the pleasure of the Queen of Scots. As soon as she was back, the agent asked for a formal audience at a sitting of the Council. On these occasions Mary had a habit of bringing her needlework. Randolph was introduced and begged the honour of instructions. What answer should he return to Berwick over the case of Lord Bothwell?

The Queen turned from her sewing to her Council. Randolph stood in respectful silence until the whispering had ceased.

"I take it in good part," the soft French voice replied at length, "that my sister's officers, for goodwill towards me, have apprehended the Lord Bothwell." Slender eyebrows forced themselves into severity. "He hath overgreatly failed towards me." A sidelong glance flickered from under heavy lids. "Wherefore, I pray you, write unto the Queen that I do desire he may be sent hither again unto Scotland."

In the pause that followed, there was opportunity for Randolph to catch the Secretary's eye. No word needed to be spoken. The agent, whose "often legations had made him exquisite," bowed and walked backwards to the door. In the privacy of his lodging he took up his pen to write to Cecil.

"In no way," he began, "should the Earl of Bothwell return, but be disposed of as shall be thought good to the Queen of England."

He thought for a moment and continued venomously:

"One thing I ought not to omit. I know him as mortal an enemy to our whole nation as any man alive, despiteful out of measure, false and untrue as the devil. If his power had been equal to his will, neither the Queen's Majesty had stood in so good terms of amity with this Queen, nor minister left alive that should be a travailer between their Majesties. If I made any account of his threatenings, your Honour had heard before this time

170

what just occasion I have had to seek the revenge that justly I ought to seek of an enemy of my country."

If anybody cares to contemplate the futility of human counsel, he may notice Bothwell and his adversaries straining every nerve to checkmate each other and seeking an identical end—that the fugitive should not be extradited, but be kept in England. It is rare to find such identity of purpose among professed associates.

John Knox gives a different version of these deliberations. "Our queen's answer was," he alleges, "that he was no rebel. Therefore she requested that he should have liberty to pass where it pleaseth him." Knox had not Randolph's access to the facts: he had, besides, other things to think about. In the words of a Victorian panegyrist, "he had sustained a severe affliction in the death of his attached wife. She died about the age of twenty-seven. Her mother, Mrs. Bowes, continued a member of the Reformer's household. Subject to melancholy, she augmented his anxieties." With incurable optimism, the prophet sought a cure for his anxieties and a solace for his affliction in remarriage with Margaret *Randolph to* Stewart, "a young lass not above sixteen years of age." *Cecil, 22* *Jan., 1563.* Forgetting the biblical precedent which the sixty-year-old Reformer indubitably followed, his theological opponents stooped to misrepresent his motives. The disparity in age and Margaret's kinship to the Duke of Chatelherault, gave scope for criticism. "The renegade and perjured *Nicol Burne* priest," they alleged, "had been repulsed in his courtship *102.* of the Duke's eldest daughter. "This most honest refusal could neither staunch his lust nor his ambition; but a little after he did pursue to have alliance with the honourable house of Ochiltree, riding there with a great court on a trim gelding, not like a prophet or an old decrepit priest as he was, but like as he had been one of the blood royal with his bands of taffeta sewn with golden rings and precious stones. And, as is plainly reported in the country, did so allure that poor gentlewoman by sorcery and witchcraft that she could not live without him."

It is to be feared that the Prophet's second flowering

171

set malicious tongues a-wag. That summer, when the marriage with the youthful Margaret hung fire, a certain "Ewfame" Dundas was guilty of "divers injurious and slanderous words, saying that within a few days past John Knox was apprehended and taken forth of ane killogye" (the space before the fire of a brick kiln) "with ane common hure and that he had been ane common harlot all his days." Confronted with authority, Euphemia (ironic name!) ate her words, but denial did not suffice and "such order was taken with her as might stand with the glory of God."

No repression, however sanctified, could still the tongues of the ribald. Reformation in morals, as well as in religion, might have done it, but there was not much to choose between the leaders of the Reformed Kirk and the prelates they had displaced. The partiality of Lord Arran for Alison Craig has been mentioned. About this time the habits of one of the ministers began to attract notice. Under the heading, "Messans, a superintendent, hath a bastard," an unsympathetic historian retails the scandal. "The ministers' business," he writes with gusto, "was somewhat interrupted by a slip of a chip of their own block; for Paul Messans, a superintendent and married, was questioned for getting a bairn on his maid Bessy. Who in the end confessed all, though he was Knox's great companion."

From such hypocrisy it is pleasant to return to the transparent failings of the Earl of Bothwell. Not that, in his captivity at Berwick, his weaknesses found much scope. At Randolph's orders, his gaolers sought any pretext for continuing to detain him. Hoping to find compromising papers, they searched the ship that had brought him to Holy Island. A packet roused their hopes, but only produced a letter written by the aged Bishop of Ross to France for a surgeon to cut him for the stone.

They fell back on John Rively. With the best will in the world, all examination could extract was a guess that during the three days Bothwell had been hidden at his house "he might have practised some offence against this realm." From the Forster family they gleaned a vague story "that the Earl and certain others had made a 'draughte' to have set fire in two places in this country about this time."

These meagre results encouraged Valentine Browne, Treasurer of the Garrison, to deliver the Earl to Sir Henry Percy for confinement in his Castle of Tynemouth, until the Privy Council of England should signify their pleasure.

Percy to the P.C., 24 Jan. 1563.

Bothwell's new prison stood on a headland lashed by the North Sea. Some years before the Percies had added a new wing to the tower of the thirteenth century, but in January it was a depressing place. Even the chanting of the monks who had once filled the Priory on the point of the promontory would have fallen gratefully on the prisoner's ears, assailed by the ceaseless din of the elements. His enemies could heave a sigh of satisfaction, tempered by one regret. Where injustice was the first consideration, Sir Henry Percy's reputation for fair dealing made him an unsatisfactory gaoler.

Randolph to Cecil, 31 Jan., 1563.

Misgiving was well-founded. Before Percy had had charge of James Hepburn for three weeks, he was writing to London on his behalf.

"The Earl of Bothwell," he informed Cecil, "is in great heaviness because of the enmity of his prince, the hatred of his enemies and from being in captivity."

Percy to Cecil, 13 Feb., 1563.

One Borderer had sympathy with the misfortunes of another; moreover, the prisoner had won the gaoler's regard. "The Earl is very wise," he wrote, "and not the man he was reported to be." He understood the dilemma between extradition and exile in which his captive stood. "He has several times lamented that he feared lest his unfriends should devise his deliverance, which he thinks will be his ruin;" at the same time "his poor living would be hindered by long absence from his country."

Percy went on to explain that he had suggested an appeal to Queen Elizabeth. Bothwell objected that he had not "the means of obtaining some mercy from the Queen of England or from the nobility and governors of the State." How could he prevail on her either "to make peace for him with his prince" or alternately, to let him remain at liberty in her country on parole? So Sir Henry took on himself to write this letter to Cecil pointing out that the Earl's friendship might be useful, "seeing that he is a man of the frontiers and a great power, for Liddesdale is his, also a good piece of Teviotdale." The best way would be for his charge to come to London for an audience.

This was a letter that Cecil might have been glad to suppress, but somehow—Henry's brother Thomas comes into the picture—it reached the eyes of Elizabeth. Impressed by its good sense, she sent immediate instructions to Tynemouth that the prisoner should be given a greater measure of liberty. Randolph shook a despondent head. He marvelled "by what good means or deserts towards her or her country he has conquered so many friendly hearts that any man can either speak good of him or write in his favour."

Randolph to Cecil, 28 Feb., 1563.

In his fuller liberty, two pieces of news that intimately touched his fortunes reached the exile. With distress he must have learnt that the Duke of Guise, whose patronage he had been on his way to seek, had been assassinated. The fullest details were to hand. Nineteen-year-old Poltrot de Méré had waited in the dusk in the vineyards of Orleans that Bothwell had lately visited. Wrapped in a tawny cloak, a hat on top of his morion, Poltrot had walked up and down for an hour until his victim approached. At a range of eight or nine yards he fired. Three pistol bullets, ingeniously notched and anointed with a mixture of brimstone and spittle, entered the Duke's shoulder. The stricken man called an attendant to lend him his furred coat and ride poste-haste to Paris with the news.

The surgeons set to work. Somebody in the camp said that without them the Duke might have lived. In the torments they inflicted his "stout courage, patience and wise words were much commended." A diet of woman's

174

milk and lily root was prescribed to no purpose and the sufferer died on Ash Wednesday.

Poltrot was caught and his sentence made the three hundred crowns that Coligny was said to have paid him look inadequate. As the horses tore his body apart, perhaps Theodore de Bèze's alleged blessing was of more help: "*Allez-vous-en*; *prenez courage*; *les anges vous assist-ront.*"

The Duke, whose *manes* it was thus sought to appease, received posthumous tributes even from his enemies. "He was the best general in France," testified Sir Thomas Smith, "some say in all Christendom. He had a ready wit, a body to endure pain, great courage, courtesy in entertaining men, eloquence to utter his mind, liberality in money and honour." Among those who mourned him Bothwell had cause to lament the death of a pros-pective patron. He had less reason to regret at about the same time the loss of a recent mistress.

For Anna Throndsen, her lover safely lodged in Tynemouth Castle, applied for a passport. A compre-hensive document granted her and all her goods the Queen's protection. She had permission to dwell in Scotland, to leave it as often as she liked, and to return to it. A "voyage to Norway for necessary business" was authorised, on which foreigners were invited to use "all kindly offices" and to grant her every privilege that Scottish subjects enjoyed. The nature of her business was not filled in—bureaucracy had not found its feet in the sixteenth century—but it is agreeable to suppose that Anna went home to try to raise money for her protector's hour of adversity. If that was indeed her object, it is disappointing to record complete failure. The summer of this calamitous year found Bothwell destitute, in Randolph's savage phrase, "a very beggar, stark naked, naught." Out of the Scandinavian North he received "a Portugal piece for a token." A token of what? Of failure and despair? Randolph does not say. Anna may have sent the coin to celebrate an anniversary of happier days —it might have formed part of the Spanish costume she

P.C. Register xiv. 211.

Randolph to Cecil, 3 June, 1563.

175

liked to wear. A less sentimental solution discerns a gesture of mockery, deriding the depths her betrayer had touched. Randolph's bleak comment on the sender of the token favours the last explanation—"a gentlewoman," he sneers "that, if she ever be a widow, shall never be my wife." The intellectual pretensions of the Admiral's daughter do not seem to have impressed the sophisticated agent.

So Anna was not among the visitors of both sexes who were allowed to come from Scotland to enliven Bothwell's *Randolph to Cecil, 28 Feb., 10 April, 1563.* wider liberty at Tynemouth. Their company helped to pass the weeks that elapsed before an answer came to his suit for an audience in London. His prospects there were none too bright. Lethington had ridden South to negotiate the succession to the throne of England. Disregarding Queen Mary's written instructions to take the opportunity to arrange Bothwell's repatriation, in his fear lest the returned prisoner would be "reserved for an ill instrument," he added his hostility to Cecil's spite. For once Elizabeth did not take long to make up *Q. Elizabeth to Percy, 18 March, 1563.* her mind. On the 18th March she sent orders for Sir Henry Percy to bring his captive with all speed to London.

As the two Borderers jogged down the Great North Road, they had plenty of time to exchange guesses at the fate that was waiting at the end of the journey. Nobody could predict the workings of the Tudor mind. The Virgin Queen might be "mortally intended." On the other hand, she had ever an eye for an enterprising young man!

CHAPTER EIGHTEEN

A NY flattering dreams that Bothwell nursed were quickly dispelled as the little procession reached London and was directed on the road that led to the Tower. The reasons for putting him in that ominous building were vague. Somebody said he was "taken to be a great papist and enemy to England, to which he intended some mischief." Another theory was even wilder—"his takers were in controversy who took him, and that he should be judged." With Latin love of mystery the Spanish Ambassador circulated a story that Elizabeth wanted to sow dissension between the Queen of Scots and her protestant nobles. How she gained her end by throwing Bothwell into the Tower to be "examined and well guarded," the diplomat did not explain. A hint of the truth may be gleaned from the connection in Bothwell's mind between Cecil and Rively, whom he called his worst enemies in England. The free pardon which Sir William procured the Northumbrian may have been earned by some invention of hostile deeds on the Border that would suffice to hold the Earl a suspect in the Tower.

Goldwell to Challoner, 21 May, 1563.

Quadra to K. Philip, 24 April, 1563.

Bedford to Cecil, 25 March, 1564.

That fortress (the fourth that had welcomed him in the thirteen months that had passed since his unlucky reconciliation with Arran) housed during his stay some notable guests. Edward Seymour, son of the Protector who had ravaged the Border in Bothwell's boyhood, was there with his wife, Lady Catherine Grey. She was unfortunate enough to be a potential successor to Elizabeth's crown ; he was unwise enough to have fallen in love with her. Arthur Pole, a son-in-law of Northumberland, was there, expiating a rash offer he had made on the Continent to set up as a pretender. The Provost of Paris with three other French hostages made, if their subsequent performance at Eton College is evidence,[1] exuberant neighbours. Taken all round, the Tower of London was an improvement on the isolation of Tynemouth. It was at least near the centre of government and Sir Henry and his brother Thomas were in London to urge the prisoner's case. The favour of the Percies stood high and on St. George's Day Northumberland was made a Knight of the Garter. Besides these friends at Court, Bothwell had succeeded in mobilising the help of France. Philibert du Croc, the French envoy to Scotland, was allowed to visit the prisoner on his way through London and "promised much for him at his return."

Middlemoor to Cecil, 17 May, 1563.

While his well-wishers were busy, his adversaries' influence was on the wane. Lethington had seized the chance of his trip to London to discuss with the Spanish Ambassador Mary's hopes of marrying Don Carlos. Word reached Elizabeth and shook her confidence in the Scottish Secretary. His fall from her favour, the efforts of the Percies, perhaps even the prisoner's complete innocence combined to procure a release. By June 3rd news reached Edinburgh that Lord Bothwell had been let out of the Tower on parole.

The heavy months of unmerited captivity had left their mark. He emerged harder and more callous. To make him desperate, he was "extreme poor." The last bit of land had been mortgaged. The Hermitage command had been given to the head of the Elliot clan. Haddington Abbey had passed into the tenacious hands of Lethington. The destitute Earl tried to borrow money from Scottish merchants in London, but met with a firm refusal. Freedom, had he been permitted to enjoy it, might have made up for any financial misery. But his liberties were still closely restricted. He was not allowed to leave England without the permission of

---

[1] Later in the year they were transferred to Eton, where their butler "attempted to enforce" a young woman who brought their food. They were responsible for the presence of "a lewd woman, taken in a barn." They put stones in the Fellows' keyholes and committed nuisance against their doors. They cast the lead of the roofs into bullets for their "hand guns" and took daily toll of pheasants, herons, mallard, teal and doves.

its Queen and he could only stay in approved quarters. Randolph was his merriest on the subject. His spirits ran high. He was due for leave and the prospect "did him more good than any pleasure he could have taken in the saffron shirt or Highland plaid," that an imminent visit to the Highlands in Queen Mary's train had threatened.

"I advise all my friends to take heed how they lodge such a guest," he sneered, hearing of Bothwell's predicament. His thoughts travelled to his brother Edward, governor of Dover Castle, and with mock terror he begged Cecil to put the released prisoner where he would, "saving in Dover Castle, not for fear of my old mother, but my sister is young and hath many daughters."

It was not possible for the object of his wit to linger in London. A summer epidemic of the plague, which had started at the siege of Le Havre, was raging. Over twenty thousand people succumbed. One of Queen Elizabeth's maids died and the Spanish Ambassador, but the principal class to suffer were "very poor men who ate bread made of corrupted corn." Once again Sir Henry Percy came to Bothwell's rescue with the offer of a refuge at his Border Castle of Norham. *Randolph to Cecil, 31 Dec., 1563.*

At Norham he found compensations. To begin with, the Percy deputy who kept the Castle while Sir Henry was south, fell foul of the Berwick officers. Sending a detachment to seize his goods, they found the Castle ready to resist a siege. It is difficult to imagine the distinguished guest playing a passive part. The disorders did not end there. Soon Berwick itself was at loggerheads, and the Marshal, was accusing the Treasurer of summoning a riotous meeting of armed men to throw fire-balls and squibs on the walls of the city. It is impossible to resist the reflection that the affairs of any one who had meddled with the Earl of Bothwell were apt not to prosper.

Some such deduction may have influenced the authorities, for soon the paroled prisoner was moved to Alnwick. During Northumberland's absence at Court, his castle was in charge of Sir John Forster. At Alnwick Bothwell *Randolph to Cecil, 13 Dec., 1563.*

Randolph to
Cecil, 13
Dec., 1563.
Randolph to
Cecil, 31
Dec., 1563.

found congenial and harmless occupation. English geldings were popular in Scotland and his eye for a horse was useful in sizing up likely material. Randolph, on his way back from London, heard of the traffic and wanted to stop it. He stayed a night with Forster and could not avoid meeting the man he had wronged. Adversity had taught Bothwell prudence. He saw he must stop the agent's bitter tongue if he hoped for a hearing at Edinburgh. Disclaiming any ill-feeling he tried to put his visitor at his ease. The other affected to accept his assurances and "passed lightly over."

Politeness satisfied, the exile came to earth with a hint that Randolph might be disposed to take a more friendly line. Unfortunately his poverty precluded the argument that might have appealed to the agent who was "rich of children and therefore poor of purse." Randolph professed surprise that he should be supposed to have meddled with the Earl's affairs in the past or be willing to do so in the future. If a go-between was wanted, there were plenty of noble compatriots able to officiate.

Bothwell saw at once that he was wasting his time. He remarked that if his sovereign proved obdurate, he meant to ask leave to quit England. Here he found his visitor more sympathetic. Thomas Randolph could bear the British Isles without Lord Bothwell. "Little good," he meditated, "he does where he is." The geldings rankled and perhaps Valentine Browne's fire-balls. "I wish he were out of the country, for neither can he afford it good word, nor never will do it a good deed."

Two pieces of news, both of the obituary order, had helped to turn the exile's thoughts to foreign parts. His brother-in-law, the Commendator, had lately gone to Inverness to temper the justice of the Earl of Moray. After a couple of witches had been burnt, proceedings were interrupted by the Commendator's sudden death. The Queen wept bitterly when the news reached her and, remembering the Duke of Guise, cried out that God always took from her those persons in whom she had the greatest pleasure. If only for selfish reasons, Bothwell had to lament the loss of his best friend at Court. His sister was left with an infant son and a mourning robe presented by a sympathetic sovereign.[1] Her power to advance her brother's return was gone.

The other death that suggested a move to France was, from Bothwell's point of view, less lamentable. An appointment at the French Court fell vacant at the end of November with the demise of the Captain of the Scottish Archers. Although for the moment a Frenchman was given the post, he might be glad to retire from a delicate situation, since Gallic opinion was alive to the character of the Scots—"a wild, obstinate and war-like race, which will not be tamed by force, unless total extermination is resorted to." The patronage lay nominally in the hands of Queen Mary. She might not be able to get her advisers to consent to Bothwell's recall; she need not consult them about his appointment to a post at the French Court. And it carried a salary that would at least provide a living.

So Bothwell began a campaign to find backing for his petition to leave England. Before the end of the year, besides sounding Randolph, he had written to the Earl of Lennox in England. He may have heard from his friends at the English Court how well Elizabeth liked the son, young Henry Darnley, and his lute-playing. Nor did the petitioner neglect the Court of Scotland. Queen Mary, whose conscience cannot have been easy, gave wholehearted support. She promised a despatch to her cousin of England recommending his request "to pass out of the country into France or some other place." An access of royal geniality at a Twelfth Night Ball coaxed even Randolph into writing to Cecil and Leicester. *Miss Strickland from Dawson Turner MSS.*

Mason to Challoner, 19 July, 1563.

The agent was left to square his conscience in a private note giving his opinion that Bothwell was "of so little worth that it is no matter where he is," while the formal letter that he left open is a model for suggesting shades of hidden meaning.

[1] It was a black knitted frock with a squirrel cape. (Inventories.) That it helped to assuage her grief is suggested by her re-marriage within a year or two.

"Your Honour's favour to all noblemen—in special to those whose cases are to be lamented—is such that I doubt the less to write in favour of the Earl of Bothwell. *His case is sufficiently known to you* and he will declare his suit, as others have written. At their request, *with the goodwill I have myself that his Lordship were well*, I trouble you with my desire that by your means he may find favour at the Queen Majesty's hands."

The Earl's popularity with women secured him the backing of yet another opponent, when Maitland, "to oblige friends he could not refuse," wrote on his behalf to Cecil. The identity of the friends was an open secret. "Our secretaree wyf is dead," gossiped Grange, "and he a sutor to M. Fleming, quha is als meit for hym as I am to be paipe!" As Mary Fleming was generally agreed to "contend with Venus in beauty, with Minerva in wit and with Juno in worldly wealth," it is not surprising that the lean and bearded Lethington, at twice her age, could refuse her nothing.

Mary Fleming was a good friend to Bothwell. Was it she who jogged her mistress's memory? Here is a second letter Mary Stuart wrote to Elizabeth:—

"Right Excellent, High and Mighty Princess, our dearest Sister and Cousin, we commend us right heartily unto you. We wrote to you lately at the desire of certain of the Earl Bothwell's friends here, that it might please you to grant him liberty to pass forth of that your realm to the parts beyond sea, where he liketh best. And because they understand that he is to repair to your Court for obtaining of the same, have made new suit unto us to put you in remembrance of our former request. Wherefore we pray you, Dearest Sister, to give command that the said Earl may have freedom to depart forth of your Realm to such countries as shall seem to him most convenient, as ye will do us acceptable pleasure in that behalf. And thus, Right Excellent, Right High and Mighty Princess, our dearest Sister and Cousin, we commit you to the tuition of Almighty God."

At last Bothwell had collected all the letters he needed,

but the weather did not favour an immediate start. The rain, says the emphatic Knox, "fell in such abundance and froze so vehemently, that the Earth was but a shot of ice. The fowls, both great and small, freezed and might not fly. Some were taken and laid beside the fire that their feathers might dissolve." The sea was frozen and the *aurora borealis* provoked the Reformer's prophetic powers. A blizzard blocked the roads to Berwick, while, farther south, people walked across the Thames. All these rigours could not stop Helen Barron's pursuit of self-expression. Finding married life with Bothwell's principal creditor unendurable, "she rebelliously separated from his society and deserted the realm." James Barron complained to the General Assembly and got Knox to write to the Archbishops of Canterbury and York, but there is no record that either presbyterial or episcopal fulmination ever brought Helen back across the Border.

Other wayfarers on those wintry roads included Michael Balfour (once more in possession of Melrose Abbey), Black Ormiston, John Wemyss of Pittencrieff and Mr. David Chalmers, who made their way to Alnwick for a last conference with the Earl before he started on his travels. The departing exile was uneasy about his papers. With everything "sold to the uttermost penny," they were all he had to put in safe keeping. John Mosman, the goldsmith, took charge of various deeds of reversion; a cousin Jane, lady of Wedderburn, lent her services, and later on Sir Walter Robertson, ("alias Douny") put his strong-box at the traveller's disposal. *Randolph to Forster, 6 Feb., 1564.*

While he was thus peaceably engaged, wild rumours filled the air. Did Mary pay an unexpected visit to Dunbar, all Moray's servants and supporters were mobilised by the story that she had gone to a secret rendezvous with Bothwell. Protestant circles held that she intended to recall him as soon as her plans for a catholic revival were complete. Word leaked out that Lennox was coming north to push his son's suit for Mary's hand. The Lennox Stewarts were catholic and the more nervous of their opponents began to feel uncomfortable. "Things begin to grow to a ripeness," they whispered. "The Queen thinks to have Bothwell at all times ready to shake out of her pushet against us protestants." With young Darnley and his mother across the Border—"the Mass shall up. Bothwell shall follow with power to put into execution, and then shall Knox and his preaching be pulled by the ears."

When eighteen months later part of this programme was realised, the political prophets could for once claim some foresight. But at the beginning of March, 1564, Bothwell was only interested in his journey. He left Alnwick and Forster's hospitality, proudly displaying the addresses of the letters he had so laboriously collected. His host, who prided himself that "we that inhabit Northumberland are not acquainted with any learned or rare phrases," added a testimonial that his guest "had behaved as to him appertained all the time of his abode," and sped him on his way to the scene of his recent confinement at Tynemouth. Percy was home and proved his friendship afresh by taking up his pen to assure Cecil that the exile's "behaviour has been both courteous and honourable, keeping his promise." He pressed the well-established claims of youth and poverty and again urged the Secretary to let handsome treatment win a friend for England.

Forster to Cecil, 10 March, 1564.

Percy to Cecil, 18 March, 1564.

From the March morning that saw Bothwell ride from under the Tynemouth portcullis with Sir Henry's letter in his pocket, to the September day that gave him his congé, the exile disappears. Elizabeth's Court was enlivening Richmond-on-Thames. Stags were hunted and killed on the Green. The new Spanish Ambassador was rowed up-stream and allowed to surprise the Queen of England demurely playing the virginals. (Sir James Melville, who was soon to be given the material for his much-quoted account of her girlish ways, was not there to warn him of that favourite pose.) She had *The Battle of Pavia* performed by the band, a compliment that forty years of usage had not staled. She translated the jokes of a play "whose plot as usual turned upon marriage."

184

Dancers revolved, splendid in the royal black and white. There was a recitation—an ode in Gloriana's praise. There was a buffet laid with preserved fruits and sweetmeats—and somewhere with increasing ill-humour the Earl of Bothwell waited for permission to sail.

Elizabeth, murmured the moralists, "was entirely given over to love, hunting, hawking and dancing, consuming day and night with trifles." They were ignorant of certain undercurrents. For the invincible spinster was determined that the Queen of Scots should not marry a foreign prince. Feminine jealousy apart, her foreign policy demanded a weak and divided neighbour and recognised royal marriage as the surest means to acquire territory or influence. Arran and his Hamilton pretensions had been the right pawn to unsettle the Franco-Scottish entente; Darnley and the far weaker Lennox Stewart claim to the succession now offered a move that might checkmate a Spanish wedding.

Challoner to Sir Thos. Cecil, 18 Dec., 1563.

Jebb ii. 460.

Elizabeth liked Darnley better than Arran. He had been carefully brought up by his mother and had "learnt from his youth to play the lute, to dance and other honest exercise." Before he was nine, his tutor reported his "towardness in the Latin tongue and the French, and in sundry other virtuous qualities; of his good wit, gentleness, beauty and favour. So, if it may please God to send him a long life, he shall prove a witty, virtuous and active, well-learned gentleman."

Although the pedagogue's programme did not receive divine endorsement, Darnley lived long enough to disappoint his enthusiasm. By the age of nineteen he was unkindly likened to "a great cocke-chicke." Knox, naturally prejudiced against his religious views, mentions that "he was much given to hunting and hawking and running of horses, likewise playing on the lute and also to Venus's chamber. He was somewhat given to wine and much feeding and likewise to inconstancy." Critics were disarmed by his good looks—"he was a comely prince of a fair and large stature of body, pleasant in countenance"—though a less partial observer states that he "more resembled a woman than a man, for he was handsome, beardless and lady-faced." Melville's standards of masculine beauty were evidently hirsute.

Lord Darnley's appearance and his sketchy claim to succeed to the two crowns made him suitable bait to lay before the Queen of Scots. Skilfully encouraged, she could be led to confuse a natural fancy for a youth she heard was good-looking with profundity of statecraft. So Darnley's father, who ranked as an English subject, received licence from Elizabeth and finance from Cecil to push his son's suit at Holyrood. In the long run his venture proved more expensive than the Secretary had reckoned. "Of the seven hundred pounds that the Earl of Lennox brought," Randolph had soon to report, "little is left. If he tarry long, he may be a dear purchase." Again a few weeks later—"Lennox must shortly be supplied with more money."

Randolph to Cecil, 24 Oct., 1564.

Randolph to Cecil, 18 Jan., 1565.

Thus the snare was spread at Mary's feet which was in the end to be her ruin. For all her quickness of wit she never saw it. After some months of Darnley's courtship first by proxy and later in person, Mary Stuart, ingeniously provoked by the thinly-veiled commands of the daughter of Anne Boleyn, flew into a temper and cried that she would exert what she pathetically called her own choice. In the words of an English diplomat analysing the marriage, "the foundation was despite and anger." Only Randolph knew what pains had gone to lay the foundation stones. "My whole care," he remarked, as the match grew inevitable, "is how to avoid suspicion that the Queen's Majesty was the mean and worker hereof." When at last the dice were cast, he gloated over Mary's challenge to Fate—"a greater plague to her there cannot be. A greater benefit to the Queen's Majesty could not have chanced." It needed all Randolph's irony to use the word "chance."

Randolph to Cecil, 18 April, 1565.

Darnley was selected for his high and fatal destiny while Bothwell in England waited for licence to sail.

186

HENRY STEWART, LORD DARNLEY
(*By courtesy of the Duke of Devonshire*)

There are signs that he was in sympathy with the young man's hopes. His name is entered on a list of Lennox supporters; he had been recently in correspondence with the head of the clan; John Wemyss of Pittencrieff and Murray of Tullibardine, both Lennox men, were in his circle. He clearly stood to gain if any new influence displaced Moray. But no account has been preserved of any intercourse in England between the two men whose lives were later to cross so disastrously. The Hepburn fortunes were at too low an ebb for Bothwell's movements to attract much notice. *Memorial of the friends and enemies of Lennox, 3 Feb., 1565.*

It was not until the 12th September that he at last succeeded in cornering the Queen of England at Harrow-on-the-Hill, where she had not yet allowed a farmer to erect a tall red brick building for use as a school. To the man who had commanded a Scottish army she condescended to grant leave to cross the Channel with a bundle of letters for her Ambassador in France. Truly her intelligence department seemed justified in putting against Lord Bothwell's name the note "of no force now." *Sir Thos. Smith to Queen Elizabeth, 9 Nov., 1567.*

CHAPTER NINETEEN

THE exile's enemies were not yet satisfied. They had ruined him, put him in prison, driven him from his home—as long as he was alive they feared him. His restless energy, his value to the Queen as her man of action might at any moment lift him on a half-turn of Fortune's wheel to any eminence. The weapon of judicial murder had broken; the domestic variety remained to be tried.

By the beginning of November Bothwell had reached France. In his scanty luggage letters from Mary recommended the King and Council of France to give him command of the Scottish Archers, inappropriately known as "the bodyguard of the Virgin Mary." His natural refuge, now that the Duke of Guise was dead, lay with the Queen's other uncle, Charles, Cardinal of Lorraine. That dignitary, nicknamed "The Tiger of France," appears in the pages of protestant historians as the spearhead of catholic repression. His contemporaries were less confident of his zeal. A Spanish Ambassador heard with horror that he "was damned and a heretic; or to speak plainly, one of the protestants." The damaging insinuation took colour from the Cardinal's proceedings at the Council of Trent, where he presented the thirty-four articles that permitted communion in both kinds and the study of the Scriptures in the vulgar tongue. Such a mind could appreciate the exile's unorthodox views and loyal service. While strings were being pulled to win the coveted command, the Cardinal's protection would be valuable.

But no patronage could insure against intelligent assassination, inspired by the Machiavelli of Scotland. Maitland had enlisted a willing tool in John Wemyss, Laird of Pittencrieff, who arrived in France about the same time as Bothwell. If the laird had himself no

Les Affaires du Comte de Boduel. 9.

Vargas to Philip II., Jan., 1561. Pollen 8.

Forster to Bedford, 3 April, 1565. Teulet Lettres 85.

particular flair for murder, he knew where one could be bought. With Scottish thoroughness, he corrupted six of the victim's servants. Bothwell's barber, whose profession carried a knowledge of drugs, held the key position. As accomplices, "all of one confederacy and mind," he had his Lordship's French page, Nicholas Hubert; his confidential man, Gabriel Sempill;[1] Walter Murray, Dandie Pringle and the head groom. At first everything went smoothly. The barber had "the puson ready mixed for ministering." But Wemyss neglected the personal equation. At the last minute the poisoner's heart "would not serve him to do his feat!"

The workings of conscience, the memory of past kindness, perhaps mistrust of the efficacy of his mixture —one of these considerations restrained him. A hurried council of war decided that for their master a knife was as good as a glass. "They devised to have slain him in his own chamber and when they were going up the stairs, being three steps up and none in the chamber but the Earl himself, they dallied and grew in fear of the matter and so passed it over without proceeding any further." It is a pretty story of treachery and cowardice, the five menials hiding behind each other on the stairs, the Earl sitting quietly in his room, his force of personality dominating them as they slunk away unnerved.

With one exception they went back quietly to their jobs. Dandie Pringle was the son of that Sandy Pringle who sold information to the English about the late Earl of Bothwell. Perhaps Dandie's nerves were weaker than his fellows; perhaps he had played too conspicuous a part in the plot. Leaving the Hepburn service, he attached himself to James Murray of Purdorvis, younger brother of William Murray of Tullibardine, who was shortly due to cross the Channel.

Randolph to Cecil, 15 March, 1565.

Bedford to Cecil, 25 March, 1565.

The plot had collapsed ignominiously and Bothwell might never have learnt how near Maitland's lethal

[1] Nicholas Hubert and Gabriel Sempill seem, confusingly, to have shared a nickname. The latter, finding perhaps the name selected by his god-parents too much to live up to, adopted the less exacting pseudonym of "Paris." Nicholas Hubert was known as *French* Paris.

designs had been to fulfilment, if some months later the delinquent head groom (Bothwell cannot be said to have chosen his servants well) had not helped himself to a couple of his master's shirts. Detected and thrown into prison with a promise of the gallows, the thief bought his pardon by an offer to "open matters of more greater importance." Under pressure, French Paris confirmed the confession and implicated Wemyss and Maitland.

Il Barchingo to Alava, 20 May, 1565. Dr. Wilson's Actio.

Rather late in the day the story reached secret service circles in Paris and was ultimately used as propaganda against Bothwell, "whose house," wrote the pamphleteers, "was in France defamed of poisoning and whose servants were there for the same cause, some tortured, some imprisoned and all suspected." To an impartial eye, it seems a little hard that Bothwell should be blamed for being nearly poisoned, while there is every indication that he treated his treacherous servants very mercifully.[1] French Paris was soon back in his service, Gabriel Sempill was well enough the following year to steal four horses, the property of a lady, while Dandie Pringle lived happily at Newcastle to do his utmost, as will be seen, to blacken his master's name.

This poison plot was not discovered until the last days of March, 1565. Plenty happened in Franco-Scottish circles before then. The old Bishop of Ross had his operation in Paris and died "of the flux." The Cardinal of Lorraine was told to avoid friction with huguenots and to keep his men outside the gates of Paris. The Governor of Ile de France, himself "a huguenot or little it lacks," sent fifteen hagbutters to see that it was done. They were surrounded by the Cardinal's people (Bothwell could be counted on not to miss the excitement), a hundred shots were exchanged and one of the soldiers was killed. The Cardinal wrote an account of the encounter to his niece and sent it to Scotland by the hand of James Murray of Purdorvis. Bothwell took the opportunity to include a

---

[1] Walter Murray, Bothwell's guilty servant, came to a violent end in the following August. The name of his slayer was Sinclair. As Bothwell's mother was a Sinclair, Highland blood may have been less forgiving than Border.

letter. If he had to be kept in exile, he begged the Queen to remember his hope to command the Archers so that he might preserve "the countenance and condition of a man of his calling and birth." With a characteristic mistrust of the power of the pen he enlisted the eloquence of James Murray to press his plea. *Randolph to Cecil, 1 Mar., 1565.*

The choice looked sensible, for James Murray was to develop into an expert propagandist and a pioneer in the use of pictorial advertisement. But Bothwell reckoned without the man's inherent treachery. A compatriot, James Murray enjoyed the hospitality every nobleman, however poor, dispensed. Bothwell was known by his enemies for "a blasphemous and irreverent speaker" and his habit of saying what he thought helped to lighten a heart full of bitterness. His caustic tongue spared no one who had contributed to his downfall. Moray was the main object of his indignation, but if his guest can be believed, Mary's lukewarm support and Elizabeth's condescension were remembered without gratitude. The publicity expert sat drinking in the flow of indiscreet invective. Bothwell took him for a Lennox man, no friend to the Moray-Maitland regime. Had he guessed that his listener's route to Scotland lay past Cecil's house in Westminster and that Dandie Pringle, specialist in poison, chemical and verbal, was in his service, he might have set a watch on his words.

James Murray left Paris with his letter-bag soon after the fracas with the hagbutters. Holding an English trading permit that let him visit any town or port of England on foot or horse, or in a boat under one hundred tons, and combining the occupations of merchant and messenger, he made his way home by slow stages. Before he had been gone a month there was every probability that the exile's hope of commanding the Archers would be independently realised. The French were dissatisfied with the behaviour of the mercenaries. Many refused to go to Mass and some had served in the English ranks at the siege of Le Havre. It was proposed to replace them by "such as are of the old religion and have never served *Passport to James Murray 24 Aug., 1564.*

Sir Thos. Smith to Cecil, 10 Feb., 1565.

nor would serve England." As an additional reform, the Queen of Scots was to nominate James Hepburn as their Captain.

Les Affaires du Comte de Boduel 9.

To Bothwell's laconic memoir a marginal note has been added in his own hand: "I was made Captain of the Scottish Guard." Allowing for certain important suppressions that record of his life is reliable. Although his claim lacks outside corroboration, it can be accepted with the proviso that he only occupied the office for a matter of weeks.

No longer period is possible. On the 10th February the English Ambassador gives the rumour of the appointment. By the 5th March, to every one's amazement, the Earl is signalled at Edinburgh. What took him there? He had every reason to stay in France. He had just won the post he coveted and the emoluments he needed. He was still "wanted" in Scotland. The enemies who had vowed his destruction were still in power. The reason for his rash return can only be found in the latest moves in the royal marriage game.

On 17th February Elizabeth's secret choice, young Henry Darnley, rode to Wemyss Castle on a horse borrowed from Randolph. Queen Mary "took well with him and said that he was the lustiest and best proportioned long man that she had seen; for he was of high stature, long and small, even and brent up." In France Bothwell's patron, the Cardinal, felt differently. Darnley, he cried, was a nincompoop and no fit match for his niece. Feverishly he sought alternatives—the Duke of Orleans, the young Duke of Guise, even Charles IX., with his "great knees and ankles and little legs." Is it improbable that, anxious to leave no stone unturned, the prelate invited a *protégé*, who was always ready for anything, to risk his life in a sudden descent on Scotland to find out what was really happening? May not the impatient exile have felt that Darnley's progress spelt the end of Moray's power and, encouraged by the premature optimism of friends at Court, have decided to take a chance?

The West Coast was his best route, for the roads from the Eastern ports were blocked by a blizzard. That on his arrival in the capital he granted a charter to some lands in Lanarkshire, also suggests an approach from that direction. Edinburgh was too hot to hold him and he hurried to the Hepburn country, to his mother at Morham, and to Haddington (where the free-thinking schoolmaster had just shocked everybody by baptising a cat in the name of the Father, the Son and the Holy Ghost). *Les Affaires du Comte de Boduel, lxv.*

Meanwhile James Murray at last reached Holyrood House with the adventurer's out-of-date petition. He had not wasted the weeks that had passed. In London he had met a friendly welcome from Cecil and had been warmed by the sympathetic atmosphere into betraying his compatriot. Cecil heard with pleasure of Bothwell's indiscretions and saw at once what good uses they would serve. Dandie Pringle was called in and invited to add his share of highly-spiced reminiscence. He needed little pressing to promise evidence to ruin the master he had already tried to murder. *Randolph to Cecil, 1, 15 March, 1565. Bedford to Cecil, 10 March, 1565.*

Once at the Scottish Court, James Murray lost no time telling Moray the "great and injurious words spoken against him by Bothwell in France in his hearing," threatening both him and Lethington "that he would be the death of them at his return to Scotland." The Earl was furious and ran to his half-sister, whom he found busy with plans for "banqueting, balling and dancing" to entertain her suitor.

"Is it by your will," he demanded, "or your advice that my enemy is come home?"

Mary answered composedly that Bothwell was a nobleman who had done her service, and that she could not hate him.

"Scotland will not hold us both!" blustered Moray. "Either he or I must leave it."

He demanded that the adventurer be "put to the horn," a ritual which proclaimed outlawry with three blasts and by a statute of James V associated the outlaw with

thieves, foreigners and wolves for any citizen to capture
or expel. But the Queen, who was "not evil affected"
towards the returned adventurer, avoided a direct
answer.

The plan that Cecil had hatched now entered its
second stage. James Murray was sent for to tell the
Queen how Bothwell, not content with threatening her
brother, "had spoken divers dishonourable words"
against herself. Here the informant affected a scruple.
He would not soil his lips—but Dandie Pringle, "dwelling
in Newcastle," would no doubt oblige.

So Moray and Randolph wrote to the Earl of Bedford,
the new governor at Berwick, to send Dandie along with
all speed.

Bedford to
Cecil, 25
Mar., 1565.
Randolph to
Cecil, 30
Mar., 1565,
and 13 Oct.,
1565.
Randolph to
Throckmorton,
31 Mar., 1565.

Pringle is hurried to Court and ushered by the eager
Randolph into the presence. In Mary's outraged ears
he distils his venom. In his hearing the Earl of Bothwell
actually said that the queens of England and Scotland,
taken together, "could not make one honest woman."
Pressed by his appalled but delighted hearers for further
revelations, he alleges that his master called the Queen
"the Cardinal's hoore." As this monstrous libel seems to
need some amplification, he quotes the actual words:
"If she had taken any but a Cardinal, it had been better to
be borne with."

This was too much for the Stewart temper. Swearing
upon her honour that Bothwell should never again receive
favour at her hands, she gave orders that he should be
"summoned to underlie the law or, if he refuses to do so,
to be pronounced rebel."

Murray's and Pringle's charges might readily be dismissed as the inventions of a treacherous acquaintance
and of a discharged servant. But it must be admitted
that the first jibe, "that the two queens could not make
one honest woman," has the genuine Bothwell ring.
If the Earl was guilty of the sneer, his offence was not
altogether without provocation. After years of faithful
service, Mary had apologetically thrown him to the lions.
Elizabeth sent him to prison without the shadow of a

cause. Released, she let him hang about her Court like a lackey. Is it surprising that the Border noble felt less veneration for good Queen Bess than her adoring courtiers?

But while no one can claim that in Bothwell's case either queen acted like an honest woman, what mud could be thrown, even in that unreticent century, at Mary's relations with her uncle, the Cardinal of Lorraine? The slander is so wild that it is hard to believe it was ever spoken. Who will believe that Bothwell, then dependent on the Cardinal's favour, would be stupid enough to tell an unsavoury lie about him and his niece? If Pringle's revelations had any solid foundation at all, may not Bothwell in the privacy of his dining-room have mentioned the old scandal about Mary of Lorraine and Cardinal Beton? May he not have quoted his father's lament over a failure in a field where the Church was said to have met more conspicuous success—"If she had taken any but a Cardinal, it had been better to be borne with!" The greedy ears of the servant caught the ecclesiastical title and the Christian name and his dirty mouth spread the story that Bothwell called Mary Stuart the Cardinal's whore.

The man had not finished with his master's good name. The tale of threats against Lethington, Cecil and Rively was probably true. Over a bottle or two of claret, it would be natural to discuss plans for the glad days when exile was past; without an informer on the hearth the relaxation would be harmless enough. A more serious accusation, started by Pringle, has been repeated in awe-struck footnotes. It is grave enough to demand examination.

Francis Russell, second Earl of Bedford, had lately been put in charge at Berwick. He was, an appreciative foreigner records, "liberal to the soldiers and the well-deserving. In peace there is no gentleman more pleasant than he, nor any who pays more attention to historical studies, which he stores in his tenacious memory." *Bedford to Cecil, 25 March, 1565.* To this free-handed nobleman fell the task of preparing

195

Pringle for his visit to Court. To him Dandie opened the treasures of his mind. Bedford could hardly believe his ears. "I assure you," he hastened to write of Pringle's late master, "he is as naughty a man as liveth and much given to that vile and detestable vice of sodomy."

Before sharing the Governor's indignation, it must be asked whether Bedford did not provide one more instance of the failure of historical studies to develop a critical sense. He knew well that the accusation started from the servants' hall on the lips of a man who had run away after trying to murder his master; that the charge was the commonplace of political and religious controversy of the century. Deplorable instances of this can be quoted on either side. "I dare be bold to say," affirmed Sir Ralph Sadler, "that unless your monks be more holy in Scotland than ours are in England, there reigneth nowhere more Carnality, Incontinency, Sodomy with Lechery and other Abominations than is to be used in Cloisters among Monks, Canons, Nuns and Friars." On the other side of the fence, Nichol Burne was no less emphatic. "As for the practice of bougrie and sodomitical sin, I remit you to the verse of your Paraclet, Theodore de Bèze." He proceeds to quote some unrepeatable stanzas which, if they were authentic, would certainly inculpate de Bèze. "Siklike Calvin," he continues brightly, "was marked with the *fleur de lys* upon his shoulder for the horrible sin of Sodomie." If the irritable but certainly ascetic Genevan could not escape the imputation, what chance had Bothwell?

It is noteworthy that, although Pringle launched this charge in 1565, in all the abuse that was showered on Bothwell during the remainder of his life, it was not repeated. Possibly the common sense of his assailants saw that while they were proclaiming his "inordinateness towards women" the alternative charge lacked verisimilitude. The subject cannot unfortunately be left without mentioning one piece of evidence which historians have quoted to confirm Bedford's accusation.

After Bothwell's fortunes had touched their zenith

and had suffered their final collapse, his page, French Paris, passed nine months in his enemies' power. The statement which resulted bears witness in its inconsistencies to the blind terror of the deponent. One passage in it charges Bothwell with "terrible vices," which are generally assumed to be unnatural, although the equally common sixteenth century accusations of witchcraft or poisoning would adequately fill the bill.

"I knew his very terrible vices," quavered poor Paris, *Teulet Lettres, 81, 85.* "especially one in which I am said to be so good a minister. I told him more than six years ago that it would be his ruin. Of the truth of that, ask the Laird of Pittencrieff, who knows why I left his service out of England. He beat me and kicked me in the belly to force me to an act which I refused. Afterwards he thanked me in Scotland for protecting his honour when I had occasion to harm it."

That complicated word "honour" does not necessarily carry a sexual connotation in Paris's mouth. Twice he talks of "honour" being compromised by complicity in murder. The Laird of Pittencrieff's name suggests a connection with the poison plot, and the pamphleteer's charge that the servants were ill-treated may allude to kicks that Paris earned. If the whole story of the attempted murder were known, it is probable that the page's terrified babblings would be explained without introducing homosexuality. In quitting the subject with relief, it may be mentioned that, whatever the Earl's treatment, French Paris was soon back in his service.

Pringle had done his work thoroughly, inflaming authority and posterity against his master. Mary sent a herald "with letters to summon James Earl of Bothwell at his dwelling-places of Crichton, Hailes, Morham, Haddington, Duns, Lauder, Selkirk, Hawick, Hermitage and Jedburgh to appear before the Justice and his deputies in Edinburgh, to underlie the law for certain points of *lèse majesté* the second day of May next to come, within six days, under pain of rebellion and putting him to the horn." That there might be no mistake "twelve copies of great volume" were made at a cost of thirty-six shillings.

By now the Earl, "finding no safety anywhere," had disappeared into the seclusion of the Hermitage, from which he had first to displace an Elliot. His conscience was clear and he submitted to the Queen's summons, depositing a caution of two hundred pounds Scots to appear at the Tolbooth on the appointed day. His enemies were convinced that he would bolt. Berwick and Edinburgh combined to stop the earths and took steps to catch the fugitive the moment he appeared on English soil. Hints are not lacking of a plot to kidnap him where he was. Bothwell for one believed the danger and rallied to his protection "all the outlaws, thieves and rovers" of Liddesdale.

One night about ten o'clock while he was eating his supper, a voice was heard outside the barricaded gates, shouting: "Horse! Horse!"

Bolts were pulled and Gabriel Sempill, Bothwell's confidential man, tumbled in. He had been to Edinburgh on business, which his master "did accredit him with, more than any other servant or friend that he had." His exhausted state proclaimed "the most speedful manner" of his return.

"The Earl of Moray," he gasped, "is coming towards your Lordship with a great company of horsemen and all the surname of Kerr and Scott do mind to be in your way."

Bothwell believed in Gabriel. He did not believe in fortresses. His Border instinct inclined him to "take present order for the keeping of his house, and himself to horse and ride to the hills all that night, where all the Liddesdales did accompany him."

After an uncomfortable night, dawn revealed no trace of the Earl of Moray or the surnames of Kerr and Scott. So the Borderer returned quietly to his castle and sent Gabriel, with the few appropriate words that may be guessed, back to Lothian.

But the false alarm, which Moray had started by riding out of Stirling in force, had its results. The next night Bothwell, to be on the safe side, absented himself again. It was then that the head groom saw his chance to steal the shirts that led to the discovery of the poison plot and exposed an elaborate system of treachery.

The proof that he could trust no one among his friends or servants may have decided Bothwell's next move. He left the Hermitage and paid a brief visit to his castle of Crichton and his mother's home at Morham. He was getting ready for a longer journey. By now the Queen's intention to marry Darnley was admitted in Court circles and no duty to the Cardinal detained Bothwell in Scotland. The second of May was close. Moray was collecting "a great train of his kinsfolk and friends" whose presence at the trial was calculated to influence the impartiality of any jury. Associated with him was his brother-in-law, the unstable Earl of Argyll, who conveniently held the office of Lord Justice of Scotland.

On the 30th April, the Marchmont Herald summoned an assize. The following night Moray and Argyll led six thousand men into Edinburgh. With the verdict thus plainly indicated, the court sat in the Tolbooth. The summons of treason was read for all to hear how James, Earl of Bothwell, had conceived a treasonable enterprise against the Queen's noble person, which would have succeeded had not the Grace of God moved the heart of James Lord Arran to reveal the same. As a sequel, the Earl of Bothwell, knowing himself most guilty and his conscience being record against him, treasonably and contemptuously broke out of the Castle of Edinburgh and departed forth to his liberty.

The impression left by the rolling periods would have been deeper had the Earl been standing at the bar of Justice to hear them. Unfortunately for the full vindication of the majesty of Law, his unalterable regard for liberty had taken him several days earlier to North Berwick. As the charges were read, a favourable wind wafted him towards the coast of France.

In his place his cousin, Sir Alexander Hepburn of Whitsome, known as the Laird of Riccarton, stood up. His opening phrases entered a formal repudiation of the indictment.

"But," continued the Laird, "the personal absence of the Earl should not be prejudicial to him. He has absented himself for just fear which might happen in the heart of any man, since he has so potent an enemy as the Earl of Moray." He paused to let the clang of pikes and broadswords give point to his words.

Riccarton sat down and the Court deliberated. At length the Justice Clerk announced a verdict. Bothwell's caution was forfeited, but in his absence he would not be outlawed. Protestant circles openly complained that the sentence was inspired by the Queen. Her quick resentments never lasted and already she regretted the heed she had paid to back-stairs gossip. At any moment her marriage might open a breach with Moray and lead to civil war. In a tight corner she knew she could count on Bothwell. The rumour that she "wald him good" was not far from the mark.

CHAPTER TWENTY

A FEW days before the abortive trial at the Tolbooth, the royal marriage situation took a fresh twist. The unromantic impetus was an attack of measles. No ingenuity or far-sighted policy could have had better results. Only this infantile ailment was needed to release the mother instinct which is said to lurk in every woman's heart. Devotedly Mary smoothed Darnley's pillow. Her care was "marvellously great and tender." She had no fear of infection and commonly stayed by the bedside until midnight. The long hours of intimacy with almost the only young, good-looking and eligible man at her Court had the inevitable result and by the end of the three weeks' illness, Mary was head over heels in love. The match which had originally been conceived in England to side-track a foreign alliance, and accepted by Mary in a moment of artfully-provoked irritation, developed into a royal romance.

Nothing was too good for her sweetheart. Johnnie Dabrow, "Portingale Hatmaker," was commissioned to design a model to cost £4. William Hoppringle, tailor, set to work on £73 worth of black velvet, silk, taffeta, satin and silver lace. Fleming Allayard, shoemaker, soon had footgear to the value of £42 on his lasts. Alexander Henderson, spongemaker, booked an order for "twa great spungis and twa rubberis." A doublet and hose of chamois leather and an overcoat of buffalo hide were put in hand. Seventy-three yards of Holland cloth was cut into shirts, ruffs and nightcaps and cost over £90. Two dozen feathers were curled to decorate hat or bonnet—and each piece of finery as it was ready went into a wardrobe hung with French green to house the bridegroom's *trousseau*.

The Queen was too deep in love to mind what Court

gossip was saying. She only smiled when the superstitious diagnosed sorcery—"the saying is that she is bewitched; the tokens, the rings, the bracelets are daily worn that contain the sacred mysteries." The terrible Lord Ruthven, whom the Queen herself suspected of this unhallowed traffic, was supposed to be "stirring coals as hot as fire to have these matters take effect." In her infatuation, Mary laughed at the opposition of her relations. Kinsfolk widely separated by every interest and tenet saw in the marriage the ruin of their hopes. The Cardinal of Lorraine had counted on his niece's beauty to contribute to the aggrandisement of his house. In France they saw that the royal widow was "in the flower of her age, admired and adored by her subjects, courted by all her neighbours. So there was no high fortune and alliance to which she could not aspire, for she was cousin and heir of the Queen of England and gifted with grace and the fullest perfection of beauty

Bain ii. 233.

of any princess of her day." In the opposite camp the Earl of Moray beheld the destruction of his hope to be legitimized and, if Mary should die, to succeed to her crown. He foresaw the danger to the religion that gave him his popularity and the end of the domination he had enjoyed since his sister's return from France.

Too late Elizabeth realised the damage the success of her red-herring tactics must cause her anglophile allies. Too late she tried to undo her work by an abrupt summons to Darnley and Lennox to return to their adopted country. Their hopes ran high and her authority seemed remote. "Mr. Randolph," cried Darnley, when the message was delivered, "this is very sore and extreme! What would you do, if you were in my case?"

Her tardy alarm was shared by the protestant party in Scotland, which dreaded the reinforcement popery would draw from a catholic wedding. To religious zeal political assassination is apt to seem a legitimate weapon and soon designs against the bridegroom were

Randolph to Cecil, 3 June, 1565.

forming. "God must send him a short end or themselves a miserable life. To see so many in hazard of life, lands and goods, it is great pity to think. Only to remedy this mischief, he must be taken away."

Randolph began to get inquiries whether, if Lennox and Darnley were brought prisoners to Berwick, the English would take delivery. His reply enlarged the scope from kidnapping to murder—"we could, nor would, not refuse our own, *in what sort soever* they came unto us" —and an attempt on the liberties, if not the lives of the young lovers and their beaming chaperon, the Earl of Lennox, was put in hand.[1] On the first of July, Moray informed the agent that "my Lord of Argyll, my Lord Boyd and I have this day convened together to determine upon some matters of consequence, the which we are willing to communicate to you." In spite of the pious ending of the letter which inevitably commits its recipient to his Maker, the nature of the business to be discussed is easily detected. A few hours before it was written, warning had reached Mary of an ambush designed by Lord Rothes to trap the royal cavalcade on its way from Perth to Callander.

Danger always brought out the best in Mary. She took horse at five in the morning and rode with great speed, with only three women in her train. A hastily-gathered bodyguard of three hundred horsemen convoyed the rest of the party and the early start took them safely through the pass under the hill of Benarty before the ambush at the Parrot Well was set. When Randolph presented himself at the rendezvous, instead of three captives or corpses, he was met with a demand for a loan of £3,000 to finance the rebellion to which Moray was thus committed.

So failed that attempt to kidnap the lovers which is known, from a church near the scene, as the Raid of *P.C. Reg. i.* Beith. Moray tried to excuse his share by pretending that *340.* Darnley had "conspired and devised his death in the back gallery of her Highness's lodging" at Perth. The

---

[1] For the *Raid of Beith* see: Randolph to Cecil, 4 July, 1565 (Keith 291); Blackwood in Jebb ii. 200; Simancas 479; Argyll and Moray to Randolph, 1 July, 1565; Melville 108.

young idiot's tongue—it must be remembered that he was only nineteen—had got him into trouble already. Poring over a map of the Highlands, his innocent remark that my Lord of Moray owned too much land had caused the royal bastard to withdraw from Court in a sulk and to refuse his signature to the speaker's marriage. With equal infelicity he had outraged the powerful house of Hamilton, already sensitive on Lennox Stewart claims, by threatening to rise from his bed of sickness and "knock the Duke's pate."

Mary Stuart, kindly though she regarded her young Adonis's failings, had sense enough to see that, unaided, he could not make head against his enemies. In her need her thoughts turned naturally to the man she had wronged. From the safe distance of Paris, Bothwell was waiting to see what would turn up. He was thirty years of age and his career, which had opened with such distinction, seemed extinguished. Even on his resilient temperament disillusion had left its mark. He had watched his enemies triumph, his friends desert, the servants plan his murder; no wonder that "suspecting almost every man, he was not in great assurance of his life." He had measured the value of Justice and knew that the blindfold eyes could see the intimidating sword. He stored that lesson for future use. The Queen had engraved another precept on his memory, one that Francis I out of a wide experience had scratched with a diamond on a window-pane at Rambouillet:

Knox v. 3.

> Souvent femme varie,
> Malhabille qui s'y fie.

In deepening cynicism, Bothwell decided that if a second chance were granted, he would not permit such variation a second time to ruin him.

His recent expedition had done nothing to improve his fortunes. No more was said about the command of the Scottish archers, which passed in July into the hands of an uncle of Darnley's. If he turned in his discouragement to the sex that recognised his qualities, he found a new spirit abroad. "Orders are made that no gentleman shall talk with the French Queen's maids, except he be married. If they sit on a stool he may sit by her, and if she sit on the ground he may kneel by her, but not lie long as the fashion was." People said he surmounted these obstacles to collect "ane uther wyf" in France, allotting him already not only the hearts but the hands of Janet Beton and Anna Throndsen. While it is gratifying to learn that his intentions, if trigamous, were always honourable—his aim ever matrimony, however frequent and simultaneous—it is curious that when the day of his authenticated marriage came, the Church preserved so tactful a silence about the previous ventures. *James Mait-land's Apology (Misc. of Scot. Hist. Soc. ii.)*

If the shadowy French "wyf" ever existed, she did not enjoy much of her husband's society. The situation in Scotland was developing fast. The royal lovers were secretly married, so said one of the celebrating priests, on the 9th July in the presence of a few friends. A few days earlier Mary had made up her mind, if gossip can be believed, to send for the exile and employ him in repressing the rising that was now inevitable. It was rumoured that she had her horse saddled for a night ride to Seton to meet him, but Bothwell's letter of recall was not actually signed until the 16th July. It was entrusted to his cousin, the Laird of Riccarton.

Randolph's spies were busy. Orders went out to detain the Earl, "enemy to all honest men," in England, should he choose that route. Riccarton, on his way South, innocently supposing that he was travelling through a friendly country, fell with his letter into Bedford's hands.

The high-handed act escaped notice in the excitement of the official wedding which was celebrated on Sunday, the 29th July, 1565. Between five and six in the morning, the Queen was escorted by her catholic lords to the Chapel Royal. "She had upon her back the great mourning gown of black with the great wide mourning hood." The bridegroom was introduced by his father and the

Earl of Atholl. The momentous words were spoken by
the future Bishop of Brechin, three rings were put on the
bride's finger, prayers were murmured and a Mass
celebrated.

Mary retired to her room to change into gayer clothes.
The happy pair were escorted to the midday meal amid
a blare of trumpets and the distribution of largess
"to such as were happy to get any part." Lord Darnley,
who had already been invested in various titles and
honours and had sworn "to be leel and true to his Princess
and never to fly from her in time of need," was proclaimed King Henry of Scotland. His name was to appear
with his wife's on all state documents, and a medal was
struck with the ironical legend:

QUOS DEUS CONJUNXIT HOMO NON SEPARET.

CHAPTER TWENTY-ONE

Where Wit is over-ruled by Will,
And Will is led by fond Desire . . .

FRANCIS DAVISON might almost be referring to the marriage of his father's hapless victim.

Plenty of excuses can be found for Mary's infatuation for "yonder long lad." He was young, handsome and pleasure-mad. With his lute and his verses, he had an artistic facility which was bound to appeal to the beauty-loving Stewart. He seemed to offer an escape from the dour circle of middle-aged men that hedged the gay, impetuous girl. None of them gave her any disinterested advice. Her half-brother had been driven away by Darnley's rise; Maitland stepped back to see which party, by winning, should earn his support. She listened, while the clouds gathered, to the flattering counsel of "crafty and wily strangers, chiefly two Italians, Davy and Francisco," who encouraged her to follow her inclination.

David Rizzio, the more famous of the two, had come to her Court three years before in the train of Robertino Solaro, known as Moretta, agent of Savoy. "Her Majesty had three varlets of her chamber that sang three parts and wanted a bass to sing the fourth part; therefore they told her Majesty of this man to be their fourth." Living as mortals must, under the domination of trifling chances, Mary took the momentous step of engaging the vocalist. That evening her clerk wrote up his book: "Item the 8th day of January, 1562, to Anthony Geddes for keeping her Grace's dogs, twelve pounds. Item to David Rizzio, varlet in the Queen's Grace's Chamber, one pound . . ."

David's person was not attractive; "he was misshapen, *Blackwood 9.* evil favoured and in visage very black," but he was a poet, *Birrel 5.* a musician, (his guitar of tortoise-shell, mother-of-pearl, *Melville 103.*

ebony and ivory hangs in the Royal College of Music)
and "a merry fellow." With these qualities a man
might go far at a Renaissance Court. Rizzio's chance
came in December, 1564, when the secretary in charge of
the Queen's French correspondence showed himself "too
familiar with one" and was discharged. Thenceforth
Secretary Davy "began to grow great in Court." His
rise was not popular with the barons, who held the view
prevalent almost to our day that the place of musicians is
the servants' hall. Some of the nobility would "glowm
upon him and some would shoulder him and schut him
by when they entered the chamber." Perhaps they
found with a Victorian biographer that "no dress could
make him look like a gentleman." At the same time they
were willing to use his advocacy and pay for it.

Common interest as well as natural sympathy drew
Rizzio and Darnley together. Both were strangers at
the Scottish Court, which disliked and suspected both.
They had a faith in common (Rizzio was called by many
an agent of the Pope) and a love of music. Did David
teach the boy new songs to woo his princess's ear? Certainly, from Darnley's first appearance at Court, all the
Italian's influence was thrown into the scales. How
could a foreigner understand the complicated national
reasons which should have forbidden the match? How
could he guess that love-making and lute-playing would
be interrupted by the noise of war?

Four weeks after the marriage saw two armies in the
field. The Hamiltons, led by the aged Duke and the un-
ecclesiastical Abbot of Kilwinning; extreme protestants,
like Glencairn, Pitarrow, Ochiltree and Grange; hereditary enemies of the Lennox, like Boyd and Maxwell;
Moray and his supporters, Argyll and Rothes, were
"riding in armour to and fro in the country." They had
the backing, moral and financial, of England.

Mary and Darnley came to their senses, put away
their lutes and took steps to meet the danger. Moray and
the ringleaders ("God," perceived Bedford, "suffereth
His own to be afflicted,") were put to the horn. Loyal

forces were mustered: Lennox with his ally, Home, and Atholl, whose religion kept him faithful, rallied to their sovereigns. George Gordon, heir to the Huntly earldom, was released from prison and gleefully took up arms against the man who had ruined his family. Bothwell, on whom Mary counted more than any, at last received his summons. By the 27th August a messenger, more fortunate than Riccarton, got through to Paris to announce to the exile his pardon and his queen's necessity.

He had been expecting the call and made a lightning start—"he is gone from Paris," reported the English Embassy, "no man knows whither." Cecil's network *Sir Thos. Smith to Cecil, 27, 29 Aug., 1565.* of spies fell to work. They were no match for the Earl's mobility. He was heard of in Brussels, in Antwerp, in *John Marsh to Cecil, 9 Sept., 1565.* Flushing. It was whispered that he was collecting munitions, subsidies. Nothing could be more likely. Both *de Foix to Q. Catherine, 18 Sept., 1565.* sides, royalists and rebels, were short of money. Moray counted on England. He was allowed to draw one thousand pounds from Elizabeth's coffers "in the most secret sort he can," while three hundred hagbutters were surreptitiously put at his disposal. Elizabeth's parsi- *Bedford to Q. Elizabeth, 19 Sept., 1565.* monious heart must have felt a glow when Bedford congratulated her on an act "redounding to God's glory and her own high honour." Mary and Darnley were roused to tap the reluctant reservoirs of Spain and Rome. The nearest point of contact with Spain was the Hapsburg dependency of the Netherlands. Thither Darnley's English secretary was sent to take instructions from Mary's cousin, the Duchess of Aershott. Aershott is a *Teulet ii. 54* few miles from Brussels. There is no record that Bothwell's and Yaxley's business overlapped, but their presence in Brussels within a few days is suggestive.

Elizabeth put two and two together and made a scene with the Spanish Ambassador. What did Bothwell's welcome in the Netherlands mean? Was he not lading ships at Flushing with arms and gunpowder? Their objective, she had discovered, was Ireland, where O'Neill's *Teulet ii. 85.* rebellion was supposed to have the good will of the Queen of Scots. Alas, the angry Tudor had fallen into the

Borderer's favourite trap. Bent on catching the man who possessed the knack of upsetting her best-laid schemes, she detached four warships to patrol the West coast of Scotland and the route to Ireland. Meanwhile the Admiral of Scotland, who had repeated the feint that served him in the valley of the Till, was scudding up the East coast of England in a pinnace, making for the little bays of the Border.

Anthony Jenkinson to the P.C., 6 Oct., 1565. de Foix to Q. Catherine, 11 Oct., 1565.

Either word leaked out, or it was Cecil's habit of making sure that sent H.M.S. *Aid* with a hundred men on board and Anthony Jenkinson[1] in command to cruise up the coast as far north as the Firth of Forth, keeping a look-out for the Admiral.

Nor was that all. An idea of Bothwell's reputation may be gleaned from the measures England took to catch a single, friendless adventurer. A couple of privateers, with letters of marque from the King of Sweden, had anchored off Berwick. Their captain, Charles Wilson, had an understanding with the rebels. He had fired on Yaxley's ship, though a foul keel frustrated a capture. He had better luck with the Earl of Sutherland, whom he caught on his way from Flanders to help the royalists. Bedford saw what further uses Wilson's ships would serve. He wrote to Elizabeth, excusing their captain's reputation as a pirate and praying her "to be his good lady and not think upon such things as may be brought against him." Wilson, too, could make himself useful in the hunt for the Admiral of Scotland.

Bedford to Q. Elizabeth 1 Sept., 1565. Bedford to Cecil, 1, 19 Sept., 1565.

But four fighting ships on the West coast and three on the East were not enough to catch Bothwell's two pinnaces. Without difficulty he out-distanced the *Aid*. On 17th September, 1565, he reached the mouth of the Tweed, where Wilson's privateers were waiting. The wind fell. Watcher and blockade-runner lay becalmed, the distance between them so small that the pinnaces lay under Wilson's guns. Luckily his aim was bad. Unperturbed, the

---

[1] Anthony Jenkinson had recently been exploring Central Asia. He had rounded the North Cape of Russia, sailed up the Dwina, sledged to Moscow, gone on by water to Astrakhan and visited the King of Bokhara.

Admiral gave orders to man the oars and every one bent his back. Wilson, firing futile salvos, watched in impotent fury as the light craft rowed out of range.

A few hours later Bothwell with six or eight followers landed at Eyemouth. He wasted no time in that sad little harbour. Quarter of an hour was long enough to put ashore the light armament he had brought and to commandeer horses. Off rode the Earl and with him Mr. David Chalmers, faithful companion of his exile, though "to speak good of him for virtue, knowledge, truth or honesty," said Randolph cattily, "would be as great a slander unto him as reproof to myself."

The feelings of the English can be imagined. Bedford vented his rage in abuse of the man who had outwitted him, in his opinion "fit to be minister to any shameful act either against God or man." Wilson's despair was more personal. His employers abandoned him to the stern hands of Anthony Jenkinson to be taken South where he was fortunate to escape the yard-arm which pirates, if unsuccessful, could expect.

Such news of the campaign as Bothwell gleaned from the horsemen who joined his triumphant progress was fairly satisfactory. After some weeks of marching and countermarching, Moray had occupied Edinburgh in the early morning of the 30th August. Though he had only some twelve hundred horse, the royal troops in superior numbers fell back to Stirling and Glasgow. He hoped to find reinforcements with the protestants of the city but the Governor of the Castle turned his guns on the town and showed the burghers they would be well advised to give "neither help nor comfort." After a couple of disappointing days, Moray ordered his men to evacuate the place at three in the morning, proclaiming a purpose "after this, if they found any likelihood to make their part good, to adventure their lives and leave the success to God." He was in a sanctimonious mood, dubbing his disgrace "the day of my cross and persecution."

It is true his position was not enviable. He had shown

his hand and ventured into open insurrection to find his calculations at fault. He had not expected that Argyll and Boyd would want to operate in isolation in the North, or that the Lowlands would show such disposition to hang back. He had underestimated the Queen's forces. Besides a considerable body of horse she had "five hundred hagbutters and certain field pieces," while Moray "had neither shot nor ordnance," a deficiency he had hoped England would make good. Still less had he foreseen Mary's energy. A spate of proclamations summoning supporters, denouncing opponents, guaranteeing the religious *status quo* had rallied the greater part of the country. She showed herself an inspiring leader, braving the elements to ride with her troops. The ingenious Randolph produced the inevitable plan to kidnap her. "It may easily be brought to pass that one country may receive both queens before it be long. It will not be done with a pound or two," but an outlay of eight to ten thousand would work wonders.

Randolph to Cecil, 4 Sept., 1565.

Ignorant of this plot, which came to nothing, Mary left her army recuperating at Stirling, while the rebels withdrew to the west. After a tiring but inconclusive three weeks, the comfort of Holyrood was welcome. Thither on the 21st September came the Earl of Bothwell with Mr. David Chalmers. The one man who would know how to exploit an advantage was granted a very gracious reception. He "gave his presents" (presumably the rather meagre store of munitions he had landed at Eyemouth, which, Heaven knows, he had found hard enough to pay for) and made the most of an offer he brought from France where his old comrade-at-arms, Sarlebous, had two thousand men ready in case they were wanted.

Pitscottie. Diurnal of Occurents. Bedford to Cecil, 19 Sept., 1565.

He need not have felt anxious. Mary knew that at last she had a leader she could trust. His unfortunate remark about two queens and one honest woman was conveniently forgotten. Policy called for short memory and royal condescension, "whatsoever the Queen can do by authority, by suit, by request, favour or benefit, it is all one." Bothwell was agreeably surprised in the King. He had heard of his arrogance and lack of tact; personally he found him "very gracious and polite." Perhaps the warmth with which he was welcomed coloured his judgment. In proof that the past was forgotten, his old office of Lieutenant of the Border was restored. His pleasure may have subsided when he heard that the state of emergency called for two other lieutenants, Lennox for the west and Atholl for the north. *de Foix to Q. Catherine*, 29 *Sept., 1565.*

Plans for the campaign were discussed. Bothwell's name meant the accession of many of the Border families, and he calculated that if the Queen was ready to start for Stirling on the last day of the month, she would find an army of fifteen thousand men ready to march against the rebel concentration at Dumfries. The enemy he reckoned at about a thousand horse and he promised to round them up or drive them before him over the Border.

In spite of the ground Mr. David Chalmers had covered that month, it was decided to send him to London with despatches to the French Ambassador. He seems to have learnt the secret of his master's mobility for he covered the four hundred miles on horseback in not more than four and a half days. The Earl obtained leave to attend to his affairs at home and to collect a following for the coming battle. Before he left Edinburgh, he was assured of the devotion of "the barons and gentlemen of Nithsdale and Annandale"—the families of Johnstone and Jardine —who promised "truly to serve the King and Queen and whatsoever person their Highness gives their power, in especial James Hepburn, Earl of Bothwell." A couple of days later the barons and gentlemen of Teviotdale —Kerrs, Turnbulls and Rutherfords—took a similar pledge. *Castelnau to de Foix*, 27 *Sept., 1565.*

When the reinstated exile reached Liddesdale, he found the Elliots in an awkward mood. While he was languishing in the Tower of London, the head of the family, Robert Elliot of Redheugh, was given command of the Hermitage, where his branch claimed an almost *P.C Reg. i.* 240.

hereditary captaincy. The Earl's premature home-coming in the spring of 1565 displaced him and sent him to the English warden irritably offering the allegiance of his clan to the Queen of England. So at first Bothwell's patriotic exhortations met a cool reception. Promises and threats were of no avail for Sir John Forster had been before him with the potent argument of hard cash. As the sums involved were not large (fifty pounds was as far as Sir John would go), and Bothwell's arguments were forcible, "some of the 'Elwoods'," it is recorded, "are shrunk away and gone to him." But the partial defection angered his loyalty and hurt the vanity which had held out high hopes at Court.

Bedford to Cecil, 2 Oct., 1565. Castelnau to de Foix, 27 Sept., 1565.

Four or five days on the Border and Bothwell was back at Holyrood. He was given a seat on the Council and Mary wanted to put him in command of her army, to which end she had recalled him from exile. She met the unexpected opposition of her husband, who claimed that since his father was Lieutenant of the west, he had the right to lead an action near Dumfries. Lennox was not even immediately available. At the head of two thousand men he was preventing a junction of Argyll's Highlanders with Moray's cavalry in the west, and incidentally stopping Campbell inroads on Lennox lands.

Cockburn to Cecil, 2 Oct., 1565.

Nevertheless the King vehemently maintained the family claims. Mary, if Cecil's intelligence system was well informed, as vehemently supported the rights of the better man. Bothwell himself expressed confidence of being able to put a speedy end to the rising. As he had as many Borderers at his back as the total rebel forces at Dumfries, his optimism was well-founded and could ignore Randolph's sneers at "a fit captain for so loose a company as now hangs upon him."

de Foix to Charles IX., 16 Oct., 1565.

But the King's obstinacy won the day. Mary was too deeply in love to oppose him long. The army had to wait for Lennox and got its orders to march from Biggar a week late. This blunder of Darnley's saved the rebels from extermination and let them start an un-opposed withdrawal to Carlisle.

A forced march was made to Castlehill, the site of a Castle of Robert the Bruce, ten miles from Dumfries. Mary wore mail under her cloak, a light helmet on her head and pistols at her saddle. Darnley made a fine show in a gilt breastplate and a gilt morion. (The headgear was entered at eight pounds; his winter gloves, perfumed and lined with velvet, cost six pounds). On 10th October a council of war was held at Castlehill and the order of battle was drawn up with as much care as a hostess devotes to a diplomatic dinner-table. The vanguard *Keith Ap 115.* must be led by Lennox in recognition of his claim to command. The rearguard took orders from the Earls of Atholl, Huntly and Crawford. The main body was commanded by the King, accompanied by the Earls of Bothwell, Morton and Mar. These preliminaries would have been still more imposing if the enemy had not by now been half-way to Carlisle, where Bedford had a force waiting to prevent pursuit. A circumstantial story of a dashing engagement with a full list of casualties reached the Spanish Ambassador. Bothwell, with two thousand men, it related, had intercepted the retreat and inflicted heavy loss. But no confirmation is forthcoming and the withdrawal into what should have been neutral country was apparently accomplished without bloodshed. Mary, whose humanity was in advance of her day, was no doubt content. The Chase-about Raid, as Moray's insurrection is called, had ended with the ring-leaders chased out of the country.

Thus ended in ignominious failure the first of Moray's three great attempts to dethrone his sister. It collapsed for two main reasons: Mary, in spite of anything that contemporary history-books written by Genevan ministers and party hacks may say, was very popular with her people. In her time of need they rallied. She had also, when she cared to employ him, an efficient leader in Bothwell who commanded the personal loyalty of most of the Border.

CHAPTER TWENTY-TWO

ONCE the rebels were over the Border, the royalist forces broke up and returned to their homes. The lieutenants of west and north relinquished their shadowy commands of vanguard and rearguard and followed the royal couple to Edinburgh. Bothwell was left at Dumfries with his eleven hundred Borderers and three hundred hagbutters. His duty was to see no counter-attack was launched from Carlisle. He had instructions "to appoint watchers in every high passage" in the Border hills to stop communication between the vanquished leaders and the country they had quitted. "Our authority prospered so well in his hands," wrote Mary later, "that our whole rebels were constrained to remain in England."

Before the insurrection had collapsed, Bothwell had been able to secure the pardon of a fellow Borderer whose feud with the Lennox had led him to back the losing side. This was the Warden of the Western Marches, afterwards Lord Herries. When it was clear that no further action need be feared from the neighbourhood of Carlisle, the Warden had orders to relieve Bothwell and his garrison at Dumfries. At the end of October James Hepburn, at the head of his moss-troopers and the three hundred hagbutters, marched back to Edinburgh.

*P.C. Reg. i.
403, 474.*

Even in time of peace his military knowledge had its uses. He served on a committee, instructed to see "that all the artillery of the realm might be perfectly mounted, ordered and put into double equipage to serve as well in the places upon the walls as to be carried to the fields." Bothwell's hand may be seen in this proposal to make siege guns convertible into field batteries. He had grasped the advantage a strong field artillery gave the Crown in handling a turbulent but lightly-armed nobility.

The committee had to start from the beginning.

John Chisholm, the Controller of Artillery, was instructed "to pass over all places nearest the fortresses of the realm with wrights and gunners." He was given authority over the gentlemen, "to whom woods and orchards belong, to cut such timber as he needs—elm, ash and oak for stocks, wheels, axles and limbers." The treasurer had orders to supply seasoned oak for platforms, iron for mountings, lead for projectiles. Bothwell's practical touch may be found in a stipulation that all back wages and current wages were to be paid, provided the tradesmen were kept "continually labouring, every man according to his craft and vocation." The winter was spent felling timber on the Tay to be carried by sea to Leith. From the port the logs had to be dragged to the Castle "to be laboured and put to work." Bothwell divided the carriage among the people of his sheriffdom. Though never doubting that "every nobleman, gentleman and yeoman will voluntarily and with glad will obey in this so needful a cause," yet to make sure of an equal distribution of labour, he specified the number of draught oxen to be sent by each stockowner to Leith sands with a penalty of twenty shillings for each beast missing.

At the beginning of the New Year his name was proposed for a more important and difficult duty. The normal Border friction between England and Scotland —sheep-stealing or rick-burning—that winter was aggravated by the presence of the rebels at Newcastle and Berwick and by the "sure watching" which Bothwell kept on their sympathisers. His "rank riders" interfered with Scots selling meat at Berwick. The English pursued the raiders and fell into an ambush at Churnside, losing half a dozen prisoners and eight horses. A strong counter-attack was launched, a boy was killed and sixteen Scots with forty-one horses were led triumphantly to Berwick.

The Elliots, too, were active. Bothwell, to punish the defection of the autumn, burned their peels and vowed he would have Martin Elliot's head. Martin went to the English Warden for protection, but Elizabeth was seeking reconciliation with the Queen of Scots. Her fear that Bothwell would reach Scotland had been justified. The rebels she had supported had been no match for him. She fell back on the idea of a commission "to conclude a firm and perfect league." Her motives were not governed by any abstract love of peace. Her Scottish policy was hampered by the absence from their country of her usual tools, and a conference might offer an opportunity to engineer the exiles' return. To this end she chose Bedford and Forster for her commissioners and instructed Randolph to see that tractable—she meant corruptible—officials were appointed on the other side.

Elizabeth to Randolph, 10 Jan., 1565.

The little agent hurried to the Palace. Mary was spending a day in bed, but the agent was admitted to her room. London, he reported, had replied. The Earl of Bedford and Sir John Forster were chosen "for the good trust her Majesty hath in them."

The Queen of Scots smothered a groan.

"I looked," she said wearily, "for little better. How feat these men are to do good in these matters, I refer me to yourself."

Randolph tactfully changed the subject. Mary explained that a bad night had kept her in bed. The Englishman's outspoken suggestion "that she had something in her belly that kept her waking" must have made her blink. She decided to accept it as a compliment.

" Indeed," she smiled, "I may speak with more assurance than before I could." Thus unceremoniously was the future Solomon of the British Isles announced.

Next day Sir James Balfour, who was doing most of the work of the disgraced Secretary, and Sir John Bellenden, the Justice Clerk, called at Randolph's quarters as he was finishing his midday meal. Sir James ("Blasphemous Balfour" to his friends) opened with a few well-chosen words on his mistress's goodwill and desire to live at peace. But Elizabeth, she must point out, by choosing two of her Wardens, had reduced the suggested peace conference to the status of a Border meeting. On the Scottish side two Wardens must also be chosen, Lord Home and Kerr of Cessford.

The agent looked blank. Neither nominee was pro-English. Home had been known to refuse a bribe, and Kerr drew a pension from the King of Spain, whose policy Elizabeth was just then trying to checkmate. Randolph improvised the objection that his Queen would expect a commissioner of equal rank to the Earl of Bedford.

Next day he saw his blunder. His visitors returned with their mistress's second thoughts. Appreciating the difficulty, she had substituted "the Earl of Bothwell, of equal degree with the Earl of Bedford."

Randolph's jaw dropped. For all his subtlety, he had paved the way for the one man in the country who would never take a bribe and who had sworn to hunt Moray out of Scotland! Venomously he retorted that the Borderer was personally odious to the Queen of England and a notorious enemy to peace. He washed his hands of any consequences that might follow the selection.

Mary laughed. She had not, she remarked, found Bedford very peaceably disposed. Had she known what Elizabeth had written to him the week before, she might have used stronger words. "There can be no complaint coming out of Scotland," her affectionate cousin had assured the peace commissioner, "which can alter any part of my good judgment of your true and faithful service, but rather will I think your service more faithful because it is misliked of them."

In spite of Randolph's protests, Queen Mary stuck to her guns. She insisted that Bothwell should represent her, though if the Queen of England cared to add a third delegate, she was willing to follow suit. But the agent knew of a plan hatching which was calculated to bring home the exiles quicker than any conference intrigue. A pretext soon offered for a trip to Berwick. Its governor did not appreciate the Border January. "Being subject to rheum and catarrhs," he complained, "as Dr. Hewick who knoweth best the state of my body can declare, this winter will make an end of me." At the moment "he was troubled with a rheum and the evil." Perhaps

Dr. Hewick wanted a second opinion on a common cold with scrofulous complications; in any case, Randolph offered to accompany a physician from Edinburgh.

He found the invalid perturbed at Bothwell's appointment. "As long as he is continued in the commission," growled Bedford, "I see not what good can be done. For if he either feared God or loved justice, there were some hope that somewhat would be amended."

But Randolph had not ridden from Edinburgh to listen to the governor's views on Bothwell. If his mind had not been occupied with darker business, he could have given some interesting news of that nobleman. For at last Bothwell had made up his mind to marry. He was thirty-one and his wanderings, moral and geographical, he hoped were over. Timely service had recovered his sovereign's favour. His enemies were scattered. A wife, he considered, would complete the smiling picture.

Reg. of Deeds VIII. 232. 12 Feb., 1566.
In his choice he had the help and approval of the Queen; so she allowed it to be stated in the marriage contract, passed "with her advice and express council." The girl was one of her ladies, and high hopes were based on her steadying influence. Moreover, the alliance united two important elements of the loyal party, Highlands and Border.

Birrel's Diary.

Bishop of Norwich, 1st series Parker Soc. lxxx.

Drury to Cecil, 16 Feb., 1566.
Lady Jean Gordon was a daughter of that Earl of Huntly who met a sudden death in the rising crushed at Corrichie. The new Earl, George, was her brother. She was a pale-faced, long-nosed girl of twenty. Her eyebrows were fashionably high and arched, her lids heavy, her sandy hair grew low on the temples. People said she was "a good, modest, virtuous woman." So thought an English bishop who declared her "an excellent, noble lady." The Marshal of Berwick joins the chorus of praise on the grounds that she was a "proper and vartuous jentylwoman" and a protestant. Although the unanimity of protestant opinion in the matter of her virtue confirms this version of her religious views, historians have agreed to call her a life-long catholic. They produce a portrait of a middle-aged lady devoutly handling a rosary and

LADY JEAN GORDON IN 1566
*(Enlarged from a miniature, by permission of the Scottish National
Portrait Gallery)*   [*Annan Glasgow*

repeat charges that in later life Jean harboured Jesuits and was "vehemently suspected to have had a Mass." *Dr. John Stuart 6 ss.* But these aberrations occurred after her second marriage with the catholic Earl of Sutherland and do not necessarily over-ride the Marshal's description of her faith at an earlier period. Like her brother, at the time of Bothwell's courting, she had no doubt embraced the Reformed faith. Knox's eloquence found ready fuel in the enthusiasm of youth. What lady of the Court could listen unmoved to that master of prose addressing her sisterhood? "Fair Ladies, how pleasant were this life of yours, if it should ever abide! But fie on that Knave Death, that will come whether we will or no. The silly soul, I fear, shall be so feeble that it can neither carry with it gold, garnishing, targating, pearl nor precious stones."

If Jean had fallen under the spell of the Prophet's periods, her conversion from the faith of her fathers may explain her suitor's conduct at Candlemas. At that feast the Queen "used great persuasions to divers of her nobility to hear Mass with her and took the Earl of Bothwell by the hand the rather to procure him in." But Bothwell, as usual failing to behave like a courtier, resisted the appeal and took his future brother-in-law to hear Knox preach.

If in some curious way the doctrines of the Reformation formed a bond between Bothwell's unorthodoxy and the girl he was seeking to marry, more mundane considerations were not lacking.

Marriage in the great Scottish houses was arranged on strictly business lines. Property and political connection found a readier market than grace of body or mind. Since his recent reinstatement, Bothwell had political advantages to offer. His financial standing was less brilliant. All the rewards his services in the field had *Hay Fleming 370.* won were some tithes that used to be paid to Moray and an annuity of five hundred crowns that Melrose Abbey had contributed to Glencairn. The transfer of these sums only tided over his most urgent needs.

Gordon finances, in spite of the blow the family had recently suffered, were in better state. Huntly could offer a substantial dowry in exchange for the royal favour that Bothwell's ascendant star might secure.

In Lady Jean, the prudent bridegroom chose the ideal wife to re-establish impoverished grandeur. It was his misfortune that her talents came only to be exercised to the benefit of his successor. The child of that later union may be quoted on her abilities. Owing to the Earl of Sutherland's sickly disposition, "she was constrained to take upon her the managing of all the affairs of that house, which she did perform with great care to her own credit and the weal of the family, all being committed to her care by reason of the singular affection which she did carry to that house, as likewise for her dexterity in management of business." Instances of her hard-headed administration are given. She started coal mines and exploited salt pans on her second husband's estate; "by her great care and diligence she brought to a prosperous end many hard and difficult businesses of great consequence." Hints of practical, if not very profound, wisdom gleam out of her letters which show her preoccupied by the domestic cares that harass the women of to-day. "Honest and faithful servants," she writes, "are hard to be found." She can have no peace, she assures her son, "by oft changing of servants."

Sir Robert Gordon's History of the Earldom of Sutherland 169.

Hints, it is true, are dropped of a reverse side to the picture. "The Earl of Sutherland," it is recorded, "is wholly governed by his wife." But when every allowance for filial piety has been made, the creditable character emerges of a "virtuous and comely lady, judicious, of excellent memory and of great understanding above the capacity of her sex." (Feminism had not yet reared its head.) "She always managed her affairs with so great prudence and foresight that the enemies of her family could never prevail against her. Amidst all these troublous storms and variable courses of fortune, she still enjoyed the possession of her jointure, which was assigned to her out of the Earldom of Bothwell. . . ."

Account of the Nobility of Scotland, 1577.

That provision had been made in the marriage contract which formed such an important part of the wedding preliminaries. The bridegroom was "before the completing of the marriage to invest Mistress Jean Gordon in her pure virginity for all the days of her lifetime, for sums of money to be mentioned, in the town and mains of Crichton with the house, tower and fortress of the same." But as these and other lands were in the hands of creditors, eleven out of the twelve thousand marks of the bride's dowry were to be employed in their redemption.

The document received the Queen's blessing and signature. The bride's brother, her mother, who could not write and had her "hand led on the pen" by her brother-in-law, the Bishop of Galloway, Lord Seton, Lord Home and others added their names. Among the witnesses figured the Earl of Atholl, Sir James Belfour and the indispensable Mr. David Chalmers.

Parchment and ink had not yet finished their task. Four generations earlier an Earl of Bothwell had married a daughter of an Earl of Huntly and created a kinship within the degrees forbidden by the canon law. Normally such relationship was taken as a convenient loophole should a change in government or a loss of lands dictate a dissolution of marriage. Perhaps Jean and James were hoping for a more permanent union; perhaps the Dowager Countess's orthodoxy insisted that the position should be entirely regular; for some reason application was made by these two protestants for a Papal dispensation.

All the forms were observed. After the existence of the legal obstacle had been duly established, the Pope's[1] legate *a latere*, John Hamilton, Archbishop of St. Andrews, granted liberty to the related couple to marry. It may be claimed that every precaution which lawyer and theologian could devise to secure the legality, permanence, and irrevocability of the union was taken.

---

[1] In the dispensation a mistake has been made in the name of the Pope, whose legate granted it. To some writers this error suggests that the document is "ridiculous forgery."

Wardrobe-mistresses and dressmakers did not neglect their parts. Old Lady Huntly had a clever sewing-maid, Bessie Crawford, a girl with a white skin and very black hair. Bessie was set to work on the trousseau and her quick hands sewed pearls and braid on the gorgeous dresses. The material for the wedding-dress came from the Queen's own cupboards. Twelve yards of cloth of silver she gave Jean, and six yards of white taffeta to line the wide sleeves and train. Queen Mary herself had two new dresses. One was white satin—she looked her best in white—lined with white taffeta and braided with damasked cloth of silver. The second was a splendid crimson, with a taffeta lining that came from Lyons, a little fringe of gold, and black and gold tracery. One frock would do for the ceremony and one for the banquet that she and King Henry were to give. But in Scotland religious prejudices were always upsetting the Queen's plans. She wanted the marriage to take place in the Chapel Royal during the Mass. The bridegroom (or was it the bride?) refused the favour and insisted on the Kirk of the Canongate and the rites of the reformed Church.

Queen Mary shrugged her shoulders and decided to wear the dress she liked better at the banquet. There was a great crowd in church; some of the guests could not get a glimpse of the young couple standing hand-in-hand in front of the Bishop of Galloway, Jean's uncle, who had chosen not to climb the pulpit to deliver his sermon. When the knot was tied, the company streamed out of church up the Canongate to Kinloch House, the home of a rich burgher high in the royal favour. Five days the banquets lasted, with the interruption of jousting and tournaments to keep satiety at bay and indulge the bridegroom's love of chivalry.

Bothwell engaged a French artist, living in Scotland, to paint his wife's portrait and his own. Either from modesty or economy he ordered two miniatures, each less than an inch and a half in diameter. Jean "sat" wearing a blue and gold cap and the frill of a little ruff outlining the oval of her pale face. James wore his gold doublet of ribbed silk with puffed shoulders. Little gold studs buttoned it up to the lean, muscular throat that a narrow lace ruff encircled. In spite of his weather-beaten skin, he fancied himself in bright colours. His enemy, George Buchanan, called him "an ape in purple." Like most effective abuse, the gibe contained a residue of truth. There was something a little simian in the long, mobile upper lip that a wild moustache did not hide, the square jaw, and the low, back-sloping forehead that the painter flattered to the best of his ability. Long, powerful arms added to the resemblance. This suggestion of the anthropoid clearly did not repel women. Men differed. Brantôme said he was the most ungraceful and the ugliest man you could see. A Venetian ambassador contradicts him and mentions a handsome presence. George Conn expatiates on pre-eminent gifts of body and mind. It is likely that none of the three had ever seen him. (Brantôme, it is true, stayed at Holyrood after the Queen's return from France, but at that time Bothwell was forbidden the Court.) The wedding miniature suggests that truth lay, as usual, midway. Misfortune has scored deep lines from the prominent nose to the corners of the wide, sardonic mouth. Hard, out-of-door life has fined away the flesh from the cheeks and fitted the skin close to the skull. Anxieties have bared the temples. Short, chestnut hair straggles to a peak on top of the head. Dark, deep-socketed eyes dart a sleepless glance that seeks to unmask the stratagems of enemies and the treacheries of friends. Lady Jean had married no iron-hearted gladiator, but an adventurer with an imagination who lived on his nerves and never was sure what the next moment would bring.[1]

The first week of the honeymoon was passed at Seton.

[1] The description of Bothwell is made from inspection of the Boyle miniature in the National Portrait Gallery of Edinburgh and the mummy in Faarevejle Church. Scrutiny with a magnifying glass of the Kirk o' Field and Carberry Hill drawings reproduced in this book, suggests that in 1567 he grew a dark beard. The Buchan-Hepburn portrait of a red-faced desperado cannot be accepted. Not only does the man's character discredit it, but the clothes are wrong for the period. The "close" ruff which the subject wears did not come into use until a decade after Bothwell had left Scotland for good. Sir James Caw concluded that the costume of this picture is of the late 1570's or more probably of the 1580's, by which time Bothwell was dead.

Future revelations, which will be dealt with in their place, suggest that it was a disappointment. The days, however, brought Bothwell one minor satisfaction. Randolph returned from his visit to Berwick to find his presence no longer welcome in Scotland. An Edinburgh lawyer had repeated to Queen Mary an old but damaging story. "On his conscience and as he should answer before God," John Johnstone declared that the English agent had sent for him to his quarters during the period of the rising. There, in the presence of an envoy of England, he had given him three thousand crowns in three sealed sacks to take to St. Andrews and give to Lady Moray, then occupied with one of her frequent pregnancies, for the use of her rebellious husband.

Randolph, "perceiving himself narrowly compassed," tried a flat denial. He pointed out that the lawyer was compromised by his own story. He offered to stand his trial in England. Mary for once was inexorable. The agent must leave the country. The order came at an inconvenient moment. The matter discussed at Berwick needed all his attention. He shut himself in his quarters ("save the time I was at the sermon") and refused to budge. Repeated messages failed to dislodge him. At last on the 2nd March, about ten in the morning, James Ormiston called and remarked that he was ready. The Black Laird had a compelling manner, and within an hour a little party of half a dozen was on its way. A quarter of a mile out of Edinburgh Ormiston broke the silence. His patron, Lord Bothwell, wanted to know why the Queen of England objected to him as a member of the Peace Commission.

"I have no will to speak," was Randolph's circumspect reply. "Things are verified by the Earl's own countrymen. If true they are unhonourable; if false, he may revenge it on the speakers."

The allusion was to the scandal Dandie Pringle had repeated. Ormiston asked if Randolph would care to hear Bothwell's own version.

"I will speak with any that speak with me," came the

lofty reply. Ormiston gave a sign and a gentleman spurred his horse to a trot.

Bothwell received the message at Seton, and caught up the party a little way beyond the Castle. A chilly greeting and the Earl "took God to witness as a gentleman born of a noble house that he had never spoken but honourably of the Queen of England. He would oppose his body" (the formula was unfailing) "to any man who spoke the contrary, desiring her Majesty to be satisfied with his purgation."

"I will report your speech," was Randolph's stiff reply. "But the sooner your Lordship justifies himself and has the matter tried, the more it will be to his honour." He changed the subject to his own expulsion.

"It is the Queen's will," said Bothwell briefly, "procured by others than myself."

"*That* I know to be true!" assented Randolph, aware that "some one else" was "the chief cause and adviser" of his downfall. It was pleasant to think of the fate that was brewing for "that poltroon and vile knave, Davie." The same week he was able to report to Elizabeth that "a matter of no small consequence is intended in Scotland. We hope by this means my Lord Moray shall be brought home without your Majesty's further suit; and therefore we have thought good to stay the sending of your Majesty's letters on his behalf." The peace commission scheme had given place to a more sanguinary project.

Randolph and Bedford to Q. Elizabeth, 6 March, 1566.

CHAPTER TWENTY-THREE

Randolph to Leicester, 13 Feb., 1566.

BEFORE Randolph was turned out of Scotland, but when his hours were already short, he had picked up his pen to vent his malice on Mary and her consort.

"I know now for certain," he wrote to the Earl of Leicester, "that this queen repenteth her marriage, that she hateth (Darnley) and all his kin. I know that he knoweth himself that he hath a partaker in play and game with him. I know that there are practices in hand contrived between the father and the son to come by the crown against her will. I know that if that take effect which is intended, David, with the consent of the King, shall have his throat cut within these ten days. Many things grievouser and worse than these are brought to my ears, yea of things intended against her own person. . . . This your Lordship shall know for certain, that this queen to her subjects is now so intolerable that I see them bent to nothing but extreme mischief and I believe that before it be long, if she take not up in time, you shall hear of as evil as yet you have heard. There is a bait laid for Signor David, that if he be caught, howsoever his mistress be offended, others will be pleased."

The agent's spite had got the better of his prudence to give a pretty accurate summary of the conspiracy to murder Rizzio and to scare the Queen into a fatal miscarriage. Wheels, however, moved so discreetly within wheels that it is necessary to examine briefly the various motives that were woven into one bloodstained pattern.

Although he overstates Mary's feelings, Randolph was right in deducing that all was not well between her and the King. As soon as the rebellion collapsed, Darnley showed how unfitted he was to fill the position his good looks had won. His intemperance was common talk and reduced his wife to the humiliation of public tears. An *Pietro Bizari.* Italian visitor alleges a love affair with a Douglas lady and a child by one of the Queen's women. It is certain that for long periods he was absent from Mary's side and from all public business. Her over-exertion during the rebellion and her pregnancy made her feel ill. She did not make allowance for the impatience of youth, which preferred hawk and hound in the forests of Peebles and Fife to tedious councils and the bedside of an ailing wife.[1]

Nevertheless, he was greedy of power and coveted the "crown matrimonial" which would maintain him on the throne in the event of the Queen's death. This insurance Mary refused to grant, acting by the advice of Rizzio, who understood by now his former ally's political incompetence. Darnley's friendship gave place to a hatred that was inflamed by jealousy of the Italian's intimate footing.

It is clear to-day that Mary's relations with Rizzio were those of a sovereign with a confidential servant. As ever she stood in need of competent advisers. David had the quick intelligence, if the easy venality, of his countrymen; as a secretary he had proved his efficiency. His deformity and his subordinate rank seemed to the Queen's innocence to permit the familiarity to which the Stewarts as a family were inclined. Her affability gave her enemies the chance they wanted. Five months before the crisis Queen Elizabeth heard Moray's disgrace attri- *de Foix to King of France, 16 Oct., 1565.* buted to his impulse "to hang an Italian called David whom the Queen of Scots liked and favoured, giving him more credit and authority than her business and her *State Papers* honour warranted." About the same time Randolph's *For. Ser. 1587. 1565.* despatches hinted at the same libel. But it was not until the beginning of 1566 that the King's jealousy could be fanned to the heat required.

Nothing could have better suited the plans of Moray and Cecil. Here lay the seeds of a first-class political

---

[1] Mary was ill with the pain in her side, which was usually worse in the late autumn, from the 14th November to the 1st December, 1565. Darnley was expected to return from Fife and Falkland on the 4th December, but by the 20th his father was looking for him at Peebles.

crisis which could be exploited to the Queen's ruin. Self-interest produced allies in every direction. Mary's instinct had been to treat the recent rebels with her usual clemency and to Darnley's disgust she had pardoned the Hamiltons within two months of the collapse. But her Guise relations urged her to try the effect of severity and she summoned a Parliament for the 12th March to denounce the remaining exiles as traitors who had forfeited life, lands and goods. Their natural anxiety to save their property made them ready to join any conspiracy, however atrocious.

The handicap of their physical absence from the scene of action was made good by active auxiliaries. The Kirk was roused by the belief that Rizzio was working to get Mary's signature to a Catholic League. If the murder plot did not secure the actual co-operation of John Knox, it won at least his sincere approval, and one Robert Hamilton naïvely accused the Reformer of being "as great a murderer as any Hamilton in Scotland." Maitland, too, had an early finger in the plot. A month

Maitland to Cecil, 9 Feb., 1566. before the deed he could see "no certain way unless we chop at the very root ... remitting the success to Him who hath their hearts in His hands and shall move them as it pleaseth Him." Jealousy and ambition enlisted the King. The Douglases, his mother's kinsfolk, were always game for anything that would harm the royal Stewarts. The acting head of the clan, the "slow and greedy" Earl of Morton, hung back until he was allowed to make the discovery that Rizzio, probably prompted by the King, was tampering with his prerogatives.

Till now James Douglas, 4th Earl of Morton, has moved in the background of the story. The Rizzio conspiracy brings him into the limelight. Godscroft draws an impressive picture, "comely, of middle stature, square rather than tall, hair and beard yellowish flaxen, face full and large, countenance majestic, grave and courtly. Affable and courteous to all, he yet held encroachers at a proper distance. Slow of speech, his language sounded somewhat to the English." But a sight of the little eyes, bushy red whiskers, boneless nose and pudgy hands of the portrait in the Edinburgh Portrait Gallery suggests that his eulogist was making the best of a bad job. Much credence need not be placed in an anecdote of his youth, how to the distress of his nurse young James swallowed a toad except for "a little of the legs"; nor how his father, philosophically remarking, "The devil chew thee or bust thee, there will never come good of thee," encouraged his little treasure to finish the mouthful. In later life a period of exile caused James Douglas to assume the name *Crawford's* of Innes and to "serve a gentleman in the capacity of *Chancellors.* steward," thus becoming "acquainted with the humours *Hume of* and disposition of the vulgar and inferior sort of the *Godscroft.* common people."

Sir James Melville found him proud and disdainful, ungrateful to his old friends and servants. By his acts when he came to wield the power of Regency he may be judged cruel, licentious and rapacious. He had a minister tortured and hanged for rebuking his adultery with the widow of Captain Cullen (whose widowhood he had himself procured). He hanged two poets for an uncomplimentary pamphlet. By 1574 three of his bastards were drawing pensions. At the end of his life backstairs gossip credited him with 100,000 crowns and £36,000 concealed underground in the castle-yard of Dalkeith, beside four puncheons of silver under a stone in the gate at Aberdour, and twenty-eight pounds of uncoined gold at Leith. Nevertheless his dying moments were edifying. The minister, assured that the Earl had read "all the five books of Moses, Joshua and Judges and was now in Samuel," offered to pledge his health upon the condition "that you and I shall drink together in the Kingdom of Heaven of that immortal drink that will never suffer us to thirst again." Morton answered confidently, "Truly I pledge you, Mr. Walter, on the same condition," and walked firmly to the scaffold.

In the conspiracy to murder Rizzio, this engaging character was only a very able executant. Above his head there were, so to speak, two gangs of creative plotters.

There was the old gang, dominated by the policy of Cecil and Moray, who consistently designed the downfall of the Queen of Scots. The return of the exiled rebels, the integrity of their lands, the security of the Reformed Faith formed a subordinate part of the programme. The new gang was led by Lennox and Darnley, both catholics, who drew their man-power from the Douglases. Their objects, as Randolph's letter to Leicester exposes, were the punishment of Rizzio and the elimination of the Queen and her unborn heir. The shock of assassination under her eyes might be hoped to leave the throne vacant for the wearer of the crown matrimonial.

To this end a bond was signed between the King and the banished Lords. This extant document provides for the pardon and restoration of the exiles, who undertake in return to procure Darnley the crown matrimonial, to fortify him in his ultimate title to the throne, and to spare neither life nor death "in setting forward all things that may be to the advancement of the said noble prince." Little trust, however, was felt in Darnley's promise by the Edinburgh ringleaders—Morton, George Douglas the Postulate, and two husbands of Douglas wives, Ruthven, and Lindsay. These extracted a ready-signed proclamation whereby the King assumed full responsibility for the murder of "Rizzio the Italian, though it were in the very palace and presence of the Queen."

Nearly everybody seems to have known that this "just act and worthy of all praise," was imminent. At the English Court Cecil was able to whisper the story in the ear of Darnley's mother the day before the event. The only people in ignorance were the victim and the loyal lords. Bothwell, whose intelligence system was usually efficient, heard nothing. He had returned from Seton with the royal pair to take his place in the procession that opened Parliament. To him fell the honour of carrying the sceptre, to Huntly the crown, and to Crawford the sword. At the last minute an astrologer delivered a warning, but the traditions of his science compelled ambiguity. Rizzio, he urged, should be

Misc. of Maitland Club iii. I. 188.

Keith App. 122, 167.

Silva to K. Philip, 11 April, 1566.

wary of the Bastard. The Italian, reassured by Moray's absence at Newcastle, disregarded the hint. He ignored the qualifications of George Douglas to that not uncommon designation. To quiet David's fears Darnley, with a refinement of treachery, spent the afternoon playing tennis with him.

The tale of that Saturday night has often been told. Its events are conveniently summarised in the death sentence that was afterwards passed on one of the actors. Henry Yair, ex-priest, was convicted "for gathering our sovereign's lieges to the number of five hundred persons, armed as well with secret armour, and entering within their Majesties' palace purposely to have put violent hands on our sovereign lady's most noble person. On the 9th day of March, under silence of night, at eight hours of even, they most treasonably rushed and entered the said palace, reft the keys of the porter, closed the gates and most cruelly with drawn swords, whingers, bended pistols and other weapons invasive pursued the late Secretary David Rizzio, then in company within her Highness's chamber, and slew him treasonably and unmercifully in presence of our said sovereign. And put violent hands on her most noble person, held, detained and pressed the same most awfully and treasonably, till they had committed the said slaughter in her presence (her Majesty being then great with child) giving to her Majesty occasion, by the sight of the said cruel slaughter and by the detaining and thirsting of her person in violent manner, to part with her birth."

The bloodlust of Lord Ruthven had raised him from a sick bed where for three months past three doctors had been tending "an inflammation of the liver and a consumption of the kidneys." He limped to the Queen's chamber. A little table had been laid for supper. Lady Argyll sat at one end; at the other the Italian. He was wearing an evening robe of damask trimmed with fur, a satin doublet and russet velvet hose; his hat was on his head. Between them sat Lord Robert Stewart and the Queen. The King had slipped a treacherous arm round

233

her waist. A couple of courtiers completed the company, and servants filled the space left in the little room. Though it was Lent, by the doctors' orders they had set meat in front of the Queen.

In the doorway Lord Ruthven appeared, "lean and ill-coloured by reason of his long sickness, and yet in armour."

"Let it please your Majesty that yonder man David come forth of your privy chamber where he hath been over long!"

"What offence hath he done?"

"He hath offended your honour, which I dare not be so bold as to speak of."

The sinister invalid turned to the King.

"Sir, take the Queen to you!"

But Darnley stood "all amazed and wist not what to do."

Mary rose and, placing her body between her servant and his danger, commanded Ruthven, under pain of treason, to go. Courtiers and domestics took a step towards him.

"Lay no hands on me, for I will not be handled!" he shouted.

The cry brought a swarm of accomplices. They upset the table and the candles on it. Lady Argyll caught one as it fell and lit the scene by its single light.

Rizzio clung to the Queen by the plaits of her dress. Kerr of Fawdonside bent back his middle finger until from pain he loosed his grip and let Ruthven lift the Queen and pass her to Darnley. Rizzio, dagger in hand, crouched in the window until George Douglas the Postulate was moved to fulfil the mandate of the stars. Snatching a dagger from Darnley's thigh, he buried it in the Italian's body.[1] The gang seized their screaming victim and carried him to be dispatched in comfort in

---

[1] The Queen's own story and the sentence passed on Henry Yair state clearly that the killing took place *in the room*. Ruthven's not disinterested "Narrative" asserts that David was murdered in the outer chamber. Perhaps the truth is that the first blow was struck in the Queen's sight and the remaining fifty-five outside.

the doorway of the outer chamber. Such enthusiasm was displayed, that fifty-six wounds were afterwards counted.

The corpse, with the King's dagger ostentatiously sticking in its ribs, was thrown down the palace stairs. The porter stripped it in his lodge. "This was his destiny," he remarked unsympathetically, "for upon this chest was his first bed when he came to this place, and there he lieth a very niggard and misknown knave."

When Rizzio had breathed his last, Morton led his Douglases downstairs to block any attempt to rescue the Queen. Bothwell was in the palace supping in his quarters with Huntly and Atholl. The meal was interrupted by the war-cry, "A Douglas—a Douglas!" Shouting to their servants to follow, and calling the cooks to bring their spits, the diners hurried in the direction of the noise. They hurled themselves against the gallery door, which Morton's men were holding.

Word of the struggle reached Ruthven, who "being sore felled with his sickness and wearied with his travail, desired her Majesty's pardon to sit down, calling for a drink for God's sake." When a Frenchman had satisfied his needs, the sick man consigned the Queen to her husband's keeping and dragged himself downstairs with a servant to support him by either armpit. He found that Bothwell had failed to force the gallery door and had retired to his quarters. Thither he made his laborious way to show "the whole proceedings of that night" and to fasten the responsibility on the King. He added the unwelcome news that Moray and the exiles would be in Edinburgh before dawn. The loyalist, obliged to profess himself content with what he later stigmatised as a wicked and detestable act, had to drink with the murderer.

As soon as Ruthven was on his way to placate Atholl, Bothwell set to work. Taking his brother-in-law with him, he found a window that gave on "the little garden where the lions were lodged." A trifling matter like a lion pit proved no obstacle to the Earls' hurried exit from the palace.

235

The escape was of vital importance. Had Bothwell and Huntly been detained or disposed of, the Queen's cause was doomed, for Atholl and the majority of her party tamely consented to withdraw to the safety of the mountains. Bothwell had a more vigorous purpose. Two measures could restore the situation. The Queen must be extricated from the power of her captors and forces raised to overcome them.

A half-hearted effort at a rescue had been made by the Provost of Edinburgh and its well-disposed citizens. The common bell, struck with hammers, had given the alarm, and thirty-five torches lit a crowd of hastily-armed burghers down the hill to Holyrood. Finding the gates locked, from the outer court they demanded to see their queen. Mary's hopes rose, but the Lords promised, if she showed herself, to cut her in collops and throw her down the wall. The ineffable Darnley, stomaching this threat to his wife, appeared at the palace window and exhorted the crowd to return home "for he and the Queen were in good health."

Bothwell's attempt at rescue was more enterprising. Mary spent the night of the murder watched by eighty armed guards who did not allow even her servants to enter her room. She touched no food until four o'clock on Sunday afternoon when the dishes were examined by Lord Lindsay. In the meantime Bothwell's mother-in-law, the Dowager Lady Huntly, had secured leave to visit the captive. Their intercourse was closely watched until, under pretext of bodily needs, the two women secured a brief privacy. Then the Queen, seated on a *chaise percée*, heard of the escape of the two loyalists and of their efforts to raise troops. She learnt that, reckoning without Lindsay's attention to detail, they had taught the dowager the classic trick of introducing a rope "between two dishes as if it had been meat." By this means "these noblemen, being without fear, and willing to sacrifice their lives," intended to lower their sovereign in a chair from the window which the Countess indicated.

To the mercurial Borderer who had climbed the

Q. Mary to K. of France. (Copy sent to Venice, 13 April, 1566.)

Castle Rock in the dark, the difficulty of lowering a closely-guarded Queen, six months advanced in pregnancy, from an upper window (according to one account from a clock tower) seemed negligible. To Mary certain objections presented themselves. To begin with, as she told Lady Huntly, soldiers were stationed over her room, opposite the window in question. She had already formed her own plan and she scribbled a note to Bothwell and Huntly, bidding them wait for her at a village near Seton on Monday night.

Even her present situation could secure the Queen no longer privacy and the omnipresent Lord Lindsay made his appearance. Perhaps Blackwood does not exaggerate in calling him "a raging, furious, rude, ignorant man, nothing differing from a beast." Brusquely he ordered the Countess to leave the suite and not to come back. He was not quick enough to prevent her slipping the note to Bothwell under her shift.

So far the rebel Lords could claim unbroken success. The Queen and her unborn infant lay at their mercy. Rizzio was dead; so was the Dominican Father Black. The Friar had been confessor to Mary's mother, and had served her as a secret agent, passing under the name of John Noir. He was murdered in his bed the same night as Rizzio and by the same interests.[1] There was some idea of hanging Sir James Balfour, but that astute lawyer stood too well with the King to suffer the fate he was so richly to deserve. The politics of the plot went as smoothly as its mechanics. On Sunday, by proclamation at the Market Cross, the King dissolved the newly-assembled Parliament. Its members were charged under pain of

[1] But for Bedford's authoritative statement that the Dominican was killed "by like order" as Rizzio, a private motive might be suspected. Father Black must have made enemies. Some years before he had been banished for his part in "two several advouteries." Some months before his death he met late at night "two or three blows with a cudgel and one with a dagger." The indignation his morals excited knew neither rhyme nor metre:

> "A certain Black Friar, well surnamed Black,
>   For black were all his works,
> He took a black whoor to wash his black sarks
>   Committing with her black fornication."

237

death to leave Edinburgh within three hours, and the danger which threatened the lands of the recent exiles was lifted. The same evening the Earls of Moray, Rothes and Glencairn; John Knox's father-in-law, Lord Ochiltree; the Lairds of Grange and Pitarrow, made a public appearance in Edinburgh and joined forces with the murderers of Rizzio. Mary sent for her half-brother; her plight moved him to hypocritical tears. On Monday morning a council was held which decided to remove her to a stronger prison at Stirling. A fresh Parliament was summoned to confer on Darnley the crown matrimonial and the government of the country. The pact between the two gangs of conspirators was being loyally kept: Darnley arranged the return of the exiles and the integrity of their lands; they took the contracted steps to satisfy his ambition.

Mary had to act quickly, if she was to avoid a cell in Stirling Castle from which she might never emerge alive. Warning her husband that a miscarriage was imminent, she begged him to allow her the company of her ladies. After dutifully referring the request to Morton and Ruthven, Darnley consented. The ingenious Ruthven, suspecting that the Queen planned escape in the dress of one of her attendants, gave instructions that no gentlewoman was to go out "muffled." But Mary's design was at once simpler and more profound. During her few months of marriage she had, like any other wife, plumbed the depths of her husband's weakness. For all his arrogance, brutality and lack of scruple, he lacked the hardness that could draw profit from villainy. "He was so facile," it was said, "that he could conceal no secret although it might tend to his own evil." Getting him alone at last, not only was Mary able to charm out of him the full story of his associates' designs, but to implant suspicion of their fair dealing towards himself, "certifying him how miserably he would be handled in case he permitted the Lords to prevail." She played, moreover, on his catholic principles and his sensitiveness to catholic opinion—"how unacceptable it would be to other princes

238

in case he altered the religion!" Briefly, by exploiting his fears, his suspicions and his uxoriousness, she persuaded him to desert his confederates and once more join his fortunes to hers.

This finesse took Mary more than one session, but by midday on Monday she had won the King to her plan. Its success hung on overcoming the rebels' mistrust. Darnley sought out the ringleaders and assured them that "he had obtained of her Majesty that the earls and lords should come into her presence and she would forgive all things bypast and bury them out of her mind."

"Her fair speaking is but policy," retorted their spokesman pessimistically, "and little or nothing will be performed." He might have added that since they meant to shut up the Queen at Stirling, her forgiveness did not much matter. The King seemed full of confidence; he told the doubters to draft any document they liked for signature. The chance of covering their violent acts by some show of legality was attractive, and between four and five in the afternoon Moray, Morton and Ruthven were waiting in the ante-room. Darnley fetched the Queen and the three conspirators knelt, Morton on the bloodstain that marked the spot of Rizzio's slaughter. A perfunctory plea for pardon and the restoration of estates received the Queen's assurance "that she was never bloodthirsty nor greedy upon their lands and goods." Her half-brother added his views on the value of such clemency.

"It is advantageous and necessary to kings" (a pause pointed his meaning) "for their own safety and the preservation of the state."

The Earl of Morton's eye was caught by the stain near his knee.

"The loss of one mean man," he remarked broad-mindedly, "is of less consequence than the ruin of many lords and gentlemen."

Mary's reply has been variously reported. It is clear that she made some promise of a pardon, which she subsequently kept. A queen fighting a lone battle to preserve the life of her unborn heir may be allowed some latitude in her choice of weapons. She is said to have told the rebels to draw up their own safeguards which she promised to sign. Then for an hour, while the paper was drafting, she paced the ante-room with Moray on one side and Darnley on the other. The insincerities that were bandied have not been preserved.

By six o'clock the document was ready. The King took charge of it and promised to secure his wife's signature. Now came the critical moment. Would Ruthven and Morton withdraw their men? Darnley promised brightly to "warrant all." Reluctantly and under protest the lords took themselves and their followers out of the palace and withdrew to Morton's house for supper.

Mary lost no time. Sending for the Stewart captain of her guard, through the door of the King's chamber she gave him whispered orders to bring horses to the Abbey burial-place. All danger was not past. An imprudent move and Darnley's men would report to the supper party at Douglas House. At last everything was quiet; Mary led Darnley down a stairway to the "office of her butlers and cup-bearers." They were French and could be trusted to join in no local conspiracy. From this pantry a door opened to the burial-ground. It was fastened but in so bad a state that the fugitives were able to squeeze through. As midnight struck, with thumping hearts, they skirted the grave where David's mutilated body had found peace. His murderer's emotions cannot have been enviable. The captain of the guard and the master of the horse were waiting with "a tall and stout gelding" for the Queen, and three other horses; Mary mounted behind her master of horse; the captain of the guard took Margaret Carwood, her woman; the King and his equerry, Anthony Standen, rode together, and a certain Sebastian Browne brought up the rear.

As soon as he had cleared the town, the King began to canter and did not draw rein until he had covered the ten miles to Seton. On the outskirts of the village Bothwell had posted a picket. Taking the soldiers for enemies, Darnley spurred his exhausted horse.

"Come on! By God's blood!" he swore as he flogged the Queen's mount on the quarters, "They will murder us both!"

The Queen protested the danger to her child.

"Come on!" screamed her husband, "if this one dies we can have more!"

By now Bothwell and Huntly, Fleming, Seton and Livingstone had ridden up. Bothwell decided there was no safety from pursuit nearer than Dunbar, another fifteen miles on, where the royal pair arrived by daybreak. The soldiers lit a fire and Mary had energy left to cook some eggs. The high spirit which she showed throughout these terrible three days has moved even her enemies to admiration. A woman, naturally delicate and in the seventh month of her pregnancy, beset by a gang of greedy and bloodthirsty assassins, faced with the discovery that the husband she loved was a treacherous coward, had never faltered. By her hardihood and resource, she defeated the overwhelming combination that designed her ruin.

Bothwell's exertions to raise the Border bore speedy *Les Affaires* fruit. Within three days four thousand spears gathered *du Comte de* *Boduel, p. 10.* at Dunbar. The news depleted the rebel ranks. Two of the recent exiles, the Earls of Glencairn and Rothes, appeared at Dunbar to offer their submission. The former was a Cunningham and had a connection with the Lennox family. Mary, who understood the maxim *divide et impera*, readily forgave them and stretched the pardon to Argyll and Boyd, who had stayed in the Highlands since the Chase-about Raid and had played no part in the Rizzio disorders. To split the alliance between Moray and Morton, she let the former know that her attitude towards him was not inexorable.

After a week collecting forces at Dunbar she marched with Bothwell on Edinburgh. At Haddington she found Melville with the humble thanks of the Earl of Moray. Her half-brother promised he had severed relations with

Bedford and Randolph to Cecil, 27 March, 1566.

"such as had committed the vile act." This separation did not prevent him sending a man to Bedford to desire the Englishman's favour for "his dear friends," Morton, Lindsay and Ruthven, who "for his sake had given this adventure."

For the murder gang soon decided that the loss of their trump card in the Queen's person, and the progress of Bothwell's levies had ruined the chances of the rebellion. Lindsay and Ruthven, Morton and his Douglases made their way independently over the Border to the welcome that awaited them at Newcastle. Maitland, who had kept in the background, thought it well to retire to the Highlands. John Knox, openly proclaiming the virtues of those that "gave counsel to take just punishment on that knave David," disappeared into Ayrshire.

Knox, i. 43.

Lord Ruthven did not long survive his exertions on the night of the 9th of March. A martyr to his sense of duty, he died at Newcastle in the middle of May, "exclaiming that he saw Paradise opened and a choir of angels coming to take him." At his friend's decease Morton felt "no small grief, and yet the same was so godly that all men that saw it did rejoice." It was an age when crime and sanctimoniousness walked hand in hand.

Queen Mary's return to her capital offered a striking contrast to her midnight flight. Bothwell rode at the head of the Borderers and four companies of professional infantry. The nobles to whom his example had given courage led their retainers—the Earls of Atholl, Huntly, Sutherland, Crawford, Cassilis, Caithness, Marischal, and the Lords Seton, Fleming, Livingstone and Home. (A week earlier the last-named had acted as Moray's escort.) At Musselburgh the Primate of Scotland trotted out at the head of the Hamiltons. The town of Edinburgh turned out to welcome the victor. They escorted her to the Bishop of Dunkeld's house, then in the occupation of Lord Home. Field-guns (the Bothwell touch) were unlimbered at its doors. The professional infantry was billeted in the town.

The next day kept Queen Mary and her Council busy

on the work of punishment and pardon. All of the rebel party who had not been actively concerned in the murder were formally forgiven and required to keep away from Court for the present. Morton and the Douglases, Ruthven and Lindsay and their partisans were outlawed. From this doom Bothwell, who was not a good hater, secured the exemption of three lairds of Lothian, one of them his old enemy, John Cockburn. Giving further rein to his humanitarianism, he procured the reprieve of a merchant and a saddler who had been sacrificed by Darnley and sentenced to death for their share in holding the Queen a prisoner. Her ex-gaolers were standing at the foot of the gallows when Bothwell rode up to show the Provost the Queen's ring. Only two rebels suffered the extreme penalty—Tom Scott, "a trusted gentleman of the Earl of Ruthven, who died very well and stoutly," and Henry Yair, another Ruthven retainer. Scott's head decorated a tower of the palace—the stomachs of the sixteenth century were strong—and Yair's the Netherbow Gate.

Knox ii. 527.

Les Affaires du Comte de Boduel p. 11.

Darnley had still to be dealt with. That ingenuous young man made matters easy for his wife by protesting before her Council his absolute innocence of the conspiracy, "how he never counselled, commanded, consented, assisted nor approved the same." A signed declaration to the effect was posted "at his desire" at the Market Cross. His wife accepted for form's sake his assurances, but from that time forward allowed him no practical share in public affairs; "he cannot obtain from the Queen the authority he had before the late tumults, that is to sit by the side of his wife in council and in public places, to set his name with hers in treaties and public affairs."

Q. Mary to the Archb. of Glasgow, 2 April, 1566.

Mondovi to Cardinal of Alessandria, 4 Nov., 1566.

Thus was liquidated a plot "sufficient to dishonour a nation and to characterise an age." The men who conceived it regarded its failure with different degrees of depression. Moray had at least the consolation that his exile was over and his lands were safe. Cecil took vengeance for the collapse of his hopes in telling the French

Ambassador that "a deformed and base menial" had been killed in the Queen's arms. Darnley had only disaster to deplore. His wife and unborn child were still alive; his hopes of the crown matrimonial were shattered; he had discredited himself with Mary, had lost his public authority, and had earned the deadly hatred of the accomplices he had betrayed.

CHAPTER TWENTY-FOUR

PARADOXICALLY, the only man to gain by the Rizzio murder was the Queen's champion and defender. At last his mistress began to appreciate the contrast that Bothwell's loyalty and resource afforded. "All her people," said a French Ambassador on his return from Scotland in May, 1566, "are barbarous, strange and changeable. The Queen has little confidence in them and few whom she can trust." She began to feel the greater respect for Bothwell's dependability, which had surmounted the tests of prison and exile. She saw his genius for prompt, decisive action. Months later she was still praising his "dexterity," and describing "how suddenly by his providence not only were we delivered out of prison, but also the whole company of conspirators dissolved and we recovered our former obedience. Indeed we must confess that service done at that time to have been so acceptable to us that we could never to this hour forget it."

A change followed in Bothwell's standing at her Court. The part he played in the Chase-about Raid had been spoiled by Lennox's appointment to the High Command. The artillery commission and the peace deputation were the returned exile's unexciting rewards. The lead he took in suppressing the Rizzio rebellion won a more personal gratitude. "The Earl Bothwell had now of all men greatest access and familiarity with the Queen, so that nothing of importance was done without him."

He has left no record of his theories of government, but during the period when "all things passed by him," the Acts of the Privy Council may legitimately be taken as bearing evidence to his administrative ideals. They

245

are more statesmanlike than the usual view of his character would suggest.

There is a Currency Act designed to check the import of false money from Flanders. There are a couple of Game Laws, the first to stop shooting deer with culverins, half-hags, pistols or bows; the second to prevent foreigners fishing in the Highland lochs. To discourage piracy on the high seas an order cancels all letters of search including those issued to two of the Admiral's own captains, William Blackadder and George Fogo. To check disorder on land, there is a decree for Courts of Justice to be held on all royal progresses.

P.C. Register 1, 471, 477, 481, 482.

Two measures aim at defending Mary from her own generosity. "Their Highnesses, at the shameless and indiscreet asking of divers their subjects, are oft-times moved to make disposition freely of that whereon their Majesties' own living consists." A halt is therefore called to the indiscriminate granting of escheats, wards, marriage feus, taxes. Again, too many pardons have been granted to "wicked manslayers, murderers and other unworthy persons; for their Majesties of their clemency have been cruel to none, but have oft-times shown mercy without occasion. This has not moved the wicked to desist from their mischief, but, continuing in their bloody cruelty, they cease not daily, without fear of God or their Prince, unnaturally to put hands each in another's blood." Accordingly pardons for such violent crimes are to be limited. It must be granted that the ruffianly character which historians have ascribed to Bothwell has left curiously little trace on the statute book at a time when by common consent he "had a great hand in the management of affairs."

Bedford to Cecil, 27 July, 9 Aug., 1566.

Nor, though "he carried all credit in the Court," did he exploit his chance to get rich. Here he has been libelled by some who had access to the truth. Moray's tithes which Bothwell had been given on his return from France, and the Glencairn pension out of the revenues of Melrose reverted to their original beneficiaries on their pardon in March, 1566. When the hero of the Rizzio rising

Chalmers ii. 248.

was appointed Governor of Dunbar Castle in place of Simon Preston, the Provost of Edinburgh who had failed Mary in her hour of need, he was granted certain lands to contribute to the upkeep of the Castle. Some feudal payments due to the Crown by his father and himself, "whereof no account had been made," were remitted. Finally, at the expense of the disgraced Maitland, he recovered the hereditary Hepburn patronage of Haddington Abbey, which carried certain revenue. "With all ceremonies and toys that can be used," his cousin, Isobel Hepburn, was installed abbess in place of his father's nominee, Elizabeth Hepburn, recently deceased. Bothwell certainly had cause to be "surprised at his own moderation."

But the hey-day of his influence was short. After a few weeks of rustication in the Highlands, Moray and Argyll were allowed to return to Court. On the 21st April they appeared in Edinburgh and were received by Mary at the Castle, where the prudence of her Privy Council ordained her infant should be born. To mark her forgiveness, the Queen gave a banquet in their honour and invited Bothwell and Huntly. Anxious to appease the feuds that distracted the country, she used all her influence and charm to reconcile the rival parties. A proclamation attested the official success of her amiable intentions "to soothe the enmity that was between the Earls."

Beneath the surface the lifelong hatred between Bothwell and Moray simmered. At one time an ingenious proposal brought the Hepburn into line with Darnley, whose resentment at the exiles' return surpassed his own. Darnley knew that the allies he had betrayed felt for him "such misliking as never was more of man." Seeing a way to discredit them, he and Bothwell set to work to procure the pardon of George Douglas the Postulate, "the shameless butcher" of Rizzio. If brought home, Douglas was expected to be willing "to declare that the Earl of Moray, the Laird of Lethington and some others, whom the Queen knew not of, were designers and purposemakers of the slaughter of David." Two obstacles ruined a

Randolph to Cecil, 13 May, 1566.

Morton to Forster, July, 1566.

Leicester to Cecil, 11 July, 1566.

247

Sir J. Forster
to Cecil, 13
July, 1566.

hopeful project. Queen Mary refused to pardon the man who had struck the first blow, and was equally loath to inquire too closely into her half-brother's guilt. As a final disappointment, Queen Elizabeth, warned that a full exposure of the Rizzio intrigue was imminent, hurriedly sent orders to the Warden of her Marches "to stay George Douglas from going into Scotland and put him under guard."

The same desire to discourage the indiscreet led to the elimination of William Kerr, Abbot of Kelso. That Silva to K.
Philip, 17
Aug., 1566.
P.C. Reg. i.
470. "learned and worthy person" seems to have known something which compromised the recently-pardoned Earl of Glencairn. He was imprudent enough to speak "of him infamy and words of dishonour, unworthy to be rehearsed, which ought not to pass over unpunished." So two Kerr relations, undeterred by the memory of an old man holding one of their sons over the font, visited him and "smote off his head Bedford to
Cecil, 17
July, 1566. and his arms." Rumour said this savage act was inspired by Moray. In any case, it effectively shut the Abbot's mouth.

What had started as a Court intrigue to discredit Moray was developing into something grimmer. The royal bastard, who always hit hard, carried the war into enemy territory and started work on the Border. There his ally, Morton, was spending an enforced leisure travelling rapidly and obscurely between the two countries. Plans were afoot to repatriate him and his companions Killigrew to
Cecil, 4
July, 1566. in adversity. "Many," reported an English agent, "were like to venture all for their relief." Moray developed the situation with his usual skill and economy of effort. Bedford to
Cecil, 2 and 3
Aug., 1566. The ranks of Bothwell's enemies could be stiffened by the accession of Morton's friends. The Cessford Kerrs and Buccleugh's Scotts were ready. Two Wardens of the Marches, Home and the future Lord Herries, joined. The latter had secured pardon for his share in the Chase-about Raid through Bothwell's good offices, but now, after a long friendship, turned against him. The Elliots, eager for any move that might hurt their enemy,

obtained leave from England to operate from the southern side of the Border.

Bothwell believed that Moray was plotting to restore Morton at the moment of Mary's *accouchement*. He made her a party to his suspicions, but although "his credit with the Queen was more than all the rest together," she did not take his alarms seriously. She was right in thinking her half-brother too prudent to risk another premature coup. He was content that the activity on the Border should keep up Morton's spirits, serve as a protective screen for the Abbot's murderers and undermine Bothwell's influence. There is a hint at something more deadly afoot in a letter of Bedford's. "I have heard that there is a device," he writes casually, "working for the Earl of Bothwell, about which I could indeed obtain precise information. But since such things are not addressed to me, I do not wish to hear any more of them. He hath grown of late so hated that he cannot long continue."

*Killigrew to Cecil, 24 June, 1566.
Melville 127.*

Bedford to Cecil, 12 Aug., 1566.

Bothwell's counter-stroke was a model of prudence and legality. As Lieutenant it was his duty to ride against the Kelso murderers and bring them to justice. But the opposition he met made a backing of royal authority seem desirable. It was easy to arrange a Border "progress" to be attended by all loyal subjects, with a Court of Justice at Jedburgh. "The King and Queen," so the decree ran, "considering the universal disorder and unquietness and cruel murder become as it were common, not only among them that has quarrel but kinsfolk unnaturally slaying others without fear of God, reverence for their Majesties and as there were no authority above their heads," contemplated "progresses" throughout the realm. The Borders were selected for a start, and earls, lords, barons, freeholders and landed men summoned to appear at Peebles on the 13th August for the ride to Jedburgh, where meat, drink and lodging for man and horse would be kept at reasonable prices.

Such were the steps that Bothwell devised to cope with the forces of disorder his enemy was organising.

But before Mary could attempt to "do justice to our poor oppressed subjects" on this considerable scale, her infant had to be born.

She waited in the gloom of the Castle in some trepidation for an event that the terrors of the Rizzio week-end might well have prejudiced. They tried to buy a parrot to beguile her hours of waiting, but its French owner sold it for two crowns to the wife of the Marshal of Berwick. Mary filled in the time making her will in triplicate. To her husband, whose treachery she was trying to forget, she made twenty-six bequests of jewellery. Against one of the entries—a diamond ring enamelled in red—she wrote, "It is with this that I was married. To the King, who gave it me." To Bothwell she left a table-cut diamond enamelled in black and a figure of a mermaid set in diamonds with a diamond mirror and a ruby comb in her hand. To his wife she left a head-dress, collar and cuffs, set with rubies, pearls and garnets. To the Crown of Scotland, to her kinsfolk in France, to her connections by marriage and her illegitimate brothers and sisters, to her privy councillors, to her lords and ladies, her attendants and servants, she made the remaining two hundred and twenty-five bequests of jewellery.

Randolph to Cecil, 7 June, 1566.

With her in the Castle were lodged the Earls of Moray and Argyll. Bothwell and Huntly applied for quarters but were refused, no doubt to avoid the risk of quarrels. The King had his suite in the building, but, if a royal

Nau. History of Mary Stewart.

secretary of a later date may be believed, "vagabondised every night."

Incredible as it sounds, it is to this period that Darnley's father chose to ascribe the beginning of a liaison between the Queen and Bothwell. In the "Narrative" which Lennox afterwards composed, and on which nearly all the stories not derived from the manipulated Casket letters are based, he alleges that Mary and Darnley "passed to the Castle where they abode till she was brought to bed. During which time although they accompanied at bed as man and wife, yet that innocent lamb who

250

meant so faithfully unto her as his wife, had but an unquiet life. Insomuch that he, being overcome with inward sorrow of heart by her most strange and ungrateful dealings, was forced to withdraw himself out of her company oftener than he himself would have done. In the meantime Bothwell waxed so great that he, supplying the place of the aforesaid David, was her love in such sort that she, forgetting her duty to God and her husband, and setting apart her honour and good name, became addicted and wholly assotted unto the said Bothwell. Not only for lust of body, but also to seek the blood of her dear husband in revenge for the death of her servant David."

Lennox's reputation for intelligence was not high among his contemporaries. He certainly chose an improbable moment for the prelude of a love epic that has engendered so much hysteria among historians and novelists. It is not necessary to call evidence of the day to the Queen's virtue; to quote the French Ambassador *le Croc to Archbishop of Glasgow, 15 Oct., 1566.* who wrote that autumn that he never saw her so much beloved, esteemed and honoured; to cite the solemn oath of her father confessor that up to her fatal marriage he *Silva to K. Philip, 26 July, 1567.* had never met a woman of greater virtue, courage and honesty. It is not even necessary to ask the common-sense question—does a woman who has known a man for five years of blameless widowhood suddenly fall crazily in love with him? Nor to wonder whether the weakness of a lady whose claim to beauty was European, but who failed to enslave the easy senses of either of her grown-up husbands for longer than a few weeks, was not rather frigidity than the fervid temperament her enemies have imagined. A survey of the weeks when Lennox avers the guilty connection began demolishes his story.

The Queen was in the last stages of her pregnancy, an automatic safeguard, it might be thought, to her virtue. She was living in the restricted area of Edinburgh Castle under the watchful eyes of her husband, her half-brother and his brother-in-law. Not one of these three interested guardians of her honour has left on record any breath of scandal. Did the King, who had shown to some purpose his jealousy of Rizzio, ignore or condone the adultery of a wife in her last weeks of bearing him a child?

Secret access to the Queen in those close and inconvenient quarters was impossible, and Bothwell had been refused a lodging under the same roof. He may not have regretted his exclusion, for he must have wanted to keep an eye on the Border. He had at least two other women on his hands. There was the wife whom the Queen had given him four months before; there was a mistress of no royal rank, Bessie Crawford, the smith's daughter. Granted all Bothwell's energy, is it not superfluous to invent an additional amour with a queen?

James's and Jean's marriage had not made a good start. The failure does not seem to have been the fault of the bridegroom. Jean's affections had been won before marriage by a less exciting but more reliable suitor. This was Alexander Ogilvie of Boyne. That he is harshly *Sonnets iv.* described as "a tedious fool" would not necessarily make the girl feel more kindly towards his supplanter, when, dragooned by her brother or driven by her ambition, she gave Alexander his *congé*. Ogilvie accepted his loss with fortitude and promptly transferred his suit to one of the Queen's Maries. Mary Beton was also at a loose end. Her red-gold curls had tossed and her dark eyes had flashed at the flattery of Thomas Randolph. The agent's expulsion and Lady Jean's marriage left two lacerated hearts to find common consolation. Bothwell must have heaved a sigh of relief as he added his bold signature to the Beton-Ogilvie marriage contract. But parchment could not make Jean forget her Alexander. In her hus- *Sonnets v.* band's presence she wore mourning for her suspended romance, and thirty-three years later, other matrimonial engagements on either side then permitting, she took her first suitor to be her third husband.

So Bothwell's early married life, in the words of a nineteenth century historian, was "neither fruitful nor

252

fortunate." From Seton, after the interruption of the Rizzio episode, he took his wife to Crichton. There the possession of a young if absent-minded bride, the cares of an estate, the anxieties of politics did not prevent the Earl's restless eye falling on Bessie Crawford. He found *Bodleian Add. MS. c 27.* himself watching for the black gown and white petticoat of his wife's sewing-maid and catching the dark eye that smouldered in a white face. He liked the gay taffeta handkerchief she wore on her head.

About the 17th May the household moved to Haddington Abbey. The beauties of its architecture were not lost on Bessie. Some curiosity took her up the steeple. It may have been the same urge that brought the Earl there too. A quarter of an hour later the couple were noticed coming down. The black dress was dusty; so was the Earl's bonnet.

Word of these architectural interests reached the Countess. She felt that Bessie's enthusiasm would be better employed outside her service. But Willie Crawford's smithy lay close by in Haddington town. One afternoon Bothwell sent Patrick Wilson, a Haddington merchant, to suggest that the smith's daughter might care to explore another Abbey building. St. Paul's Work stood in the Cloisters. Two or three steps led up to its principal room. In a vaulted space underneath stood some old beds, covered with arras. Pat Wilson showed this intriguing place to the dark-haired little sempstress. To make sure her interest did not wane, he locked the door on her. When half an hour later the Earl, with a cloak thrown over his black hose and white doublet, came from the hall, the obliging Mr. Wilson handed him the key. . . .

The cloisters seem to have been busy. There was an old friend, Gabriel Sempill; there were the Craigwallises, father and son. Through the locked door the father could hear, so he said, the amateurs of architecture whispering. He was the more intrigued for, although he was Bothwell's porter, he had not seen his master "have ado with any woman since he was married." Half an hour later

253

the three idlers missed none of the details of the Earl's departure.

With so many witnesses it was too much to hope that the Countess could be kept in ignorance. It may be guessed that her Gordon pride did not take the hurt tamely and Bothwell had to make his peace as best he could. He found a satisfactory formula. Soon after the visit to St. Paul's Work he had a deed drawn up. On the 11th June, 1566, it was signed and sealed, giving to "his beloved wife (for the favour and love he bore her)" the lands of Nether Hailes with the Castle and houses appertaining for the period of her life. It had not taken the young husband long to grasp his wife's practical point of view.

These efforts at conciliation met some measure of success. In later years Cuthbert Ramsay bore witness that he had watched James and Jean living peaceably together. George Livingstone said the same. He was an old friend of both parties who had known the husband since boyhood at home and abroad. Lady Jean he knew at her mother's house and later in Queen Mary's train. His story carries some weight when he says that the pair "lived friendly and quietly together, like man and wife as the saying is." The saying is a wide one, but it is difficult to think that it could be stretched to include simultaneous adultery with the sewing-maid and the Queen.

Between ten and eleven in the morning of the 19th June, Mary's baby was born, "albeit dear bought with the peril of her life, she being so sore handled that she wished she had never been married." Darnley came to her room and wanted to see the future King of Scotland and England. The young mother could not forget his suspicion of Rizzio.

"My Lord," she said, "God has given you and me a son, begotten by none but you."

254

The King blushed and kissed the child. Mary took her baby in her arms and uncovered his face.

"Here I protest to God," she went on, "as I shall answer to Him in the great day of Judgment, this is your son and no other man's son. I am desirous that all here, with ladies and others, bear witness. For he is so much your own son, that I fear it will be the worse for him hereafter."

The citizens of Edinburgh did not share their Queen's misgivings. That night five hundred bonfires reddened the Edinburgh sky.

In five weeks Mary was well enough to stay with Lord Mar at Alloa Castle. His neutral attitude in the maelstrom of Scottish politics as well as the Erskine family tradition, indicated him as the guardian of the little prince. That the Countess was a catholic commended her more to Mary than to Knox, who thought her "a very Jezebel" and "a sweet morsel for the Devil's mouth." Bothwell cannot have liked the choice, for Annabella, described as "wise and sharp," was sister to that James Murray of Purdovis, who had betrayed his indiscreet confidences in Paris.

"The sweet seat of Alloa" stands on the north coast of the Forth, six miles from Stirling. The easiest approach for a convalescent woman was by water, and Bothwell, Admiral of Scotland, had orders to provide transport. He detailed Captain William Blackadder and his crew, whom George Buchanan no doubt correctly describes as "famous robbers and pirates"—language that was applied to more famous sailors of the date. When Buchanan was later hired to write up the libellous material provided by the Earl of Lennox, he made a feature of Mary's trip to Alloa. "How she behaved herself," he hints, "I had rather every man should with himself imagine than hear me declare it. This one thing I dare affirm that in all her words and doings she never kept any regard, I will not say of queenlike majesty, but not of matronlike modesty." Would his readers' imagination have been baulked, had Buchanan seen fit to disclose that Bothwell, supposed partner in her "unprincely licentiousness," did not go with her to Alloa, while the Earls of Mar and Moray did? Nor that the "pastimes" of these days of debauchery included an audience for Bothwell's returned enemy, Maitland, and a reception for the French Ambassador, sponsored by a bishop.

In truth, for the time, relations between the royal couple improved. Mid-August found them hunting together on the edge of Ettrick Forest, where Bothwell, Moray and Mar joined them. Sport was bad and after a week the Sovereigns were back in Edinburgh. The Queen took the opportunity to make her husband a present of a newly-reconstructed bed of "violet-brown velvet, enriched with cloth of gold and silver, with cyphers and flowers sewn with gold and silk, furnished with roof and headpiece." It had curtains of violet damask, pillows of violet velvet, a blue taffeta quilt and Holland linen sheets. A costly and intimate gift.

Inventories 19, 31, 165, 166, 178.

From Edinburgh Mary took the baby prince, under escort of a strong guard of hagbutters, to the care of the Mar family at Stirling, traditional nursery of the Kings of Scotland. She had made Bothwell, a man she could trust with that precious life, one of the two captains of his bodyguard. Another royal hunting trip, this time in Perthshire, a joint visit to Drummond Castle, and Mary and Darnley were back with the baby at Stirling.

Bishop of Mondovi to Card. of Alessandria, 23 Aug., 1566.

Their better understanding did not last. Darnley's unquiet spirit could not be happy without intrigue, and at the end of the first week in September his wife returned alone to Edinburgh, "to sit at her Exchequer to understand her revenues." This sudden financial interest sprang from her plans for the christening of the Prince. Every penny the treasury could spare was to dignify the occasion. What dreams did not the girl cherish for the baby who was to reconcile two warring kingdoms and even, she may have fondly hoped, two rival religions!

Forster to Cecil, 8 Sept., 1566.

When she had "understood her revenues," she called a Privy Council meeting at Holyrood House and secured a vote of £12,000 for christening expenses. Next she sorted

Forster to Cecil, 19 Sept., 1566.

her jewels and had a happy thought for a colour scheme on the great day. Each nobleman should dress his retinue in one colour. To give a start she issued Moray a suit of green, Argyll a red and Bothwell a blue. (It is perhaps significant that in blazonry the last colour stands for loyalty.) She did not forget linings, red and gold for Moray, silver and white for Bothwell.

To this genial atmosphere the Queen decided to re-admit the questionable figure of Lethington. His was the best brain in the country and for many months she had missed his subtle counsel. Discredited by his sympathy with the leaders of the Chase-about Raid, he had been dismissed for his subterranean labours in the Rizzio plot. Leave granted him to retire to the Continent had been revoked and he was told to hold himself under arrest in the Highlands. The story ran that the change of plan saved him from the Admiral's sailors. It is true that Bothwell spared no effort to harm his enemy. He quarrelled with a political associate, the Earl of Atholl, for being "a continual travailer for the Laird of Lethington" (whose sweetheart, Mary Fleming, was a connection of Atholl's by marriage). As if the long-standing feud were not bitter enough, both men claimed the revenues of Haddington Abbey, and Bothwell knew that if the exile returned to favour his pocket would suffer. Moray and Balfour suggested a compromise whose over-partial terms reached the Hepburn's ears where he stood in the Queen's presence.

"Ere I part with such lands I will part with my life," he muttered.

Moray overheard.

"Twenty as honest men as my lord of Bothwell shall lose their lives ere he rob Lethington," he growled.

The Queen listened and made no comment. She wanted the quarrel to end in one of those surface reconciliations that satisfied her amiable disposition. She needed her late secretary's help in her plans for the baby's future. Only Maitland could improve relations with England and procure the promise of its throne for the infant. Bothwell might be a faithful servant and a good general, his very name would hinder a *rapprochement* with Elizabeth. So Hepburn interests were disregarded and, in what seemed a longer-sighted policy, Lethington was restored to his post. On the Secretary's return to Court, "the Queen dined with him and liked him very well." A few days later he was able to write from Edinburgh to that tireless correspondent, Sir William Cecil:

"By your letter from Woodstock I find myself confirmed in the good esperance I had that the envy of ambitious men, which is a common sickness of all courts, should not at length prevail against me, although it might have place to exercise my patience for a time. The same day your letter came into my hands it pleased the Queen's Majesty to come to a friend's house nigh this town secretly, accompanied only by the Earls of Moray, Argyll and Bothwell, to make agreeance between the said Earl of Bothwell and me. Where, after some conference with us both in the hearing of the others, by one consent all differences betwixt us were accorded and we made friends. Whereupon her Majesty was well pleased that I should resort in her company to this town and received me to her good favour and my former place."

So Mary overruled Bothwell's instinct. Fatally, she gave her trust to the untrustworthy. "That lewd and atheistical man, Mr. George Buchanan" at present enjoyed her complete confidence. A few years later he was to describe her occupations at the Exchequer during the days that her mind was so busy with her baby's future.

"When she was returned to Edinburgh," he wrote, "she took not her lodging in her own palace, but in a private house next adjoining to John Balfour's. Thence she removed into another house, where the yearly court called the Exchequer was then kept. There dwelt hard by one David Chalmers, Bothwell's servant, whose back door adjoined to the garden of the Queen's lodging. The rest, who guesses not? For the Queen herself confessed the matter both to many other and also namely to the Regent and his mother. But she laid all the blame upon my Lady Reres, a woman of most vile unchastity, who had sometime been one of Bothwell's harlots and then was one of the chief of the Queen's privy chamber. By this woman, who now in her age had from the gain of whoredom betaken herself to the craft of bawdery, was the Queen, as herself said, betrayed; for Bothwell was through the garden brought into the Queen's chamber and there forced her against her will forsooth." Buffoonery follows about a rope that broke a few days later in lowering Margaret Reres, "a woman very heavy, both by unwieldy age and massy substance," over the garden wall to fetch Bothwell "out of his bed, even out of his wife's arms, half asleep, half naked," to repay force with force.

Upon obscene rubbish of this sort the story of the loves of Mary and Bothwell, which nine Englishmen or Frenchmen out of ten believe, has been erected. The inherent impossibilities of Buchanan's "bawdy conjectures and filthy suspicions," are hardly worth listing. If Lennox starts the legendary adultery before the birth of the Prince, how can Buchanan describe an initial rape three months later? Sir John Forster, an accurate reporter, gives the 8th September as the date of Mary's home-coming "to sit at her Exchequer," and further records that she was at Holyrood House by 12th September. These two dates destroy the remains of Buchanan's fabrication. How could Mary, between the 8th and the 12th, take up residence next door to Balfour, move house to the Exchequer, be surprised there by Bothwell (who seems to have been quite indifferent to the inevitable presence of courtiers, ladies, servants or guards) and "*within few days after*" recall her seducer to the same spot by the agency of Lady Reres? Margaret Reres was the baby's wet-nurse and was far more likely to be attending her charge at Stirling than her mistress at the Exchequer. The nature of her duties proves that she cannot have been as elderly as Buchanan says and suggests that he has confused her with her elder sister, Janet Beton, who seven years earlier, at the age of forty-three, was Bothwell's mistress. Not

259

even the *lumen Boreale refulgens* can expect his readers to accept a statement that a Queen confessed these improprieties, not merely to her austere half-brother and his less austere mother, but "to many other." He sets the final stamp of mendacity on his story when he asserts that George Dalgleish attested it before his death and that "his confession yet remains of record." While Dalgleish's dying confession is extant, it contains no sentence incriminating the Queen. Perhaps a rival pamphleteer did not far exaggerate when he calls the great Latinist "this bawdy fellow, the filthiest of men and dunghill puddle and sink of filth!"

CHAPTER TWENTY-FIVE

THREE weeks later the Queen and her Lieutenant very nearly died. Medical science, or their own will to live, saved them for misery and immortality. We may wonder if both did not subsequently find the price of the double survival a little high.

The Justice Court at Jedburgh had to be postponed until the middle of October. The official explanation gave out that the Queen did not wish to interfere with the harvests of her subjects, but she may also have been advised to allow time for unrest to subside. People said that if Bothwell tried to hold the Court without her, he would find "but a homely welcome and a worse farewell." Not until the end of September were summonses issued to well-disposed subjects to attend the Queen, armed and carrying food for twenty days. The father of the murderous Kerr, whose crime was one of the main causes for the assize, received an urgent invitation. "Traist Friend," wrote Mary's clerk to the Laird of Cessford, "we greet you well. We intend, God willing, to repair to Teviotdale to see justice ministered. And because it is our first journey in that country, it is needful aforehand that we consult upon such things as shall be there to do, whereunto your advice and presence is very necessary. Wherefore we pray you, all excusation and delay set aside, that ye fail not to be with us at Edinburgh upon the 1st day of October next, as ye will do us acceptable pleasure."

Q. Mary to Cessford, 25 Sept., 1566 (MS. at Jedburgh.)

A couple of days before the Queen was ready to start, her Lieutenant rode ahead with three hundred horsemen intent on rounding up malefactors to submit to her justice. The feud which was raging between Armstrongs of Liddesdale and Johnstones of Nithsdale gave him a good starting-point. From the Hermitage he made a "bag" of Armstrongs and shut them inside the fortress

261

to await transport to Jedburgh. The next day he meant to devote to the house of Elliot, whose peel towers dotted the marshy burns that trickle between the steep hills of Liddesdale.

Under the high, grey arch of the Hermitage and over the planks that bridged the moat, rode Bothwell and his troopers. Down Witterhope Burn they galloped, avoiding the little bogs of which the russet-coloured reeds and grass gave warning. The colours were very bright— patches of velvet-green grass, stripes of orange where the bracken had turned, and streaks of purple where the steep hillsides were dry enough for heather to grow. They rode past the peel of Robert Elliot of Shaws without molesting a man who was, as Elliots went, a peace-lover. The next peel, where Witterhope Burn joined Liddel Water, belonged to an Elliot with a worse reputation. The exploits of Jock o' the Park had moved Sir Richard Maitland to indignant verse. Of him and his peers the Secretary's father had written:

> "They spoil poor men of their packs,
>   They leave them not on bed or backs;
>   Both hen and cock
>   With reel and rock
>   The Laird's Jock[1]
>   All with him takes.

> "They leave not spindle, spoon nor spit,
>   Bed, bolster, blanket, shirt nor sheet;
>   John o' the Park
>   Ripes chest and ark,
>   For all such work,
>   He is right meet."

An uneasy conscience and the sight of armed men

---

[1] "The gude Laird's Jock" appears under more flattering colours in the ballads "Jock o' the Side" and "Dick o' the Cow." He died at an advanced age wrapped in blankets and watching a single combat in which his only son was killed by a Forster and his own two-handed sword lost. (Minstrelsy of the Scottish Border ii. 72.)

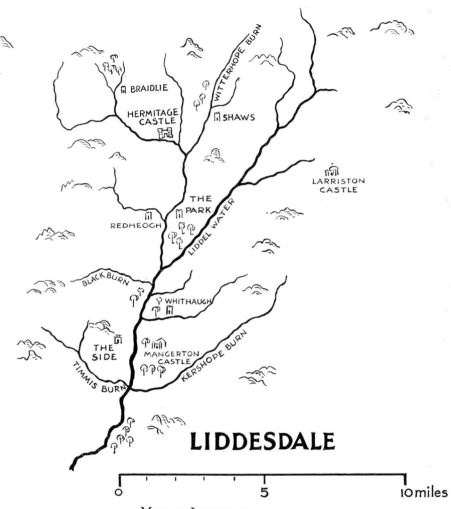

BRAIDLIE

HERMITAGE
CASTLE

WITTERHOPE BURN

SHAWS

LARRISTON
CASTLE

THE
PARK

REDHEOGH

LIDDEL WATER

BLACKBURN

WHITHAUGH

THE
SIDE

MANGERTON
CASTLE

KERSHOPE BURN

TIMMIS BURN

LIDDESDALE

0   5   10 miles

MAP OF LIDDESDALE,
SHOWING THE ELLIOT AND ARMSTRONG PEEL TOWERS

converging on his tower pointed to this hero the advantages of the hills. Down Liddel Water he galloped, past the Armstrong peels of Whithaugh and Mangerton, whose owners had preceded him to the Hermitage prisons. Jock's horse was fresh and soon the thunder of pursuing hoofs grew faint. Looking over his shoulder he saw one horseman ahead of his fellows. The Elliot could spur his gelding, his pursuer steadily gained ground. When they reached the junction of Liddel Water and Kershope Burn ("Kershope of the lilly lea") the two were level and Jock o' the Park could recognise the features of the redoubtable Lieutenant.

Aware that his chance of escape was small, the Elliot attempted a bargain. If he surrendered, would his life be safe? Bothwell hesitated.

"If," he decided, "an assize will make you clean, *I* am heartily contented. But it behoves you to pass by the Queen's peace."

Jock o' the Park had horror of the law. Jumping from his horse, he took advantage of the marshy ground to attempt an escape on foot. Two shots rang out and a pain in his thigh made him stumble. Bothwell dropped his smoking pistol and, fearing to bog his horse, dismounted. A hidden stump brought him heavily to earth. Before he could get up, the Elliot turned, drawing his two-handed sword. Three times he struck the prostrate man, wounding him in body, head and hand. The Lieutenant retaliated with "two strokes with a whinger at the pap." Then he fainted. His assailant dragged himself to a hillside a mile away and collapsed.

It cannot have been long before Bothwell's followers, whom his rashness had out-distanced, found their lord in this dangerous state. They loaded him on a sleigh and dragged him home to the Hermitage. There fresh perils waited; the Armstrongs, whom he had collected the day before, had broken prison and, making themselves masters of the fortress, refused him admission. It only needed an Elliot counter-attack to make the position desperate. The life of the unconscious man was probably saved by his peace-loving neighbour, Robert Elliot of Shaws, who had the sensible idea that in exchange for the keys of the Castle, the escaped Armstrongs should be given safe passage home.

So Bothwell gained the haven of bed and word reached London and the Continent that his wounds were mortal. The Queen of Scots (wrote the premature obituaries) "has lost a man she could trust, of whom she had but few." Sir John Forster reported that the Lieutenant's life was hanging in the balance. He also chronicled the escape of Jock o' the Park, a happy event which contemporary diarists denied. One of them states that his head was brought to Edinburgh—but detached Elliot heads cannot have been uncommon and to a layman would look much alike. Forster's habit of lending a little surreptitious support to the family put him in the way of hearing the truth. His story is confirmed by a Jedburgh charge of sheep-stealing brought against Jock the following year, while a manuscript in the British Museum suggests that "Scottis Joh of the Park" survived for further conflict with the law until 1590.

B. M. Addit : MS. 33531 fol. 237.

Two days after Jock had broken into history, Queen Mary came, by way of Borthwick and Melrose, to Jedburgh to hold the long-postponed assize. A Kerr lady rented her a small house for forty pounds. On the ground floor were the servants' quarters with a big fireplace; above was a hall and withdrawing-room. A left-handed turnpike stair (the Kerrs were left-handed and had to keep their sword-hands free from the newel) led up to the Queen's bedroom on the second floor; the four Maries slept under the roof.

Mary resolved that there should be no profiteering in Jedburgh. She fixed the price of a pint of good ale at fivepence, sixteen ounces of fine bread at fourpence, stabling for a horse for twenty-four hours at twopence, bed and bedding for a shilling a night, and "a man's ordinary, being served with braised beef, mutton and and roast at the least," at one shilling and fourpence. The arts were more liberally rationed, a reward of forty

Harwick Arch. Soc. Proceedings, 1925.

shillings being paid to John Home, player on the lute, and four pounds to James Heron, player on the pipe and whistle.

On the 10th October the Court of Justice opened. The statement of a contemporary Scottish radical that "the puir men were hangit and the rich men were hangit by the purse" seems like many radical assertions to have little foundation. At first there was small recourse to the scales of justice. The Privy Council had to announce that while many complaints had been made "of the infinite crimes of slaughter, theft and open oppression and her Honour had been moved to come in proper person to see trespassers punished and justice ministered to the poor oppressed subjects, nevertheless there is no complaints presented." Such offenders as were at length produced, profited by the Queen's unfailing mercy, and Forster reported that she "has not executed one, but has put all offenders to fine." That her Lieutenant was still "in great danger from his wounds" explains the small attendance, since Jock Elliot's two-handed sword had prevented the round-up that should have filled the Court.

A week after his accident, word reached Mary that Bothwell was well enough to receive visitors. Delighted at the recovery of a servant "whose loss would have been no small one," she undertook a journey to the Hermitage to discuss the business of the Border. The fortress contained no accommodation for women, and the double journey had to be made in the day. With a start at sunrise, twenty-five to thirty miles of steep braes, peat bogs and flooded burns must have taken her and her attendant noblemen till noon. (Tradition has it that she was bogged in "The Queen's Mire" and a lady's spur that was found there is shown as evidence.) Leisure to discuss her programme with the invalid, her Secretary and Earls of Huntly and Moray must have been short. She authorised the Lieutenant to hold a Court of Oyer and Terminer next day. She also conferred a post for drafting wills on George Sinclair, presumably a kinsman of Bothwell's on his mother's side. Then it was time to

Pitscottie ii. 190.

Forster to Cecil, 23 Oct., 1566

Silva to K. Philip, 26 Oct., 1566.

du Croc to Catherine de Medici, 17 Oct., 1566.

Scrope to Cecil, 17 Oct., 1566.

Harwick Arch. Soc. 1925.

265

be off, in order to cover the difficult miles to Jedburgh and to arrive splashed with black peaty mud, and wet to the skin, before sunset a little after five.

The visit furnished fresh powder and shot for Buchanan. His version may be quoted without comment. After sneering at Bothwell's discomfiture at the hands of "a poor thief," he tells how the news was brought to Mary at Borthwick, and how "she flings away in haste like a mad woman by great journeys in post in the sharp time of winter, first to Melrose and then to Jedburgh. There though she heard sure news of his life, yet her affection, impatient of delay, could not temper itself, but she must needs display her outrageous lust and in an inconvenient time of the year, despising all discommodities of the way and weather and all dangers of thieves, she betook herself headlong to her journey with a company as no man of any honest degree would have adventured his life and his goods among them."

The day after this misrepresented adventure the Queen sent a boy "with a mass of writings" to the Hermitage, no doubt in connection with the Court of Justice she had empowered the invalid to hold. But Liddesdale did not trust itself to the uncertainties of convalescent temper, and stayed away from the seat of judgment. The results to the Queen's health were even less happy. To a body never robust and exhausted by child-bearing, to a mind troubled by her husband's obscure manoeuvres, the sixty-mile ride proved nearly fatal. Next morning the pain in her side, which had been more frequent since her confinement, became acute. It lasted for several days and was accompanied by frequent vomiting. She was sick more than sixty times and in the later spasms produced a quantity of blood. She lost consciousness more than once, and at times the use of her eyes and voice failed.

On the seventh day a slight improvement allowed her to make her confession and submission to the will of her Maker, and to declare her adherence to the Roman Catholic faith. She called her nobles to her bedside and implored them "to keep love, unity and charity among

Scrope to Cecil, 17 Oct., 1566.

266

themselves, rehearsing what great goodness comes of unity and concord, and by the contrary, of discord, all desolations." She recommended her son to their care and begged them "not to suffer him to take any evil conditions which may fall to him through his father, mother or any his natural parents." She spoke of the state of religion and urged her lords "to press no man in his conscience." She advocated friendship with France and asked for rewards to be paid to her servants.

Next day she was worse. The Bishop of Ross's account of her treatment is a sidelight on the medical knowledge of the century. "At ten hours at even her Majesty swooned again and failed in her sight. Her feet and her knees were cold, which were handled by extreme rubbing, drawing, and other cures by the space of four hours that no creature could endure greater pain; and through the vehemency of the cure her Majesty got some relief. About six hours in the morning on Friday her Majesty became dead and all her members cold, eyes closed, mouth fast, and feet and arms stiff and cold." It was at this stage that her servants, thinking their mistress dead, opened the window to let her spirit depart. Her more practical half-brother started to collect her silver and rings. But the surgeon, "Master Naw," whom the Bishop testifies was "a perfect man of his craft, would not give the matter over, but of new began to draw her knees, legs, arms, feet and the rest with such vehement torments, which lasted the space of three hours, until her Majesty recovered again her sight and speech, and got a great sweating, which was held the relief of the sickness, because it was on the ninth day, which commonly is called the crisis of the sickness and so here thought the cooling of the fever." The weakness which ensued may be attributed as much to the drastic treatment as to the illness, for the remedies included binding cords about her shackle bones, knees and great toes, pouring wine into her mouth and administering a glyster.

Modern medical science has discovered the name of

Sir George
Turner.
Forgotten
Forgeries 46.

hæmatemesis for the vomiting of blood which occurs in cases of duodenal ulcer, and declares that Mary's later symptoms, even the appearance of death, are compatible with this diagnosis. The pain in her side seems due to indigestion arising from the ulcer or to uric acid, and not to some morbid state of the spleen, as was commonly believed.

The causes which "Mr. Buchanan's Roman"—if venal —"pen" assigns for her "sore and dangerous sickness" are as usual disallowed by the calendar. He states that on the Queen's return from the Hermitage she sent for her wounded lover and that "their nightly and daily travails, dishonourable to themselves and infamous to the people," provoked her illness! As Mary returned on the night of the 15th October to take to her bed on the 16th, while Bothwell could not be moved to Jedburgh for another five days, the theory does not demand very careful consideration.

Forster to
Cecil, 23
Oct., 1566.

A "horse litter" was used to transport the Earl. Total lack of roads must have made the journey grievous to a wounded man, but he was well enough by the crisis of Mary's illness to attend the meeting of the Privy Council that decreed emergency measures for the preservation of public order. Nor did he neglect his own affairs, putting his signature next day to an agreement with Michael Balfour about the lands that belonged to Melrose Abbey. His left hand that had sought to stop the Elliot sword was to trouble him for several months. The cut on his forehead left a scar for life, but there seems no authority for nineteenth century French statements that he lost the sight of an eye. His body wound may have been responsible for a "flux of blood" which inconvenienced him fourteen weeks later.

Bibliotèque
National,
Paris.
Collection
relative à
M. Stuart.

Lamartine.

Teulet
Lettres. 80.

The Queen's recovery was rapid, although a perfunctory visit from her husband, who came for one night to Jedburgh, did little to advance it. By the end of the month she took enough interest in life to order red silk brocade, white plaid, white taffeta (the royal colours were red and white) and black velvet to be sent from Edinburgh. She needed the material to dignify the progress she still meant to make through the towns of the Border. By the 9th of November she was able to ride out of Jedburgh, where she left twenty pounds to be given to the poor. Moray, Maitland, Huntly and Bothwell trotted behind her; Home, Warden of the Eastern Marches, commanded her guard of a thousand horse. In the week they visited Kelso, Home Castle, Langton and Wedderburn, and halted on the high ground above Berwick. Sir John Forster, at the time in command, had the guns fired and cantered out to meet her with sixty captains and burghers "doing all the humanity and honour to her Highness that was possible to him." He escorted the party almost to Eyemouth, whence they proceeded to Dunbar, by way of Coldingham. That ended the Border progress. In spite of its long postponement, in spite of Bothwell's accident and the Queen's illness, it seems to have helped the end desired. Nothing more is heard of the plot to bring Morton home, and Kerrs, Elliots and Armstrongs seem to have ceased for a time from troubling.

From Dunbar Queen Mary and her lords went to Craigmillar, a couple of miles south-east of Edinburgh. *du Croc to Archb. of Glasgow, 2 Dec., 1566.* Fresh breezes and wide prospects of distant moorland and gleaming sea made the Castle a better place for convalescence than the more urban palace of Holyrood. At Craigmillar she stayed for a fortnight "in the hands of physicians," profoundly depressed at the pass to which her marriage had come. The lords in attendance openly discussed its dissolution, as the next chapter will detail. Darnley even let it be known that he did not mean to attend his child's christening. His unexplained absence would amount to a public charge of bastardy, which Mary, if only for the boy's sake, could not allow. Moreover, national policy demanded an outward show of unity on an occasion which was to be graced by the presence of the ambassadors of England, France and Savoy.

In Darnley's default, somebody had to make the preparations at Stirling, where tradition demanded that the *Forster to Cecil, 11 Dec., 1566.*

six-months-old prince should be baptized. Somebody had to receive the ambassadors. The duty fell on Bothwell, who could be trusted not to intrigue.

Two of the ambassadors were already in the country and had brought valuable presents from their sovereigns. The Comte de Brienne, who had been staying at Craigmillar, gave the Queen a diamond chain and pendant in the name of Charles IX. On Elizabeth's behalf, the Earl of Bedford presented a font of massive gold, of exquisite workmanship with many precious stones "combining elegance with value." It was big enough to immerse her god-child. Robertino Solaro, known as the Sieur de Moretta, was late with the Duke of Savoy's tribute—a large fan with jewelled feathers. The retinues of the ambassadors filled the streets of Stirling. Bedford had an escort of eighty horsemen, and among his staff rode Sir Christopher Hatton, the "frisking" favourite of Elizabeth, Mr. Carey, great nephew of Anne Boleyn, and Mr. Lignish to represent the Duke of Norfolk.

A splendid spectacle had been prepared to gratify their eyes. Caparisons for the royal horses had been cut out of cloth of gold with a silver fringe. The baptismal Cloth of Estate was made of crimson velvet "of high colour," edged with gold thread, crimson silk and gold braid. The baby's bedspread took ten yards of figured cloth of silver. At the ceremony the full pomp of the Roman Church was to be deployed, though Mary had refused to allow the use of the spittle. That she deemed "a filthy and an apish trick rather in scorn than in imitation of Christ. And her very own words were that she would not have a pocky priest to spit in her child's mouth." The disease for which the Primate had been treated by Dr. Jerome Cardan of Milan at a fee of 1800 gold crowns made Mary's epithet anything but symbolic.

At five o'clock in the evening of Sunday the 17th December, 1566, the infant prince was carried by the French Ambassador from his room to the Chapel Royal. He passed between two rows of barons and gentlemen with wax candles in their hands. The catholic nobility

270

of Scotland followed, bearing the great serge, the salt, the cude cloth, the basin and ewer. Bothwell, with his unalterable distaste for ritual, stopped with Bedford, Moray and Huntly at the chapel door to watch the Popish proceedings from a distance. He saw an archbishop, three bishops, a prior, various deans and archdeacons waiting "in their several habits and copes with the singers of the Chapel." He watched the Ambassador hand the baby across the golden font to the Countess of Argyll, who was acting as the Queen of England's proxy. He saw the Primate's lips move as he gave the names of James and Charles. He heard heralds with their trumpets proclaim these names three times, with the Prince's titles. To the strains of music he saw the infant carried back to his crib. He noticed the absence of the young father, who lurked morosely in his quarters.

The King did not emerge for supper in the great hall. The Queen sat at a small table between the English and French ambassadors, facing the proxy of the laggard from Savoy. Another table accommodated sixty guests, their nationalities tactfully divided by the Queen's ladies. Dancing followed the meal, and Mary, resolutely enjoying her day of happiness, took part. When the dancers tired, Sebastien Pagez, her Auvergnat *valet de chambre*, "in great favour for his cunning in music and his merry jesting," had prepared what the entertainment world would now call a "number." It seems to have puzzled a spectator who describes "three or four men, coming in like hobby-horses and yet sitting as upon a tailor's shop-band, cutting out silk to make something." If the five Italian songs that these artists sang were written by Rizzio, absence may have spared the King an uncomfortable ten minutes.

Next day's amusement was in the nature of a bull-fight—"the hunting of the wild bull"—in the park. Thursday saw a great banquet and masque to which the Queen had bidden ambassadors and nobles. The spectacle was provided by collaboration of the Auvergnat valet, Sebastien Pagez, and the hireling scholar, George

271

Buchanan. "Bastien's" contribution was a platform decorated with laurel on which reclined six singing naiads. This rural scene was piled with the first course of the banquet, and pulled into the hall by twelve satyrs, torch in hand, while rustic gods danced round. As they reached the round table where the Queen sat with thirty guests, the satyrs handed their torches to bystanders, and taking the dishes from the naiads, served alternate ambassadors, ladies and earls.

Meanwhile the nymphs were singing the well-turned compliments that Mr. George had contrived.

> Virtute, ingenio, Regina, et munera formae
>   Felicibus felicior majoribus,
> Conjugi fructu sed felicissima, cujus
>   Legati honorant exteri cunabula:
> Rustica quem donis reverentur Numina, silvis
>   Satyri relictis, Naiadesque fontibus.

No thought of the open depravity which he was afterwards paid to disclose, seems to have embarrassed the poet's appreciation of his victim's beauty, wit, motherhood and virtue.

The Satyrs animated by their success, nearly provoked an international episode. Not content to perform their duties as waiters, they "put their hands behind them to their tails, which they waggit with their hands." Englishmen were touchy on the subject of tails, conscious of the inaccurate but widely-held continental belief that their countrymen of Kent were born with tails in token of divine disapproval of the murder of St. Thomas à Becket. So Sir Christopher Hatton, genially remarking to Sir James Melville that, but for the Queen's presence, he would put a dagger to the heart of that French knave, Bastien, sat down with Mr. Lignish on the floor behind the table, so as not to witness the slight. It took the Queen's tact and the Earl of Bedford's authority to get this dignified protest withdrawn.

The platform reappeared under different disguises to

serve the succeeding courses. A rocky hill which Buchanan's classical fancy may have transformed into Parnassus; a fountain in which the same readily inflamed imagination may have seen the Castalian spring; a globe out of which a child emerged, whose symbolism sounds complimentary to the infant James, made in turn a brief appearance. The final spectacle, sad to relate, "could not be brought to pass because the stage broke."

From the great hall the company passed into the December night. A fortress had been constructed near the churchyard and was assaulted by a regiment of centaurs, moors, highlanders, lanzknechts and demons. To repel the attack, defenders of the fort shot "fire-balls, fire-spears and all other things pleasant for the sight of man." The pyrotechnic display had taken Johnny Chisholm forty days to prepare. It cost the treasury £190 17s. 5d.

Bangs, shouts, music, laughter reached the King's ears where he sat in his room brooding on imaginary grievance, plotting clandestine revenge, aching with disease. They had borrowed his silver plate, no doubt to meet the demands of the banquet and had replaced it with pewter; the time would come when he would show them who was king. The French agent had been rude and had refused to listen to his complaints. When he had insisted, the wretch had remarked pointedly that there were two doors to his suite and he would leave by one as the King came in by the other. Never mind; there were other countries more powerful than Mary's eternal France. Mary—she didn't seem able to forget that miserable night last March. What did David matter? A servant and a foreigner! If only he hadn't screamed when they carried him out of the room. . . . That was Ruthven's doing and Morton's, not his. Anyhow, it was months ago and still Mary treated him like a dog. He had only to whisper to one of the lords and she would think he was hatching something. That was the worst of women, once you made them suspicious. That quarrel about the men his father brought to Stirling! Why

Inventories lxxxviii.

Diurnal of Occurents 105.

Bishop of Mondovi to Cardinal of Alessandria, 13 Feb. 1567.
du Croc to Archb. of Glasgow, 23 Dec., 1566.
Wilson's Actio.

du Croc to Archb. of Glasgow, 2 Dec., 1566.
Melville 143.

*Silva to K.
Philip, 20
Dec., 1566.*

shouldn't he? All honest men of Lennox. And the endless
wrangle about the christening and keeping up appearances. It was to get her way that she took her meals
with him now. What was the use of that, if she kept her
bedroom barred? He hated her ... or did he love her?
He didn't quite know. He knew he was ill and unhappy.

A burst of cheering, an orange flash reflected on the
wall, and a sonorous report. They had blown up the fort
the servants had been gabbling about. Fireworks. Gunpowder. Gunpowder to blow up a sham fort ... it would
blow up a house, wouldn't it?

CHAPTER TWENTY-SIX

TO understand Darnley's thoughts, his doings since the murder of Rizzio must be followed. That tragedy was staged at the intersection, so to speak, of two intrigues. There was the long-standing purpose of Moray and Cecil to dethrone the Queen of Scots and remove at one stroke Elizabeth's rival and the obstacle to Moray's greatness. There was the more recent aim of Darnley and his father to sacrifice Mary to the Lennox Stewart pretension to the throne. Darnley's weakness and Bothwell's strength brought the Rizzio operations to a disastrous halt, but neither branch of the temporary amalgamation abandoned its dark objective. For the future the work was done separately.

During the remaining nine months of 1566 the Moray-Cecil gang attempted no fresh aggression, but worked quietly to recover lost ground. Moray, Maitland and Argyll regained their footing at Court and intrigued to repatriate their exiled accomplices. How far Bothwell was right in believing that a forcible restoration was planned, is uncertain. Some activity on the Border, a murder of an Abbot, an immature plot against James Hepburn's life—these preliminaries subsided into the more lawful expedients of diplomacy.

The agents of the King of France, Castelnau de Mauvissière and Philibert du Croc, were working "very earnestly and effectually" on Morton's behalf; while on the other side of the Border Bedford was anxious that "a Douglas should be called home rather by England's means." *Bedford to Cecil, 3 Aug., 1566.*

The other gang, with Darnley's youth to set the pace, scorned the patient realisation of ambition. Quick results were needed to forestall the enemies whom the King's treachery had created. The hope of finding a new ally in

275

Bothwell petered out. Greater names and more grandiose fancies filled Darnley's shallow brain. A startling project was evolved which aimed at the re-establishment of the Roman Church in Scotland, the removal of the Queen who had failed to revive catholicism, and the execution of the protestant leaders.[1] If Darnley was lukewarm about religion, he cared greatly for his own rise to supreme power and for the elimination of the enemies he had made. Nor were the means to prosecute his programme out of his reach. He had reason to believe that Pius V, first Pope of the Counter Reformation, and King Philip of Spain would be glad to subsidise and even to assist so devout an undertaking. Spain's whole policy was directed at limiting the power of France and as long as Mary sat on the throne of Scotland that country was a potential French ally.

The Spaniard was master of hiding his diplomatic tracks, but Darnley was less discreet. A hint at his mood comes from the exiled Morton, posted no doubt by some Douglas relative. In May, 1566, Darnley was "minded to depart to Flanders and such other places as he thinks will best serve his purpose to complain of the Queen." May was the month that saw King Philip's wish to visit his troublesome provinces crystallise. Before long he was telling the Pope his plan to ship an army to the Netherlands to overawe the malcontents and their supporters in England. It is not hard to see why Darnley wanted to visit Flanders.

Morton to Bedford, 24 May, 1566. " *The Tragedy of Kirk o' Field*" 248 ss.

In June the boy's uneasy fancy took a twist. William Rogers, an English spy, won his confidence by proficiency in the chase and frank admission of a criminal past. Rogers reported to Cecil that his new friend had a chart of the Scilly Islands and designs on Scarborough Castle. He was in communication with that Arthur Pole who had been a fellow-prisoner with Bothwell in the Tower, and who now claimed to be able to raise the West of England. If these straws show the quarter of the wind, they suggest

---

[1] The details of this plot were first worked out by the late Major-General Mahon in his most valuable book, *The Tragedy of Kirk o' Field.*

that Darnley had ideas of joining King Philip in a descent on the English coast. What his reward was to be was outside the knowledge of William Rogers.

The scene shifts from the Netherlands to Paris. There Vincenzo Laureo, Bishop of Mondovi, chosen as his Holiness's legate to Scotland, was waiting for encouragement to start on his uncertain mission. Queen Mary was quite anxious to receive a papal subsidy (the first and only instalment of which she diverted to defray the expenses of her baby's baptism), less enthusiastic about the papal nuncio. Laureo was broad-minded enough to understand the obstacles to his reception, and at the same time clear-sighted enough to suggest a simple, if bloodthirsty, remedy. "These difficulties," he wrote in a secret and confidential letter which won the Pope's cordial approval, "might be obviated if the King of Spain should come, as is hoped, with a strong force to Flanders or, as certain people of weight believe, if justice were executed against six rebels whose deaths would effectually restore peace and obedience in that kingdom. These are the Earls of Moray and Argyll; the Earl of Morton; the Laird of Lethington; Bellenden, Justice Clerk; and James MacGill, Clerk Register.... The King himself (Darnley) could execute it without any disturbance arising and with the assured hope that afterwards the holy Catholic and Roman religion could soon be restored.... The danger is that the Cardinal of Lorraine and the Queen in their excessive kindness, would not consent to such an act." *Bishop of Mondovi to Cardinal of Alessandria, 23 Aug., 1566.*

Their lack of religious fervour seemed to the prelate inexcusable. Twice he went to see Mary's uncle and suggested pressure (a prettier word than blackmail) calculated to bring the Queen to her senses. Had not his Holiness given him express orders not to disburse the moneys of the Apostolic See except in the service of religion? (The Cardinal's expressive lips tightened. He saw what was coming.) "But," insinuated the nuncio, "as soon as something notable should be done for religion," he would be surprised if his *Bishop of Mondovi to Cardinal of Alessandria, 21 Oct., 12 Nov., 1566.*

277

Holiness did not release the full subsidy, or even a greater sum.

That was a powerful argument, but Laureo reports great difficulty in persuading his host that "there ought to be no further delay in doing something signal for the service of God in Scotland." At length the Cardinal agreed to send a gentleman to his niece with advice "to decide on restoring the holy religion. As there seemed to be no more expeditious remedy than the punishment of a few seditious wretches," the messenger was to urge the Queen to "execute with a brave heart this most just punishment for God's glory."

Laureo had met such lack of enthusiasm that he felt nervous lest cardinal and queen should double-cross the vicar of Christ and draw the subsidy on the strength of sanguinary promises which they did not mean to keep. Failure in his mission and recall to Rome were threatening the nuncio; in his anxiety he took the further step of dispatching the Bishop of Dunblane and the Jesuit Hay "to give courage to the Queen to prosecute the holy cause of religion." Both these churchmen had helped him formulate the "expeditious remedy."

Thus was launched the Paris Plot. It may be shown in conventional form as a triangle. At the apex in Paris, for all to see, stands the Papal Legate. At one angle, in the Netherlands, the figure of King Philip may be with more difficulty detected ("if the King of Spain should come to Flanders," wrote Laureo blandly, "the Queen could with no great difficulty arrange the affairs of her realm.") At the other angle, in Scotland, Darnley's erratic enthusiasm is manifest.

Even before the black list left for Rome, Darnley set at work. He was imprudent enough to tell his plans to his wife, who promptly sent a warning to her half-brother. She had him awakened at midnight, hurried into a dressing-gown, and brought in disarray to her room. "The King," she whispered, "boiled in deadly hatred against him and was fully determined, so soon as any possible opportunity served, to murder him."

278

That is Buchanan's story. His opponent Blackwood purports to give Darnley's threat. The language contains a curious echo of the nuncio's private and confidential letter. "The death of such a traitor," Darnley is reported to have said of Moray, "would bring peace to the kingdom, security to the State, and relief to the people." *Jebb ii. 210.*

In September the King retired to Stirling. One day Lennox rode over from Glasgow. Nobody knows what father and son discussed, but the upshot was a letter to the Queen, telling her that her husband had a ship manned to take him abroad. *P.C. to Catherine de Medicis, 8 Oct., 1566.*

Mary got the letter at Edinburgh on Michaelmas Day. At ten the same night Darnley himself drew rein outside the palace. When he heard that "three of the greatest lords of the kingdom" (two would be Moray and Argyll) were with the Queen, he refused to dismount. Mary came into the courtyard and led him in by the hand. That night "when he and the Queen were abed together, her Majesty besought him to declare to her the ground of his designed voyage, but in this he would by no means satisfy her." Puzzled and anxious, next morning she called a meeting of the Council in her room. Everybody begged the King to state his reason for "relinquishing so beautiful a queen and so royal a realm." Darnley sulked and refused to own "he intended any voyage or had any discontent." He left melodramatically without kissing the Queen. "Adieu, Madam!" he cried. "Ye shall not see my face for a long space." *du Croc to Archb. of Glasgow, 13 Oct., 1566.*

The gesture did not forbid letters, and from Corstorphine on his way west he wrote "in a sort of disguised style," complaining of the nobles' lack of respect. He could not, he grumbled, "obtain such things as he seeks, to wit such persons as the Secretary, the Justice Clerk and the Clerk of Register to be put out of their office." It is significant that all three officials figure on Laureo's list. *Book of Articles (Hosack i. 526).* *R. Melville to Archb. of Glasgow, 23 Oct., 1566.*

No doubt the King was hesitating between two equally discreditable lines of conduct. He might actually sail to Flanders and get in direct touch with Philip, or he could use the threat of departure to coerce a wife who badly wanted him to be at the christening.

Knox ii. 533.

All the time his pen was busy. "He wrote to the Pope, the King of Spain and the King of France complaining of the state of the country, which was out of order, all because that Mass and Popery were not again erected; giving the whole blame to the Queen as not managing the catholic cause aright." The corollary can be supplied. With a little help from the catholic powers, a more vigorous successor could replace the inactive Queen.

Silva to K. Philip, 13 Nov., 1566.

She heard of these letters, and entered a protest at the Spanish Embassy in London against the charge that "she was dubious in the faith." Her position invites sympathy. She was barely convalescent. Darnley had paid her a flying visit and had spent the night in the bed of the obliging Bishop of Orkney. A day or two later the messenger arrived whom cardinal and nuncio had sent from Paris

Bishop of Mondovi to Cardinal of Alessandria, 12 Nov., 1566.

with the sanguinary "test." He had left Laureo in a state of optimism, inclined to believe that the dangerous illness with which God had visited Mary had touched her heart and inspired her "with some good and holy resolution." It is painful to record that the Queen of Scots proved herself unworthy of the pious hope. Surely she must have seen that the assassination of half a dozen heretics and conspirators would not only rank as a measure of good government but a proof of religious zeal? Surely she must have known that refusal automatically closed

Bishop of Mondovi to Cardinal of Alessandria, 3 Dec., 1566.

the Papal pocket? Nevertheless, "the remedy was not found good by the Queen," as the disillusioned legate gloomily records. "Her Majesty did not consent to it." It must be owned that a queen whom historians have represented as a bigot and a wanton, showed at a time when she was ill, isolated and sorely tempted, a standard of civilisation several centuries in advance of her time.

Her answer was on its way to Paris when a letter arrived from Darnley. She read it and, if Buchanan may be believed, "cast a piteous look, as if she would have incontinent fallen down again into her former sickness."

In despairing tones she vowed that she would as soon kill herself as live in such sorrow. The letter is lost. A glance at its contents might show how brutally her husband had negatived her clemency by offering himself as figurehead of the Paris Plot.

Disheartened, she put herself under medical care at Craigmillar, but du Croc believed "the principal part of her disease to consist in a deep grief and sorrow. Still she repeats these words, 'I could wish to be dead.'" A visit from Darnley did not help. On Saturday, 30th November, he was still hanging about the Castle and met du Croc half a league off. This Saturday, if the present writer is correct, is the real date of the vital letter on which the Casket forgeries were based. *du Croc to Archb. of Glasgow, 2 Dec., 1566.*

Suppose that under the forger's pen was placed a genuine letter of Mary to Bothwell. It carried no indication of place of origin, its only date was "ce samedi." It was child's play to add "à Glasgow." The two words supplied a change, not only of place, but of date and interpretation. What was written in all innocence at Craigmillar before the christening takes a different accent post-dated to Saturday, 25th January, when Mary had gone to Glasgow to fetch Darnley. It is only necessary to read the awkward English translation, which is all the Casket manipulators have left of Mary's original French, to see how much damage the two interpolated words could do.

"It seemeth," runs what is known as the Short Casket Letter, "that with your absence forgetfulness is joined, considering that at your departure you promised to send me news from you. Nevertheless I can learn none. And yet did I yesterday look for that that should make me merrier than I shall be. I think you do the like for your return, prolonging it more than you have promised."

Bothwell, we have seen, had the sole charge of the preparations for the christening. There were only three weeks left and he could not attend to his duties from Craigmillar. What would be more natural than to ride *Forster to Cecil, 11 Dec., 1566.*

281

to Stirling after the Council meeting on Sunday, 24th November? He did not keep his promise to report progress and the Queen was disappointed when Friday the 29th came without a letter.

"As for me," she continued, "if I hear no other matter from you, according to my commission I bring the man Monday to Craigmillar, where he shall be upon Wednesday. And I go to Edinburgh to be let blood, if I hear no word to the contrary."

du Croc to Archb. of Glasgow, 2 Dec., 1566.

Unless she got a letter from Bothwell that made her change her plans, she was going to send somebody to fetch the King. He was only a couple of miles away, telling du Croc that he meant to miss the christening. Mary was determined he should attend, and she was going to keep him under her eye at Craigmillar until Wednesday. On that day he was to accompany her to Edinburgh, where she was going for treatment. (It is worth mentioning that on the Monday after the Glasgow visit, there was no question of Mary or Darnley being anywhere near Craigmillar.) The letter goes on:

"He is the merriest that you ever saw and doth remember unto me all that he can to make me believe he loveth me. To conclude, you would say that he maketh love to me, wherein I take so much pleasure that I never come in there but the pain of my side doth take me. I have it sore to-day. If Paris doth bring back unto me that for which I have sent, it should much amend me."

She gives an account of Darnley's conduct during his visit to Craigmillar that week. The hypocritical overtures of the man who meant to brand her child with bastardy made her feel ill, but Paris, the page, had gone to Edinburgh for medicine, in which she had faith. The description of Darnley's good spirits contrasts with the misery depicted in the Long Casket Letter of 24th-25th January ("he desires nobody should see him; he has ever the tear in his eye"). Is it conceivable that the two accounts were written within a few hours, as a Glasgow allocation of the short letter implies?

"I pray you send me word from you at large, and what

I shall do if you be not returned, when I shall be there. For if you be not wise I see assuredly the whole burden falling upon my shoulders. Provide for all and consider well first of all. I send this present to Lethington to be delivered to you by Beton, who goeth to one day of law of Lord Balfour. I will say no more unto you, but that I pray God send me good news of your voyage. This Saturday morning."

The Queen is in a hurry for Bothwell's report so that she can make her own plans and fix the date for the formal entry to Stirling. If he fails her or does not exercise sufficient forethought, the whole burden of the baptism preparations will fall on her. Where is the trace of the passion to be expected of a woman in the throes of an illicit intrigue? Where is even the anxiety she would show, writing when her lover was on his way (as was Bothwell at the time of the Glasgow week-end) to a dangerous encounter on the Border? Is this the love letter of a partner in crime, or the routine note of a devoted mother?

Soon after the departure from Craigmillar, the Jesuit Hay and the Bishop of Dunblane, a recent guest of the Jesuit College, reached Scotland, commissioned by Laureo "to prosecute the holy cause." The zealous bishop pursued the Queen to Stirling and presented the legate's letter, "but was unable to converse about anything, her Majesty being entirely taken up with the baptism." Darnley had more leisure and the story that the Queen tried to keep the "ambassadors" away from him may well have been true of the nuncio's envoy. *Bishop of Mondovi to Cardinal of Alessandria, 24 Jan., 13 Feb., 1567.* *Lennox Narrative Mahon, 124.*

Lennox had filled the streets of Stirling with his supporters, and the quarrel they caused between Mary and Darnley shows she was nervous of a Lennox Stewart conspiracy. The need for peaceable conduct at a time when so many nobles, foreigners and their servants were collected in the town, provided the excuse for an edict forbidding culverins, dags and pistolets or any weapon except a sword and whinger. Mary's relief can be imagined when the week was over without serious *P.C. Reg. i. 43.*

conflict between the various clans, nationalities and sects.

For it was not to be expected that the protestant leaders were quietly waiting until the Paris Plot, of which Darnley's indiscretions kept them informed, was ripe. For weeks they had been strengthening their position and preparing a counter-stroke. Their first move was to isolate Darnley and cut off the support which Bothwell had lent him over the scheme to bring back the Postulate. It is significant that Moray and Maitland visited their old enemy after the break-up of the Michaelmas Council that met to probe the threatened trip to Flanders. Three days later saw another Council, followed by another conference of the same unusual trio. The upshot was the signature of a bond by which Moray, Bothwell, Argyll, Huntly and probably Maitland and Atholl agreed to support each other in not obeying the King when his orders conflicted with the Queen's wishes. Both parties had reason to feel pleased with the compact. Moray had deprived his enemy of the potential backing of Bothwell and the Border; while Bothwell had bought a little peace at the price of a promise to obey his Queen.

Lang,
Mystery of
M. Stuart
87 ss.
A. Douglas to
Q. Mary Apr.
1583.
Keith Ap.
139.

So far Moray was on safe ground. He meant to stay there. Darnley must go, but constitutional methods were to be employed. Moray had no unmanly prejudice against assassination, but to kill a king was dangerous. If Darnley ceased to be king . . . if he were divorced, for instance . . . At the end of November, during the Queen's visit to Craigmillar, an informal meeting was held to discuss the possibilities. An account of the proceedings is found in the so-called "Protestation of the Earls of Huntly and Argyll." This paper was drawn up two years later from the futile[1] Bishop Leslie's recollection of what Huntly had told him. It was sent to the two

Moray's
Answer, 19
Jan., 1569.
Buchanan
Detection
Spottiswood
196-8.

---

[1] A perusal of the Bishop's *Defence of Queen Mary's Honour*, with its allusions and analogies—Vortiger and Constance, Seleucas and Heliodorus, Duncan and Macbeth, Onias of Jerusalem—will justify the epithet. One of his most imprudent arguments may be quoted: "I find that King David was both an adulterer and a murderer. Yet I cannot find that he was therefore by his subjects deposed."

noblemen for signature, but on the way fell into enemy hands to end in Cecil's omnivorous files. To accept, therefore, its assertion that Bothwell was present at the divorce conference, when "that grave and reverend prelate" Archbishop Spottiswood, not to mention "that notable man, Mr. George Buchanan" omits his name, is unsafe.

Moray, Argyll, Lethington and Huntly carried the discussion from bedroom to bedroom. Could not the Queen be brought to exchange a divorce from Darnley for a pardon for Morton? The idea bears the stamp of Moray's labour-saving mind. They put the suggestion to the Queen. Suppose she divorced on the score of adultery the man who was threatening to brand her baby a bastard? What more effective answer could she make? Mary at once put her finger on the weak spot: would her Church recognise the grounds? Somebody suggested an annulment on the usual plea of consanguinity. Mary shook her head. If her marriage was illegal from the start, her baby might be illegitimate and lose his claim to the double throne. Somebody cited the case of Bothwell,[1] whose mother's marriage had been dissolved without hindrance to his rights. But the Queen was nervous. Better show patience and perhaps her husband was young enough to mend his ways. Maitland of Lethington intervened.

"Madame," he protested, "fancy ye not we are here of the principal of your Grace's nobility and council, that shall find the means that your Majesty shall be quit of him without prejudice to your son? And albeit that my Lord of Moray here present be little less scrupulous for a protestant than your Grace is for a papist, I am assured he will look through his fingers thereto."

Use has been made of Maitland's words to incriminate him and Moray in the Gunpowder Plot of 9th February, 1567. But was not the "means" that Maitland thought satisfactory to Mary's catholic scruples and tolerable to

[1] The "Protestation," which asserts Bothwell's presence, attributes the argument to him.

285

Moray's protestant conscience, beyond doubt the re-establishment of the catholic Archbishop's abolished court? That Consistory, which Lethington believed would find a safe formula to dissolve the marriage, was in fact restored two days before Christmas. With the General Assembly of the Kirk registering violent indignation, until it was bribed to silence by increased stipends, the austere Moray can be reckoned to have "looked through his fingers."

Privy Seal Record Book 35 fol. 99. Hosack i. 177.

At the time the Secretary did not explain his thoughts and failed to convince his mistress.

"I will that you do nothing whereto any spot may be laid to my honour and conscience," she insisted.

"Madame," answered Maitland, his thoughts still on the Consistory, "let us guide the matter. Your Grace shall see nothing but good and approved by Parliament."

There the matter rested. It is usually related that at Craigmillar the associated lords signed a bond for Darnley's murder. The story rests in part on the confession of a kinsman of Bothwell. The Earl, said John Hepburn of Bolton before his death, showed him a bond which contained "some light causes against the King, such as his behaviour contrar the Queen," and was signed by Huntly, Argyll, Lethington and Bothwell. But does not this description clearly fit the bond which engaged the signatories not to obey the King's orders when they were in conflict with the Queen's? John Hepburn made no mention of any murder clause. The gap, however, was filled by the minister who handled Black Ormiston's scaffold confession. "After long conference and prayers made for about the space of an hour," the Reverend John Brand extracted a promise from his penitent, "as he should answer to God, with whom that night he hoped to sup," to tell the truth. He proceeded to give proof, if the minister can be believed, of a remarkable memory that could quote nearly a hundred words of a bond, which Bothwell had read once through to him seven busy years before. This extract provided for the murder of

Suppressed part of Hepburn of Bolton's Confession. Lang xiv.

"the young fool and proud tyrant." Having unburdened his conscience, Black Ormiston, reassured that he was one of God's elect, went to his death crying, "My Lord Jesus, sweet Jesus, have mercy upon me, as You have had upon other sinners."

With all respect to the Reverend John and his powers of consolation, it is difficult to believe in the feat of memory which alone vouches for the existence of a highly improbable murder bond. Who can admit that in those treacherous days, the heads of two opposing parties, temporarily associated, would trust each other to the extent of signing an agreement to murder a king? Would the prudent Moray (who categorically denied that he had ever signed such a bond) allow his incalculable enemy the custody of this deadly weapon? It is surely time to bury an ill-verified legend.

If a divorce could be contrived, there is evidence that the protestant leaders planned another legal move that might avoid the dangers of straight assassination. Darnley, no longer king, could be impeached for his treasonable proceedings. If he happened to be killed resisting arrest, no one could be blamed, and the danger that inconvenient facts might emerge at his trial would be avoided.

A coalition makes for indiscretion, and word went round that some such idea had been discussed. Lennox heard in Glasgow of "an enterprise to the great peril and danger" of his son. The information was not very precise; either the Privy Council had signed a warrant for Darnley's arrest, or they had asked the Queen to sign and, so near the christening, had been refused. The Spanish secret service heard the same story of the Queen refusing to allow a plot to be formed against her husband. Minto, Provost of Glasgow, warned Darnley that "some of the Council" had unsuccessfully petitioned her to sign a mandate for his arrest, and planned to kill him if he resisted. The Provost got the story from his Town Clerk, who had it from one of Lord Eglington's servants. Nothing very authoritative, but enough to send Darnley

Lang, Mystery of M. Stuart. 99 ss.

Silva to K. Philip, 18 Jan., 1566. Long Casket Letter. Crawford's Deposition Q. Mary to Archb. of Glasgow, 20 Jan., 1567.

hot-foot out of the gates of Stirling as soon as the christening party was over. Another bit of news hastened his departure. Morton and the Douglases were coming back to Scotland.

For months England and France had put pressure on Mary to pardon the criminals most directly concerned in the Rizzio murder. Until her own nobles joined to urge a general amnesty after the baptism, she resisted the request. Negotiations were already on foot between the associated lords and the exiles, whose clerical representative, Archibald Douglas, was admitted to the country *sub rosa*. This ecclesiastic is described by a French envoy as "almost impossibly prudent, circumspect and far-seeing." He was given the credit of "knowing good and evil," but there is no recorded instance that he ever applied the former knowledge. He was spy, traitor, forger and assassin. Soon after his induction as parson of St. Mungo's, Glasgow, he employed a confidential servant to shoot his cousin Morton—unfortunately "the gun made no service." At his examination for the benefice, "when he had gotten the psalm book, after looking and casting over the leaves thereof for a space, he asked the minister to make the prayer for him, 'for,' said he, 'I am not used to pray.'" Mr. Archibald shared with Sir James Balfour the hardly-won distinction of being the worst man in Scotland.

A. Douglas to Q. Mary, April, 1585.

After crossing the Border to negotiate with the Lords, Douglas says he learnt the existence of the bond to obey the Queen and "have nothing to do with her husband's command." He was asked if his cousin Morton would add his signature in exchange for the Lords' promise to work for his pardon. The story has a hollow ring and some essential term in the bargain has been suppressed, but the Yuletide sequel may be told in the words of the English Ambassador's letter to Cecil. "The Queen hath now granted to the Earl of Morton, the Lords Ruthven and Lindsay their relaxation and 'dresse.' The Earl of Moray hath done very friendly towards the Queen for them and so have I, according to your advice. The Earls

Bedford to Cecil, 30 Dec., 1566.

Bothwell and Atholl and all other Lords helped them or it would not have been so soon gotten."

It is clear that the initiative came from the Moray-Cecil junta. Their plans were working out. Moray had secured the co-operation of the loyal lords. He now closed the ranks of his party with the return of the exiles. Moreover, should he need it, in the homicidal instinct of the Douglases he had a tool to cut the web of the Paris Plot.

CHAPTER TWENTY-SEVEN

B Y Christmas, 1566, the stage was set for the long
tragedy that took twenty years to finish. Fate, far-
sighted propertyman, had ready the powder barrels
of Kirk o' Field, the axe of Fotheringay, the fetters of
Dragsholm.

On Christmas Eve, before Darnley was well clear of
Stirling, the disease with which he was infected declared
its presence. He rode painfully to Glasgow and sought
his bed. The official diagnosis was smallpox, scandal
whispered poison, and the truth seems to have been
syphilis. The documentary evidence and the marks on
a skull, preserved as his, have been carefully examined
by Dr. Karl Pearson. His verdict, "we may conclude with
a high degree of probability that the poison was syphil-
itic," is all that it is necessary to repeat.[1] One point
must not be missed. Bothwell knew and carefully
recorded the real nature of the disease.[2] Such knowledge
helped him to judge the young man's worth as a husband.
The Queen showed her habitual tolerance, sending her

[1] Three passages may be added to the contemporary testimony to the
nature of Darnley's complaint collected by Dr. Karl Pearson in his admirable
Skull and Portraits of Lord Darnley.

Blackwood (Jebb ii. 240) says: "Les pustules s'engendrent au corps des
hommes non seulement par poison, mais aussi par plusieurs autres accidents
. . . et principalement ceux de son age."

On 12th March, 1566, a man called Sheres the Scot reports Randolph as
writing to the Privy Council in England, "she (Mary) the falling sickness,
he (Darnley) lepre." (Bain ii. 266.) Leprosy, like smallpox, was in those days
confused with syphilis. Darnley was ill in the spring of 1566, and a blue
satin coat was made for him to wear in bed. (Inventories 164.) As for Mary's
epilepsy, this has been fully discussed by General Mahon. (*The Tragedy of
Kirk o' Field,* 179.)

Pitscottie states (ii. 191) that the King "was stricken with a great fever
of the Pox, but it was judged that he should have been poisoned, but God
knows the verity thereof."

[2] In his memoir "Les Affaires du Comte de Boduel," p. 12, Bothwell's
secretary wrote "*le Roy tumba malade de la petite vérole.*" With his own hand
Bothwell crossed out *vérole* and wrote *roniole. Rognuel* or *roigne* seem to have
implied syphilis.

own doctor to Glasgow to treat the sufferer and giving orders for linen to be cut into "ruffs for the King's sark." *Hay Fleming, 505.*

But whether the figurehead of the conspiracy was in sickness or health, subterranean preparations did not stop. From every quarter warning reached the Queen. From the Earl of Moray to a humble retainer of the house of Beton—all told the same story. Lennox, Glencairn and others were plotting to dethrone the Queen, throw her into prison, crown the prince and make Darnley regent. William Walker, whom his Beton patrons declared was "il nostro amico e non della fortuna," secured an audience and repeated what he had heard, but his witnesses lost their nerve and would not tell their story. A solemn warning, alarming in its vagueness, was despatched from Paris to arrive too late to avert the catastrophe. From that city the Archbishop of Glasgow sent one of the Scottish archers with an urgent message to the Queen "to advertise you to take heed to yourself." The hint had come from Don Francisco de Alava, Spanish Ambassador in Paris. That diplomat may have been instructed by his master to prepare him an alibi by uttering a warning too late to prevent a tragedy. He refused to give particulars, merely stating that "there be some surprise to be trafficked to the Queen's contrar." Rather impudently he admitted that he had written to his master for details; he probably felt the indiscretion of implying that Philip knew something would be covered by the impossibility of any answer coming in time to prevent the "surprise." That Don Francisco took the report seriously is shown by the letters he wrote to the Duchess of Parma in the Netherlands and to the Spanish Ambassador in London stating that "he had news of a plot forming in Scotland against the Queen." *Q. Mary to Archb. of Glasgow, 20 Jan., 1567. Blackwood (Jebb ii. 214.)* *Archbishop of Glasgow to Q. Mary, 27 Jan., 1567. (Keith viii.)* *Silva to K. Philip, 17 Feb., 1567.*

The Archbishop hurried to Catherine de Medicis hoping to learn more. The Queen Mother professed bland ignorance. Had he watched her restless eyes, the irony of her words might not have escaped him. "She thought there was nothing to be feared, and approved greatly the ruth and pity the Queen had for her own." Her flat features must have worked to conceal a smile as she counted the price her rival was to pay for tenderness to her protestant subjects. The Scottish Archbishop was no match for Florentine subtlety. He went home to write his letter of warning and to urge his mistress "to cause the captains of her guard to be diligent in their office." It was a pity he did not think of calling on the representative of England. Sir Henry Norris had valuable information, or why did he write from Paris that tantalising sentence after the catastrophe of Kirk o' Field had startled the world, "as at first I thought, therein I remain not to be removed, which was that the original of that fact came *from hence*"?

Norris to Throckmorton, 5 April, 1567.

But though the Archbishop's letter came too late, the warnings that reached Mary, the story of a mystery ship lying in the Clyde, the watch Darnley's agents were keeping on her movements, made her anxious. "Always," she said, "we perceive him occupied and busy enough to have inquisition of our doings." Uneasy, she resolved to bring her child from Stirling to the capital. Stirling was too near the storm centre, and Lady Mar, in whose charge the baby lay, had family ties with the Lennox Stewarts. The night of the 14th January, 1567, found mother and child sleeping safely at Holyrood House.

Q. Mary to Archbishop of Glasgow, 20 Jan., 1567.

The next stage in Mary's programme was to remove her husband from the plot-thickened atmosphere of Glasgow. She wanted his impressionable mind under her influence and his eccentricities under her eye. Letters were no use, nor messengers; health would furnish an excuse to stay where he was. She must go herself and fetch the invalid as soon as he could be moved. She had two new frocks made (satin and velvet lined with red taffeta), and started west on Tuesday, 21st January, taking Bothwell and Huntly to escort her out of Edinburgh. That night she slept at Callendar, the Livingstone place, whence the Earls returned to the capital. On Wednesday she reached Glasgow.

Hay Fleming 505.

Bothwell's improved fortunes had in no way impaired

his old mobility. Newly returned from a visit to Whittingham in East Lothian, he escorted Mary most of the way to Glasgow, returned to Edinburgh, and a few days later was heading a raid in Liddesdale. Whittingham was the seat of William Douglas, Archibald's brother, and there Bothwell had ridden for a conference in the garden with Morton, Archibald Douglas and Maitland. The true story of the discussion has not been, and cannot now, be written. It was probably concerned with the steps that the protestant party were contemplating to checkmate Darnley. Morton and Archibald Douglas in after years alleged that Bothwell "came to Whittingham to propose the calling away of the King." Morton declares that his own answer was "that I would not in any way meddle in the matter because that I am but newly come out of a great trouble." It is a suspicious fact that in Bothwell's memoir, written years before Morton's confession, an identical sentiment is to be found. "When I had procured them their pardon"—the epoch of the conference is clearly in his mind—"and they were allowed to follow the Court, I took thought for rest and a peaceful life after the imprisonment and exile I had suffered, without idea of vengeance or quarrel." It is probable that Bothwell used the excuse under the trees at Whittingham, and that Morton in his account of the conference reversed the rôles. *Morton's Confession Holinshed's History, 1587. A. Douglas to Q. Mary, April, 1583.* *Les Affaires du Comte de Boduel 12.*

Archibald Douglas, says Morton, took sides with Bothwell, though according to Douglas's own story—"what speech passed there among them, as God shall be my judge, I knew nothing at the time." In this innocence he was sent to Edinburgh to find if the Queen would give a written authority to get rid of her husband, as Bothwell, so Morton alleges, had promised. That answer (again "as God shall be his judge") was definite, "Show to the Earl of Morton that the Queen will hear no speech of the matter."

Given witnesses as profoundly dishonest as the two Douglases (and Morton's confession reeks with insincerity), it is not possible to arrive at any certainty. In the garden at Whittingham some project prejudicial to Darnley was no doubt discussed, whether divorce, indictment or murder. The attitude of the disputants was probably the reverse of Morton's account. The hitherto humanitarian Bothwell, who had no quarrel with the King nor was threatened by his intrigues, probably advised legitimate measures. The Douglases, who had recently been betrayed and who stood under the shadow of the Paris Plot, would only be true to character if they claimed a sanguinary vengeance. Maitland's technique was notorious: "to throw the stone without seeming to move the hand." He would see how the Douglas savagery could be used to dispel the danger which threatened the protestant leaders. Somebody tried to compromise the Queen. May not Bothwell have attended the conference in order to call a Douglas bluff? A direct appeal was demanded. Her answer was unequivocal; she would hear no speech of the matter.

It is impossible to suppose that Bothwell cared very strongly what was done to Darnley. He seems to have dismissed the whole matter easily from his mind. He went with the Queen to Callendar, returned to Edinburgh, but did not linger. Before the 27th January he had reached Jedburgh. On that day he led a raid of eighty moss-troopers into Liddesdale against the Elliots. His hobby was the Border foray, not the palace intrigue. He captured a dozen law-breakers, one of them "an Elliot of the best sort." As he was riding home with his prisoners, Martin Elliot of Braidley led a strong counter-attack. In the fighting a brother of Black Ormiston's was killed and "if good hap had not chanced, the Earl himself had been in great peril." The picture does not tally with a passionate liaison with a queen and the stealthy preparation of a death-trap for her husband.

Scrope to Cecil, 28 Jan., 1567.

By now Mary, assured that the January cold offered no danger to Darnley's health, was taking him in a litter to Edinburgh. Her stay at Glasgow had lasted about five days. Part of that time she had spent drawing up a memorandum on the attitude of Darnley and his father.

Drury to Cecil, 26 Jan., 1567.

This paper may have been intended for Maitland, who was handling the divorce and who would be Mary's natural confidant in her fears of Lennox Stewart agitation. That it was not addressed to Bothwell is proved by a note at the end, "remember you . . . of the Earl of Bothwell," an otiose reminder had her correspondent been that nobleman. Nevertheless, if the theory of this book is correct, the Queen's enemies took this memorandum and, interpolating a few passages of love letters received by Bothwell from other women, and a few paragraphs forged for the occasion, produced that perennial subject of discussion, the Long Casket Letter.

Interpolations and all, it runs to five thousand words and is too long to quote. The gist of the original genuine memorandum, however, can be extracted to recover Mary's report on her momentous visit to Glasgow.

Four miles outside the town a Lennox retainer had met her with excuses from her father-in-law, who stated that he did not dare come in person after the sharp words she had given Cunningham. (Glencairn, whose share in the Paris Plot has been mentioned, was a Cunningham.) Lennox himself received the tart reply that there was no recipe against fear. If his conscience was at ease, he need not be afraid.

The names and conversation of the gentlemen who rode to meet the Queen follow, with a comment on the absence of the pro-Lennox burghers of Glasgow.

The memorandum's first mention of Darnley records his efforts to find out from the royal servants the object of the visit. It goes on to record his expressions of delight at seeing his wife. Next comes a verbatim record of the young man's promises of amendment. Mary was not impressed; perhaps she had heard the excuses too often. She asked about the mysterious ship in the Clyde and wanted details of the Town Clerk's warning. Darnley admitted that he had been told that some of the Council had applied for a warrant and meant to kill him if he resisted arrest, but he absolved his wife of any evil intentions. He was annoyed by William Walker's report of the plan to proclaim a regency, and denied its truth. He also denied that any scheme to harm the Lords was on foot.

Mary succeeded in extracting information about "the Bishop" and the Earl of Sutherland, to which she obviously attached importance. Unfortunately she does not report her discovery. The Bishop of Dunblane was Laureo's emissary and held the strings of the Paris Plot, while Sunderland, as a catholic nobleman, may have been involved. Throughout the memorandum Mary expresses her distaste for the deception she was obliged to practise to get Darnley to talk. These passages were picked on by the forger for distortion and expansion, until the result reads like a confession of guilt. She also regrets that, in order to persuade Darnley to come with her to Edinburgh, she had to promise to share a bedroom there. The invalid was unnaturally insistent on this condition to which he repeatedly recurred. The events of the night of the 9th February explain his eagerness.

Such in brief was Mary's memorandum. The rest of the paper is omitted in the confident belief, based on style and content, that she never wrote it.

The journey back to Edinburgh was only remarkable for the ominous company of a raven, which hovered over the travellers and finally settled on the King's lodging. Other sinister figures were collecting at the capital. Signor di Moretta arrived, who had once before brought death in his train in the person of Rizzio. He was more than two months late for the christening, at which he had been deputed to represent the Duke of Savoy. A familiar of the nuncio, he joined fortunes with the jesuit, Father Hay. He tried to see Darnley "about a horse," but Mary prevented the interview. Remembering the very close link between Savoy and Spain, is it unfair to see in the Savoyard the emissary of Spain? The steps which, according to Buchanan, were taken to bring him

Simancas 622.

into touch with two of the leaders on the black list, Moray *Lethington to Cecil, 8 Feb., 1567.* and Morton, and to detain a third, Maitland, in Edinburgh, suggest that his function was also that of a decoy.

Another suspicious character steps a little way out of the shadows, the "*vrai traitre*" whom du Croc stigmatises. Sir James Balfour had a shrewd head and a black heart. John Knox, who rowed in the same galley when the couple were implicated in the murder of Cardinal Beton, found in him "neither fear of God nor love of virtue, further than the present commodity persuadeth." In those days a protestant, Sir James was subject to conversion whenever advantage prompted. As a catholic *Teulet ii. 106.* he was created Privy Councillor in 1565 during the short period of Darnley's ascendancy. From that time he seems to have stayed a King's man, and it was to him *J. Hepburn's Confession. (Lang xv.) Nau. History of Mary Stewart.* that the King now listened when the question of accommodation in Edinburgh arose.

Whatever the nature of Darnley's sickness, the official bulletin said smallpox and some degree of quarantine was expected. Mary, some say, made preparations at Craigmillar; others claim that "she had already prepared a *Sebastian Davelourt in Q. Mary's Divorce Proceedings, 1575.* lodging for him at the palace of Holyrood." But the invalid was told "by certain lords who were in his suite that a house of better air had been prepared and that it would be better for his health to go there." It was Sir James Balfour who explained that his brother Robert, Canon of Holyrood, had an empty house just inside the city wall at Kirk o' Field which was suitable for his purpose. So Darnley over-ruled his wife and, still accompanied by the raven, made his way to the south side of the town.

"The whole building, sometime called Kirk o' Field,[1] *Records of the Burgh of Edinburgh, 21 June, 1563.* with lodgings, buildings, mansions and yards" had been an ecclesiastical foundation before the Reformation. It *Blackwood 29.* is described as a "place highly situate, pleasant and in good air, environed with pleasant gardens and removed from the noise of the people." A contemporary placed it

---

[1] Major-General Mahon's ingenious reconstruction of the house and precincts should be studied in the first part of his *Tragedy of Kirk o' Field.*"

as far from Holyrood as the Palace of Westminster from St. James's. The Church of St. Mary in the Fields had been allowed to fall into ruin, but the old Provost's House, as the King's lodging should be called, was a substantial building some of whose stones are said to have measured ten feet by four. It formed the south side of the quadrangle, where the ecclesiastics who served the foundation—provost, precentor and prebendaries—once lived. Behind the house ran the Flodden wall with only a narrow passage or court between. Through the town wall was a postern gate, by which "it was possible to go into the country." This convenience made the house particularly suitable for Darnley's purpose. At the east end of the building was a garden, to which another door gave access from the house. A third entrance opened on the quadrangle.

History of James Sext.

J. Curl in Q. Mary's Divorce Proceedings, 1575.

A long, narrow reception-room with an outside door, probably originally a separate hall for the prebendaries, formed the western half of the premises. Joining this wing with the main building was a turnpike stair which gave entrance to two east bedrooms, one above the other. The lower room was the Queen's, the upper the King's, with a gallery projecting to the south that rested on the city wall. An ante-chamber was used for sanitary purposes. A basement would underlie both parts of the house, whose floor levels varied with the steep pitch of the ground to north and east. Here were servants' quarters, kitchens, cellar and storage vaults. A red-tiled roof, dormer windows and crow-stepped gables may be inferred in a house of the date.

The nearest house, also owned by Robert Balfour, was the new Provost's House at the south-west corner of the quadrangle. Hamilton House stood "about a stone's cast distant," and Douglas House as far away again.

Birrel's Diary.

Inventories 49. Book of Articles. Nelson's Deposition.

When Darnley arrived on the last day of January he had to sleep in a bed with figured black velvet hangings and gold and silver fringes that had been brought with some tapestry from Holyrood House for the use of the visiting Earl of Bedford on his way to the christening.

The bed had been taken into palace use soon after the Queen's arrival from France, and Darnley preferred the newer violet bed his wife had given him in the summer. It was not until February that the wardrobe-master could arrange the transport of Darnley's furniture from Craigmillar or Holyrood or wherever he had been expected to pass his convalescence. For the Queen's own use a little green and yellow bed with a green quilt was erected in the lower bedroom, where she slept to please her husband on the nights of Wednesday and Friday, the 5th and 7th of February. *Inventories 177.* *Nelson's Deposition. Book of Articles.*

The next Sunday was Carnival Sunday. There were two functions to amuse the Court. The more humble, but possibly the less tedious, was the morning marriage between Sebastien Pagez, who had designed the masque of satyrs and naiads, and Christina Hogg, one of the Queen's women. The church ceremony was followed by a midday dinner; that night there was to be a dance at the palace. The more formal entertainment was a banquet given by the Bishop of Argyll in honour of Moretta. The scene of this supper, which the Queen had signified her intention to attend, was Balfour's Canongate house, which had been lent to the Savoyard for his stay in Edinburgh. That stay was timed to end the next day. Three notable figures were missing. One of his Countess's convenient pregnancies provided the Earl of Moray with an excuse, Lethington was inexplicably absent—his recent marriage to Mary Fleming may have kept him at home —and the Earl of Morton was not yet welcome at Court. In Moretta's eyes the presence of Argyll, Huntly, Cassilis and Bothwell did not compensate. *Book of Articles.*

By nine supper was over. The Queen washed her hands—French Paris stood behind her to attend to her wants—and gave the signal to adjourn to the old Provost's House, where she had promised her husband she would pass the last night of his quarantine. *Book of Articles. Nelson's Deposition.*

There was a little snow on the ground; the moon had been new at six that morning and the February night was dark and cold. There would be *Lennox Narrative.*

braziers to warm the waiting servants and torches to light the way.

Under the tawny light the snow would tread into a copper-coloured slush as Campbells, Gordons, and Kennedies scrambled to find their lords' mounts. Somebody led a horse to the doorway, where the Queen stood keeping her feet dry and somebody bent to lift her easily to the saddle. Distance swallowed the sound of hoofs, and houses soon hid the lights, as Moretta returned to his packing.

The scene inside the Provost's House has lived down the centuries. The long, narrow reception-room, hung *Inventories 177.* with tapestry and dignified by a royal dais and canopy of black fringed velvet, was filled with ladies and gentlemen in attendance on the Queen and her nobles. Only the very great were allowed to approach the King's bedroom through the ante-room hung with the Rabbit Catcher tapestry where the King's commode stood in majestic isolation. (A formidable piece of furniture, it *Royal Wardrobe and Jewels 98. Inventories 33, 178.* was upholstered in velvet, fitted with twin pans and surmounted by a canopy of yellow shot silk with a red and yellow fringe, the former property of a Cardinal.) The King's bedroom was indescribably stuffy. It was small and no windows were ever opened. Not counting servants, at least six people were present. Sitting on red velvet cushions, Bothwell, Huntly, Argyll and Cassilis were playing dice at a little table with a green velvet cloth. They wore their carnival costumes, and Bothwell *Bishop of Mondovi to Cardinal of Alessandria, 27 Feb., 1567.* was splendid in black velvet and satin, trimmed with silver. On a high chair, upholstered to match the violet bed, sat the Queen. She had drawn her chair to the bedside, pulling it over the little Turkey carpet that served to keep the King's feet warm when he got out of bed. Her tone was friendly as she laughed with Darnley. His expression she could not see, for, drawn down over his face, he wore a piece of taffeta to hide the disfigurement of his disease.

For nearly two hours her visit lasted. Suddenly she *Cockburn to Cecil, 19 March, 1567.* declared, or perhaps a reminder came from Lethington, that she had promised to go to Bastien's wedding dance.

Darnley protested vehemently. Had she not agreed to spend the night in the room below? Mary only laughed. Next night the quarantine would be over and they could share a bedroom at Holyrood. To satisfy his strange importunity, she took a ring from her finger and gave it him as a pledge. *Venetian Calendar vii. 389.*

She was not allowed to stay long at the dance. Soon after midnight the two officers in charge of her bodyguard—Bothwell and the Laird of Traquair—wanted word with her. What threatened their charge that the two men who were responsible for the Queen's safety cut short her evening of festivity with conversation so long and so earnest? The Laird was the first to leave; still Bothwell pursued the argument.

Back in the Provost's House, Darnley was preparing for the night. There was talk about the three great horses Lord Seton had given him. They were to be ready saddled at five in the morning. There were many guesses about a remark of the Queen's. Why had she mentioned Rizzio, dead these eleven months? He had hoped that treachery was forgotten. One of the servants had a psalm-book and, to change the subject, his master suggested that he should sing. The man asked Darnley to accompany him on his lute, but the King refused. He did not feel in the mood. They sang, it is said, the fifth Psalm: *Lennox Narrative (Mahon: Mary Queen of Scots 128).*

Lead me, O Lord, in Thy righteousness because of mine enemies; make Thy way straight before my face. Destroy Thou them, O God; let them fall by their own counsels . . .

Then Darnley called for wine and drank a good-night health. William Taylor, his valet, slept in the room. Symonds and Taylor's boy had the gallery overhanging the town wall. Two grooms, Glen and MacCaig, were somewhere within call. The rest of the servants had leave of absence. Soon all sounds in the house had ceased. A single light burned in a window of Hamilton House. *Nelson's Deposition.* *Buchanan's History 214.*

Proceedings in
Queen Mary's
Action of
Divorce, 22
Sept., 1575.

An hour and a half later a great roar was heard "as if twenty-five or thirty cannon had been fired in a volley." Sebastian Davelourt, Keeper of the Ordnance, said so and likened it to thunder. The houses of Edinburgh were shaken by the violence of the explosion. Paris, the French page, declared that every hair of his head stood up like an awl. "As many as were awake were afraid and as

Herries,
History 84.

many as slept were awaken." One of the former, William Blackadder, the sea captain, was drinking in the house of Willie Henderson, whom his friends called Bloody Wits. The Captain left his glass half-full and ran out into the High Street. "The great uproar in the town" had called out the magistrats. Marching down the street and finding Captain Blackadder agape, they arrested him on chance.

The solitary watcher at the window of Hamilton House had blown out his candle. "Amazedness and confused fear of all sorts of people" abated, and the bolder crept in the direction of the explosion. The old Provost's House was completely demolished. Appalled, they searched the rubbish-heap where the King had lodged. A mutilated body met their gaze. They peered at the distorted features. A shout came from the garden on the south side of the town wall. The King had been found. Under a pear tree on the snowy ground in his night-shirt the unhappy boy lay dead. His valet, Taylor, lay a little further on. There was no mark on either body.

CHAPTER TWENTY-EIGHT

ABOUT midsummer the tormentors set to work on the wretches suspected of the murder. The torture chamber of the Tolbooth echoed with the soft thud of mallets driving wedges between the iron of the "boot" and the shrinking flesh. Rack pulleys creaked. Deliberately the screws of capsiclaws and pilniewinks were tightened. Hooks and pincers glowed red-hot. The skinning knife slipped in a wet hand. And over and over a relentless voice repeated its questions. . . .

The result did not repay the trouble taken. From Geordie Dalgleish, Bothwell's tailor, and from Willie Powrie, his porter, some sort of a story was extracted, but the helpful hand of the examiner shows through the sameness of the phrases. Later in the year it became possible to apply similar pressure on two of Bothwell's kinsmen. Reluctantly John Hepburn of Bolton and young Hay of Talla yielded further details. The atrocious method of winning the evidence inspires no more confidence than the secret nature of the tribunal that collected it or the false attestations of the Justice Clerk who took it down. Nor is the story that emerged, even when contradictions between the four versions are ignored, credible.

Here is the official story on which Bothwell has been found guilty of Darnley's murder by his contemporaries, by tradition and by history.

During the days that preceded the explosion Bothwell, it was alleged, discussed with John Hepburn a project to murder the King. Later young Hay of Talla and Black Ormiston were taken into the secret. The first idea was to do the killing "in the fields" where, the Earl assured his henchmen, a syndicate of nobles meant to be represented by two servants apiece. It was not until Friday that this co-operative technique was abandoned in favour of a gunpowder plot, which was to be Bothwell's unaided responsibility. For some unexplained reason, gunpowder had *already* been brought from Dunbar Castle and was lying in the hall of Bothwell's quarters at Holyrood. This powder was to be transferred to a barrel, stood in the Queen's bedroom at the Provost's House, and ignited by a fuse. The day fixed to spring this surprise on Lord Darnley was Saturday, the 8th February. But except that Geordie Dalgleish innocently borrowed three foot of fuse from an unknown soldier, Saturday passed without incident.

On Sunday at dusk John Hay's man collected an empty powder-barrel, which his master, determined to leave no clue unindicated, had already ordered. About the same time a meeting of conspirators was held, a trifle melodramatically, in the room with the gunpowder. From there they went to Black Ormiston's apartment in Blackfriars' Wynd to discuss details with the laird and his uncle Hob. This was the first Hob had heard of any plot to blow up the King, but he, good, easy-going creature, made no difficulties. Black Ormiston, too, was quite unprepared. He was "going belted in a gown," inappropriate costume for desperate adventure.

Ormiston's Confession (*in Howell's State Trials*).

At some not very clear moment Bothwell left his accomplices in order to attend the Moretta farewell party. At ten o'clock Willie Powrie and Pat Wilson (who pimped for Bothwell in the Bessie Crawford affair) had their orders to carry the gunpowder to the Blackfriars Gate, some two hundred yards from Kirk o' Field. The powder was packed in "polks"[1] inside a leather portmanteau and a trunk; it took two trips of a grey nag to carry this deadly luggage and the empty powder barrel from Bothwell's quarters to the Gate. There they found the other conspirators waiting, their ranks swelled by French Paris and three men with cloaks about their faces and "mules" or slippers on their feet. The Gate stood open, for James Ormiston had climbed through a gap to

[1] A "polk" was a leather bag.

304

unbar it. The gang carried the "polks" by candlelight to the east garden of the old Provost's House. Wilson and Powrie were sent back to Holyrood with the empty luggage. They had to walk, for the horse had bolted, and they saw the torches of the royal procession pass up Blackfriars' Wynd in front of them. The other conspirators carried the "polks" to the back door of the Provost's House which Paris unlocked. Black Ormiston went in first and with his uncle chose a convenient moment for the gunpowder to follow. Bothwell seems to have gone upstairs to the King's bedroom. The barrel proved too big to pass the door and was returned to the garden to provide another clue. By the naked light of a candle the "polks" were emptied in a "bing" or heap on the floor of the Queen's room. Remarking genially, "You know what to do, when all is quiet above. Fire the end of the 'lunt' and come away," Black Ormiston and his uncle went home, leaving Paris to lock the back door and the staircase door. Hay and Hepburn stayed in the Queen's bedroom with the powder.

The page went to the King's room to let Bothwell know that everything was ready. (Then it was, says another story, that the Queen cried, "Jesu, Paris, how begrimed you are!") After a little delay, the company left the house and Bothwell took his place in the torch-light procession that escorted the Queen to the palace.

By midnight he was in his bedroom changing his carnival clothes for a canvas doublet and a riding-cloak of sad English cloth called the "new" colour. (Dalgleish, the tailor, is speaking.) The Earl collected his page and the servants, and led them through the palace grounds to the Canongate. At the gate of the palace garden they were challenged by the sentry, and in their passion for providing evidence announced themselves as "friends to my Lord Bothwell." Up the Canongate they walked and woke up the porter at the Netherbow, who asked what they did out of their beds that time of night. Ormiston was not at his lodging, and the five conspirators made their way without him through the Blackfriars Gate to the "back wall and dyke of the town wall" at Kirk o' Field. The Earl and the page disappeared over the wall, leaving the three servants half an hour to wait in the east garden.

At two Hepburn and Hay, locked in the Queen's bedroom, felt that the time was ripe for the big event. They lit the fuse and left the house. As they had fourteen duplicate keys, including two for the back door, they carefully locked all doors behind them. Bothwell they found, apparently in the little yard or passage between the house and the town wall. Together they rejoined the party in the east garden.

Fifteen minutes passed and Bothwell became impatient. Was there any part of the house through which he could see if the fuse was burning? They told him the only window by which he could see looked on the quadrangle. The impetuous Earl wanted to explore, though John Hepburn assured him there was no need. "I will not go away until I see it done," declared Bothwell obstinately. At that moment the conspirators "saw the house rising and heard the 'crack.'" Taking to their heels, all seven bolted for a gap in the town wall in Leith Wynd. Finding the place too high for Bothwell's wounded hand, they once more roused the Netherbow porter and once more gave their lord's name. Splitting into two parties, they ran down the hill, some by the Canongate and some at the back of the Canongate gardens. At the palace they were again challenged by sentries and again gave Bothwell's name.

Safe in his lodging the Earl called for a drink, took off his clothes and went to bed. Within half an hour he was disturbed by Mr. George Hackett's knock. Admitted, Mr. George could not find a word to say.

"What's the matter, man?" asked Bothwell.

"The King's house is blown up," stammered Hackett, "I trow the King be slain."

Bothwell sprang out of bed and began to dress. Huntly called for him and together they hurried to find the Queen.

When this story had been extracted by torture from Hepburn, Hay, Powrie and Dagleish, one day saw them tried, sentenced, hanged and quartered. Their limbs were carefully packed in wicker baskets and sent to be stuck on the gates of the major towns of Scotland.

French Paris did not fall into the hands of his enemies until October, 1568. Some months in a dungeon and a taste of torture produced two picturesque statements, which agreed so badly with the evidence already won that the prosecution had to discard them. The page was hanged in haste without a trial.

James Ormiston reached the scaffold in 1573, and his dying confession was secured by the same pastor who had brightened the final moments of the first four to suffer. For that reason, perhaps, it generally supports their statements, without providing any new facts. It is pleasant to reflect that Pat Wilson and Hob Ormiston were never caught.

There are three reasons why this official story of the King's murder, provided by the torture depositions, cannot be true. It conflicts with all psychological probability; with all physical possibility; and with the known facts.

What are the known and undisputed facts? Unfortunately for any honest attempt to solve the puzzle, there are only two small groups. In the first place, the old Provost's House in which Darnley was last seen alive by his visitors at about eleven on Sunday night was blown up in the early hours of Monday morning *and totally destroyed*. This complete destruction is attested by unimpeachable evidence. The Privy Council version states that the house "was in an instant blown in the air . . . with such force and vehemency that of the whole lodging, walls and other, there is nothing left unruinated and dung in dross to the very ground-stone." This comprehensive account is supported by the Queen's letter to the Archbishop of Glasgow on the 11th February ("there is nothing remaining, no not one stone above another"); by the Privy Council's letter to Catherine de Medicis

P.C. Reg. i. 498.

307

("there remains nothing, all being carried to a distance and reduced to dross not only the roof and floor, but the walls down to the foundations"); by the French eye-witness Clerneau's description of the house as "totalement rasé"; even by the court's sentence on Hay, Hepburn and the rest, which states that the "whole lodging was raised and blown in the air."

The second fact which cannot be disputed is that the bodies of Darnley and his valet, William Taylor, were found under a tree at a little distance from the house. They were in their night-shirts. Darnley's purple velvet dressing-gown, furred with sables, and his slippers lay nearby. There was no mark on either body. Buchanan in his History describes the condition of Darnley's corpse very clearly. "No fracture, contusion or livid mark appeared on his body . . . His clothes, which were lying near, were not only not singed with the flames nor sprinkled with the powder, but were so regularly placed that they appeared to have been carefully put there and not either thrown by violence or left by chance." This account is confirmed by Knox's History, which states that the corpse "had no mark of fire," and by Melville's report that Bothwell invited inspection "how that there was not a hurt or mark on the body."

Is it possible to believe that two men were blown up by an explosion violent enough to obliterate a house, that they shot through the shattered roof or wall, that they fell through a tree on the frozen ground sixty or eighty paces away, but that their nearly naked bodies showed no mark? Or that a folded dressing-gown and a pair of slippers passed through the same experience to land intact beside their owner?

The reader who is not prepared to accept this miracle is forced to admit that Darnley was not inside the Provost's House when it was blown up. If he holds to the belief that Darnley was murdered by Bothwell and his men, he is placed in a dilemma. He must discredit the depositions which state that Hay and Hepburn fired the fuse in the Queen's room, that they locked the doors and that, as the house blew up, the whole Bothwell party ran home. He must make a frank assumption that Darnley got out of the house to be murdered by Bothwell in the south garden before or after the explosion. But he can find no witness to support his theory, for the sole evidence in any way implicating Bothwell is contained in the depositions which have been abandoned.

Before following the clue to the mystery which the two known facts provide, the case against the depositions on grounds of physical possibility and psychological probability may be stated.

How much gunpowder could be carried in a portmanteau and trunk on the back of a horse making two journeys? (The grey nag, it will be remembered, also carried a barrel.) How efficient was the gunpowder of that unscientific century? If this comparatively small amount of inferior gunpowder was loosely heaped in the ground-floor room of a stone-built basement house and exploded, would that house be "dung in dross"?

Major-General Mahon goes carefully into the question of the quantity and quality of powder available and gives the following answer: "It can be said quite definitely that 250 lbs. of indifferent gunpowder exploded on a floor over arched masonry vaults would in the first place not crush these arches downwards, and in the second place would probably not destroy the walls. . . . It is yet certain that any person in the upper room would have been mangled beyond recognition. . . . It is absolutely impossible that the effect could have been produced by placing a comparatively small quantity of bad gunpowder in the Queen's room." *"The Tragedy of Kirk o' Field" 60, 61.*

Again, is it physically possible that gunpowder could be introduced without detection into a house that sheltered the two sovereigns of the country and four of its principal nobles? These august presences would necessarily imply a host of kinsmen, dependents, retainers, bodyguards, servants, pages, grooms, torch-bearers and horse-holders;

the house servants must also be counted, some eight of whom are known by name. Even were it credible that Wilson and Powrie could bring their barrel and trunks through the streets and gates of the capital, unchallenged by town watch[1] or citizens, could three or four of the gang conceivably carry the "polks" into a small house, whose layout they did not know, through a crowd which, indoors and out, must have numbered at least fifty persons? Here again the objection is forcibly presented by Major-general Mahon.

If the physical facts play havoc with the official story, so does the psychological aspect. What sort of character has emerged from this review of Bothwell's life? Do not two traits seem to contradict the charge that his mind planned the Gunpowder Plot of Kirk o' Field? So many of his actions prove him a good-natured man, reluctant to take human life. A qualm lest mercy should look unmanly and the slang of the day explain an occasional threat to hang a dishonest servant or to cut the throat of a treacherous Englishman. Up to the night of this Carnival Sunday, in spite of considerable provocation, in no single instance has he been seen to kill, or have killed, any individual. After the age of thirty, character does not suddenly change. It is hard to believe that during this week James Hepburn's nature so far altered that in cold blood he planned the atrocious murder of a man with whom he had no quarrel and risked the deaths of half a dozen innocent menials.

If the depositions are accepted, a second psychological contradiction is implied. Bothwell's efficient coups have been in frequent evidence. His unaltering technique has been displayed—mobility, secrecy and economy of effort. Why at the most important moment of his life should his dexterity be replaced by a clumsy routine of "bings" of gunpowder on bedroom floors? No more conspicuous or wasteful way of despatching a single man can be con-

[1] In August, 1565, the town watch consisted at night of thirty-two men, six at the gap in the town wall in Leith Wynd, four at Kirk o' Field Gate, two at the Netherbow Gate and ten perambulating the streets. (Records of Burgh of Edinburgh.)

ceived. The ludicrous scheme did not in fact succeed in killing its victim. The only sensible use in murder for gunpowder must be to destroy a large number of people and, spreading panic, to engineer a revolution. Of neither object has Bothwell ever been accused.

Even if the grotesque idea of putting powder under the King's bed be conceded, the depositions describe every blunder in method that the efficient Borderer could be trusted to avoid. Would a master of secrecy admit a dozen accomplices (the three masked men at Blackfriars Gate must be counted), when a single indiscretion would cost him life and lands? Would he advertise his crime by buying a powder-barrel in the open market, parade it through the streets, and leave it on the scene of action? Could he hope that his deadly freight would escape attention carried through the town on Carnival Sunday or smuggled into a house humming with life? What chance of concealment was there with his name broadcast at various gates before and after the explosion? Was the Bothwell responsible for the Till Valley foray, the All Hallows' Eve raid, the Castle escape, the return from France, the Rizzio recovery—was that successful leader of desperate causes guilty of this string of imbecilities? Surely the untenable position held by the official story of Kirk o' Field must be abandoned and with it the only evidence that convicts Bothwell of a premeditated plot to kill the King.

Some of our objections were felt by the writers of the day. But, as they had already made up their minds on Bothwell's guilt, their attempts to explain away an explosion that did not mark its victims were doomed to absurdity. The King and his valet, say Melville, Pitscottie, Camden, Holinshed, and the authors of the *History of James Sext* and the *Speculum Tragicum*, were strangled in their sleep by the Bothwell gang who gained admission by the use of false keys. They carried the bodies into the garden and proceeded to blow up the house. This improbable version follows the Narrative of the Earl of Lennox, which provides the picturesque detail that the

King was suffocated "with a wet napkin steeped in vinegar." Its ineptitude hardly calls for exposure. Why go to the trouble, expense and risk of introducing gunpowder, when all that was needed was a napkin and some vinegar? Did the clumsy keys and locks of the sixteenth century turn so silently that not one of the seven sleepers in the doomed house was wakened? How heavily must Nelson, Symonds and Taylor's boy have slumbered in the little gallery that opened out of the King's room! They neither heard the approach of sixteen murderers counted by Lennox, nor the performance of the horrid deeds, nor the noise of carrying two corpses downstairs. The gallery which rested on the town wall was saved in the cataclysm, and Nelson could testify that they "never knew anything until the house (room) wherein they lay was fallen about them."[1] Two further actions, unparalleled in the annals of murder for silliness, have to be swallowed. The assassins, it must be supposed, reverently laid the deceased's slippers and dressing-gown beside him before they blew up the house to tell the world they had finished!

It is a relief to emerge from the quicksands of fancy to the refuge of the solid ground of fact. The explanation of the "first known fact" of the total demolition of the house is simple. The gunpowder was never smuggled into the Queen's bedroom; it was introduced into the vaults that the steep slope of the site created in the foundations. Only on this supposition, or on the kindred theory of an underground mine, can the effect of the explosion be explained. The deduction has the support of contemporary opinion.

Simancas 635. On the 19th April Moray told the Spanish Ambassador in London that the King's house had been "entirely

[1] On 22nd February Melville told de Silva that five servants escaped "who only knew that they had heard the noise." The Privy Council version, after mentioning Taylor's death, alludes to "some others that through the ruin of the house were oppressed and some at God's pleasure preserved." In the latter group were Nelson, Symons and Taylor's boy, sleeping in the gallery on the wall. The former included Andrew MacCaig, whose death is recorded in the sentence on Hay and Hepburn. What happened to Glen, the other groom, is not known.

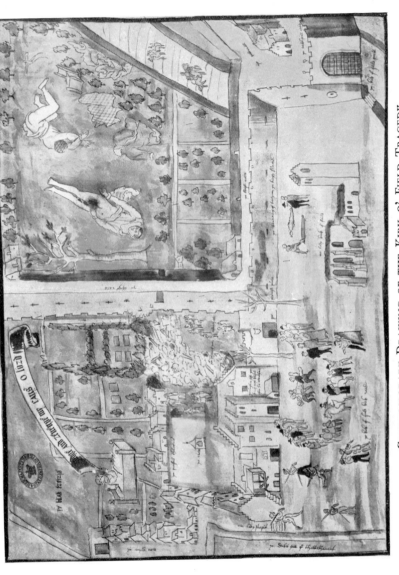

CONTEMPORARY DRAWING OF THE KIRK O' FIELD TRAGEDY

(By courtesy of the Record Office)

undermined." The Frenchman, Clerneau, reported "an underground mine." In the Lennox Narrative Darnley's father described "a place that was already prepared with *undermining and* trains of powder." The italicised words were added in his own handwriting. Dr. Wilson's incautious pamphlet refers to underminers and to undermining the wall. Finally, the death sentence, passed in 1581 on the Earl of Morton for his share in the murder, states that gunpowder was "plasit and imput . . . under the ground and angular stones and within the vaults in laich and darnit (low and secret) pairts and places." The vault theory seems preferable to the land-mine, since digging makes noise and heaps of earth, while nothing could be less conspicuous than to break through a cellar wall of the adjacent new Provost's House and to push explosives into the "laich and darnit pairts" of the King's house. Who made this secret preparation and with what object will shortly be discussed.

To the second fact of the unclad and unmarked corpses in the south garden, valuable details are added by a picture of the tragedy sent to London by one of Cecil's secret agents. This sketch is a literal representation of what the draughtsman (fulfilling the duties of the modern police photographer) saw on the morning after the catastrophe and reproduced as far as his knowledge of perspective permitted. From the sketch may be learnt, that at the time of his murder Darnley was wearing nothing but his night-shirt. He had no shoes on his feet. Taylor wore one shoe and some sort of headgear. Near the valet lay his dagger on its belt, a chair, a quilt (there were two in Darnley's room, a red and a blue), the dressing-gown, and some miscellaneous garments. The doorway into the south garden is marked and opposite it, across the road, the postern gate in the town wall that admitted to the Provost's House.

To a certain point what happened is clear. Something frightened Darnley very badly in the middle of the night. He had barely recovered from a two months' illness; it was two in the morning; it was February; it was pitch dark; there was snow on the ground. Yet the invalid did not stay for clothes to defend his weakened body against the cold, or shoes to protect his feet from the snow. Down the stone stairs he ran, through the back door, through the postern and into the south garden. He had wakened his valet, who followed without understanding what was happening. Unlike the King, he felt no overwhelming fear. He stopped to collect his dagger, his shoes and cap and the various garments which he wanted to keep his eccentric young master warm. He had no idea why he was going, or he would not have carried a heavy oak chair through several doorways and down two flights of narrow, winding stairs.

Darnley in his wild flight from some sudden and uncombatable danger, ran blindly into the south garden. He ran into the waiting arms of men without pity. Strangling, says John Webster, is a very quiet death. But, as will be shown, the boy had a short time to plead for life. He wasted that little breath. The stranglers dropped the body under a tree and caught the valet. . . .

The reports of Edinburgh residents and visitors at the time of the tragedy support this reconstruction, without developing its implications. Sebastian Davelourt says cautiously that on the day the bodies were found a rumour was current that the killing had taken place, not in the house, but in the garden. Moretta, on his arrival in Paris, gave two versions. The first said that Darnley heard the noise of people surrounding the house and trying the doors. He escaped by a gate that led to the garden and was there stifled. The second version substituted a sight of armed men from one window and an escape through another. Flight through a window, this time provoked by the smell of a burning match, was also reported by Sir Roger Ashton, who claimed in his anecdotage to have shared the attempted escape.[1] Bizari, writing the year

Giovanni Correr to the Signory, 20 Mar., 1567. Bishop of Mondovi to Cardinal of Alessandria, 16 Mar., 1567.

[1] Sir William Sanderson (born about twenty years after these events) says that Sir Roger Ashton used to tell this story after he came south with James VI. (Sir Roger was certainly alive in 1603 and attended Raleigh's trial.) He had told his story of Darnley's death so often that he had come to believe he was there himself. Nevertheless, his version contains more likelihood than any other.

314

after the tragedy, says that the King heard the noise of armed men in the house and ran with a page to the cellar. They stayed there a good while until the noise had ceased. They then came out to meet their deaths.

The instrument with which the murder was committed varies in each story and was clearly a matter of guesswork. The victim's own belt, the sleeves of his shirt, his garters, a serviette, a napkin dipped in vinegar, a waxed cord were all with equal certainty propounded. However quiet the method employed, complete silence was not realised. On the authority of the Marshal of Berwick, "the King was long in dying and made debate for his life." The story doubtless was started by "certain women who lodged near the garden and heard him cry, 'Pity me, kinsmen, for the love of Him who pitied all the world.'" *Labanoff vii 108.*

The batch of unofficial stories contains a clear element of truth. The jump from the window indeed has to be given up, since Nelson, Symonds and Taylor's boy slept through everything in the gallery with the window over the south garden. Nor will Moretta's tale of the sight or sound of strangers trying to force an entrance pass muster. Suppose a lantern flashed a beam in east garden or quadrangle, suppose a knife clattered on the stone floor, or a key screeched in a lock, would Darnley not have wakened his half-dozen servants, snatched his weapons and, barring the door, have yelled for help? More valiantly, he might have thrown the chairs downstairs and called his men to help him defend the barricade against assailants who could only approach one by one. Nothing would send him running naked and unarmed into the danger outside.

Suppose the remaining story is true and that he smelt smoke or saw the gleam of fire? Danger from ordinary incendiarism would not stop him taking some protection against the bitter elements. It is significant that Taylor, who would also smell the smoke, did not share the King's blind haste. The sight or smell of burning, which spoke to the King of instant death, conveyed no warning of very pressing peril to the valet. He was more concerned with his master's comfort than his own. As the "picture" shows, he collected shoes, dressing-gown, even a chair for the invalid to sit on.

Only one explanation covers the different conduct of the two men. They woke up and smelt smoke. To the valet smoke meant possibility of a house on fire and time for reasonable preparations. To the King, *if he knew that there was gunpowder in the house*, fire meant sudden death. Without waiting a moment, he bolted for the open country.

There were only two ways by which Darnley could have had this fatal knowledge. He could have been warned by some well-wisher. In that case, as soon as the ominous words reached his brain, he would have given orders to move house. Only one alternative remains. *Darnley knew that there was gunpowder in the house because he had allowed it to be put there.*

Once this logical inference is drawn, the whole story makes sense. Darnley was the Scottish figurehead of the Paris Plot. Queen Mary had failed in the test of catholic zeal to which the legate had submitted her. How could one blow destroy the protestants on Laureo's list and clear the throne for Darnley's Counter Reformation zeal? Gunpowder was the obvious answer. Blow up the Queen and the protestant leaders; in the panic that would follow establish the new regime. This was the conspiracy Mary was warned of. This was the "surprise to be trafficked to her contrar" which the Archbishop's messenger was riding night and day to Edinburgh to expose. When the plot miscarried, when the Provost's House blew up and Darnley died, the Queen was not without her suspicions. *Queen Mary to Archbishop of Glasgow, 11, Feb.* "Whoever has taken this wicked enterprise in hand," she wrote, "we assure ourselves it was dressed as well for us as the King. For we lay the most part of all last week in that same lodging and was there accompanied with the most part of the Lords that are in this town that same night at midnight, and of very chance tarried not all night." Her suspicion was repeated by the Privy Council in

316

the letter to Catherine de Medicis that announces the tragedy. Truth flourishes in the most unlikely soil. In March, 1587, Renauld de Beaulne, Archbishop of Bourges, preached Queen Mary's funeral sermon in Nôtre Dame. In its course he gave this substantially accurate account of the plot: "Being advised that the Queen was coming to visit the King in his house, they (the conspirators) took measures to put there certain powder and engines to blow her up. But the mine went off before they expected and the house fell before this princess had arrived."

The detailed workings of the conspiracy will never be known. Father Hay, whom Laureo had sent to Scotland, was in Edinburgh. He joined Moretta, Laureo's confidant. (Sir Walter Raleigh's dictum is worth remembering: "Savoy from Spain is inseparable.") A convenient catholic tool was available in the unspeakable Sir James Balfour, whose brother owned the buildings at Kirk o' Field. "It is believed for certain," wrote the Spanish *Silva to Philip, 6 Sept., 1567.* Ambassador in London, "that this man was one of the principal actors in the murder of the King," and that opinion persisted until Sir James's death. "Balfour is well known throughout the realm," wrote Hunsdon in 1581, "to be one of the principal murderers." It was he *Drury to Cecil P.R.O. S.P. xii. 207.* who recommended Kirk o' Field for the quarantine; it was he who from one source in Edinburgh bought sixty pounds' worth of gunpowder. Some time on Carnival Sunday (consideration for the nerves of the decoy would leave the operation to the last moment) Balfour's men must have dragged his store of explosives from the cellars of the new Provost's House into the vaults of the old Provost's House. There the gunpowder lay ready to blow up the Queen, who had published her intention of spending the night in her green and yellow bed. Next morning as her lords gathered to escort her back to the palace or to ride with her to Seton, Darnley was to make some excuse to leave the building. His great horses, which had been waiting saddled since five o'clock, would provide a quick escape. One of the features that

317

James Curl
(Queen Mary's
Divorce
Proceedings,
1575.)

recommended Kirk o' Field was the ease by which its tenant could "go into the country by a small door in the court." It was no coincidence that brought his father to Linlithgow, less than twenty miles away. It was no coincidence that Kerr of Fawdonside was waiting in the

Drury to
Cecil, 13 Aug.,
1575. Nau.
History of
Mary Stewart.

fields. (Most brutal of the Rizzio murderers, he had lately boasted that there would soon be a change at Court which would bring him back to favour. He made his meaning manifest by asking ironically after the Queen's health.)

Some one would have to give a signal, as soon as Darnley was clear of the house. Some one else (was it Captain James Cullen, afterwards arrested and tortured, whose enlightening statement was promptly suppressed?) —some one would have to light the fuse. In a few moments Laureo's hopes and Darnley's ambitions stood to be realised in an explosion that would have shaken Europe.

The failure of the scheme must be attributed to Darnley's indiscretion. "He was," said Morton, an expert in secrecy, "sic a bairn that there was nothing told him, but he would reveal it." He told everything, repeats Melville, to his servants, "who were not all honest." One of them, Sandy Durham, went to considerable lengths

Dr. Wilson's
Actio.

to escape from the doomed house. There is a story that he set fire to his bedding to get himself discharged, an effective protest in a house full of gunpowder. As Sandy had a connection with the Hepburns,[1] it may well have been he who passed on the warning. Moray and Lethington, despite Moretta's blandishments, absented themselves. Without them half the point of the explosion was gone. Darnley perhaps decided to wait for a more favourable chance. But the gunpowder was in position.

The warning whisper did its work. On the Sunday morning Moray cleared out, leaving his sister to her fate.

Blackwood 30
Caussin
(Jebb ii. 68).

Scandal quoted his remark as he crossed the Forth, that the night would see Darnley cured of all his troubles.

---

[1] Sandy Durham seems to have been the son of Alexander Durham, the Queen's silversmith. Another son, James, silversmith to James VI, married Margaret Hepburn, illegitimate daughter of Patrick, the Fair Earl. (Exchq. Rolls xxi. 548, 366.)

Lethington stayed in Edinburgh but avoided Kirk o' Field. He had sufficient gratitude to his mistress to advise a change in her plans and a bed in the palace. That is the tale Sebastien Pagez told at Dieppe. There was even a story one would like to believe, that Darnley wavered in his villainy and warned his wife to guard against people who were urging him to attempt her life. In any case she remembered Bastien's wedding masque and escaped from the doomed house.

Cockburn to Cecil, 19 March, 1567.

Nau 34.

Safe at Holyrood, she sent for Bothwell and John Stewart of Traquair. These two men commanded her bodyguard, Bothwell the horse and Traquair the foot. For a long time she discussed the vague warning she had received. It seems that Bothwell did not believe it. He went back to his quarters and began to go to bed. This statement has the authority of Geordie Dalgleish's dying confession, which conflicts with the deposition put into his mouth. "As God shall be my judge," he protested before his execution. "I knew nothing of the King's death before it was done. For my Lord Bothwell *going to his bed* (after the taking off of his hose, which was trimmed with velvet), French Paris came and rounded with him and thereafter he tarried on me for other hose and clothes and his riding cloak and sword, which I gave him." Paris was clearly the bearer of fresh tidings which put a more serious complexion on Maitland's warning. Bothwell, in his working clothes, went to discover the truth. With nothing to conceal, he gave his name at the various gates. He went up the Canongate, says Dalgleish, and called for Black Ormiston at his rooms. The unforeseen visit accounts for the laird's negligé (he was "going belted in a gown") and his uncle Hob's ignorance. John Hay was sleeping at John Hepburn's and, though Dalgleish does not mention it, their feudal superior no doubt enlisted their support. Wilson and Powrie may well have been taken on what looked like a dangerous errand.

Bishop of Mondovi to Cardinal of Alessandria, 23 Aug., 1566.

At Kirk o' Field, the present writer believes, Bothwell met Sir James Balfour. It is certain one of the brothers Balfour was noticed at the foot of Thraples Wynd near the

John Binning's statement.

scene of the tragedy. Bothwell's appearance in the middle of the night told Sir James the game was up. His victim had escaped. With his unerring instinct to join the winning side, he ratted. He told the man to whom loyalty was a creed of the King's supreme treachery. Bothwell, it is easy to guess, would not credit his words. "See for yourself!" and Balfour gave him the cellar key.

The Provost's House keys were divided, so one of the servants testified, into three lots. The keys of the Queen's bedroom and the east door into the east garden were kept by the Queen's servants. Bonkil, the cook, had the cellar door key, and the King's men looked after the rest. Bonkil, it appears, was not one of the King's servants but "went with the house." That fits with Black Ormiston's statement that the keys which admitted him and his friends were "given by him that owned the house." Balfour gave Bothwell, if this theory is right, the key that his brother's servant kept in his pocket.

Outraged, incredulous, Bothwell let himself into the basement. The contents of the vaults showed him Sir James spoke truth. The sight was too much for his indignant and bitter humour. If the treacherous, disease-ridden boy upstairs wanted an explosion, he should have one. . . .

The intruder took, it seems, no precautions for secrecy. Either the noise he made or the smell of the burning fuse awakened Darnley. It is possible that Bothwell wanted to give the household a chance.

The terrified youth dashed half-naked down the stairs. The draught from the open cellar door blew cold on his legs and pointed the way to the readiest escape. Across the little backyard he ran, through the postern door and into the south garden, to put two walls between him and the explosion he knew would come. Just as he believed himself safe, a grim circle closed on him in the darkness.

His murderers were, almost certainly, the Douglases. The few facts that have not been suppressed in the four trials of members and supporters of that family convict them. In June, 1581, the Earl of Morton was found guilty of counselling and concealing the King's murder and being "art and part" in it. "At these last words he shewed himself much grieved and beating the ground once or twice with a little staff he carried in his hand, said, 'Art and part! God knoweth the contrary!'" He confessed that his cousin, Archibald Douglas, came to him with a plan for the murder, to which he neither lent approval nor help. He admitted that he did not try to dissuade his relative and disclosed that "Mr. Archibald, after the deed was done, showed to me that he was at the deed doing and came to Kirk o' Field yard (garden) with the Earls of Bothwell and Huntly." As one of Mr. Archibald's "pantables" or slippers had been found "at the house end," the parson's active co-operation seems certain. Morton, as head of the family, knew all about the assassination, but his indignation at being accused of direct participation when he was really at St. Andrews, rings true. *Spottiswood 313. Bannatyne's Memorials. Forster to Walsingham 4 June, 1581.*

It did not save him. Soon he was lying on his face under the shadow of a guillotine of his own invention, "his body making great rebounding with sighs and sobs which are evident signs of the inward and mighty working of the Spirit of God." After the blade had fallen they left him till eight o'clock in the evening, covered with an old blue cloak, "not one appearing upon the place to shew his gratitude for some good office past or to express the least sign of mourning for his misfortune." *Crawford's Chancellors 116.*

The same year John Binning, servant to Archibald Douglas, came to a less distinguished end on the gallows at the Market Cross of Edinburgh. The details of his trial have conveniently disappeared. In his attempt to save his skin, he testified that his master was guilty "art and part" of the crime and did actually devise and perpetrate it. After supper Douglas, he declared, wearing secret armour and a steel helmet, took him and a fellow servant by the back door of his house to the murder in the garden. *Arnot 7-20.*

The next to face a jury was George Home of Sprott, another Douglas man. He was tried in 1582 on a charge of complicity before and after the crime, "knowing perfectly that Mr. Archibald Douglas and the late John Binning, his servant, were actually at the committing." More fortunate than his predecessors in the dock, the Laird of Sprott was acquitted.

At last in 1586 Archibald Douglas was brought to book. His trial comes up to the best American standards. Of the jury of nineteen, ten did not answer their names. The reasons for their absence were no doubt prudent. They were replaced by ten persons "who happened to be at the bar." Among them, by one of those lucky chances, was the Laird of Sprott!

The prosecution produced the depositions of James Ormiston, John Hay and French Paris, none of which, in its present form, makes any allusion to the accused. Binning's statement was also produced. No witnesses dared to appear. The reverend gentleman, for his defence, denied losing his "mules" at Kirk o' Field and said that the road between his house and the scene of the murder was not fit for a man in armour to walk in velvet slippers. He also pointed out some apparent contradictions in the times of Binning's story. The impartial tribunal arrived unanimously at an ingenious verdict, which it is pleasant to endorse. It declared Douglas "clean and acquit *of being in company* with Bothwell, Ormiston, Hay and Hepburn in committing the crime." When the detail is remembered that the dying boy was heard to cry "Pity me, *kinsmen!*" and that his mother was born a Douglas, the case against the family seems complete.[1]

[1] In 1571 the Primate of Scotland, John Hamilton, was hanged in his episcopal robes at the Market Cross of Stirling for complicity in the murder. He protested throughout "that he was so innocent that he would not ask God's mercy therefore." There is small reason to doubt his word. Buchanan tells the story of the light burning in the window of Hamilton House and put out after the explosion. A priest called Thomas Robinson asserted that one John Hamilton, known as "Black John," confessed on his death-bed that he had been present at the murder by the Archbishop's orders. There is no other evidence to implicate the Hamiltons. Two epitaphs of the Archbishop are worth quoting. The first was pinned on his gibbet: "Cresce diu, felix arbor, semperque vireto fraudibus, ut nobis talia poma feras." The other comes from the tolerant pages of Archbishop Spottiswood: "He was a man of great action, wise and not unlearned, but in life somewhat dissolute." That this was not an overstatement, his six children by "this harlot Sempill, neither beautiful, of gude form, or otherwise in any sort notable," bear witness.

At what stage of these complicated intrigues did Douglas receive his commission to remove the double traitor? Or did the cleric act out of his natural enthusiasm for murder? It is impossible to say. Perhaps Moray and Lethington, warned of Darnley's gunpowder, sent word to the party bravo to be ready. Douglas House was a few hundred yards from the tragic site. He may, as Morton stated, have walked with Bothwell to the scene of action. All that is reasonably certain is that Darnley bolted out of the house into his arms.

The King was dead before the house blew up. The depositions probably told the truth about the quarter of an hour that the fuse took to burn. A little-known document throws a some light on what happened in the east garden, while Douglas was finishing his work in the south. An old acquaintance, Cuthbert Ramsay, tells the anecdote. It must be remembered he had no reason to love Bothwell. He paid a visit, he relates, to the prison where John Hepburn, John Hay and the servants were awaiting execution. "From them he heard both in prison and on the scaffold that the author of the murder was the Earl Bothwell. One of them, by name John Hepburn, told the witness in prison that if he had not stopped the Earl Bothwell, he would have been smothered under the house in which the King had his lodging. For the train of gunpowder which had been made to blow up the house did not burn as quickly as the Earl thought it should. He therefore took John Hepburn near the house. Suddenly the train took fire. When he saw that, he threw the Earl back to prevent the house falling on him." *Proceedings and Evidence in action of Divorce, 22 Sept., 1575.*

This bit of evidence, which is quite independent of the depositions, makes it clear that Bothwell, disgusted by Darnley's treachery, fired the fuse. It also provides him with an alibi for the period when the King, scared out of the house by the smell of burning, was being murdered.

CHAPTER TWENTY-NINE

THAT moment of uncontrolled disgust set Bothwell's feet on a slope that hurried him faster and faster to ruin. Fight as he would to recover his balance, some force toppled him, struggling, down the hill of infamy. Each desperate expedient spun him lower. The man, who for all his failings was almost the only humane and honourable Scotsman in the history of his day, had let himself sink momentarily to the level of the brutality that surrounded him. From the consequences of his lapse, his enemies, his environment, possibly his conscience never let him escape. A modern poet might have had Bothwell's story in mind when he wrote

> Of two that loved—or did not love—and one
> Whose perplexed heart did evil, foolishly,
> A long while since.

At first Bothwell had little time for remorse. As Sheriff of Edinburgh, it was his duty to lead a party of soldiers from Holyrood to the scene of the crime to look for the assassins. Finding no one to arrest, he had the King's body carried to the new Provost's House and placed in the care of Sandy Durham, the dead man's servant. Surgeons came to inspect and members of the Council, nor does Sandy seem to have excluded the general public. In due course, the body was carried on a board to Holyrood by four "pioneers." It was embalmed by an apothecary and a surgeon at a cost of £42 6s. 0d., and lay in State for several days. Mary, as she gazed on her husband's body, gave no "outward show or sign of joy or sorrow." Her feelings are difficult to guess. Though she knew something of the dead boy's treachery, he had been her husband and once she had loved him dearly.

Karl Pearson
37.

324

Bothwell's word that she was "sorrowful and quiet" may be accepted. Without divulging his own movements that fatal morning he could not tell her the truth about the *cache* of gunpowder. Let us hope he found a better explanation than he gave Sir James Melville. "The strangest accident," he vowed, "had fallen out that ever was; for thunder had come out of the sky and had burnt the King's house."

The undamaged state of the body aroused his wonder. He remarked on it to Sir James and, fumbling after the truth, sought young Hay's reassurance. "What thought you," he asked, "when you saw him blown in the air?" His accomplice could throw no light. The King "was handled by no man's hands as he saw." Puzzled, the Earl told his retainers "to keep their tongues close and they should never want so long as he had." To Hay he gave a brown horse and to John Hepburn a white. The servants, he promised, should go to the Hermitage and be "honestly sustained."

Official investigations were on foot. The same morning the Privy Council, with Bothwell among them, met at the Tolbooth under the presidency of Argyll, Lord Justice of Scotland. A letter was dictated to the French Court, breaking the news. Next a board of inquiry was set up. Argyll sat, and William Murray of Tullibardine to represent Lennox interests, and Bothwell. Bothwell had searched the ruins and discovered a powder-barrel "which we kept, after noting the brand on it," but it is not stated that he divulged this important evidence.[1] *Les Affaires du Comte de Boduel 13.*

Neighbours gave their recollection of the fatal night. Barbara Martin had "heard" thirteen men go towards Kirk o' Field before the "crack" and eleven come back, two of whom wore "clear things." May Crockit was sleeping between her two bairns "when the crack raised." Running to the door in her "sark allane," she saw eleven

---

[1] The people who took the four depositions knew of the existence of this incriminating evidence. That is why they dragged in the improbable story of the barrel that Hay's man could carry about the town, but which was so vast that it would not pass the door of the Provost's House.

men come out of the Blackfriars Gate. She "clekkit ane" by his silk cloak, but he would not answer. Barbara's and May's sight (or hearing) seems to have been very acute to let them count so accurately on so dark a night. The survivors of the explosion repeated their stories and answered questions about the keys of the doomed house, until Tullibardine thought he saw ground to suspect the Queen's servants.

But neither Tullibardine nor Bothwell wanted truth to emerge and the inquiry produced no useful result. The Queen tried again and offered a reward of £2000 with "an honest yearly rent" and a free pardon to any informer. On the day after the murder she had written to her father-in-law promising justice, and inviting him to Edinburgh to take part in proceedings. Lennox's conscience was bad. Deeply involved in the Paris Plot, he could not tell how much the Queen knew. After a week's silence, he asked for that traditional *lucus a non lucendo*, a Parliamentary inquiry.

Diary of Events. Drury to Cecil, 19 Feb., 1567.

Lennox to Queen Mary, 20 Feb., 1567.

The Queen wrote back that Parliament was already summoned and its session would "leave nothing undone which may further the clear trial." She wrote from Seton. Her first instinct had been to seek the safety of Edinburgh Castle, but when no rising followed the night of Kirk o' Field, she obeyed the advice of her doctors to move to the country. At Holyrood House she left Bothwell and Huntly to guard the infant prince.

She had had the body of her husband carried by torchlight to what she hoped would be its last rest beside her father. (A later democratic enthusiasm dispersed the bones about auction-room and collector's cabinet.) No sooner was Darnley buried than the murdered boy, his unpopularity forgotten, became the hero of an artfully engineered agitation. A week after the explosion a placard was pinned by night to the Tolbooth door. The anonymous author declared that, encouraged by the two thousand pound reward for information about the murder, he had "made inquisition by them that were the doers thereof." His researches put him in a position

326

to "affirm that the committers of it were the Earl Bothwell, Mr. James Balfour, Mr. David Chalmers, black
Mr. John Spens, who was the principal deviser of the
murder, and the Queen assenting thereto, through the
persuasion of the Earl of Bothwell and the witchcraft
of the Lady Buccleugh. And if this be not true," the
notice ended, "speir at Gilbert Balfour."

Anonymous libel by placard was common on the
Continent, and James Murray of Purdovis, Bothwell's old
defamer, applied his experience of the practice to divert
attention from the real plotters. Adroitly mixing fact
with fancy, he used the guilty Balfours to incriminate
innocent Hepburn adherents. Black Mr. John Spens, for
all his forbidding nickname, was, as Knox testifies, "a
man of gentle nature and one that professed the doctrine
of the Evangel," whom nothing but James Murray's
random accusation ever connected with the murder. No
formal charge was subsequently lodged against Chalmers,
and Janet Beton's sorceries can have had small scope at
Kirk o' Field.

Within two nights a second poster appeared accusing
three members of the royal household, Sebastien Pagez,
Signor Francisco (Busso) and Joseph Rizzio, brother of
the late secretary. The informer offered to give his name
if the expected reward was lodged in neutral hands. All
that month an intensive libel campaign was waged.
Portraits of Bothwell with the headline, "Here is the
Murderer!" were dropped in the streets. Voices in the
darkness proclaimed his guilt. Bills were stuck on the
Tron and the Market Cross, on church doors, on city
gates, even on the portals of the palace. Some of them
announced a confession by the smith who made the false
keys; some were pictorial. The letters *M.R.* "in a roman
hand very great" surmounted an arm that brandished a
sword; *L.B.* was written, perplexingly, over a mallet.
One poster depicted the Queen as a mermaid and Bothwell
as a hare. This symbolism somehow gave a clue to the
author. "The Queen sent for the minister of Dunferm- *Drury to*
line and asked him if he knew the deviser of the *Cecil, 29*
March, 1567.

327

mermaid." In spite of the cleric's denial, Bothwell asked whether James Murray had not spoken evil of him. The dour reply came back that "he had never heard him say well."

Buchanan's Detectio.

A comparatively small number of people were able to paint mermaids or hares and a process of elimination produced evidence to convict James Murray. On the 14th March the Privy Council ordered his arrest for sticking "certain painted papers" on the Tolbooth door, tending to the Queen's slander and defamation. When the time came, the accused was not to be found, though he wrote from a place of safety offering to bring half a dozen men to support his charges, "either armed or naked."

P.C. Reg. i. 500.

From the pulpits denunciation began to rumble. Hepburn nerves were set on edge. Bothwell muttered that he would wash his hands in the blood of the bill-stickers—if he could catch them. A bodyguard of fifty never left his side. His hand went to his dagger when any one he did not know stopped him.

Drury to Cecil, 28 Feb., 1567.
19 April, 1567.

Sir James Balfour took the publicity no less to heart. He left town soon after the first placard was posted. When he came back, thirty horsemen rode with him. Even so he dismounted outside the walls and went to his house "by a secret way." He set a guard on his house day and night, and the story ran that he had killed one of his servants lest the weakling, moved "either by remorse or conscience or other folly," should let out something "that might trend to the whole discovery of the King's death."

"Conscience or other folly" was not the only fury that watched the pillow of the Earl of Bothwell. There was his chronic shortage of cash. In February he had to sell more land, this time to Alexander Home. If he was ever granted the superiority of Leith, the honour can have carried no pecuniary advantage.

Drury to Cecil, 28 Feb., 1567.

His wife's health, too, was a source of worry. Lady Jean had been ill since the beginning of February, and by the end of the month her life was despaired of. Her

328

death by poison was naturally announced in diplomatic circles. If she had not made a complete recovery and lived for sixty-two more years, a further crime would certainly have been added to the Bothwell calendar. Still, when the doctors gave up hope, it may not be unfair to guess that the husband's mind turned towards another, more splendid alliance. With Lady Jean in heaven, could not the family tradition to be kind to widow queens be revived? James Hepburn knew himself a better man than Leicester, whom Amy Robsart's convenient death had freed to aspire to the hand of the Queen of England. . . . the contemptible Darnley had won the Queen of Scots . . . then Jean began to mend, and the dream was put aside. But James cannot have been entirely discreet, for by the end of March a story reached the English Ambassador in Paris of a marriage hatching between Mary and the potential widower.

Giovanni Correr to Signory, 30 March, 1567.

Bothwell was probably at Seton—there is a shocked story of a February archery match with the widow Queen, Huntly and Seton, and even "of exercising one day right openly in the fields with 'goif'"—when a further letter arrived from Lennox. By now Mary's father-in-law felt it safe to take a firmer line and press for an immediate inquiry without waiting for Parliament to assemble. He even urged the arrest of everybody named by the placards. These demands puzzled Mary and irritated Bothwell's jangled nerves. They did not know that the protestant leaders were joining forces with Lennox's catholics. Moray, Morton and Lindsay, ardent Reformers, held a secret meeting with the catholic Earls of Caithness and Atholl at Dunkeld. From there Moray, accompanied by Argyll and Atholl, seems to have gone on to see Lennox. Their talk has not been recorded, but their aim clearly was to exploit the death of Darnley to ruin Bothwell, and through him the Queen. Henceforward Maitland's brain supplied the ingenuity that Lennox lacked, while Kirkaldy of Grange joined James Murray in organising the publicity campaign. Nor was Cecil inactive. Soon Bedford had his orders to approach any one disposed

Drury to Cecil, 28 Feb., 1567.

Silva to K. Philip, 8 March, 1567.

Mondovi to Cardinal of Alessandria, 16 Mar., 1567.

*Pembroke to
Bedford, 8
April, 1567.*

"to stand fast for the maintenance of God's honour and for
the punishment of the late murder," and to circularise all
Border notables "who seem to mislike Bothwell's greatness." So confident were the associates that, by the middle
of March, the Justice Clerk was telling Sir John Forster

*Forster to
Cecil, 16
March, 1567.*

"never to give him trust in time coming if Bothwell and
his complices gave not their lives ere midsummer."

However determined Moray might be to "maintain
God's honour and to punish the late murder," his indignation did not prevent him seeking the murderer's
company. On the 8th March an Englishman was granted
an audience by the Queen, who had returned for that
purpose from Seton, still wearing the mourning that
had cost £143. Before his admission to her conventionally

*Hay Fleming,
442, 507.*

darkened room, a dinner was given in his honour by
Moray, at which the confederates sat beside the man
they had sworn to hang. In spite of their geniality, some
warning reached Bothwell's sensitive nerves. Action
followed as promptly as usual, but an ever-present sense
of guilt obscured his judgment. He took five steps of
varying importance. Each step was attended by failure
or disaster.

His first wish was to stop the placards, and his failure
to catch James Murray has been described. His next move
was patriotic and humane, but ruinous to his interests.
As the clouds gathered on the horizon, he decided the
infant prince must be sent somewhere safe. Custom
dictated Stirling and the care of the Earl of Mar. Born
before the days of the democratic press, Bothwell did not
understand the propaganda value of royal infancy. There
is less excuse for his failure to guess the use that could
be made of the heir as an alternative figurehead to the
mother.

Even so he need not have made the blunder of estrang-
ing the nobleman into whose hands he had delivered this
precious pawn. Mar was governor of Edinburgh Castle.[1]

---

[1] For the facts about the governorship of the castle see: Silva to King
Philip, 7 Ap., 1567; Mondovi to Cardinal of Alessandria, 8 Ap., 1567; Acts
of Parliaments of Scotland ii. 547; Royal Wardrobes and Jewels, 175, 176.

Bothwell, as a soldier, recognised the vital importance of the fortress, which dominated the capital and directed the loyalty of the citizens. Its walls mounted most of the artillery of the realm, and the value of guns was one of Bothwell's tenets. With ordnance, stores, and the royal treasure it was an important repository. Bothwell thought that military considerations demanded that this key position should be held by his nominee. Mar was removed to the command of Stirling, and Edinburgh Castle was given to Sir James Cockburn. The prince's guardian never forgave the change. His indignation was fanned by his wife, Annabella, "a malevolent woman" and sister of James Murray. When the time was ripe, Mar joined Bothwell's open enemies. In the troubles of the reign he had hitherto held himself neutral and his decision gave a lead to the moderate elements. Even then, if Bothwell had left the Castle in the safe hands of Sir James Cockburn, the strategic gain might have outweighed the political loss. But, as will be seen, it was allowed to pass into less reliable hands.

Bothwell's most ruinous decision was also his boldest. Lady Jean had recovered. There was now no question of a widower achieving a royal marriage. But the vision would not fade. His fatal aspirations have inspired the pen of Shakespeare, who

> Heard a *Mermaid* on a *Dolphin's* back
> Uttering such dulcet and harmonious breath,
> That the rude *Seas* grew civil at her song
> And certain *Stars* shot madly from their spheres
> To hear the sea maid's music.[1]

Bothwell, whatever Shakespeare believed, was not fascinated by Mary. He had known her and served her too long. She had none of the warmth of temperament he demanded in a woman. It was the protection a queen could give a husband that attracted him. The memory of

[1] If a key is needed, the Mermaid is, of course, Mary, and the Dolphin, Francis II. The rude Seas are the Scottish commons or Reformers, while Bothwell is the presumptuous Star.

the night at Kirk o' Field, the nerve-fraying attacks, Lennox's untiring pursuit, the new combination to destroy him, all made safety and peace seem the most desirable ends he could attain. As the Queen's consort he believed he could laugh at his enemies, his fears, at the twinges of his conscience. Before the month was out, word went round that a divorce was to be arranged; that Jean's brother, Huntly, had given his consent; that Janet Beton, now in her ever-green fifties, would be cited as co-respondent. Gossip did not stop with the divorce; "the judgment of the people" held that the Earl would marry the Queen.

Drury to Cecil, 29, 30 March, 1567.

Before the audacious opportunism that James Hepburn had developed could soar so high, liberal application of whitewash was needed. With Hepburn of Bolton plucking his sleeve to whisper, "What devil is this, my Lord, that every one suspects you and cries a vengeance?" —with nocturnal voices in the streets calling down the punishment of heaven, the divorcee could hardly raise his eyes to the highest lady in the land. But Bothwell was never at a loss. Why not a public trial and a triumphant acquittal?

Mary's answers to Lennox grew more definite. She dropped her objection to the inconsistency of the placards "so different and contrarious in counting of the names." On the 23rd March she promised that the eight accused, with Bothwell at their head, that week should stand their trial. Five days later her Council was presented with "the humble desire" of Lord Bothwell, appearing in person, "to underlie the trial according to the laws of the realm." Statute imposed a fifteen days' notice and the hearing could not be fixed before the 12th April. Heralds rode to the market crosses of Edinburgh, Glasgow, Dumbarton and Perth summoning Lennox to appear at the Tolbooth to prosecute.

Queen Mary to Lennox, 1 March, 1567.

P.C. Reg. i. 504.

It was Holy Week, and the memory of Darnley hung heavy at Court. Forty days after his strangling there was "a solemn Mass with a dirge sung in the Chapel Royal for the said Henry Stewart and his soul by the

Birrel's Diary.

papists at her Majesty's command." Was it for this *Inventories xiv, xxvi,* 53, 175. commemoration that a bed was made for the dead king out of cloth of gold, reputed cut from the pavilions that Edward of England abandoned on the field of Bannockburn? The precious stuff, figured with white, red and yellow, had been sewn into ecclesiastical vestments; but the Queen thought the occasion solemn enough to take from her store a cope, a chasuble and four tunicles. "Three of the fairest" pieces she gave for some special purpose to Bothwell. With the rest and with cloth of silver and crimson velvet, enriched with great embroidered flowers, she furnished the memorial bed. Perhaps it was by its side that she passed the hours between *Drury to Cecil, 29 March, 1567.* eleven at night and three on Good Friday morning on her knees in prayer.

Bothwell, who knew the truth about the man thus commemorated, must have felt a spasm of impatience as he made preparations to secure vindication for his murder. He had learned the routine from Moray two years earlier, and began to fill the town with supporters. Soon he could count four thousand men. In Glasgow Lennox was proceeding on the same theory of the violability of justice. He raised three thousand men and led them to Linlithgow. There he was met by the Queen's orders to proceed to the Court of Justice with the number of attendants prescribed by law. As that number was six, his prompt return to Stirling can be understood. From that town he wrote to the Queen, pleading illness and asking for a postponement. Whereas he had before urged haste, he now protested that sufficient time had not been allowed to prepare a case. He demanded the arrest of the accused and their detention in prison until he was ready.

He saw the hand of Bothwell everywhere. He knew that the distracted little Queen left everything to the man who had saved her life. He guessed whose idea had forced him to leave his Lennox men at Linlithgow. Edinburgh, he heard, bristled with Hepburn spears. The jury, he supposed, would be recruited from Hepburn and related families. The common belief, however, that the jury was packed is not well-founded. Whether Bothwell felt that even an impartial panel would see reason when it was pointed out by four thousand pikes, or whether he had some childlike faith that his essential innocence would prevail once an uninterrupted hearing had been assured, it cannot be disputed that two-thirds of those who sat in judgment were his active enemies.

The four assessors—Robert Pitcairn ("a filthie, adulterous whoremaister, wha kept all his life ane other mannes wife"), James MacGill ("*un subtil chicaneur*"), the "blockish and brutish" Lindsay, and Henry Balnaves, Mary of Lorraine's old opponent—were all prominent in the anglophile, anti-Bothwell ranks. The Lord Justice Argyll was no friend of Bothwell's. In the jury Rothes and Boyd had opposed him in 1565; Sempill and Forbes were to fight him at Carberry Hill; Herries had quarrelled with him; Lord John Hamilton was Arran's brother; Caithness was in league with Moray; and Ogilvie of Boyne can have nourished no kindly feeling for the man who was planning to divorce his old sweetheart. Only seven members of the jury are left who can be called neutral or, like Langton, favourable to the accused. Buchanan's vivid phrase, "there sat the judges, not chosen to judge, but picked out to acquit," has dazzled the eyes of historians.

If Lennox was anxious about the issue of the trial, he found small cause for confidence in the movements of his new ally, the Earl of Moray. That astute politician, after making his will and appointing his half-sister principal executor "to see all things handled and ruled for the weel of his daughter," felt the call of foreign travel. On the 9th April he left for France, via London, where he gave authoritative news of Bothwell's divorce plans. His tortuous schemes were in order; his victims were playing into his hands. It was his cautious habit to be absent in body while his instructions were carried out. He liked to appear, an impeccable *deus ex machina*, a few days after his catspaws had done their nefarious work.

But the monkey who handled the chestnuts, in this case represented by the Earl of Lennox, must sometimes have had an anxious moment.

In England, too, a lively interest was taken in the trial.

At six o'clock on the morning of the appointed day, John Selby, Provost Marshal of Berwick, arrived at the gates of Holyrood House with a letter from the Queen of England. Not unnaturally he was told that Mary was asleep. He walked the crowded streets of Edinburgh until nine or ten, when he saw the Hepburns tightening their girths. He tried to enter the courtyard of the Palace, but word had gone round that his errand was to get the trial postponed, and the mob of men and horses would not let him pass. No one would even take charge of his letter. At last word came from the Earl of Bothwell in the palace. He had deputed his cousin, Thomas Hepburn, parson of Oldhamstocks, to advise Selby to wait till the trial was over, as the Queen was unable to attend to business. The parson probably exceeded his instructions by threatening to hang the guide who had brought the Englishman to the palace at so inconvenient a moment. A thought struck the Laird of Skirling as he marked Selby's impatience. Was the letter he sought to deliver addressed by the hand of the Queen of England or by her Council? He learnt that the former was the august source. Punctilious where royalty was concerned, Skirling went to tell his patron. At that moment Bothwell, accompanied by Lethington, appeared in the door. The waiting lairds and gentlemen jumped to their horses. But the Secretary beckoned Selby, asked for the letter and took it into the palace. For half an hour the body-guard waited in the saddle. At last the Secretary returned, avoiding the Englishman's eye. John Selby pushed his way through the crowd and demanded an answer. The Queen, he was told, was still asleep; it was doubtful if there would be an answer before the trial.

Whether the letter had been allowed to reach Mary is uncertain, but a few minutes later she was awake, stand-

335

ing with Mary Fleming at a window to see Bothwell mount. In the saddle he looked up and was rewarded with a friendly nod. Between Morton and Lethington he rode up the crowded Canongate. "A merry and lusty cheer" broke from his lips to hearten the thousands of supporters who trotted behind him. A couple of hundred hagbutters from the Castle brought up the rear of the procession.

They reached the Tolbooth before noon and the hagbutters were posted to keep the doors. The session of the Court lasted till seven at night. The jury was sworn and the indictment of the Earl was read "for art and part of the cruel, odious, treasonable and abominable slaughter of the late, the right excellent, right high and mighty prince, the King's Grace, dearest spouse for the time to our sovereign lady the Queen's Majesty, under silence of night in his own lodging beside the Kirk o' Field, he taking the night's rest."

The accused entered his formal appearance and denied the charges. He proceeded to appoint his counsel. A question of the rival jurisdiction of the Constable of Scotland and the Lord Justice was disposed of. Bothwell stood at the Bar, "looking down and sad-like." The moment of exultation had passed. A glance at the thin face of Lethington, who had ridden at his shoulder up the Canongate, at Morton's cruel little eyes, assured him these men would sacrifice him the minute it suited. In his mind's eye he could see the motionless, half-naked figure under the pear tree in the south garden. The seconds seemed to pass as slowly as when he waited outside the Provost's House for the lunt to burn. . . . He felt a hand on his cloak. Looking round, he met James Ormiston's anxious frown.

"Fie, my Lord, what devil is this ye are doing?" whispered the Black Laird. "Your face shows what you are! Hold up your head for God's sake and look blithely; you might look so an you were going to the deed!"

Bothwell did not answer.

"Alas!" growled Ormiston, "and woe worth them that ever devised it; I trow it shall gar us all mourn."

His patron woke from his depression.

"Hold your tongue!" he muttered, "I would not yet it were to do. I have one out-gate from it, come as may, and that ye shall shortly know."

His mind had shifted to his marriage plans; to win the Queen he must nerve himself for the strain of this trial.

The Court officials were shouting the name of Matthew, Earl of Lennox. Somebody stood up, a paper in his hand. There was a silence while he disclosed his identity as Robert Cunningham, servant to Lennox. He began to read.

"My Lords, I am come here, sent by my master to declare the cause of his absence. The shortness of time, and that he is denied of his friends which should have accompanied him to his honour and surety of his life..." The voice droned on, demanding a postponement for forty days to collect evidence. If the Court insisted on hearing the case at once, an acquittal would convict the jury of "wilful error and not ignorance."[1] Before he sat down Cunningham produced copies of the correspondence between Lennox and the Queen.

These letters, the Lord Justice did not fail to point out, requested summary action. Bothwell's counsel joined in demanding immediate hearing, and the Court, after the assessors' opinion had been taken, ruled that the case should proceed.

Nobody appeared to swear to the truth of the indictment. No "verification or testification" was brought to support its charges. The jury, with Caithness as their foreman, withdrew and "after long reasoning" came to a unanimous verdict. They voted, delivered and acquitted the said James Earl Bothwell of art and part of the said slaughter of the King. Their finding, which has been

[1] If a party in a Scottish case of this date protested "wilful error" the jury became liable to pains and penalties, should their verdict not afterwards be upheld. Caithness subsequently appeared before Parliament to represent this jury and succeeded in obtaining that they should "incur no strait or danger in their lives, lands or goods in respect of the protestation made the time they were on the assize."

held up to the derision of history, was justified by the total absence of evidence on which they could convict.

As soon as the Court had risen, Bothwell listened to the prosecution's entreaty that he would take no revenge, and typically made no attempt to hurt Cunningham. Lennox issued a rather dismal broadsheet about the jury:

> And other silly simple lords,
> Who fear their hanging into cords,
> God is not glee'd though him you clenge, (acquit)
> Believe me, well he will revenge
> The slaughter of that innocent lamb . . .

The lamb's father then decided on the better part of valour and took ship down the west coast to join his wife in England.

The load lifted from Bothwell's spirits. With something of his old *verve* he sent a crier round the town and stuck bills sealed with his arms on the gates, on the Tolbooth door and other noticeable places, offering to defend his innocence with his body against any man of good fame, a gentleman born, who cared to charge him with the murder. Feeling in the vein, he sent a challenge to Drury, the Berwick Marshal, daring him to prove by the law of arms certain words he had spoken two years before. The allusion was no doubt to the scandal that Dandie Pringle had started in the spring of 1565.

Val Browne to Cecil, 16 May, 1567.

But times were changing. Challenges, once an usage of high chivalry and as such still precious to Bothwell's feudal heart, could be degraded to serve as instruments of propaganda. James Murray and Sir William Kirkaldy were not slow to see their chance. The next night an anonymous "acceptance" was posted. Its author offered to prove by the law of arms that Bothwell was the "chief and author of the foul and horrible murder." Let the sovereigns of France or England appoint a place in their dominions for the contest!

338

SIR WILLIAM DRURY, MARSHAL OF BERWICK
(*By permission of the National Portrait Gallery*)

A second placard extended the meeting ground to Scotland; a third offered, if Bothwell himself were unwilling, to fight his accomplices. A completely new list followed which included the Lairds of Beanston, Ormiston, Talla and Bolton, the brothers Balfour, the Blackadders, James Cullen, Sandy Durham, Archibald Beaton, Harry Lauder and "Wanton Sym" Armstrong. What "that notable man" Mr. George Buchanan called "this jolly acquittal" had not scored the success that Bothwell hoped!

CHAPTER THIRTY

PARLIAMENT met on Monday, the 14th April, but the Queen of Scots did not attend until Wednesday. Once again Bothwell carried the sceptre before her, Argyll the crown and Crawford the sword. It was remarked that instead of the traditional escort of the bailies of Edinburgh, hagbutters were in attendance. Kirk o' Field, on top of the Rizzio affair, had been too much for even Mary's nerve.

Bothwell himself relates with some gusto and at considerable length how this assembly read the report of his trial and "declared that the proceedings had been according to right and justice and the law of the land. Further it was publicly proclaimed that on pain of death no one should after that day accuse or calumniate me or mine." On the fifth and last day of the session a number of acts were passed. One that bears the stamp of Bothwell's mind, after abolishing any relics of canon law that penalised the profession of the Reformed religion, orders all subjects to live in perfect amity whatever may be their religious differences. Bothwell anticipated the tolerance of the Edict of Nantes by thirty years.

If he had modern ideas of liberty of conscience, the modern cry of Freedom of the Press would have left him unconvinced. As an act which he sponsored premised, "by a licentious abuse entered lately and come into practice within this realm, there has been placards and bills and tickets of defamation set up under silence of night in diverse public places to the slander, reproach and infamy of the Queen's Majesty and diverse of the nobility." This disorder was judged to redound "not only to the great hurt and detriment of all noblemen in their good fame, private calumniators having by this means liberty to back-bite them," but also to tend to disturb the populace. The act decreed that any one seeing such a bill should "take it and incontinent destroy it"; failing to do so he laid himself open to the same penalty as the parties responsible for the placard.

Other measures sought to remove one of the outstanding causes of civil strife. Title to various church lands was ratified in favour of the present holders, who, nervous of being deprived of their dubiously-acquired possessions, were ever prone to take up arms in their defence. The Queen's partial knowledge of the catholic origin of the Paris Plot may have helped her to agree thus to alienate the property of her Church. No discrimination was shown in favour of Bothwell or his friends. Moray and his brother, Morton and his nephew, Rothes, Sempill, Caithness, Herries, Maitland's father, Cuthbert Ramsay's brother, Ogilvie, Michael Balfour, John Chisholm all profited. Sutherland was formally restored to his estates, as was Huntly and four other Gordons, although the actual restitution had been made nearly two years before. Titles to two castles were ratified to the faithful David Chalmers; the lands that went with Dunbar Castle were confirmed to Bothwell; these were the only advantages that accrued to Bothwell and his partisans from the measures of a Parliament, held while the Borderer's power was supreme.

Bothwell's trial and rehabilitation were only the prelude to a more ambitious programme. He could only see one "outgate" from the dangers that beset him since the crazy moment that had fired the fuse. There was no security in any condition short of the highest in the land that a loyal subject could attain. It was not his way to lose time or opportunity. The same Saturday evening that Parliament ended its labours, he invited twenty-eight of the nobles and prelates who conveniently filled the capital to supper in his quarters at the Palace. Anxious to gain their co-operation, he originated a method that has been absorbed into modern business routine. Without hinting at any ulterior motive, "he did liberally feast" his guests. At the end of a good dinner he produced a document which he suggested they might care to sign. It fell into two parts. Any of the guests, whose head was clear enough to follow the rolling periods, could read with a sigh of boredom that the noble and mighty lord had been caluminated by placards and slandered by his evil-willers. That he had been found guiltless by the country's laws of the odious crime and had shown himself ready to maintain his innocence by the law of arms. Remembering the antiquity of his house, and the honourable service of himself and his forebears, realising that noblemen were exposed to the slanders of the common people, the signatories bound themselves (as they were noblemen and would answer unto God) to take plain and upright part with him in his quarrel.

So far the more alert of the bishops, earls and barons could read without any quickening of the pulse. The second half of the document was more startling.

The Queen, they read, was now "destitute of a husband, in which solitary state the commonweal may not permit her to remain. In case the affectionate and hearty service of the Earl and his other good qualities may move her Majesty so far to humble herself as (preferring one of her native-born subjects unto all foreign princes) to take to husband the said Earl," the undersigned promised to further the marriage by vote, counsel and assistance. They would hold its adversaries their enemies, would spend life and goods in its defence. If they failed to do so, the document condemned them "never to have reputation or credit in no time hereafter, but to be accounted unworthy and faithless traitors."

Bothwell's guests, whatever their secret reservations, received this cool proposal with outward approval. Eight bishops, nine earls (among their number Morton and Argyll), and seven barons (including Boyd and Herries) meekly set their names to a paper that handed over their queen to the man most of them professed to believe a murderer.

Afterwards, when the tide had turned, they felt some

excuse was needed to colour their complaisance. Eighteen months later they declared that they had not signed, until a warrant from the Queen had expressed her consent. Two hundred hagbutters, they said, posted at the door of the dining-room, left them no choice. The dinner, they alleged, was given at Ainslie's tavern, where soldiers could readily surround the guests. A final apocryphal detail stated that Moray had signed the bond, ignoring the truth that he was in London. *Norfolk to Q. Elizabeth, 12 Oct., 1568.*

None of these latter accretions had any basis in fact. Hagbutters or warrants were not needed to win the nobles' consent. Bothwell's audacious demand was just what they were waiting for. Marriage with a bridegroom hopelessly compromised in the eyes of the people would implicate the Queen in the murder. Give Bothwell rope and he would hang himself and her. With a minimum of trouble, Moray's ambitions and Cecil's nationalism would find their long-postponed reward. Not only must Moray have told his subordinates to do nothing to hinder the wedding; he even wrote to his half-sister advising it and explaining the dangers of a refusal. His letters her party claimed afterwards to be able to produce. *Blackwood (Jebb ii. 217, 247).*

Les Affaires du Comte de Boduel 16.

By the hour of the notorious supper party, Mary Stuart had left for Seton. She seems to have had a horror of Edinburgh since the Paris Plot and Darnley's death. Bothwell, who never wasted time, followed her. He took with him Maitland and Bellenden to back his suit. An unfortunate scene gave him a bad start. The hagbutters of the guard (who were at Seton with the Queen and not at Ainslie's tavern) had not recently been paid. They came into the hall where the Queen was sitting to demand their wages. Bothwell "stepped to one, laying hands on him to strike him." His comrades came to his rescue "so that the Earl was glad to let him go." The strong man whose violence fails to gain its end does not cut an impressive figure. As one of the captains of her guard, he should have seen that pay was not in arrears. He cannot have failed to notice an *Nau. History of Mary Stuart.*

Drury to Cecil, 24 April, 1567.

343

edge on the royal voice that bade him give the men two crowns apiece.[1]

Bothwell chose this unpropitious moment to open his suit. For some weeks he had been trying to ingratiate himself. His technique had been, as the observant little Queen had noticed, "continuance in the awaiting on us and readiness to fulfil all our commandments." He had profited, she remarked, by "everything that might serve his turn and was content to entertain our favour by his good outward behaviour." Alas! his amiability only showed, as the disillusioned girl remarked, "how cunningly men can cover their designs when they have any great enterprise in head."

Queen Mary to the Bishop of Dunblane, May, 1567.

That Sunday at Seton he came to the point. The lover of Janet Beton and Anne Throndsen, the husband of Jean Gordon should have known how to handle women, should have waited for the bad effect of the hagbutter incident to wear off. Alas, he was in a hurry! He could not forget the placards, the shifty look in Morton's restless eye, some double meaning in Maitland's smooth phrases. He wanted to feel safe. "He began afar off," says Mary, "to discover his intentions unto us and to essay if he might by humble suit purchase our good will." The result was an answer "nothing correspondent to his desire."

The ardent lover proceeded to make a second blunder. He told the Queen about the deed that burned his pocket. Nothing could have been more fatal. No woman, let alone a Stewart, Dowager of France and Queen of Scots, cares to be told that eight bishops and sixteen noblemen have been discussing over their wine whom she is to marry. Her refusal of his preposterous suit was very firm. It left no hope that she would ever change her mind. She pointed out that her friends and his enemies would never allow the match; that he could not count on the vinous signatures of his temporary associates; finally that she did not care for him.

[1] Arnot says that the pay and maintenance of a soldier at this date was four pounds Scots a month, so the guard had not been paid presumably for at least two months.

344

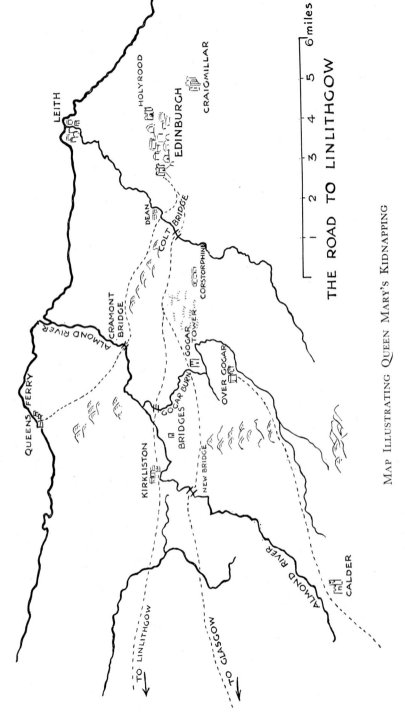

FIRTH OF FORTH

LEITH

HOLYROOD

EDINBURGH

CRAIGMILLAR

DEAN

COLT BRIDGE

CORSTORPHINE

CRAMONT BRIDGE

ALMOND RIVER

GOGAR TOWER

QUEENS FERRY

OVER GOGAR

GOGAR BURN

BRIDGES

KIRKLISTON

NEW BRIDGE

ALMOND RIVER

CALDER

TO LINLITHGOW

TO GLASGOW

THE ROAD TO LINLITHGOW

1 2 3 4 5 6 miles

MAP ILLUSTRATING QUEEN MARY'S KIDNAPPING

To her relief the rejected swain seemed willing to drop the subject. She felt no surprise when he asked a few questions about the visit she was paying her little son at Stirling. He elicited that she was leaving quietly next morning with a small escort and that she hoped to be back by Wednesday. There his interest lapsed. He began to talk of his plans to punish "the Liddesdale thieves" who had been raiding Biggar. Eight hundred to a thousand horsemen he calculated would give them the lesson they needed. *Forster to Cecil, 24 April, 1567*

Next morning, with a light heart, Mary started off to see her ten-months-old baby—as it proved for the last time in her life. She called the visit a secret one and only took with her Huntly, Maitland, Melville and some thirty horsemen. The journey to Stirling passed without incident. She spent Tuesday there, played with little James and wrote in her own hand to the Papal Legate at Paris, piously expressing her devotion to the catholic religion and promising to send a messenger on her return to Edinburgh. *Pollen 386 note.*

On Wednesday, 23rd April, she started home. On the road she was seized by a violent pain and took refuge in a cottage. Still, she was able to make Linlithgow that night and slept in the palace.

The story went round that Bothwell paid the town a midnight visit and had a long talk with Huntly. He was urging his brother-in-law, it appeared, to join him in some adventure. The Gordon was appalled and refused to play any part. Bothwell rode back to Calder House in a bad temper. *Drury to Cecil, 30 April, 1567.*

It was at Calder that Bothwell was unconvincingly concentrating his forces for the raid into Liddesdale. The house with its walls seven feet thick, its great hall paved with stone standing on arches, and its tradition of a secret passage to the church, had come into his hands in the previous autumn. It lay to the south of Kirkliston, which is a little more than midway between Linlithgow and Edinburgh. A worse place could not be found for a base of operations on the Border, or a better if the *C. Ramsay's Evidence in Divorce Proceedings, 1576.* *Johnson's Protocols 481, 491.*

objective was the Linlithgow-Edinburgh road. From Calder a map of the next century marks a track leading to Over Gogar. Near that village used to stand a farm, The Bridges, so-called from its proximity to the New Bridge that spanned the "Almond River and also to the little bridge over the Gogar Burn.

Decree of Forfeiture, 20 Dec., 1567.

"Near the bridges, commonly called Foulbridges," was the point to which Bothwell led his eight hundred horse. He had chosen a spot whence he could watch the two crossings of the Almond River, the site of the New Bridge (which was built at least by 1607) and the ferry a mile or so farther north, that continued to carry Linlithgow traffic as late as the middle of the eighteenth century. Which way would Mary come? From Foulbridges, Bothwell could command both routes; moreover, the junction of the Almond River and the Gogar Burn would hamper a flight to the north, east or west.[1] For the most faithful servant that Mary possessed, had "resolved with himself to follow forth his good fortune and all respects laid apart, either to lose all in an hour, or to bring to pass the thing he had taken in hand."

He did not succeed in keeping his plan a secret.

Lang 180; Kirkaldy to Drury, 24 April, 1567.

Lennox on the Tuesday, Grange on the Wednesday, had word of his intention, the date of the *coup* and the place to which he meant to take his captive. Perhaps Maitland, who rode with him from Edinburgh to Seton, was indiscreet; perhaps some of the eight hundred men he needed to overawe the Queen's bodyguard without bloodshed knew too much. Whatever the means of intelligence,

---

[1] The scene of the interception has been the subject of much dispute. To support the site suggested above, the following additional authorities may be quoted:

"Outside the Castle of Calder distant from Edinburgh about a league and a half." (Cuthbert Ramsay. Divorce Evidence, 1575.)

"Between Kirkliston and Edinburgh at a place called the Briggis" (Diurnal of Occurents). "Near the water of Almond" (Andrew Reidpath's Remission, 1st Oct., 1567). Other authorities cite *Almond Bridge* (Buchanan, Herries), which might mean the New Bridge if it was then built. *Cramont Bridge*, which Birrel gives, is on the road between Edinburgh and Queensferry and does not seem to enter the picture. Strickland places Foulbridges "between Colt Bridge and the West Port, within three-quarters of a mile of the castle," which does not fit with Ramsay's "league and a half," or de Silva's "six miles" from Edinburgh.

neither Lennox nor Grange attempted to save their sovereign.

It was on St. Mark's Eve, the ninth anniversary of her marriage to the Dauphin of France, that Mary rode into the trap. Bothwell spurred forward and took her horse by the bridle. His manner was respectful. He explained that he had come to warn her of grave danger that threatened and to take her to Dunbar Castle where she would be safe. Huntly, Lethington and Melville should come too. Mary's experience of Bothwell's intervention at the critical moments of the Rizzio and Kirk o' Field plots inclined her to believe him, but before she agreed to follow, she sent James Borthwick, a member of her escort, to Edinburgh to call the citizens to arms. Bothwell, who had alleged a rising, could not object. *Memoir to Cosimo I., June, 1568.*

Borthwick galloped to the city and told the Provost that the Queen was being carried to Dunbar. He did not believe Bothwell's story, and begged the citizens to arm and attempt a rescue. He got the common bell rung and the burgesses running "to armour and weapons." He had two guns moved out of the Castle and fired at Bothwell's troops, which could be seen cantering across country less than a mile from the city. The artillery of the day was little use against a moving target and one that was rapidly drawing out of range. The town bands made a demonstration and marched through the city gates, but as they had no cavalry they were useless against a mounted enemy who was rapidly disappearing over the horizon. "As was commonly agreed in the town, there was no help for the Queen." *J. Cuthbert's, C. Ramsay's Evidence in Divorce Proceedings, 1575.*

It was midnight when she reached Dunbar; by then she knew the truth. The success of his exploit had loosened Bothwell's tongue.

"I will marry the Queen," he boasted, "who would or would not. Yea, whether she would herself or not."

Mary's indignation knew no bounds. "How strange we found it of him," she complained, "of whom we doubted less than any subject we had, it is easy to be imagined." She did not fail to voice what she thought

347

of his ingratitude. The Earl felt the time had come for an explanation. Whatever his actions had been, his words, as his captive recorded, were gentle. "He asked pardon of the boldness he had taken to convey us to one of our own houses, whereunto he was driven by force, as well as constrained by love, the vehemence whereof had made him to set apart the reverence, which naturally as our subject he bore to us, as also for safety of his own life." The Earl knew enough to follow an appeal to vanity with a plea for help. His passionate love was only equalled by his desperate need.

He seems to have pushed his search for sympathy to extremes. He began, says Mary, "to make us a discourse of his whole life, how unfortunate he had been to find men his unfriends whom he had never offended; how unable he was to save himself from conspiracies of his enemies, whom he might not know by reason every man professed himself outwardly to be his friend; and yet found he such hid malice that he could not find himself in surety, without he were assured of our favour to endure without alteration." The truth was out, though protestations of passion were meant to hide it from Mary. He wanted to marry to save his skin.

His intentions, it was perhaps a relief to know, were entirely honourable; "other assurance he could not trust to, without it would please us to do him that honour to take him to husband; protesting always that he would seek no other sovereign but to serve and obey us all the days of our life, joining thereto all the honest language that could be used in such a case."

But the Queen was not moved by honest language; even a sight of the famous supper-party bond left her unappeased. She was left to think over her position. Her companions in adversity were little help. They were quarrelling among themselves. Huntly was out for Maitland's blood. The first night at Dunbar he tried to kill him. The Queen had to save her Secretary's life by swearing that if a hair of his head perished, his assailant

Drury to Cecil, 6 May, 1567.

348

would lose goods, lands or life. Kidnapping does not seem to have touched her spirit. Melville was no more use. He had been told by his captor, William Blackadder, that the abduction was with the Queen's consent. He believed the story, not perceiving that Bothwell had to lie to get his men to risk their necks in so treasonable an adventure. Had Melville known that his fellow captive *Silva to* was sending secretly to the Provost of Dunbar to come *Philip, 3 May, 1567.* to her help, he might have doubted Blackadder's tale. As it was he was glad when Bothwell gave him permission to go home on the Friday morning and leave the little Queen to her fate.

It is sometimes said that she welcomed it; that she connived at, or even directed, her capture. To add verisimilitude to their story, her enemies produced three more letters from the Silver Casket, which they said she wrote in quick succession on the Tuesday she spent at Stirling. This time the manipulators of the Casket had no partially genuine documents to build on. In concocting the whole of the three short letters, they made several obvious blunders. For one thing there was the characterisation of Bothwell. That enthusiast had just got himself acquitted on a murder change; he had collected the signatures to his marriage project of everybody who mattered in Scotland; he was on his way to kidnap a queen—all this he did in under a fortnight. But the letters draw the portrait of an irresolute fumbler whom the Queen's energy has to stimulate. He cannot make up his mind; he fails to communicate his intentions; he cannot decide the time of the *coup* or even the place; he is baffled by the problem of disposing of the escort. The discrepancy is glaring between the inertia that the Sixth Casket Letter paints and the lightning decisions that the calendar proves.

The forger did not even get his facts right. Lord Sutherland and Lord Livingstone with three hundred horse accompanied Mary, says the last of the three letters, on her journey. No other account mentions their presence. Huntly, Maitland, Melville were there and the visit was

349

called a secret one. With two more noblemen and their men, how could it merit that description? Worse mistakes follow. Maitland rode with the Queen, but the forger trips up by placing him in Bothwell's company. He blunders worse over Huntly, making Mary call him "your brother-in-law that was." The Gordon did not cease to be brother-in-law to the intending divorcee until eleven days after the letter was supposed to be written!

Even if the letters could be accepted as satisfactory evidence that Mary connived at her abduction, logic will not allow Bothwell to be cleared of the stain on his ten years' loyalty. No anxiety on a biographer's part to relieve his subject of the guilt of abusing Mary's trust and forcing on her the marriage that proved her ruin can provide her with a motive for a fake kidnapping. What would Mary gain? Marriage with her captor can be the only answer. But if from passion or policy she wanted to marry Bothwell, why should she resort to this trick? Everywhere was plain sailing. The dignitaries of her Church had signed their approval; so had her lords temporal; if the gentry and populace might murmur at so hasty a union, how could a simulated rapine placate them? Would it not make them more indignant with the kidnapper and less inclined to accept him as a bridegroom? The disadvantages to Mary were so manifest, the gains so non-existent, that it is difficult to believe that her brain, often injudicious but never cretinous, conceived or consented to the plan!

Bothwell would see the question in another light. Here was he, an ideal bridegroom, the favourite of women, whitewashed by the courts, guaranteed by the peerage and the bench of bishops! One thing stood between him and the safety he desired so desperately—a woman's fancy. He liked women, without thinking much of them. He did not mean to let Mary's ill-considered refusal upset his plans. She would, he felt sure, come to appreciate him and she would be the better for a husband who knew his mind. Once married, his influence would rule her, as her uncles had ruled her in France, and Moray when she first came to Scotland. Bothwell had not forgotten how he had been overboarded when Arran went mad. He did not mean to allow that to happen again.

At Dunbar he had his way. The method he employed is another disputed question. Some launch a charge of rape. The issue is obscured by the ambiguity of language. When contemporary writers say that Bothwell "ravished" Mary, they usually mean that he carried her off on her way from Linlithgow. "Abducted" is the modern equivalent. But Melville, present at first at Dunbar, goes further. "The Queen could not but marry him, seeing *Melville 149.* that he had ravished her and lain with her against her will." Melville was an enemy, but his categorical statement cannot be dismissed without examination. Other members of the anti-Bothwell party expand the charge. An English envoy was told later "how shamefully *The Associated* the Queen was led captive, and by fear, force and (as by *Throckmorton,* many conjectures may be well suspected) *other extra-* *July, 1567* *ordinary and more unlawful means*, compelled to become bedfellow to another wife's husband."

The words italicised hint, of course, at the vague sciences the Earl was supposed to practise. Witchcraft was the accusation that leapt to the lips of the century when it met any unconventional personality. Ruthven was accused of it, Janet Beton, the Bishop of Orkney, Lady Atholl, John Knox himself. The charge launched against the Reformer of winning his sixteen-year-old *D. Chalmers;* bride by magic, has been mentioned. David Chalmers *fortitudine* asserted quietly that "Knox was a wizard as appeared *276 N. Burne* in many instances throughout his whole life." Even *102.* Queen Mary half-believed that. Stories were whispered of *Knox ii. 276.* the prophet's dealings with the devil; "a young woman in my Lord Ochiltree's place fell almost dead because she saw his master Satan in a black man's likeness with him through a bore of the door." His claims to the more respectable powers of prophecy and exorcism lent colour to the darker charges. "He dispossessed an evil spirit out *Tweedie's* of a chamber in the house of Ormiston in East Lothian." *Select* While no particular inspiration was needed to foretell the *Biographies.*

violent end of any prominent person in Scotland, his predictions of the deaths of Thomas Maitland, Grange, Morton, Mary and Darnley established a prophetic reputation.

With random charges in the air, it is clearly dangerous to rationalise Bothwell's witchcraft into any scientific or chemical knowledge which gave him illicit influence over the Queen's mind or body. Some such explanation, however, is suggested by the mysterious hints of his contemporaries. A Frenchman alludes to "the trade which he professed more than any other, during his time at the schools, reading and studying sorcery and black magic." France was commonly the scene of his magical experiences, as a poem called *The Legend of Mary*, written by Thomas Wenman about the time of his heroine's flight to England, relates. After beginning his epic with the topical exhortation of "Baldwin awake!" the author puts this anecdote of Bothwell into the Queen's mouth:

La Mothe Fenelon to Charles IX., 29 Mar., 1568.

> For when of late in France he did remain,
> As one too curious his success to know,
> By sorcerer's mouth he heard he should attain
> Unto my favour . . .

Paralipomena ad Historiam: J. Leslie.

John Leslie, the silly Bishop of Ross, shows how the magic lore was applied. "It must be added," he explains gravely, "that Bothwell threw the Queen's mind into a confused state by means of magical arts and so brought her to agree to the marriage." As time went by, it suited Lennox to whitewash his daughter-in-law and to allege that her good qualities were corrupted by the necromantic Bothwell "with charms, potions, spells, poisons and other evil arts." At last the day came to fake the magician's death-bed confession and to crystallise the theory into the statement that "all the friendship which he had of the Queen he gat always by witchcraft and the inventions belonging thereto, specially the use of sweet water."

T. Buchanan to Frederick II., 19 Mar., 1571.

In the desire to make sense out of superstition and to forge a key to the riddle of Mary Stuart's imprudent

352

marriage, it has sometimes been supposed that in Paris, where Catherine de Medicis' example encouraged the rather deadly scientific dabblings of the day, Bothwell got some knowledge of the use of narcotics or the principles of hypnotism, and that he did not scruple to employ this dangerous skill at Dunbar.

This lurid explanation cannot be taken seriously. It did not occur to a servant of the Bishop of Ross at a time when all the evidence that could be urged against the validity of the marriage was collected. "Whether the Queen made this marriage under force and compulsion," John Cuthbert could not say; "although certain people stated that consent was lacking and that she was brought to it by force. Others said the contrary and that she lent consent." The student need not be quite as cautious as John Cuthbert, for Queen Mary has put on record her own account of how her captor overcame her resistance. She and Bothwell were the only people in the position to know what really happened and her story over-rides Melville's sensationalism and Leslie's superstitions. *Divorce Proceedings, 22 Sept., 1575.*

"Seeing ourselves in his puissance," wrote the Queen a few weeks after her detention, "sequestered from the company of our servants and others of whom we might ask counsel—yea, seeing them upon whose counsel and fidelity we had before depended . . . already zealded to his appetite, and so we left alone as it were a prey to him, many things we resolved with ourself, but never could find a way out. And yet gave he us little space to meditate with ourself, ever pressing us with continual and importunate suit." Bothwell was only exerting a moral pressure but Mary knew she was in his power and dependent on his forbearance. *Queen Mary to the Bishop of Dunblane, June, 1567.*

"In the end, when we saw no esperance to be rid of him, never man in Scotland making a move to procure our deliverance . . . we were compelled to mitigate our displeasure and began to think upon that he propounded."

Other considerations influenced her. She knew that she would have to remarry. The country needed a man to "take pain upon his person in the execution of justice and suppressing their insolence that would rebel, the travail whereof we may no longer sustain in our own person, being already wearied and almost broken with the frequent uproars and rebellions raised against us since we came to Scotland." She believed the Scottish temper would not accept a foreign consort, and remembering her captor's past services, supposed, perhaps pessimistically, that no Scot could be preferred to him "either for the reputation of his house or for the worthiness of himself as well in wisdom, valiance as in all other good qualities."

Mary was a realist. Seeing that she was in no position to refuse Bothwell's demands, she decided to make the best of a bad job. "He partly extorted and partly obtained our promise to take him to our husband." Even then he was afraid she would change her mind and pressed for an immediate ceremony. "As by a bravado in the beginning he had won the first point, so ceased he never till by persuasions and importunate suit, accompanied not the less by force, he had finally driven us to end the work begun, at such time and in such form as he thought might best serve his turn, wherein we cannot dissemble that he has used us otherwise than we would have wished or yet deserved at his hand." This is Mary's summing up of the whole manœuvre. The original "bravado" was the supper party and the bond; the subsequent "force" was the interception at Foulbridges. The allusion is surely too casual to imply a violation.

Though no excuse can be found for conduct that put the Queen in a position where at the mildest she was gravely compromised, Mary may not have suffered the agony of mind that some of her panegyrists have painted. Some women, it is said, like to be coerced. She may have felt a thrill that was not unpleasurable to find herself at the mercy of a strong man, determined to have his way. After the immature Francis and the imbecile Darnley, the virile Hepburn might seem a husband worth submitting to. She was very weary and in his arms she may have hoped to find security and peace. Swinburne may

354

have been right to put the sentiment in her mouth: "How good it is to have a *man* to love you!"

To believe that some such sigh rose to Mary's lips is not to accept Grange's version of her feelings. At the beginning of this fatal week the head of protestant propaganda wrote to England asking for copies of the placards to be printed for distribution on the Continent. He quoted Mary as saying of Bothwell "that she cares not to lose France, England and her own country for him and will go with him to the world's end in a white petticoat." That Grange was the paid spy of England is proved by Bedford's request to Elizabeth to "send him somewhat as a token of remembrance" in exchange for the intelligence he supplied, and no credence need be placed in his word. The quotation, however, is interesting as it seems to contain the germ of Casket forgery. *Grange to Bedford, 20 April, 1567.*

Bedford to Cecil, 3 Aug., 1566.

Just such love-sick phrases were said to be contained in a compromising letter of Mary's that Moray and Lennox were soon to report. Lennox quoted it as proclaiming undying love for Bothwell, "though she should thereby abandon her God, put in adventure the loss of her dowry in France, hazard such titles as she had to the crown of England and also the crown of her realm." Moray reported a similar extract. But when the time came to produce the Casket and its scandalous contents, no such detailed list of sacrifices appears. Have we been admitted for a moment to the forgers' workshop? Has Grange been detected inventing a picturesque vow, which at first seems good enough to incorporate in the earlier drafts of the compromising letter, but which is dropped from the finished article? *Lennox Narrative (Mahon, Mary Queen of Scots, 129).*

Further material may have sprung from the same fertile brain. Writing of the abduction, Grange states of the Queen: "She was minded to cause Bothwell to ravish her that she may sooner end the *marriage which she promised before* she caused Bothwell murder her husband." When two months later the Silver Casket was captured, out of it appeared certain papers purporting to be signed by Mary in which she promised to marry Bothwell. One *Grange to Bedford, 26 April, 1567.*

of them, says Buchanan, bore no date but "upon credible grounds" was "supposed to have been made and written before the death of her husband." The least power that Grange could claim, was intelligent anticipation!

The text of two of the Casket "contracts" has been preserved. One without a date alludes to Darnley's death and so seems distinct from the promise described by Buchanan. This document, which lies among the Cotton Manuscripts, is probably the sole survivor of the actual Casket series. Of the twenty-two papers which were credited to that dubious receptacle, one was never returned to it and probably stayed in Cecil's hands. The deed in question is in bad French. At the foot stands Mary's "signature." The handwriting has recently been examined by the Editor of the *Analyst*, who made use of modern research methods. His verdict, like that of earlier investigators, is that the signature is a manifest forgery. He goes further and suggests an identification of the craftsman.

Receipt of Morton to Lennox, 22 Jan., 1571.

"If the various 'lapses' in that document," Mr. Ainsworth Mitchell[1] decides, "are compared in photographic enlargement with the corresponding characters in Maitland's writing, the points of resemblance cannot be missed. Not only do letters show the same mode of formation but the method of holding the pen and applying pen pressure also agree." Our brief glimpse of the forgers at work seems to show Sir William Maitland of Lethington bending, pen in hand, and at his shoulder Sir William Kirkaldy of Grange whispering what he should write.

Of the second "marriage contract," dated the 5th April, only a copy remains. It may well have been a genuine document with a fraudulent date and place inserted—a weakness of the forgers that has already been noticed. It cannot, as the opening states, have been signed

---

[1] The opinion of this expert may be quoted on the whole question of the Casket Letters. "Mary Queen of Scots has been found guilty of the murder of her husband, mainly on the evidence drawn from the Casket Letters. But a verdict, based on inconsistent documents, which she denied having written but was not allowed to see and the only one of which now extant (still bearing her alleged signature) is demonstrably spurious, can only be regarded as a travesty of justice."

"at Seton, the 5th day of April, the year of God, 1567," for on the previous day the Queen left Seton for Holyrood House. On the 5th April Bothwell could not have promised "that in all diligence he shall prosecute the said process of divorce *already begun.*" The machinery of divorce was not set in motion until Saturday the 26th April. It is reasonable to suppose that at Dunbar Bothwell, to prevent any change of mind, insisted that the Queen should sign this promise to marry him with the date and place left blank. The witnesses, the Earl of Huntly and the parson of Oldhamstocks, were in residence, and the wording and argument of the "contract" follow the lines of the letter the Queen wrote to the Bishop of Dunblane giving her reasons for her reluctant marriage.

No long or brutal pressure was exerted by Bothwell on his prisoner. He brought her to Dunbar at midnight on Thursday; he won her consent by Saturday, for on that day he allowed his wife to start divorce proceedings.

Tongues were busy. Janet Beton, said somebody, was to be cited as co-respondent. She would claim, said some one else, that her handfast marriage invalidated the later union. This was more than Lady Jean could stand. Refusing to admit that her marriage had never been legal, she vowed that she would "die with the name of Lady Bothwell."

Cynically Bothwell changed his plans. On Tuesday the 29th four commissioners of the protestant court heard the wronged wife's counsel plead that in May and June, 1566, the Earl of Bothwell had committed adultery with the sewing-maid, Bessie Crawford. Acts had taken place "diverse times in the Abbey of Haddington, in a part thereof called St. Paul's Work," where the guilty pair were together "*solus cum sola* the doors being locked." So Lady Jean was petitioning "to be no longer repute bone of his bone, nor flesh of his flesh."

Bothwell's lawyers (neither of the principals appeared in person) went through the form of denying the charges, and Lady Jean's witnesses were called on Wednesday and on Thursday. They included Patrick Wilson and George Dalgleish, whose names have become notorious from their presence at Kirk o' Field and Gabriel Sempill, the Earl's confidential man. In small details their stories differed, but on the whole they were as convincing as collusive divorce court evidence can be expected to be. On Saturday the 3rd May the commissioners gave judgment and declared the noble Earl separate, cut off and divorced from the noble lady who was set free to marry in the Lord where she pleased. Nothing was said about any similar liberty for the noble Earl.

To be on the safe side and to put his affairs in order for remarriage with a catholic princess, Bothwell had already started proceedings before the catholic Consistory. The Archbishop's court, it may be remembered, was restored when the question of a dissolution of Mary's marriage with Darnley had arisen. Its jurisdiction was now convenient to annul Bothwell's marriage. On Saturday the 27th April, the day after Lady Jean had opened her case in the protestant Court, a commission was granted by the Primate of Scotland to two bishops and four other ecclesiastics to hear the suit, brought this time by Bothwell. On grounds of consanguinity he sought to establish the nullity of his marriage. As the Primate had provided a dispensation to permit the marriage a little over a year before, archiepiscopal memory must charitably be supposed to have been short. The members of the court felt more diffidence. Neither of the bishops ever took his seat, and when the hearing was begun on Saturday, 3rd May, only two dignitaries were there to receive the commission at the hands of the untiring parson of Oldhamstocks. On Monday, 5th, John Manderston, canon of Dunbar, made a solitary appearance. He may have thought Bothwell too near a neighbour to make absence wise. The same lawyers, who had appeared in the protestant court, represented the couple. Among the witnesses called was the Bishop of Galloway, who had solemnised this transitory union,

358

Sir John Bellenden, and the inevitable Mr. David Chalmers. On Wednesday the canon gave his sentence in favour of the Earl. The marriage, he declared, was null from the beginning, because no dispensation had been previously obtained to permit marriage within the forbidden decrees!

From the start the question of the divorce was handled by all parties with the utmost cynicism. At no stage of his career had Bothwell any regard for the sanctity of marriage. He used that sacrament as a convenient tool for getting his way. He won the favours of Janet Beton under colour of a handfast; going a little further, he seduced Anna Throndsen under promise of a marriage; for the Gordon connection he had to pay the price of a legal union; when that marriage stood in his way, he freed himself from it by the double shift of a condoned adultery with a maid-servant, and a blood relationship for which he held a dispensation.

Lady Jean stood on moral ground that was hardly higher. She had known about Bessie Crawford for the better part of a year. She kept the suppressed dispensation in her possession and, when she remarried, took the paper with her to her new husband's charter chest. She knew that the annulment was illegal and made no attempt to stop it. _{Dr. John Stuart 24.}

How much the Queen understood is uncertain. She was doubtful of her legal position and consulted "two or three catholic bishops" before the marriage. Their verdict was favourable "because Bothwell's wife was related to him in the fourth degree." She did not listen to her father confessor who urged her to have nothing to do with the marriage. A dispensation on grounds of consanguinity was a commonplace in Scottish marriage, and it is curious that it did not occur to her to inquire whether one had not been granted. At the same time it must be admitted that when later the question arose of dissolving her connection with Bothwell and a document that would automatically invalidate the marriage would have been convenient, no discovery was made. _{Silva to Philip, 26 July, 1567.}

Most to blame were the bishops and the archbishop in whose peculiar province lay the investigation of such matters, but the primate was a Hamilton and had an interest in the succession. It would be prudent to keep a piece of knowledge up his sleeve that would illegitimise any offspring of the Bothwell-Mary marriage.

To modern eyes the whole episode of abduction, divorce and forced marriage apppears deplorable. It did not present itself in such dark colours to the Earl of Bothwell. His stomach was strong, although it might have turned at some of the features of modern civilisation on which we daily congratulate ourselves. To no less distinguished a critic than the Archbishop of Glasgow, the Queen's Ambassador in Paris, he penned the complacent comment, "We trust no nobleman, being in our state and case, would have left anything undone that we have attempted."

Bothwell to Archbishop of Glasgow, 27 May, 1567.

CHAPTER THIRTY-ONE

ONCE the Queen had consented and the divorce was under way, the strain at Dunbar was lifted. Bothwell discarded his mourning and sported his finest clothes. An English visitor saw him out walking with the Queen under an escort of hagbutters, and noticed that he "showed tokens of mirth." He dismissed the troopers his friends had provided with instructions to keep themselves ready in case they were wanted. He arranged for the normal appearances of Court life. There was archery practice and horseback exercise. The Queen had her embroidery and her ladies—the Beton sisters, Janet and Margaret, and Bothwell's widowed sister. Mary liked Janet Hepburn better than the other two. Perhaps the stories about the Lady of Buccleugh and the future bridegroom now seemed a little embarrassing; perhaps Janet Hepburn was kinder. The little captive gave her a black taffeta cloak with long sleeves, a square collar and a silver border. Another present was a crimson satin petticoat with sequins and a border of crimson velvet. She even recommended Janet's fatherless boy Francis for the vacant Abbey of Kelso.

Drury to Cecil, 30 April, 1567.

Drury to Cecil, 4, 6 May, 1567.

For form's sake the machinery of government was kept in motion. What is described as a Privy Council was held, and upwards of a dozen charters were granted, none to Hepburn interests. Maitland was available to perform the duties of Secretary, as well as the dangerous double rôle in which his indirect spirit delighted. He had almost certainly helped Bothwell over the abduction; at the same time he kept in touch with the men who were vowing the kidnapper's destruction.

S. Cowan, ii. 202.

Even they did not trust the Secretary. He told them he was a prisoner at Dunbar and produced a plan to escape during an archery match, riding "between the marks on a good nag to a place where a fresh horse and company tarries." Nothing came of it and his associates began to "muse much" on his long delay. They "judged that his constraint of liberty is not altogether against his will." Their headquarters were at Stirling, where his friend Atholl was expecting him daily. Already Morton was there, with Mar, Glencairn and Argyll. When news of the abduction was brought, their first thought was that their moment had come. "Forces were even raised and armed for an advance on Edinburgh, but when the Earl's strength was known, they were obliged to return to Stirling."

J. Cuthbert's Evidence in Divorce Proceedings, 1575.

On the 1st May they met and drafted the inevitable bond. They "considered the great and heinous attempt in taking the Queen's Majesty captive, which not being put order unto, opens the door to all impiety." Accordingly they bound themselves by the faith and truth in their bodies to put the Queen at liberty, to secure the person of the Prince and to punish the murderer of the King.

P.C. Reg. xii. 315.
Grange to Bedford, 8 May, 1567.

These resolutions were a sop to the semi-loyal members of the coalition. Mar was leader of this section, which "sent to warn the Queen to consider deeply about her marriage." It did not disturb them that their associates had bound themselves less than a month before to support Bothwell's marriage plans. They diverted their leisure with a drama, acted by boy players, of the Murder of Darnley and the Fate of Bothwell. Rarely can realism in the theatre have been more patiently pursued. The actor who represented the Earl was hanged with such perseverance that "hardly in a long time could life be recovered."

Silva to K. Philip, 10 May, 1567.

The extremists of the coalition had other ends than the freeing of the Queen and the punishment of her captor. They "considered the raising of the child to the throne, the government being carried on by them in his name." To this end they asked for English support, alleging that, if refused, they could get help from

Silva to K. Philip, 10 May, 1567.

France. Through the fog of conspiracy looms the figure of the absent Earl of Moray, whose supple fingers held the threads. From France he kept in constant touch with the Stirling coalition. His henchman Grange was urging him to come to Normandy "that he may be in readiness against my lords write to him."

Grange to Bedford, 8 May, 1567.

Bothwell can hardly have been unaware of the danger, but the steps that he took show that he minimised it. He wanted to form the nucleus of a small regular army by supplementing the Queen's guard of two hundred hagbutters with a further five hundred horse and two hundred foot. Their pay was a difficulty, but five thousand crowns were raised by breaking up the golden font that Elizabeth sent as a christening present. He tried to consolidate the Border by offering the Cessford Kerrs a pardon for the murder of the Abbot of Kelso, in exchange for their co-operation. Publicly the fullest confidence was expressed and her Majesty was declared to be "contented with all her nobility (praise to God), no trouble or insurrection standing within her realms."

After ten days at Dunbar, on the evening of the 6th May, Bothwell took Mary back to her capital. As he neared the city he gave the escort orders to put away their spears, wishing to signify that the sovereign was no prisoner. He dismounted and himself led her horse with every mark of deference. None too sure of his reception, he decided not to enter by the Netherbow with the full length of the High Street to reach the Castle. He preferred a less conspicuous entry by the West Port and the Grassmarket.

For the week Mary stayed in the Castle opinion in the town was divided whether she was a free woman. The uncertainty ended on the 12th when Bothwell let her go back to Holyrood. By then he had made the blunder which was to ruin his cause. As long as the fortresses of Edinburgh and Dunbar with their garrisons, stores and artillery were in his hands, Bothwell and his borderers could laugh at the Stirling coalition. What madness drove him to relieve the faithful Sir James Cockburn and

J. Cuthbert's Evidence in Divorce Proceedings, 1575.

give the command of Edinburgh Castle to the traitor Balfour?

Two reasons may be offered. As Bothwell galloped the kidnapped Queen past the Castle rock, two guns were brought into action against him. Did he resent that tactless loyalty and feel the need of some one in the Castle a little less impetuously devoted to the Queen? But on the 1st June the displaced keeper was given the post of Controller of Customs, an appointment that does not support the theory of a disgrace. More subterranean influences may have been at work. Did Sir James Balfour blackmail Bothwell into giving him the command? If he chose the eve of the wedding to declare who lit the fuse, there could be no doubt that the Queen would cancel the ceremony. Although his own hands were far from clean, although Bothwell could guess that he had laid the powder in the vaults, the lawyer was clever enough to leave no proof. Until Bothwell had established his position by the royal marriage, Balfour had him at his mercy.

The moment the marriage contract was signed, his stranglehold was broken. On that very day word got out that Bothwell meant to replace him with a Hepburn. After the marriage, says Melville, "there were some jealousies arisen" between borderer and lawyer. Melville warned Balfour "that the Earl intended to have the Castle out of his hands to have committed the charge thereof to the Laird of Beanston." Knowing the importance of the post and the scope it gave to a traitor, Melville "dealt with Sir James Balfour not to part" with it. Forewarned, nothing would shift the man. An attempt was made to ease him out with the offer of the honourable task of announcing the marriage in England. But Balfour's vanity was not to be caught; "he doubted of his entertainment in passing and returning" and stayed where he was.

Bothwell's anxieties came thick and fast. The morning after his return from Dunbar he had sent the parson of Oldhamstocks to see about the banns. To his surprise

Drury to Cecil, 14 May, 1567.

Drury to Cecil, 20, 25 May, 1567.

both the reader and the minister of St. Giles's refused to call them. The strong-minded Mr. John Craig wanted to see the Queen's signature to a statement that she had not been kidnapped and kept prisoner against her will. Back went Thomas Hepburn and back came Bellenden with a signed assurance.

John Craig was not satisfied. "He durst proclaim no banns without consent and command of the Kirk." Next morning the Kirk Assembly met. "After long reasoning," it agreed to publish the banns on the three following Sundays in St. Giles's and in Holyrood Chapel (the efficient parson had already called them at Oldhamstocks as a precaution). But the Assembly flatly refused to allow the wedding to be solemnised on the following Friday. Not content with the havoc he had wrought in Bothwell's plans, the sturdy minister declared that "to give boldness to others," he wanted to speak his mind in the presence of the bridal pair.

The same afternoon he was admitted to a meeting of the Council at which Bothwell was present. "I laid to his charge," the intrepid preacher declared, "the law of adultery, the ordinance of the Kirk, the law of ravishing, the suspicion of collusion between him and his wife, the sudden divorce and proclaiming within the space of four days, and last the suspicion of the King's death, which his marriage would confirm."

Bothwell kept his temper and gave him a fair answer which was, however, "nothing to his satisfaction." In his Sunday sermon, the tireless Mr. Craig "took heaven and earth to witness that he abhorred and detested that marriage because it was odious and slanderous to the world." The sermon taxed Bothwell's patience, and on Tuesday the preacher was called before the Council. His remarks on the Queen's marriage were claimed to have passed the bounds of his commission.

"I answered the bounds of my commission (which was the Word of God, good laws and natural reason) was able to prove whatever I spoke, yea that their own conscience—but, while I was coming to my probation, my lord put me to silence and sent me away." It is difficult to know which most to admire, the courage of the minister or the patience of his audience.

John Craig's bold words showed Bothwell what more timid folk were whispering. To placate public opinion he persuaded the Queen to make a formal appearance at the Tolbooth before the Lord Chancellor, the Lords of Session and various dignitaries of church and state. There she made an official pronouncement on her attitude to her abductor. She had been angry, she said, when he held her against her will at Dunbar, but in view of "his good behaving towards her" and his former services, she now was content and forgave "him and all other his complices all hatred conceived by her for the taking and imprisoning of her."

Besides the effect on opinion in the country, two objects are said to have been served by this amnesty. As the law of Scotland then stood, the guilt of rape was effaced by the woman's subsequent acquiescence. Bothwell's lawyer, who had the pardon duly recorded, may well have advised his client to take the precaution. Lethington gave another, further-fetched, explanation. The murder of Darnley, he said, could only be covered by a pardon for the major offence of treason. We must leave experts to settle whether regicide is not in itself so treasonable as to discount this subtlety.

The Queen was in a pardoning mood, and Bothwell did not forget the horsemen of Foulbridges. He also obtained her signature to a statement that she had seen the supper-party bond, and her word as a princess not to hold it against the signatories.

The cornucopia of royal benevolence was not empty. Three days before the wedding the Queen of Scots created her future husband Duke of Orkney and Lord of Shetland, titles his ancestor the first Earl had borne. With her own hands she placed the ducal coronet on his bended head. Away in London, Thomas Randolph had his joke. Leith, he declared, was to be a free borough, under the name of Marianburgh, and James Hepburn to be duke of it. The new creation altered the Bothwell arms. To his former quarterings he added three chevronels gules on ermine for Lord Soulis, and a ship *or* with sails furled argent on azure for Orkney. At his investiture, four of his followers were, as was customary, knighted. His cousin, James Cockburn of Langton; the Captain of Dunbar, Patrick Hay of Whitelaw; the nominee for Edinburgh Castle, Patrick Hepburn of Beanston; and James Ormiston of the ilk, better known as the Black Laird, were chosen for the accolade.

Two days later, on the 14th May, the marriage contract was ready. A weight lifted from Bothwell's spirits as Mary affixed her signature. Witnesses included Huntly, Crawford and Fleming among his friends, and Lindsay, Lethington and Bellenden among his enemies. The wording of the deed was ingenious—the literary Mr. Chalmers may have lent a hand—and made the match sound advantageous to Mary Stuart. "And now her Majesty being destitute of a husband," it read, "living solitary in the state of widowhood, and yet young and of flourishing age, apt and able to procreate and bring forth children, has been pressed and humbly required to yield unto some marriage. The most part of the nobility naming the noble prince, now Duke of Orkney, for the special personage, her Majesty has allowed their nomination, having recent memory of the notable and worthy acts and good service performed by him." Mention is made of the noble and potent prince's "magnanimity, courage and constant truth," which had preserved her Majesty's person from evident and great dangers and had conducted high and profitable purposes, tending to her Highness's advancement. Provision is made for a protestant form of marriage and for the ratification of the bridegroom's title to the earldom of Orkney and the lordship of Shetland. But a clause insists that all documents shall be signed by the Queen and the Duke, and none by the Duke alone.

A glimpse is granted us of James Hepburn *en pantoufles* on one of the three evenings between his elevation to the dukedom and the wedding. The critical Sir James Melville had arrived at Court for the ceremony and can be allowed to tell his story in his own words.

"I found my lord Duke of Orkney sitting at his supper, who welcomed me, saying I had been a great stranger, desiring me to sit down and sup with him, the Earl of Huntly, the Justice Clerk and divers others being sitting at table with him. I said I had already supped. Then he called for a cup of wine and drank to me, saying, 'You had need grow fatter for,' says he, 'the zeal of the commonwealth hath eaten you up and made you lean.'

"I answered that every little member should serve for some use, but the care of the commonwealth appertained most to him and the rest of the nobility, who should be as fathers of the same.

"'I knew well,' says he, 'he would find a pin for every bore!'

"Then he fell in discoursing of gentlewomen, speaking such filthy language that I left him and went up to the Queen, who expressed much satisfaction at my coming."

R. Melville to Cecil, 7 May, 1567.

Her satisfaction might have been less had she known that the fastidious diarist's brother had just written to Cecil to beg English help for the Stirling conspirators.

Thursday, 15th May, was chosen for the wedding. The credulous thought May an unlucky month and with a glance at Janet Beton's favour at Court, muttered that witches and sorcerers had a hand in the choice. Somebody, whom knowledge of the classics had not freed from superstition, stuck a line from Ovid on the palace gates, *mense malas maio nubere vulgus ait*:

> The people say
> That wantons marry
> In the month of May.

Before it was dawn Bothwell was up and waiting for the event that was to crown his desperate adventures and to reward an ancestral ambition. His forebears had been the lovers of widow queens; his father had courted a royal dowager; he was the first Hepburn to slip a ring on the reigning finger. Mary was ready for him by four. Again she wore mourning, as if she were looking back, not forward. The knot was tied in the great hall at Holyrood that was normally used for Council meetings. The form employed was protestant. The sermon, the principal feature of Calvinist nuptials, was preached by Adam Bothwell, Bishop of the Orkneys. He was no kin of the bridegroom but "a man most apt and ready to serve all worlds and turns." Harder things were said of him by the enemies his instability had created: "the venerable, often perjured and foresworn father, a camelion, a sorcerer and execrable magician, a perfect atheist." This dubious ecclesiastic chose his text from the second chapter of Genesis. If his choice was the eighteenth verse, "it is not good that the man should be alone, I will make him a help-meet," he showed a nice taste in irony at the expense of one who seldom managed long without feminine society. Conscious of the Duke's reputation, in the course of the sermon he proclaimed the bridegroom's penitence for his past life, "confessing himself to have been an evil-liver." A good number of the nobility, protestant and catholic, were there to enjoy these revelations. Huntly, Sutherland, Crawford, Boyd, Fleming, Livingstone, Oliphant and Glammis were remarked, and of churchmen the Primate of Scotland with the Bishops of Ross and Dunblane.

If the wedding was by no means the hole-in-a-corner affair some writers have alleged, there was none of the public merry-making the populace expected; "there was neither pleasure nor pastime as was wont to be used when princes was married." The only relaxation was the marriage feast where the public was admitted to watch the Queen eating her dinner at the head of the table with the Duke at the foot. *James Curl's Evidence, Divorce Proceedings. 1575.*

It is difficult to get a fair picture of Mary's and James's relations once they were wed. The only direct information comes from sources bitterly hostile. There is no hint of that passionate affection the Queen was afterwards supposed to have lavished on her subject.

Just before the wedding, Drury told a story of "great unkindness" that lasted half a day. The Duke he reported "the most jealous man alive," and the quarrel occasioned by a horse his fiancée had given Lord John Hamilton! Melville adds some unflattering touches to his portrait of Bothwell. "He was so beastly and suspicious that he suffered her not to pass a day in patience"; he even caused her, says the diarist, "to shed abundance of salt tears." Lethington supplies an explanation. "From her wedding day, she was ever in tears and lamentations, for he would not let her look at anybody, or anybody look at her, though he knew that she liked her pleasure and pastime, as well as anybody."

It must be remembered that all three witnesses hated Bothwell and that, before the love story was invented, the cue was to paint him as a brutal ravisher. Still, when every allowance has been made for the hostility of the evidence and for the easy working of Mary's lachrymal glands, clearly all was not well between the newly-wedded pair.

Some people reversed the rôles and found an explanation in Mary's jealousy. She resented, it appeared, the ex-wife staying on at Crichton. London gossips claimed that the Duke spent several days a week there. Scotland went a little further and pretended that he preferred his first wife to the Queen. Maitland was spiteful enough to tell an incredulous Mary of a letter (he did not explain why it was necessary to write in view of the frequent visits), telling Jean that he looked on her as his wife and on Mary as a mistress. Du Croc spoils that story by reporting that James Hepburn denied he had ever married the Gordon but kept *her* as his mistress. Common sense discredits both tales and substitutes some jest about sweethearts and wives, which could be distorted at the reporter's will. The gossip about the preference for Jean may have grown out of the Duke's obligation to let her stay at Crichton, which her dowry had redeemed.

Whether jealousy was a cause of unhappiness or no, it is certain that the Duke's wish to isolate his bride from outside influence must have irritated the pleasure-loving girl. "No nobleman nor other durst resort to her Majesty to speak with her, or procure their lawful business without suspicion, except by him and in his hearing, her chamber doors being continually watched with men of war." Had the flattering motive been that her husband wanted her uninterrupted society, the restriction might have been tolerable; but Mary could see that his aim was to maintain the absolute ascendancy that every woman resents. *Bond of 16 June, 1567. (Keith 405.)*

Other serious grounds for discord existed. Mary was a practising catholic and her friends on the Continent were catholic. She disliked the hurried protestant ceremony that Bothwell had forced on her and was nervous of its effect abroad. Immediately she sent the Bishop of Dunblane to the French Court to explain, almost to apologise.

Her husband, she said, was more concerned with pleasing his protestant associates "than regarding our contentation, or weighing what was convenient to us that has been nourished in our own religion and never intends to leave the same for him or any man on earth." That half-day of pre-nuptial unkindness may well have been bred by a quarrel about the marriage service. "On her return from that unlawful ceremony," relates her confidant, "the Queen could not help weeping. At once she sent for the Bishop of Ross and with many tears unlocked the secret of her heart; she showed many clear signs of repentance and promised that she would never again do anything opposed to the rites of the Catholic and Roman Church." *Leslie's Paralipomena.*

That Church cherished some improbable hopes that the Queen, "to amend her error," might convert her husband. People who had known Bothwell in France even declared that such a change of heart was not impossible. It is true that the husband's essential tolerance made religious questions no lasting danger to married peace. But another point at issue was the future of the little prince. The Duke's enemies did not scruple to assert *Bishop of Mondovi to Cardinal of Alessandria, 1 July, 1567.*

that the only future he contemplated for the boy was an early grave. No confirmation of this atrocious purpose exists. Would he, had his intentions been evil, have allowed the child to be committed to the care of the anti-Hepburn Earl of Mar?

Randolph to Leicester, 10 May, 1567.

Queen Elizabeth heard a more likely tale. The Duke, with his bias towards France, wanted to send his stepson to be brought up in that country. The education would be better than any that Scotland could afford, and if the stepfather had had his way James I of England might have been less uncouth. A more immediate advantage was the temporary removal of a rallying point for Mary's enemies, ever anxious to dethrone her and to proclaim a regency. But to a mother the thought of separation was intolerable. She could not guess that during the twenty years of life that lay before her she was not to see her baby again.

Such are the probable reasons for Mary's general unhappiness at the time of her wedding. There is also a well-substantiated story of one sudden access of grief that demands a separate explanation. "A strange formality," was noticed on her wedding day, "between her and her husband, which she tried to excuse and said that if she seemed sorrowful, it was because she did not want to be merry. And she said she never would, but only longed for death." Two days later "when she was shut in a dressing-room alone with the Earl Bothwell, she cried out for a knife to kill herself. The people in the room outside heard her and thought that without God's aid she would do something desperate." In the presence of Arthur Erskine, Melville heard her ask for a knife to stab herself, "or else," said she, "I shall drown myself." These stories bear the stamp of truth and are supported by visitors who found in Mary after the marriage "the most changed woman of face that in so little time, without extremity of sickness, they had seen."

du Croc to Catherine de Medicis, 18 May, 1567.

The cause of her despair is obvious. As soon as he was safely married, Bothwell meant to be quit of Balfour's blackmail. He told Mary the truth about the explosion

372

at the Provost's House. To her horror Mary learnt that the bridegroom she had reluctantly married had been concerned in the murder of her late husband. She had loved Henry Stewart and the atrocious discovery that she was tied to a man whose hands were not clean of his blood made her wish for death. Now that her belief in the Duke's innocence was shattered, her political sense told her how desperate her case looked in the eyes of Europe. No wonder she called for a knife!

Bitterly she remembered how different had been her emotions when she married Darnley, worthless though he was to prove. Better than from the prejudiced accounts of contemporaries the contrast may be measured in the wardrobe and jewellery returns which her century kept so meticulously.

A woman's clothes are said to show what she thinks of the man who is principally privileged to see them. It was actually on her wedding day that Mary had time to go through her cupboards. She sent an old yellow silk gown and bodice to be lined with white taffeta. She had a black taffeta petticoat relined and a black figured velvet gown done up with gold braid. For a woman who cared a good deal about what she wore, Mary could hardly have taken less trouble. *Hay Fleming, 511.*

Presents are another test by which it is sometimes sought to gauge affection. When Mary married Darnley the pages of the inventories mirror her emotions. Yards of his favourite violet velvet to make a dressing-gown, crimson velvet to upholster his saddle, a cupboard to house his perfumes, fur to cover his hats, pillows and pillow-slips, Turkey carpets, a cloth of gold caparison for his horse, bedding for his squire, blue bonnets with feathers for his fools—anybody connected with her beloved roused her generosity. At the time of the fatal May wedding, only one entry marks the day: the genet fur off the collar and hem of a great black cloak of her mother's was issued to the Duke of Orkney to use on a dressing-gown! The extravagant gifts of princely furs which historians have bestowed on a luxurious *Inventories 156 ss.* *Inventories 23, 26, 176.*

paramour, when entries are traced back, boil down to some "bits.

Royal Wardrobes and Jewels. Thompson 278.

If the husband did not profit largely by his bride's wonted generosity, it must be admitted that his own purse did not open very wide. He sent indeed the customary gift to his stepson at Stirling. On a gold chain, enamelled green, red, white and black, were threaded one hundred and twenty-nine pearls grouped into nine bars. From it hung a pearl pendant and a diamond *fleur de lys*, A royal present indeed—since it came out of his wife's jewel-case!

Queen Mary to Archbishop of Glasgow, 27 May, 1567. Drury to Cecil, 23, 25, 27 May, 1567.

Whatever the Queen felt about her new marriage, she had sense and spirit enough to make the best of it in public. The event, she said, was strange and other, she expected, than people would have looked for; but "we must take the best of it and so, for our respect, must all who love us." So when she went out walking with her husband, the curious saw her hanging on his arm. For his part the Duke showed "great reverence to the Queen, ordinarily bare-headed; which she seems she would have otherwise." Sometimes she took his cap from his hand and put it on his head. They used to go for rides together and "make outward show of content." Often with royal affability they invited themselves to dinner at the tables of subjects. There is a pleasant picture of daily outings when they were "quiet and merry together." The emotion which Mary was to feel when the time came to part shows that, had fate allowed, there was happiness to be won.

CHAPTER THIRTY-TWO

T
HE acts of the Duke of Orkney during the few weeks he was allowed to perform his functions as consort of the Queen of Scots suggest that he would have filled the station to which he had called himself with dignity and ease. He made no attempt at dictatorship or unconstitutional authority. Five meetings of the Privy Council were held in the week that followed his wedding. The Duke attended all except the first, when the purely formal business of admitting Lord Oliphant as member of the Council and the parson of Oldhamstocks as Master of Requests was transacted.

Under the new regime the machinery of the Council was overhauled. Its members were divided into four batches, each batch to attend six weeks of sessions. Eighteen weeks of repose followed, while the other groups sat; then came another six weeks of duty. Any member of the Council temporarily at Court was to attend meetings, even if his own period of service was complete. Special provisions were made for "other Lords of the Council admitted of old, some forth of the realm, some aged and not able never to travel, some otherwise occupied in high and weighty matters." In view of the average habits of the Scottish nobility at this date imagination is baffled by the allusion to high and weighty matters.

James Hepburn showed the same interest in currency reform that had marked his first period of power. An act was quickly passed to limit "the great scathe and detriment of the commonweal" caused by the "home-bringing of false, corrupt and counterfeit coins struck and forged within Flanders and other parts beyond sea." This bad money was passed in payment "for victuals and other goods and lawful merchandise," not only by Scots ("treacherously and avariciously"), but by the English townsmen of Berwick and Newcastle who had "daily and continual trade with the inhabitants of the Border."

The Council next busied itself issuing summonses to various Border lairds to appear by a given date under pain of treason, and in cancelling a sentence of outlawry on a priest who had gone to Rome without the Queen's permission. The tolerance implied by this remission makes the anti-catholic bias of the remaining decree a little puzzling. "The Queen's Majesty has found by certain experience that nothing has so effectually nourished and entertained the public quietness as the Act made at her arrival by which all men were commanded to contain themselves in quietness and that none privately or openly should make alteration or innovation of the state of religion." So far the sound administrative sense of maintaining the reformed doctrines is obvious. The conclusion is surprising, especially as it is enacted "with the advice of her Majesty's dearest" (and usually broad-minded) "husband." Certain people, the decree goes on, have procured from her Majesty private permits to practise their own form of religion. These exemptions have thrown some doubt on the sincerity of her intention to make no religious change. The permits are accordingly revoked, annulled and discharged. Whether the Duke's motive was concern over a possible ground for breach of the peace, desire to penalise some individual, or inveterate distaste for the ceremonies of Rome cannot be decided. The signature of the Bishop of Ross at the foot of the Act proves the equanimity with which it was received in catholic circles.

The help in the good government of the country which, under happier circumstances, Mary Stuart might have drawn from her new husband is indicated by the statesmanlike quality of his letters to the French and English Courts. He took advantage of the Bishop of Dunblane's despatch to France to send a letter to Charles IX, and a longer one to the Scottish Ambassador. On the lean, red-haired and demented youth who spoke no tongue but his own, and that with a "fast and thick" utterance, the Duke did not spend many words. Professing his continued "affection and zeal to do him humble service and to his crown," and expressing a pious hope that "the Creator would have him in his holy and worthy keeping," he left the Bishop to do the rest. He well knew that it was with the Queen Mother (that "bloudie Jezebel to the sancts of God") that he had to reckon. Believing two episcopal tongues to be better than one, he wrote to James Beton, the Scottish Ambassador, begging his "advice, convoy and assistance" for Dunblane in his delicate task of formally announcing the marriage to Charles, to Catherine and to the Cardinal of Lorraine.

"Now for ourselves," he proceeded, "somewhat we speak, although briefly . . . We cannot marvel indeed that this marriage and the rumour that preceded it appear right strange to you . . . The place and promotion truly is great, but yet with God's care neither it nor any other accident shall ever be able to make us forget any part of our duty to any nobleman or other our friends, and chiefly to you whom we have had good occasion always to esteem with the first of that number.

"Her Majesty might well have married with men of greater birth and estimation, but, we are well assured, never with one more affectionately inclined to do her honour and service; nor more willing towards you in all things that may gratify you or do you or any of yours advancement and pleasure. We desire and pray you to bestow and extend your will, engine and labour in the convoy and accomplishing of this message so far as possible may be, for the honour and contentation of the Queen's Majesty. The blame indeed we must confess and underlie, in so far as some things may appear omitted in ceremonies and counsel-taking as otherwise than of duty ought to have been done. Yet the wisdom and diligent care of a faithful servant and friend is able to remove and set by the force of many great accusations and make the excuses to be taken in good part, which we doubt not but ye will at your possibility. Further the

377

Bishop of Dunblane will show you at length." After which piece of judicious flattery, James Duke of Orkney signs himself his lordship's loving and assured friend.

Although the Duke hoped to win golden opinions on the farther side of the Channel, he did not ignore the need to stand well with England. When Robert Melville rode South with Mary's letters to the London Court, he carried the Duke's compliments to Elizabeth and her Secretary. It is perhaps worth noticing that in approaching these less impressionable personages, the consort of Mary Stuart dropped the regal "we."

With a suavity which Cecil would be the first to appreciate, the Duke reminded him of "his good will when I happened to be forth of my country." That memory encouraged him to take advantage of Robert Melville's mission "to visit you with this short letter of hearty thanks." Seeing that God" (the modesty of the writer more admirable than convincing) "has called me to this place, I heartily desire you to persevere in all your good offices touching amity," between the two countries. A reminiscence of Border routine marks the signature, "Your right assured friend *lawfully*, James D."

The letter to Elizabeth was more difficult. The Virgin Queen had a long memory which did not forget that sneer at her honesty. James Hepburn may be said to have emerged from the test with dignity and sense.

"Your Majesty will please a-pardon me that at this present have taken the boldness to write unto your Highness, knowing your Majesty, through misreports of my unfriends and evil-willers, at sometimes to have been offended with me. Which, as I never justly deserved, so now, being called to this place, I think ever to bestow my study and credit to the entertainment and continuence of the good amity and intelligence which heretofore has stood between your Highnesses."

Credence, he continues, can be given to Robert Melville, who carries the full instructions of the Scottish Court. The formula which had already given satisfaction in the letter to the archbishop serves once again. "I will thus far boldly affirm that, albeit men of greater birth and estimation might well have been preferred to this room, yet none more careful to see your two Majesties' amity and intelligence continued by all good offices, nor more affectionate to your Highness's honour and service, could have entered therein. Your Majesty's right humble with service to command lawfully, James D."

The question may be put whether a man of the intelligence these letters suggest would not have served his country better than the series of rapacious, bloodthirsty or incompetent regents who replaced him.

All the time swords were sharpening at Stirling. Some word of his danger reached Bothwell's ears, for the day after the two envoys had started for London and Paris, proclamations summoned earls, lords, barons, freeholders, landed men and substantial yeomen to report with arms and fifteen days' provisions to the Queen and her dearest husband at Melrose on the 15th June. Disorder in Liddesdale was the pretext given for this wholesale mobilisation. There is, however, no trace of any abnormal activity, while the force to be concentrated exceeds the demands of Border discipline.

At Stirling the hint was taken. The plotters hurried on their counter-measures and started fresh propaganda. The Queen's subjects were summoned, they murmured, not for service on the Border but to engineer a *coup d'etat* against the laws of the country and the person of the Prince.

To combat these rumours a royal proclamation promised that, as God knew the Queen's mind, she never meant the subversion of the laws. "As for her dearest son, of whom shall her Majesty be careful if she neglect him that is so dear to her, on whose good success her special joy consists and without whom her Majesty could not think herself in good estate but comfortless all the days of her life?" Her protests fell flat. Four months of incessant propaganda had done their work. Public opinion, that blind but far from deaf force, which, mobilised by experts, can so easily justify any crusade,

379

persecution, massacre or war, was inflamed. Bothwell's responsibility for the Darnley murder had become an act of faith and the woman who could marry him was believed capable of destroying her own child. Whatever may have been the case about Cæsar's wife, Bothwell's was suspect.

A political barometer is offered by Maitland's habit of waiting until he could pick the winning side. On the 5th or 6th June he left Court "without leave-taking" to join Atholl in the west. The Duke "used some choler" towards him before he went, "wherewith the Queen was somewhat offended." This not unnatural irritation the Secretary magnified into a charge that his enemy "thought to have slain him in the Queen's chamber, had not her Majesty come between." A less sensational story is given in Maitland's letter asking Cecil for money to finance the rebellion. He states that he found "the best part of the nobility resolved to look narrowly into his (Bothwell's) doings and being by them required, I would not refuse to join me to them in so just and reasonable a cause."

A few days later he was deep in a three-hours' conference with Balfour at the Castle, which resulted in a draft bond between its Governor and "certain noblemen." The anonymous committee, "being informed that the Earl Bothwell as yet remains in his wicked intention to keep our sovereign's person in thraldom and subjection, environed with men of war and his friends, so that none of the nobility may resort to her presence without their most extreme and utter danger, opened this most lamentable case to Sir James Balfour, who has faithfully promised to aid and assist us and put order to the premises with the Castle of Edinburgh for furthering of our enterprise." In order that "his honour might be safe," the meticulous Sir James had a proviso inserted that when the confederates arrived at Edinburgh his treachery should not be publicly exposed. He stipulated that the contracting parties should take plain part with him "*in all and whatsoever his actions he had had to do before the date of these presents*," thus securing indemnity

Drury to Cecil, 7 June, 1567.

Maitland to Cecil, 21 June, 1567.

James Beton to Archbishop of Glasgow. (Laing iii. 112.)
Registrum Honoris de Mortonis 18.

380

for the crime of Kirk o' Field. He finally extorted a promise to "promote him in any estate that he shall be meet for and maintain him in keeping of the Castle of Edinburgh." Sir James knew that its possession justified a hard bargain even when the astute Lethington was in the market.

Ignorant of the treachery that menaced the keystone of his strategy, on the 6th June the Duke of Orkney, accompanied "with artillery and men of war," took the Queen from Holyrood House to Borthwick Castle. The move to that formidable stronghold may have been the first stage of the journey to Melrose where the loyal concentration was ordered. More probably word had come from a sympathiser at Stirling of a plot to surround the palace. An advance on the capital was already planned and the advance guard under Morton and Home preceded Mar to a rendezvous at Liberton.

This was not the first time that James Hepburn had welcomed the hospitality of the high walls of Borthwick. From there he had watched the troops of the congregation sacking his castle of Crichton. The owner was a loyal servant of Mary's. Loyalty indeed was one of his rare virtues. A few years later his wife, Grissel, a daughter of the Laird of Buccleugh, had to complain that she "had continued with him in the mutual society and bond of matrimony this long time past, having borne to him seven bairns yet on life. Notwithstanding, he, being instigated by Satan, not only abstracted his company and society from her, but dealt very unkindly with her in giving her many injurious words, striking and dinging of her to the effusion of her blood in great quantities, without fear of God, pity, or compassion of her state being then great with child." Some years after these domestic scenes the impatient husband died ingloriously "of the French disease."

Supplementing Lord Borthwick's guardianship of the Queen with the chaperonage of one hundred and fifty hagbutters, the Duke left the Castle by night at the head of fifty hagbutters and as many friends as he could collect.

381

He led them to Melrose where he hoped to find the early arrivals of next week's mobilisation. His optimism disappointed, he left his hagbutters to form a nucleus and rode back to Borthwick.

He reached the Castle just in time. The same night the advance guard of the Stirling offensive had moved from Liberton to encircle Borthwick. A thousand cavalry led by Home, Morton and young Kerr of Cessford, at first tried to gain entry by a ruse. A party rode up to the gate, shouting that the rebels were after them. The trick did not flutter the pulses of one whose youth had been grounded on Sextus Julius's *Strategems and Subleties of War*. The next expedient met no greater success. With the futility of a savage tribe firing rifles against the civilising influence of an aeroplane, they "discharged several volleys of musketry" at the massive walls. In the absence of any visible result, they came near enough to the fortress for their shouts to be heard. They called the Duke traitor, murderer and butcher, "with divers undutiful and unseemly speeches used against their queen and sovereign, too evil and unseemly to be told, which, poor princess, she did with her speech defend." They taunted her husband and dared him to come outside and sustain his challenge to single combat. This touched a tender spot and the Duke had to be held back by his people.

Still the situation was serious. If James Hepburn allowed himself to be bottled up in a castle, however impregnable, there was no general fit to lead the Queen's army in the field. With one of his quick decisions, he resolved to break out at all costs. To take the Queen would be to risk her life. She had to stay in the comparative safety of the castle, under the care of Lord Borthwick and the hagbutters, until loyal reinforcements should raise the siege.

The Duke's escape had the dramatic quality he could never avoid. They said that he got past the outposts disguised as a woman. When his exploit in the turnspit's clothes in Sandybed's kitchen is remembered, the story is not impossible. He took one companion, the son of the

382

Laird of Crookston. As they saw some of Home's men coming, they separated. The patrol caught the laird's son, but the Duke, "less than an arrowshot" away, escaped. So near to Crichton every tree and footpath was familiar. Haddington was reached in safety.

Before the circle of the besiegers had closed on Borthwick, Mary had sent two messengers to Huntly for help. Both fell into the hands of Morton. He kept them till dawn before he let them go. The two men hurried to Edinburgh to give the alarm. The city ran to arms, but second thoughts counselled inaction. Mary's name had lost its magic; the Provost was disloyal; the burghers had seen the forces of the rebels ride past the town on their way to the rendezvous at Liberton.

Still the Borthwick besiegers felt uneasy; the main body under Mar and Lindsay had not arrived; Huntly might appear instead. From the capture of Crookston's son they would learn that the Duke, the official object of the raid, was safe. It was time to raise the siege. On their retreat they met Mar with eight hundred horse and decided to enter Edinburgh together.

When they had gone, Mary sent word to her husband. The next night at ten she changed into male attire, a travesty to which her lighter moments were partial. "Indecently disguised in man's clothes," as a mid-Victorian moralist complains, she made her way to the woods. The Duke was waiting a mile off with a cob and a man's saddle. Together they rode to the safety of Dunbar. The ride felt like old times with James Hepburn once again the loyal servant. It helped to restore the old atmosphere of trust on the Queen's side and devotion on the Duke's. They reached Dunbar at three in the morning.

Immediately they sent out a summons to all loyal subjects between the ages of sixteen and sixty to rally to their support. While they were waiting for a response, and for the hagbutters to make their way to Dunbar, news came from the capital. A deputation of three burgesses had been sent to keep a foot in both camps, and to "excuse the good town anent the entering of my

383

lords Atholl, Montrose, Mar, Morton and Home."
Whether the trio had the courage to deliver the rest of
the message which declared that the lords were in arms
to punish Darnley's murder, to put the Queen at liberty,
to dissolve her marriage and to preserve the Prince, is
more doubtful.

The insurgents had had an easy entrance to the
capital. Huntly, Archbishop Hamilton and Gavin
Hamilton were nominally loyal to the Queen. They
armed to defend the city while the Provost and citizens
went through the form of closing the gates. But when
the assailants climbed a low part of the wall and undid
the bolts from within, no resistance was offered. Huntly
and the Hamiltons retired to the Castle and the society
of Sir James Balfour, as, to the music of "Jacques and his
people," the confederate lords started issuing proclamations at the Market Cross. The object of the revolt was
still veiled in respectability. They said they wanted to
deliver the Queen, to punish the murderers and to protect
the Prince. Some of the simpler among them may even
have believed it.

In spite of all that propaganda could do, the response
was disappointing. Their most zealous supporters had
to admit that "the people did not join as was expected."
Their supplies of munitions were deficient; they had no
artillery; Atholl and Glencairn with the Highlanders
were late. If the loyalists at Dunbar had waited a few
more days to collect all available forces, the rebellion
might have faded away. Already the leaders had begun
to discuss disbanding, when Balfour came to the rescue.
He sent Edmund Hay, not the jesuit but the Duke's
attorney, with a message to the Queen advising her to
march at once on Edinburgh. The insurgents, he declared,
would not stand their ground with the knowledge that
the Castle would open fire on them. If the royal army
lingered at Dunbar, he would be forced to come to terms
with the masters of the city.

Convinced by his arguments, the Queen and the Duke
of Orkney rode out of Dunbar at the head of the two

hundred hagbutters, sixty regular cavalrymen and the moss-troopers who had answered their lord's call. With them went the three brass field-guns that Dunbar Castle could provide. The Queen had discarded her man's clothes and had borrowed what she could—a short red petticoat, sleeves tied in points, a muffler and a velvet hat. On her route loyal contingents fell in. By the time she had reached Haddington, numbers had risen to six hundred horse and infantry besides. Seton, Borthwick and Yester with their detachments joined the march, but an important reinforcement of Fleming and Lord John Hamilton never came. The two nobles were in touch with each other that day debating the best route to take. There is no explanation of their non-arrival. Huntly and the remaining Hamiltons stayed meekly inside the walls of Edinburgh Castle. No other great names were represented and for the most part the Duke had to rely on irregular contingents provided by the lairds of Lothian and of the Border, men like Ormiston, Langton, Waughton, Wedderburn and Bass.

Lord John Hamilton to Lord Fleming, 14 June, 1567. (Maitland Misc. ii.); Drury to Cecil, 29 June, 1567.

At Gladsmuir, a mile or two beyond Haddington, it was judged that enough supporters had joined to hear the Queen's proclamation.

"A number of conspirators" (it related) under pretext of preserving the Prince, although he was actually in their own keeping, had shown "their latent malice." Their real object was to dethrone the Queen that they might rule all things at their pleasure. Very necessity compelled her to take up arms and her hope was in the help of all faithful subjects, who would be rewarded with the lands and possessions of the rebels "according to the merit of each man."

After listening to these heartening words the army continued its march on Leith. Meeting no opposition from a reconnoitring body which the insurgents had sent in the direction of Haddington, they reached Prestonpans, where they halted for the night. Mary and Bothwell spent their last hours together at Seton House.

At two o'clock on Sunday morning the confederate

lords, reinforced at last by the Highlanders, gave the order to march. Their army moved out of Edinburgh in the direction of Musselburgh. Their numbers were about the same as the royalists', something under or over two thousand men. The cavalry was more numerous and better trained. There was no artillery. In the van was borne a white banner stretched between two pikes, the latest triumph of propaganda. Under a green tree lay Darnley, dead. Beside him knelt his infant son out of whose mouth proceeded the words, "Judge and revenge my cause, O Lord." In some respects the last Great War had nothing to teach the sixteenth century.

As dawn broke, the rebel army reached Musselburgh Bridge, where they halted until seven o'clock and ate their breakfast. A little later in the day the royal army took the field. Both sides passed the morning working south, manœuvring for the advantage of the ground. Here the Duke proved his generalship. By midday he had occupied the high ground of Carberry Hill. His field-guns dominated the slope up which the enemy had to advance. At the bottom ran a burn which their cavalry had to cross. The position was strengthened by some old entrenchments. The sun blazed off the brass of the cannon. The Red Lion of Scotland flapped lazily overhead. The Duke, well-satisfied, gave the orders to dismount and waited for the attack which could not take long to develop.

On the hillside opposite, about a mile away, he could see the advance guard of the enemy, cavalry led by Morton and Home. A little to their rear lay the main body, the infantry of Atholl, Mar, Glancairn, Lindsay, Ruthven and Sempill. Here, too, were the horsemen led by the Laird of Grange, the best soldier on the side, with Cessford's troopers and Tullibardine's. To the Duke's surprise he saw a small body of fifty horse come trotting down the hill. They passed the rebel outposts who had already crossed the burn. A parley, he quickly understood, was intended and he sent out thirty troopers to bring the mediator to the Queen.

Philibert du Croc, the French Ambassador, had spent

CONTEMPORARY DRAWING OF THE BATTLEFIELD OF CARBERRY HILL

Queen Mary is led by Grange towards the Insurgent Lords, with their cavalry and pikemen. Behind his guns Bothwell sits his black charger. His men are beginning to ride off the field. (By courtesy of the Record Office) is free to any who can win her. There is not a man of them but wishes himself in my place!"

He glanced proudly at the Queen. Her eyes, he saw, were full of tears and he turned abruptly to the Ambassador. The Queen's distress, he explained, troubled him. To spare her, to save bloodshed, would du Croc return to the lords to ask if there was any man of good family who would step out between the armies?

"I will meet him," James Hepburn added confidently, "for my cause is so just, that I am sure of having God on my side."

The Queen interrupted. Such a solution she would not accept. She would espouse her husband's quarrel. Du Croc, who had come on purpose to arrange single combat, now siding with Mary, declared it inadmissible. The Duke cut him short in the middle of his phrases. The time for parley had passed, he said, and pointed to the enemy, who seemed as if they meant to ford the burn.

"Will you," he asked the Ambassador, "imitate the man who tried to mediate a peace between the armies of Scipio and Hannibal, when, like us, they were ready to engage? Resolving to favour neither side, he took up a post of observation, where he could see the bravest pastime he had ever beheld. If you will do the same, you will have more pleasure than ever before, for you will see a fight well fought."

Du Croc's answer was in a more peaceful key; he did not look on civil war as a pastime. But when he wrote up his morning's work, he could not resist a tribute to the Duke. "I am bound to acknowledge," he confided in the King of France, "that the Duke seemed to me a great captain, speaking with undaunted confidence and leading his army gaily and skilfully. For some time I took pleasure in watching him and judged that he would have the best of the battle if his men stayed faithful. I admired him when he saw his enemies so resolute; he could not count on half of his men and yet was not dismayed. He had not on his side a single lord of note. I rated his chances higher because he was in sole command. I doubted

388

that the other side had too many counsellors; there was great disagreement among them. I took my leave of the Queen with regret and left her with tears in her eyes."

The attack which the Duke had foreseen did not materialise. The party he had noticed crossing the burn would be the corps of four hundred storm-troops who had been told off to break the ranks of the royal gunners. They took up a position at the bottom of the hill and halted. Du Croc rode back to the rebel headquarters and reported that he had found the Queen full of goodness and willing to forgive. The discouraging reply of the lords was to invite the Ambassador to let them conduct the battle in their own way.

It is probable that, though he does not admit it, the Frenchman reported the lack of fighting spirit he had noticed in the royal army. Discouragement had grown during the conferences. The troops were tired after the long march of the previous day; the sun was hot and they began to seek refreshment. Demoralisation set in and three or four hundred men quietly disappeared. Still the enemy did not move. Acting no doubt on the hint from du Croc, they saw that a waiting game would pay. The Duke in an effort to force matters moved his advance guard to the foot of the hill. The rebels moved towards them, but made no attempt to join battle. The declining sun shone in the eyes of the royalists.

The Duke could not trust his moss-troopers to fight a successful action, charging uphill against better-trained cavalry. He saw that something must be done to restore morale. The moment seemed ripe for the gesture he had dreamed of all his life. Mounting his war-horse, he rode to the front of the army and sent a herald to challenge his accusers to single combat.

The first to accept was James Murray of Purdovis. The Duke was delighted and put on his armour. The Queen, who did not share her husband's partiality to the practices of a forgotten chivalry, forbade him to meet a man of meaner birth and one who was a traitor. The objection was not unreasonable. Obviously, if the Duke was to fight the series of champions that the lords proposed, he had to concentrate on the more important. In his turn he went straight to the top, naming the Earl of Morton.

That nobleman, after accepting the challenge and choosing the broadsword as his weapon, preferred to delegate his privilege to his friend, Lord Lindsay. "The fiercest and most bigoted of the lords" sent an enthusiastic answer to the challenger. "I will fight him," his messenger declared, "what way he pleases, on horse or on foot; doublet alone or in armour; man for man, or six for six, or twelve for twelve. If the murder be not revenged with men, God will revenge it." As soon as this acceptance was received, the Duke set to work to gain the Queen's permission. Lindsay took off his armour to rest his limbs. He knelt in front of the whole army and prayed aloud "begging the mercy of God to preserve the innocent and in His justice to overthrow the vicious murderer of the innocent blood of the King." He began to rearm, and Morton clasped round his waist the great two-handed sword that Archibald Douglas, Bell-the-Cat, had carried. It was only left for the seconds, twenty gentlemen chosen by either side, to fix the conditions of the combat.

In these interminable preliminaries the rebels' wish to delay is manifest. Given time, the royal army would disintegrate. Its loyalty had worn thin; it never felt any zest for battle; it could see no point in waiting the issue of the duel. If the Duke won, there was little hope that the lords would accept the divine ruling. They would produce another champion, or resort to the more conventional method of general carnage. If the Duke was beaten his army would be leaderless and at the mercy of the foe.

By the time all the preparations were made, without striking a blow, the rebels had won the battle. James Hepburn went to the appointed place, as he afterwards declared, invoking the evidence of a thousand gentlemen. There he waited in vain for his opponent. Eye-witnesses join in testifying that all day long he was eager to fight. It was the lords who tacitly abandoned the duel when they judged their enemy sufficiently demoralised, and accused the Duke of sheltering behind his wife's opposition.

The delay had served its turn. At last the rebel army began to advance, carrying at its head the banner that advertised the King's murder. At the same time Grange, with two hundred horse, began a flanking movement. At this crisis the courage and loyalty of Mary's army failed. In vain the Duke exhorted his men to face the onslaught. Quickly he saw that a battle would mean a massacre. He advised the Queen to make the best terms she could.

Another parley in this day of parleys was called. Neither Atholl nor Lethington was willing to face his sovereign and Grange was sent to represent his side. He protested its real loyalty and offered a safe-conduct, if the Queen would leave her army and discuss terms. He had instructions to agree that her husband should be allowed to ride off the field unharmed and without pursuit.

Mary was faced with a difficult choice. The Duke told her that he could not win the battle with the troops at his disposal. To try meant useless slaughter of her subjects. Her son was a hostage in the hands of her enemies. No doubt she hoped she could repurchase their obedience as she had after Rizzio's murder. If she could secure her husband's safety, and an indemnity for his men, she was inclined to trust her person to the hands of the men who so emphatically professed their loyalty to it.

James Hepburn differed. He warned his wife against her persistent faith in human nature. He knew the treachery of the lords and guessed their purpose. Let the Queen retreat to Dunbar and allow him and such men as he could trust, to defend her there. He could not get her to listen. He gave up, insisting only that Grange should grant her a formal safe-conduct. *Les Affaires du Comte de Boduel 20.*

The laird was in a hurry. If the Queen did not send her husband away immediately, he could not promise to restrain his men. So one of the most dramatic partings the world has known was enacted in full view of two armies, condemned to shed their blood in fratricidal slaughter should the courage of the separating couple fail. Their distress was watched by the eyes of thousands ablaze with hatred, cold with curiosity, a few, it may be hoped, moist with sympathy. Had James Hepburn known it, he and his wife were to provide a spectacle more memorable than Scipio or Hannibal ever offered.

Mary looked very young and not much like a queen in a scarlet petticoat that came to her knees. Her eyes were dark with disappointment and fatigue. Her heart went out to her husband, worn by the escape from Borthwick and the preparations at Dunbar, exhausted by the long march to Carberry, grilled in his armour by the heat of the sun, nerve-racked by waiting for a battle that never came. Parting would make his defeat more bitter. It was "with great anguish and grief" that she told him sorrowfully that he must go. She forgot his faults, the harm he had done, the ruin he had brought. She was sending away the only man in Scotland she had ever trusted, the man who had risked everything to win her. She clung to him and many times they kissed.

They could delay no longer. He put her from him and in a voice that onlookers could hear asked whether she would not keep her promise to be his loyal wife. She nodded and gave him her hand. He walked slowly to where his charger stood, leapt into the saddle and with a dozen friends went galloping down the Dunbar road. His shadow thrown by the sinking sun stretched beyond him.

Before dark they led the Queen of Scots a prisoner into Edinburgh. Before her fluttered the white banner with its picture of her husband's corpse. Around her, in a daze, she heard the shouts of the rabble—" 'Burn her, burn her, she is not worthy to live; kill her, drown her!' Others of the north parts with one voice cried, 'Burn the whore!' which amazed her much and bred her tears."

CHAPTER THIRTY-THREE

THE sanguine and resilient spirit of the Duke of Orkney did not accept the disaster of Carberry as irreparable. As long as he had life and liberty he believed he could salvage the Queen's cause. He had already experienced reverses and had surmounted them. He retired to the security of Dunbar to prepare a fresh challenge to fortune.

That belief in his recuperative powers was shared by his enemies. It explains in part their harsh treatment of the captive Queen. She refused to forget the husband they had forced her to abandon. She wept over the wrong done her in separating her "from a husband with whom she thought to live and die with all the contentment in the world." If she could choose "she would leave her kingdom and dignity and live as a simple demoiselle with him. She will never consent that he shall fare worse than herself." She wrote, it was stated, a letter "calling him her dear heart, whom she should never forget nor abandon for absence." This indecent overture from a wife to her husband provided the pretext to keep her prisoner. She was hurried by night to the island fortress of Lochleven, whose lake and whose walls would tax, it was felt, the inventiveness of that specialist in desperate remedies, the Duke of Orkney. There she was left to reconsider a vow to touch no flesh till she was restored to her husband.

Besides her loyalty to the man she had married and the affection that was developing, she was tied to him by another imperative bond. When in the third week of July Elizabeth's envoy urged her for her own sake to give up the Duke, "she sent word back that she would rather die, taking herself to be seven weeks gone with child, and, by renouncing him, she would acknowledge

du Croc to Catherine de Medicis, 17 June, 1567.

Throckmorton to Queen Elizabeth, 14 July, 1567.

Melville 156.

Throckmorton to Queen Elizabeth, 18 July, 1567.

Castelnau le
Laboureur
(*Jebb. ii.*
610).

Life of Mary
Stewart C.
Nau. 60.

du Croc to
Charles IX.,
21 June, 1567.
P.C. Reg., 13
July, 1567.

Les Affaires
du Comte de
Boduel 21.

Throckmorton
to Cecil, 6
July, 1567.

herself to be with child of a bastard." There is a story that a daughter was born to Mary and Bothwell in February, 1568, who afterwards took the veil at the convent of Our Lady of Soissons. If this is true, the nun was James Hepburn's only legitimate child. Nothing is known of her life; indeed her existence is denied. The Queen's private secretary states that about the 24th July, 1567, his mistress had a miscarriage of twins which prostrated her. The absence of any corroboration of the survival of a baby at Lochleven makes it safer to believe this not infallible reporter.[1]

It is unlikely that word ever reached the Duke of his prospective paternity. As soon as he heard that the Queen was imprisoned in Lochleven, he slipped out of Dunbar, leaving the castle in the reliable hands of the Laird of Whitelaw. He chose the sea route—the fishermen of Crail seem to have run a service for the beleagured garrison of Dunbar—and sailed up the Firth of Forth, taking advantage no doubt of the darkness. He was trying to rally the Queen's vassals who were still loyally disposed. At Linlithgow he met Lord Claud Hamilton. Receiving his promises of support, he proceeded to the west coast, probably to Dumbarton Castle, which Lord Fleming, in spite of his failure to appear at Carberry, still held for the Queen. In the space of a week the Duke's energy worked wonders. The Hamiltons, Huntly, Seton and Fleming were recorded "at his devotion." Argyll and Boyd, ever uncertain in their disloyalty, had espoused the royal cause. On his list, the Duke claimed upwards of fifty imposing names. His hopes rose. Why should he not repeat the history of the Rizzio recovery? Unfortunately, now as then, the key to the situation was the person of the Queen. On this occasion she was in securer custody. Her gaolers were of sterner stuff than the facile Darnley. The loyalists assembling at Hamilton were warned that any open move might provoke a fatal reprisal.

---

[1] Mary herself alluded to James VI as "my only child." She was fond of a device showing a lioness and its whelp with a motto that flattered the British Solomon—"*unum quidem sed leonem.*"

It was, no doubt, this threat that sent the Duke back to Dunbar by the 25th June. In his safe return he was more fortunate than several other persons who had been named with him as guilty of the murder. Captain William Blackadder was taken at sea on his way to Dunbar with John Blackadder, James Edmonston and Mynart Freis,[1] a Swedish sailor. Charles Wilson, the privateer who had failed to catch Bothwell on his return from France, was their captor and tasted a vicarious revenge. He was helped by a Colonel John Clerk, a soldier of fortune, normally in the Danish service, who was destined to make a great deal more trouble for James Hepburn. The prisoners, as they came ashore, were stoned by a mob of women and boys. From Leith they were taken to the Tolbooth to be tortured. Unable to give any details of the Kirk o' Field tragedy, Captain Blackadder professed his innocence to a packed Lennox jury. As he sat in the cart that was dragged backwards to the gallows at the Market Cross, he must have regretted the impulse that took him at the sound of the explosion from his glass of claret into the deserted street. His legs and arms were broken and subsequently fixed on the gates of Stirling, Glasgow, Perth and Dundee. Behind her bandage, Justice was warming to her work. John Blackadder and Edmonston suffered in September. Mynart Freis got back in safety to his ship.

Other innocent victims of the placards met various fates. William Powrie was tortured and forced to provide one of the famous depositions. Several months passed before he was brought to the gallows. Sebastien Pagez, the Auvergnat, and Francisco Busso, the Italian, were thrown into the Tolbooth gaol. Black Mr. John Spens "had promise of his life because he uttered his knowledge of the Duke and delivered two of the Duke's coffers,

[1] In the Danish Rigsarchiv is a safe-conduct issued in 1567 by Bothwell as Admiral of Scotland to Mynart Freis of the service of the King of Sweden. It is stated that Freis had a good and sufficient letter of marque from the King of Sweden. Edmonston and Captain Blackadder had permits granted them by Bothwell to pursue the enemies of the King of Sweden (Schiern 313 n). In the light of subsequent events it is worth noticing that Bothwell was pro-Swedish in the war then raging between that country and Denmark.

wherein is not the least part of his wealth." Captain William Cullen was kept "in the irons" for the best part of a week. His statement under torture "revealed the murder of the King with the whole manner and circumstance"—and was promptly suppressed. Released, he lived four uneasy years to be found in a cupboard by Morton, who hanged him "to the end that he might the more freely enjoy the favour of his fair wife."

Scrope to Cecil, 16 June, 1569.

By far the most useful capture was Geordie Dalgleish, Bothwell's tailor. The story of his taking is significant. Morton was at dinner with Maitland at Edinburgh. An informer "in a secret manner" showed that the parson of Oldhamstocks and George Dagleish had come from Dunbar. Archibald Douglas was sent after the parson (it seemed tactful that clergyman should catch clergyman) only to succeed in capturing his horse. The search for Dalgleish had almost been abandoned when "a good fellow" offered "for a mean piece of money" to reveal Geordie's whereabouts. The unlucky tailor protested that he had only been sent "to visit his master's clothing." His captors, however, claimed that various title-deeds belonging to the Duke and including the Patent to the Earldom of Orkney were found in his hands. Dalgleish was put in the gêne, or little-ease, at the Tolbooth and threatened with more drastic tortures. Next day "before any rigorous demeaning of his person, fearing the pain and moved by conscience, he called for Mr. Archibald Douglas." He could not have made a more ironic choice. Taken out of the gêne, the tailor led his persecutors to the Potterrow where he produced from the foot of a bed a silver casket! This lucky find, opened in front of the rebel lords on Saturday, 21st June, was claimed to contain the letters and papers that proved the Queen to have been Bothwell's mistress and accomplice in her husband's murder. Its opportune discovery by the Douglas gang doubles the suspicion that enshrouds its rare appearances.

Morton's Declaration, 29 Dec., 1565.

Ignorant of the poison his enemies were distilling, James Hepburn paid a hurried visit from Dunbar to the Border. His object was to encourage his friends to harry the usurping party. He stopped a night with Ormiston, who was defying capture in the wilds of Teviotdale. The Kerrs of Ferniehurst were willing to co-operate. Langton was ready to rise when the time was ripe.

These preliminaries did not escape the eyes of the acting government, which decided that the tolerance hitherto shown the man whose punishment was the pretext of revolt, was dangerous. The Duke had made considerable headway in his campaign, but the depositions that had been wrung from his servants now provided material to damn him. There was also the backing of Knox, returned from the seclusion Rizzio's murder had imposed. The Reformer was able to "continue his severe *Throckmorton* exhortation, as well against the Queen as the Earl Both- *to Queen* well, threatening the great plague of God to this whole *Elizabeth, 27* country if she be spared from her condign punishment." *July, 1567.* The day after the General Assembly of the Kirk had met, a reward of a thousand crowns was offered for the capture of the Earl of Bothwell, who "thinks to persuade and entice simple and ignorant men to assist him." The evidence of the depositions was summarised and everybody of every estate and degree was forbidden "to supply the Earl in their houses, or to support him with men, armour, horse, ships, boats or other furnishing by sea or land." If they did, they would be judged "plain partakers with him in the horrible murder." For a start the Laird of Whitelaw was summoned to surrender the Castle of Dunbar, where the "murderer" had taken refuge.

Three days later James Hepburn was given statutory three weeks' notice to answer at the Tolbooth for the murder, for kidnapping the Queen and, "for fear of her life, making her promise to marry him." The ten days that had passed since the Casket was found had not disclosed the three Stirling letters that would have proved the abduction collusive!

The accused did not elect to stand his trial. Five days before the date fixed he was declared outlaw and rebel. During the following winter he was formally forfeited in Parliament by act of attainder, condemned to lose

397

arms, honours, offices and dignities and to underlie the pain of treason.

These severe measures ruined the cause for which he strove. Royalists hesitated to be associated with an outlaw who had a price on his head. Even Seton and Fleming, who had been consistently loyal to Mary and friendly to her husband, withdrew from the connection. Bothwell saw he could do little in the south and ran the risk of being trapped inside Dunbar, where he was useless to the royal cause. Soon after the price was set on his head, he sailed across the Firth of Forth and up the east coast. Landing, he paid a surprise visit to his late brother-in-law at Strathbogie. At first Huntly listened with some interest to plans for levying a force of Highlanders to march to the Queen's rescue. But finding how little backing his guest could command in the Lowlands, the Gordon, who had never been much help to the Queen, quickly lost heart. Gossip ran that he bore James Hepburn no good will and hoped the Queen and his sister would soon be rid of "so wicked a husband." It was not long before Lady Jean left Crichton, making her way back to her mother at Strathbogie. Passing through Edinburgh she told Lady Moray that she would never again have anything to do with her ex-husband. On this unforgiving note she passes out of the story, nearly all of whose actors she was destined to outlive. She died at Dunrobin at the age of eighty-four, the relict of two more husbands, the sickly Earl of Sutherland and the patient Ogilvie of Boyne.

From the unsympathetic atmosphere of Strathbogie Bothwell withdrew one night to find a more generous welcome from the unregenerate Bishop of Moray. The government, disapproving of this display of avuncular affection, vindictively forbade Patrick's tenants to pay their rents. That, they felt, would teach him to "defend reset, supply, fortify and maintain" an outlaw.

While Bothwell was enjoying his great-uncle's hospitality, his mind was busy with fresh projects. On land he could find neither safety nor support. Could he not

Blackwood
(*Jebb ii.*
227).

create an empire on the waves and thence defy his enemies until the moment came to strike a decisive blow for the Queen? Various factors made his maritime prospects hopeful. That he was hereditary Admiral of Scotland assured him a backing of the conservative race of fishermen, traders and pirates from whom the naval strength of the country was recruited.

A strong card in his hand was the Queen's grant of Orkney and Shetland. Those islands would provide a fresh accession of hardy and skilful seamen and the use of safe and inaccessible harbours. Here the Queen's writ would carry more weight than a sentence of outlawry passed by remote and disloyal noblemen. Again, the hereditary principle would help the descendant of the first Earl of Bothwell, former holder of that fief.

It was a generation that took readily to adventure on the high seas. Already the Englishman Hawkins was harrying the trade routes of Spain. Before ten years were up, Drake had circumnavigated the globe. The idea of a private naval hegemony founded in the Orkneys by the Admiral of Scotland was bold but not fantastic. The adventurous of all seas would flock there in an age that drew no hard line between lawful enterprise and piracy.

Necessarily the scheme had small beginnings. Bothwell got together five ships which he manned and equipped. Their complements numbered three hundred men. To collect additional stores and munitions he sent a vessel down the coast to Eyemouth, whence access could be had to Dunbar. John Hepburn of Bolton was the captain and he carried letters to his leader's friends in the South. From that mission he did not return alive. "I had ships provided," he said as he walked to the scaffold, "but I could not escape."

Ignorant of his follower's fate, the Admiral was congratulating himself on a windfall. In Cromarty Firth, sheltering from the weather, lay a St. Andrews ship, owner Allan Watson, carrying foodstuffs for the Earl of Moray. This vessel Bothwell "and his complices masterfully and violently spoiled and reft with the goods

399

and gear extending to the sum of £100." His fleet now numbered half a dozen.

A little later he enlarged it by less arbitrary means.
Proc. Soc. Ant. Scot. 1890 391, 513. Throckmorton to Cecil, 26 Aug., 1567. Les Affaires du Comte de Boduel 22.
There was a Hanseatic merchant of Bremen called Geert Hemelingk, who maintained a trading station in the Shetlands in the parish of Dunrossness, probably at the Pool of Virkie. He used to buy fish from the islanders and ship it to the Continent. To pay, he could import flax and hemp, iron or tar. A large two-masted vessel of his, the *Pelican*, which carried guns against pirates, was lading fish at Sumbergh Head. Bothwell took a fancy to her. He agreed to charter her for two months at fifty crowns a month, with compensation of 1600 crowns if she perished, or was not returned. At the same time he made a similar contract for another ship which he believed to be the property of a second Hanseatic merchant, this time a Hamburg man. The real owner, however, seems to have been a Hamburg pirate named David Wodt, whose irregular means of livelihood was later to compromise the lessee. Geert Hemelingk[1] was a bona fide trader, as the deed he signed with Bothwell shows. So does the petition he lodged the following March with the Burgomaster of Bremen, complaining that the *Pelican* had not been returned nor the promised compensation paid. But circumstances by then were outside the borrower's control.

At the beginning of August Bothwell had to leave the
Throckmorton to Queen Elizabeth, 31 July, 1567.
Bishop's Palace. His uncle was glad to shelter him, but three of the episcopal bastards made themselves unpleasant. Whether from personal dislike, fear of the consequences of harbouring an outlaw, resentment at the damage to their father's rent-roll, or anxiety to draw the blood money, they plotted against their visitor. Widening their circle, they took into their confidence the captain of the garrison and Christopher Rokesby, an English spy for many months incarcerated at Spynie.

---

[1] These Hanseatic merchants were a vigorous breed. Thirty-five years later the ever-green Geert Hemelingk was in trouble over the murder of the second son of the Foude of Shetland.

This elderly agent, who had tried to curry favour with Queen Mary by giving her an ivory tablet engraved with the Passion of Our Lord, wrote south for instructions. To save his skin, he said, he had been forced to agree to Bothwell's murder or arrest; which would the English envoy prefer?

Sir Nicholas Throckmorton gave the question his careful attention. As Bothwell had twelve to fourteen desperate followers, he doubted that he could be taken alive. It would not be agreeable, he knew, to Queen Elizabeth's "princely nature, nor to her godly mind, to consent to any murder," although she would have been well content "that the said Earl either by justice were executed, or otherwise the world were rid of him by God's hand." Sir Nicholas was in a squeamish mood and remarked severely that the proposal to kill "the ould busshope" as well, looked "a very cruel and abominable act." Not wishing, however, to be narrow-minded, he suggested that the question might profitably be referred to Maitland, who had "more interest" in the matter than the Queen of England.

Rokesby seems to have taken the hint, but in spite of encouragement from Maitland and the approval of Huntly, the outcome was disappointing. Bothwell was ready for all comers. In the fraças one of the bishop's sons was killed, the garrison put out of the castle, their place supplied by the Earl's own men. This, by the way, is the only time that James Hepburn is recorded as responsible for a killing.

Thereafter relations at Spynie were strained, and the Admiral was not sorry when he was ready for a move to the Orkneys. His enemies in the south had foreseen some such intention. They had sent a herald to warn "the gentlemen and inhabitants of Orkney" that the outlaw was likely to try "to entice and persuade ignorant folks under pretence of a pretended hereditable gift of the lands of Orkney and Shetland." They were instructed not to "answer, obey or make payment."

Certain other obstructive measures had to be

abandoned. Charles Wilson, the privateer, had volunteered "to impeach the passage of the Earl Bothwell, in case he went to the Isles." Alas! his natural desire to try his luck a second time against the Admiral was not to be realised. Wilson fell into an argument with Colonel John Clerk over the relative share his seamanship and the colonel's valour had played in the capture of Blackadder. Words led to blows and all his employers could offer the sailor was an obituary commemorating his skill, his hardiness, his honesty (in the technical protestant sense), and his willingness to tackle Bothwell.

So the little fleet had a free crossing to the Orkneys. The Admiral met a good reception and the islanders "began to lean on him." Once again his path was crossed by the Balfour family. In Edinburgh Sir James was just completing his arrangements to hand over the Castle "on a good composition." The adjective does not exaggerate. In exchange for that key position the ingenious lawyer received a priory, a pension for his son, a pardon for his actions at Kirk o' Field and five thousand pounds in cash. In the Orkneys his brother was able to do Bothwell a comparable disservice. Gilbert Balfour had been sheriff of the islands since January, 1566, and held Noltland and Kirkwell Castles. At the orders of the government he refused the Admiral admission and fired on his ships. If Bothwell had counted on these strongholds as naval bases, this meant a serious disorganisation of his plans. He lay two days in the port, or more probably out of reach of the Kirkwell guns in Scapa Flow, and decided that he was not strong enough to assault fortifications. It was then that the idea of seeking help for the Queen in Sweden, Denmark or France may have crossed his mind. For the time being he decided to try the Shetlands.

The islanders gave their feudal lord the same reception he had met in the Orkneys. Their Foude, Oliver Sinclair of Brew, was glad to welcome the son of Lady Agnes Sinclair. But clouds were gathering. If little energy had as yet been shown in pursuit of the outlaw, it was because the conscience of Morton told him that a capture and trial might provoke inconvenient revelations. The position was changed by the Queen's enforced abdication and her half-brother's return to Scotland. On 22nd August, 1567, Moray took the oath as regent and saw his patient ambition gratified. The 72nd Psalm was sung in his honour.

"Give the king thy judgments, O God, and thy righteousness to the king's son. In his days shall the righteous flourish and abundance of peace so long as the moon endureth. To him shall be given all the gold in Sheba . . ."

If the royal bastard succeeded in amassing a substantial quantity of the gold of Sheba or elsewhere, his regency was less fortunate in procuring abundance of peace.

At once he took a strong line against Bothwell. Convenient absence had left his own hands ostensibly clean and he had a long-standing quarrel to settle. Two days after his return to Scotland the magistrates of Dundee had orders to man four large ships, the *Primrose*, the *James*, the *Robert*, and the *Unicorn* with "honest, true and faithful skippers and mariners." It was said that Leith provided another four vessels. Guns were mounted and four hundred hagbutters embarked. Grange and Tullibardine were put in charge and given the help of Bishop Adam Bothwell, "the devilish magician, sorcerer of the Orcades." Not any occult powers, but a geographical knowledge of his see, which he had once visited, and his authority with the islanders were wanted. Summary justice was intended, and the bishop's knowledge of law —he was a Lord of Session—was hoped might prove useful in sentencing the man he had married three months before.

The commission that the Council granted the Lairds of Grange and Tullibardine shows what was in their minds. After preluding that God of His inestimable goodness had moved the hearts of the nobility and other faithful lieges to withdraw the Queen's person out of Bothwell's unhappy company, the deed alleged that the bereaved husband had associated himself with "notorious and manifest pirates intending nothing else but with all cruelty to oppress, overthrow and destroy all honest and true merchants and travellers." Power was given to pursue the malefactors "with fire, sword and all other kind of hostility," and an indemnity was granted in case anybody was "hurt, slain or mutilated." Provision was made for courts *in situ* to dispose of survivors. A sigh of relief would have risen in Edinburgh and Stirling, if Bothwell had been killed in battle or promptly executed without chance to testify.

In the third week of August Grange and the bishop embarked in the *Unicorn*. The laird was in high spirits. His letter to his favourite correspondent, the Earl of Bedford, exudes animosity against Bothwell. "For my part, albeit I be no good seaman, I promise unto your lordship if I may once encounter with him either by land or sea, he shall either carry me with him or else I shall bring him dead or quick to Edinburgh." Maitland was no less confident and told the French Ambassador "they had good hope of Bothwell shortly." Moray was more cautious.

Grange to Bedford, 10 Aug., 1567.

Throckmorton to Queen Elizabeth, 14 Aug., 1567.

Throckmorton to Cecil, 1 Sept., 1567.

"We cannot merchandise for the bear's skin," he remarked cannily, "before we have him."

The expedition touched at the Orkneys to get word from Gilbert Balfour of the quarry's movements. No warning reached Bothwell of his danger. As his enemy closed silently on his little fleet lying at anchor in Bressay Sound, he was eating his midday meal with the Foude. Part of his ships' complements, the captains and fighting men, were also ashore. His sailors did not wait. They knew that without Admiral or shock troops they could not engage a heavily-armed flotilla. They cut their cables and ran northwards up the channel with Grange and Tullibardine in hot pursuit.

The pursuers had the advantage of surprise. One of Bothwell's ships was a bad sailor and lost ground at every yard. But she knew the waters and skill made up for speed. Profiting by her shallower draught, she lured the *Unicorn* over a sunken rock. The fugitive's keel grated but she passed on without serious damage. Grange's flagship struck fair and square; she filled and sank like a stone. The bishop, for all the breastplate he wore under his robes, was as agile on his feet as in his political attachments. His leap to safety was remembered in local tradition down the centuries.

The *contretemps* disorganised pursuit, for the rest of the flotilla hauled to, to rescue survivors and to salvage guns. Bothwell's four ships, with the heroine of the engagement in the rear, made good their escape to Unst, the most northerly of the isles.

Meanwhile Grange had landed and was searching the mainland. Two of Bothwell's local supporters, David Willie and George Fogo, were caught, but the Admiral himself had not waited. Collecting all the men he could find, he had disappeared to the north of the island. A boat took him and his followers across Yell Sound. Hot-foot, he crossed Yell Island and over the narrow Bluemull to Unst where he found his ships. One of them he sent down the west coast to Scalloway to pick up a detachment he had not been able to carry with him on his forced retreat. Guessing that the day's fighting was not over, he chose for this duty a vessel that carried his plate, jewels, armour and personal belongings.

His guess was shrewd; there was to be no respite. It was true that Grange, for all his vows to catch his enemy, had had enough. He stayed on dry land with the bishop and let Tullibardine bring the flotilla up east of the islands. Bothwell was ready off Unst and engaged him in a running fight. Three hours the battle raged, working all the time out to sea. The lame duck could not defend herself and fell into Tullibardine's hands. Bothwell was left with two ships. Still he fought on. The mainmast of the *Pelican* was shot away. Defeat and death looked inevitable when a south-westerly squall blew up. Superior seamanship extricated Bothwell's battered survivors from their danger. Running before the wind, they showed the pursuit their heels. Before giving up, Tullibardine followed for sixty miles.

In Shetland a search for stragglers began. Hay of Talla succeeded for the moment in escaping the hunters. A fishing boat carried him to Fife, where he was betrayed to Lord Lindsay, the torture chamber and the scaffold. In a Shetland sound the *James* found the ship that had been captured from Allan Watson. "She was void and desolate of the Earl and his servants." Her only occupant was a cook, presumably a bad one. The discovery did Watson little good, for the sailors of the *James* stole his gear and tried to sell the hull.

Throckmorton to Queen Elizabeth, 20, 22 Aug., 1567.

Thus faded Bothwell's hopes to rescue the Queen and restore her throne. With Moray regent, and Bothwell fugitive, the activity of the royalists soon subsided. Most of the leaders, Huntly, Fleming, Livingstone, made overtures of peace. For a little time Dunbar held out. Guns were brought from Edinburgh and the castle capitulated. On the first of October the names of sixty-two of Bothwell's adherents appeared in a summons of forfeiture. The lords had broken every one of the terms to which they had agreed at Carberry.

CHAPTER THIRTY-FOUR

ALL day Bothwell's battle-scarred hulks ran before the wind. They needed badly to recondition; they were short of provisions; but escape from the jaws of death made these disabilities look trifles that ingenuity or luck could correct. Before night fell, they had overhauled a merchantman from the port of Rostock. Had Bothwell been the pirate his enemies pretended, here was a chance to refit and revictual. All he did was to secure the German's services to pilot his ships to safe anchorage on the unknown shores they were approaching. All night the good samaritan followed their course. *Les Affaires du Comte de Boduel 24.*

In daylight Bothwell could see the Norwegian coast, fold after fold of every shade of blue, each graduation indicating a fresh range of hills or a different headland. Remote snow gleamed on distant peaks. Lower and nearer, cliffs loomed harsh and naked. Soon the Rostock master identified the low land of Karmoi, over which towers a crag like a beacon. In Karm Sound the Scottish ships could find still water, and on the island peasants to sell them provisions. The Hanseatic ship piloted them through the channel and lent them a boat to carry their cable ashore.

Hardly had they tied up before another sail slid in sight. From its cut they recognised a warship of the King of Denmark. She proved to be the *Bear*, commanded by Captain Christiern Aalborg, one of Frederick II's ablest sailors. Norway, after a recent history that consisted of little but fire, pestilence and famine, was at this time the dependency of Denmark. The *Bear* was patrolling her waters on the look out for the pirates whose activity depleted the revenue which the King of Denmark expected to draw from the dues of the Sound and the most productive custom-house in Europe.

It was not for nothing that James Hepburn was Admiral of Scotland and had lived with the daughter of a Danish Admiral. He knew what was expected, giving orders to strike topsails and pay the salute to a Danish warship that Danish naval supremacy could exact in Scandinavian waters. His courtesy did not prevent investigation. The *Bear* sent to ask who the seafarers were and whither they were going. Bothwell, wishing to keep his identity secret, put forward the master of his ship to answer that they were Scottish gentlemen on their way to Denmark to take service with her king. The northern Seven Years' War with Sweden was in full swing and both countries were reduced to devastating where they could not conquer. Mercenaries were especially useful in this warfare, and Frederick's army of 30,000 Germans welcomed the addition of Scottish soldiers of fortune. Bothwell's improvisation sounded plausible enough.

But Aalborg knew his job. Where were the foreigners' papers? To explain the deficiency, Bothwell sent one of his gentlemen (there were forty in a total complement of one hundred and forty) to state, without mentioning names, that events in Scotland had enforced a sudden embarkation omitting the usual formalities. The Queen, who should have signed the ship's papers, was a close prisoner. But Bothwell's emissary was not very successful; soon Aalborg was obliged to send back for an interpreter.

His next invitation was to the master and some of the ship's company. He had made up his mind that the visitors meant no good and that he must use his wits to disarm them. With only half their man-power, his position was delicate. On the pretence of issuing provisions, giving his written promise to let the Scots return to their ships when they liked, he contrived to divide them into more than one party; some he kept on board the *Bear*, where his men outnumbered their guests, and some he sent ashore, where a scare of pirates had mobilised the peasants. Bothwell, who had no reason to suspect the

Dane's good faith, allowed his forces to be split and separated from their artillery. To his indignation, as soon as he had voluntarily renounced his advantage, he heard Aalborg announce that his guests were his prisoners and that he intended to take them to Bergen.

Driven into a corner, the Duke of Orkney disclosed his identity. He had had no rest and little food since he had jumped up from the Foude's dinner-table at the sound of enemy guns; he had led a desperate retreat across the islands; he had fought a three-hour sea battle and crossed the North Sea in a small ship and a gale; he had sent away the boat that contained all his worldly possessions, and he was dressed "in old, torn and patched boatswain's *Examination* clothes." With sublime self-confidence he announced that *of Bothwell,* he was the supreme governor of all Scotland, and *23 Sept., 1567* demanded his freedom. *(Les Affaires xxxviii.)*

It is depressing to record that the gesture was not a success. Captain Aalborg was frankly incredulous. The Scot would have a chance, he was told, to repeat his story at Bergen to the Governor of the Castle, to Erik Ottesen Rosenkrantz. The name had a familiar, and not a welcome, ring. James Hepburn had not known Anna Throndsen without hearing of her influential cousin, the Viceroy of Norway, senator, lord of Valsö, Arreskov, Sem and half a dozen more places. It was months since he had had time to think of Anna.

Beggars could not be choosers, even if they were also the supreme governors of Scotland, and on the 2nd September, 1567, Bothwell, his hundred and forty men and his two ships were brought to the narrow harbour of Bergen. Like spectators in an amphitheatre, rows of gaily-painted wooden houses peered down from their vantage points on the mountain slopes that encircled the harbour. The only access to the town was from the sea, and to regulate that access the Rosenkrantz Tower rose abruptly at the water's edge. Its lord was well placed to keep a jaundiced eye on the activities of the Hanseatic merchants whose narrow, wooden houses lined the water-front.

The German quarter was shut off by gates and barriers

409

from the Norwegian town and little love was lost between the nationalities. In small dark rooms to which no woman might enter, even to make the cupboard bed, by the light of evil-smelling cod liver oil lamps, the merchants drove hard bargains with fishermen, ignorant of values. The Norwegian wheeled his catch up the narrow alleys that separated each pair of houses and watched it lifted by rope and pulley to the open hatch above. The trader, fumbling under his fur-lined cloak for his keys, doled out from his store the meagre payment of cloth or corn or schnapps.

Much as Bergen, and Rosenkrantz in particular, disliked the Hanseatic guests, their importance could not be ignored, and when a board was appointed to investigate the circumstances of Bothwell's arrival and arrest, ten members of the "Counter" or trading community served. The other fourteen members included the Bishop of Bergen, the Justice of Bergen, two of his neighbouring colleagues, some magistrates of the town and commandants of local garrisons.

*Les Affaires
du Comte de
Boduel xxxvii.*

Erik Rosenkrantz sent them on board the *Bear* to find out the truth. With a certain condescension the Admiral met the solemn little procession in its best black cloaks with sable-lined sleeves and collars. He told them he had come from Scotland and was going to France, stopping on his way to visit the King of Denmark. Memory of his former mission from Mary of Lorraine to the Danish Court may have suggested this version of his movements. The next questioner inquired who he actually was; "to which he gave answer that he was the husband of the Queen of Scotland." The Board made no difficulty in accepting this statement; it was supported "by the evidence of merchants and by the serenity of his countenance." What was puzzling was the absence of documents of any sort, passport, ship's papers. . . . Bothwell's answer was magnificent.

*Turner
(Jebb i. 415).*

"Who," he asked scornfully, "can give me credentials? Being myself the supreme ruler of the land, of whom can I receive authority?"

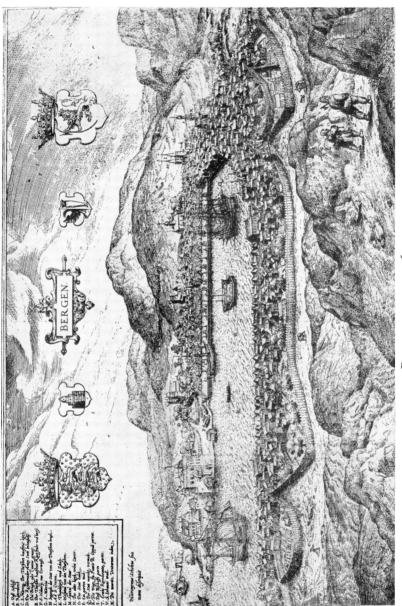

BERGEN, ABOUT 1565

(By courtesy of the Bergen Museum)

*Absalon
Pedersen
Dagbog,* 104,
107.

that saw the end of her lover's exile in France. That August she emerged from her retirement to attend a smart christening at Bergen and ten days later a fashionable wedding. The reception was given by her cousin Erik in the Rosenkrantz Tower. Although two years and a half had passed since she left Scotland, to her neighbours Anna was still "the Scottish lady." It is difficult not to conclude that she had announced her intention to recross the North Sea and take her place beside the returning exile, whose plighted wife she claimed to be. While there is no proof that she used the permission granted by her Scottish passport "to return to Scotland as often as may seem fit to her," the ascription of the Casket Sonnets to her pen makes it likely that she took the voyage. Although there is no other record of her stay, it must be noted that her previous visit from February, 1561, to February, 1563, was so discreetly managed that, but for the issue of her passport when the time came to leave, no trace of her presence in Scotland would remain.

It can therefore be supposed that her second stay between the summers of 1565 and 1567 was passed, like the first, in one of Bothwell's numerous and remote houses on the Border where her lover could pause on his way between Edinburgh or Crichton and the Hermitage. In the intervals between these rare reunions, Anna had plenty of time to write the Sonnets. It was natural for a young woman who had just left her home a second time for love's sake, to harp a little on her sacrifice—"for him I have left all relatives and friends." She lamented the slight she had inflicted on her relations and the neglect with which she had repaid her friends, until her lover must have wearied of the subject. It cannot have been with unmixed feelings that he read of a love that ignored all family opposition and meant in spite of everything to cling to him. There is no need to point out that while these sentiments rose naturally to the mouth of a homesick girl and a recent arrival in the country, they are utterly inappropriate to a queen who

Sonnet IX.
Sonnet I.

Sonnet III.
Sonnet II.

412

had lived there for five years in the middle of an admiring Court, keeping in constant and harmonious touch with her relations on the Continent.

Similarly the half-time mistress immured in some lonely Border peel, remembering happier days at the Danish Court, where she had shone as the daughter of a distinguished Admiral, might say that she wished to regain her position (*je veux rechercher grandeur*)—an *Sonnet VIII.* aspiration that could hardly be voiced by a Queen who was automatically the greatest in the land?

Poor Anna's feelings while she waited for a lover who did not always come, were different from any agony the Queen of Scots could have to endure.

"My heart, my blood, my soul, my care, you promised *Sonnet XI.* we should be together all night at our leisure here where I languish, my heart assailed by panic that springs from the absence of the aim of my desire. At one time fear of being forgotten grips me; at others I dread your dear heart hardened by the words of some tale-bearer; at another time I am afraid of some adventure on the road turning back my lover, some fresh troublesome mishap. . . . Not seeing you as you promised, I have put pen to paper. . . ."

During Bothwell's long absences, talk reached his ears that his neglected mistress was finding local consolation. He did not hide his suspicions.

"You doubt my abiding constancy," complained the *Sonnet VII.* lonely girl, "you, my only wealth, my only hope! I convince you of my faithfulness, you think me light; you suspect my love without evidence but your mistrust does me too great wrong. Forgetting the passion I bear you, you think another passion carries me away. You count my words wind, my heart you paint as wax, you believe me a woman without judgment. . . ."

Anna had made the mistake of trying to revive the past. She had left home the second time, ignorant that her lover was likely to marry and the place she hoped to occupy be filled. To the shock of discovery were added the pangs of jealousy.

"For her own profit," she insinuated of Lady Jean, her supplanter, "she is faithful; for it is no small honour to be mistress of your possessions." (The daughter of a philoprogenitive Admiral would consider the control of the damaged Hepburn fortune a more important asset than it could appear to the daughter of kings.) "By you and her marriage, she has restored her house to honour."

A foreigner who had not been long in Scotland could not know that the Gordon forfeiture had been lifted a month before Jean's future husband left Paris. Queen Mary, whose hand restored the family, would be aware how much Jean and her brother owed to the crown and how little to the marriage.

If these extracts from the Casket Sonnets point clearly to Anna and not Mary as the author, a last quotation seems to provide a pen for one of the remaining Casket
Letters. Lady Jean, the Sonnets relate, "won for a time" her husband's heart. But since she was always thinking
of Alexander Ogilvie, her reception of the marital advances proved chilling. When Jean saw what she had done (perhaps her sewing-maid showed her), she changed her tactics, and tried, the Sonnets declare, to win back her husband by a display of learning. Some of the letters penned with this pathetic object reached the Sonnet-
writer's eyes. The mistress describes the wife's effusions as "writings all rouged with learning, that does not grow in her brain but is borrowed from some distinguished author."

This account of Lady Jean's epistolary style might explain the Third ("Medea") Casket Letter, which is so involved and euphuistic that nobody has ever been able
to make sense of it. If it be assumed that the intrigue of which Bothwell suspected Anna reached Jean's sharp ears, a further stage in the triangular drama can be traced, and the "Medea" letter becomes comprehensible. Jean saw her husband bored by his plaintive little friend and glad of any excuse to end the relationship. Suppose the anonymous admirer could be brought to the scratch! Jean went in person to the scene of action.

"I watched later up there," she wrote to her husband, describing her experiences, "than I would have done had I not wanted to extract the information this bearer brings you. I find the very best convenience to excuse your affair that could offer. I have promised her to bring her to him to-morrow,[1] if you agree to put it in hand."

Lady Jean believed that all was fair in love, and her desire to recapture her husband's affections is perhaps pardonable.

". . . The thing I most desire," she went on, "and seek in the world is your good grace. . . . I will never despair so long as you keep your promise and tell me what is in your mind. Otherwise I will believe that my bad luck and the manœuvres of those who have not the third part of my fidelity and voluntary obedience have won the advantage that Jason's second lady-love obtained—not that I would compare you to so unfortunate a character, or myself to so pitiless a one."

One sees what Anna meant by the rouge of learning and the allusions to distinguished writers. They conceal a plain statement that, if her husband keeps her informed, Jean can cope with the situation. If not, Anna, who does not possess a fraction of the wife's desirable qualities, may win the day. Ovid, she recalls, relates a similar instance, how Creusa, Jason's foreign fancy, ousted Medea from her rights as his wife. And then, of course, Medea handed her rival a poisoned robe. . . .

Exactly how Anna was to be compromised does not appear, though another obscure piece of imagery gives a hint.

"Send me word early to-morrow," continues the jealous wife, "how you are inclined, for I shall be anxious. And watch carefully to see if the bird comes out of her cage, or if she stays there alone without her mate, like the turtle-dove, to lament his absence, however short."[2]

[1] This translation is made from the Hatfield French version into which Lady Jean's original Scots was no doubt turned. The French "je lui ai promise de la lui mener demain" leaves the sexes of the various parties uncertain.

[2] In order to connect the document with the Queen, the "Medea" Letter ends with an addition by the forgers of a couple of lines referring to three Court servants. It is significant that all three names appear in the part of the Long Casket Letter that Mary really wrote.

Anna, of course, is the bird; her Border home the cage; her mate the unknown Don Juan, but there is no means of knowing whether the Norwegian gave herself away as her rival intended. All that is certain is that by September, 1567, Anna was back in the Bergen district and that her love had turned to ashes. She was destined to exact payment to the uttermost farthing. The love letter, the love sonnets she had written were to ruin the cause and the reputation of the queen whose husband her lover had become. That lover was to give his chance of freedom, ultimately his reason and his life, to pay for the wrong he had done. If the name of the third Earl of Bothwell be used to point a moral and adorn a tale, the conclusion may be drawn that a man is lucky if he escapes the consequences of any of his actions.

The middle of September, 1567, was the time fixed to hear the claims and charges against the Scottish Earl and his followers. Bothwell regarded the prospect with complete equanimity. His feelings defeat description when Anna Throndsen's friends filed into Court to enter a claim for the recovery of the money she had lent him on the unofficial honeymoon in the Netherlands seven years before! No doubt there were plenty of answers he could make. The money had been a free gift; he had repaid it a hundredfold in the years he had provided for his mistress. James Hepburn had the dignity to say nothing. Anna did not exercise the same forbearance. The whole story was aired in Court. The seducer "had taken her from her fatherland and home and had led her into a foreign land away from her parents." (The language and the plaint vividly recall the words in the Sonnets and the last Casket Letter.) "Yet he would not hold her as his lawful wife, which he had promised to do with hand, mouth and letters. These last she caused to be read before him."

Bothwell's humiliation before an alien court, composed of men whose rank he despised, could be pushed no further. He looked up to hear the ironic peroration. "Whereas he has three wives living, herself first, another in Scotland, from whom he has bought himself, and last

Absalon Pedersen's Dagbog, 148; de Thou xl., 819; Les Affaires xxxix.

the Queen of Scots, the Lady Anna opines that the promise of marriage has no weight in his eyes."

What retort could Bothwell make? Since the case had contemptuously been brought on a money basis, the only possible answer was on the same lines. With a shrug of the shoulders he volunteered to pay the plaintiff a yearly rent from Scotland of one hundred dollars and to give her his smaller ship with anchor, ropes and tackle. The gesture was robbed of any particular significance by the fact that an outlaw could own no property in Scotland or dispose of a ship that belonged to somebody in Hamburg. Anna had to be satisfied with the promise and officially took no further steps. James Maitland is not *Apology for* quite correct in stating that his father's enemy "was *William* imprisoned for the wrong he had done to the said gentle- *Maitland 227.* woman in abusing, leaving and deceiving her." But Anna's suit came at a fatal moment. Erik Rosenkrantz had the power to let Bothwell proceed on his travels a free man. If no case had been brought, the Viceroy would have been obliged to speed him on his way. The injury done to his cousin provided a pretext to keep a foreigner, whose papers were not in order, under a temporary restraint which lengthened into a lifelong captivity.

Further excuse to detain the Admiral arose from a confusion over the ownership of the smaller ship. When Bothwell had wanted his name kept from Captain Aalborg, he had told the crew to say that she belonged to David Wodt, the Hamburg skipper from whom he had chartered her. There was no chance to cancel the order and the men on examination stuck sturdily to the tale, adding by way of picturesque detail that the Duke of Orkney had not left Scotland. These flights of fancy would have done little harm but for Wodt's reputation. Several of the German traders swore that only the year before he had plundered a merchantman on her way to Bergen, seizing four barrels of bread and twenty-two hogsheads of beer.

So when Bothwell, hoping that with Anna's silence his

troubles were over, applied for his passport, he met polite evasion. Ever accommodating, he offered to do without one and asked if he could hire a rowing-boat or yacht to take him along the coast to Denmark (he had never been interested in geography) for an audience with the King. A bad sailor, he protested that a journey inshore would best suit his stomach. In fact, he was anxious to avoid a passage on a Danish warship, the only alternative to the *Pelican*, which he had to leave for Hemelingk. When objections to his proposal were raised, he did not insist on Denmark, but offered to substitute Scotland, Holland or France. His hosts were sceptical, suspecting that he wanted to make Varbjerg, which the Swedes had captured two years before, and thence the enemy soil of Sweden. Blandly, Erik Rosenkrantz advised him that a Danish passport would be more hindrance than help on the Swedish territory his proposed coastal voyage would compel him to cross. He recommended one of the King's warships for transport up the Skagerrack to Copenhagen.

For a week after Anna Throndsen's calamitous inter-vention James Hepburn lingered in Bergen waiting for something to happen. He spent his nights at the inn where the barking of a score of watch-dogs that guarded the Hanseatic premises must have made sleep difficult. By day he was allowed to wander about the streets and visit the age-old fish-market where fish swim in salt-water tanks ready to be bought. On the outskirts of the town the ever-present smell of fish gave place to the scent of heather. The sight of rowan trees must have made the exile sigh, and flowers under the sparkling sun as bright as the flowers of Scotland.

One day he sent three of his gentlemen to the Ber-genhus to ask Rosenkrantz for a portfolio concealed in the ballast of one of his ships. The Viceroy sent Aalborg on board to fetch it. Next day the three gentlemen were requested to unlock it in presence of the commission. A bundle of papers, printed and manuscript, in Scots and Latin, fell out. The Board had them translated. "There was a large parchment document in Latin by virtue of

ERIK OTTESEN ROSENCRANTZ
Portrait at Gauno Castle
(*By courtesy of the Royal Library, Copenhagen*)

Sire estant parti d'escosse pour venir faire entendre au roy de
dannemare les grandts et euidens tortz qui sont faicts a la
royne d'escosse sa proche parente et a Moy particulierement pour
de la aller trouuer ey deligence vostre Maieste Jay este
par tourmente jette ey la coste de Noruuegue et de la venu
ey dennemarcts ou se trouue le seigneur de denzay vostre
embassadeur auquell Jay faict ample discours des mes
effaires et prie de vous ey aduertir par homme expres
ce quil Ma promis et ne doubtant point quil Ne
la complisse Je suppliray treshumblement vostre Maieste
da nou esgard a la bonne volonte que Jay tonte Maytie
en de vous faire seruice ey la quelle Jay delibere de
continuer et quil vous plaise Me faire tant d'honneur
de Me faire response comme a celuy qu'na apres dieu
aultre esperance qu'ey vostre Maiesté

Sire Je Me recommande treshumblement a vostre bonne
grace et suply le dieu tout puissant vous donner
tresheureuse et longue vie de copenhaguen le douzie
tour de Nouembre

Vostre treshumble et tresobeissant
seruiteur

James duc of orkmay

AUTOGRAPH LETTER FROM BOTHWELL TO CHARLES IX.,
12TH NOVEMBER, 1568

remark how "everything was conducted and governed according to his will."

This prudent counsellor was doubtful whether Copenhagen Castle was strong enough to contain for long so restless a spirit as Bothwell's. He sent Captain Aalborg to North Jutland to describe to the King the *coup* in Karm Sound with a letter of recommendations for the disposal of the captive. Frederick's reply was that "the Scottish King"—James Hepburn had clearly made an impression on Aalborg—could stay where he was until the royal return to Copenhagen.

Meanwhile Bothwell had a visitor. Charles de Dancay, the venerable French Ambassador and friend of the astronomer Tycho Brahe, undertook to get word of Bothwell's plight by special messenger to the Court of France. Like all Bothwell's letters, his plea to Charles IX was short and not without dignity. But the anxiety he felt emerges from its conventional phrases.

"Sire," he wrote in French, and in his clearest hand, *Bothwell to* "I left Scotland to let the King of Denmark hear the great *Charles IX,* and manifest wrongs done to the Queen of Scotland, his *12 Nov., 1567.* near kinswoman, and to me in particular. Intending thereafter in all diligence to seek your Majesty, I have been cast by a storm on the coast of Norway and thence have come to Denmark. Here I found Monsieur de Dancay, your Ambassador, to whom I have made full discourse of my affairs, praying him to acquaint you by express messenger, which he has promised. Not doubting the performance of his promise, I entreat your Majesty very humbly to have regard to the good will to do you service that I have shown all my life, in which course I intend to continue. May it please you to honour me with such an answer as you would give to one who has no hope in any but your Majesty, save in God.

"Sire, I commit me very humbly to your good grace and pray Almighty God to grant you a happy and long life. From Copenhagen, the twelfth day of November.

"Your very humble and very obedient servant,
                    "James, Duke of Orkney."

room. From the beech woods of Friedrichsborg he let
Bjorn Kaas, Captain of the Malmoehus, know that he
intended to send "the Scottish Earl, who is detained in
the Castle of Copenhagen, to our Castle of Malmoe there
to remain for some time. Therefore we request you to
have the vaulted room prepared where High Steward
Eyler Hardenburg had his quarters. Wall up the closet
in the room and where the iron lattice of the windows
is not strong and quite secure, have it repaired. When the
Earl arrives, put him in the room and give him a bed
and good entertainment, as Peter Oxe will further advise
you. Before all things, keep good watch and ward on the
said Earl, as you may best devise, that he does not
escape."

Two days later, on the 30th December, at Copenhagen,
Frederick had an answer ready for the Lyon King at
Arms. While deploring the murder of Darnley, he
pointed out that Bothwell's guilt was not proven, that
his accusers were in rebellion against his wife, and that
he had been acquitted by a Scottish Court of Law. Under
these circumstances and taking into account his own
royal jurisdictory rights, Frederick could not agree to
extradition. If the Regent cared to send an accredited
representative he would be allowed to take legal steps as
soon as the Council met. But as some of its members
were absent and an expedition into Sweden was imminent,
it was not proposed longer to detain the present emissary.
The King ended that he was sure this answer would give
satisfaction, especially as he was putting the accused
under stricter confinement until his case could be settled
by the rules of law and equity.

The herald bowed and was free to return to Scotland,
where a year and a half later he met a tragic and mysterious death. Condemned on a charge of witchcraft, he
was burned alive at St. Andrews. The real reason for this
savage sentence seems to have been his foreknowledge of
a plot aimed against the Regent's life. A Hepburn, yet
another illegitimate son of the Bishop of Moray, was a
ringleader and a guess may be hazarded that Stewart

426

had come in contact with the prisoner at Copenhagen and had been suborned to remove his persecutor.

For Bothwell was not kept in ignorance of his danger. *Oxe to Frederick II, 30 Dec., 1567.* The High Steward had Moray's letter read out and he understood its Latin well enough to protest vigorously against its "unfair accusations" and "lying stories." He was told that the King of Denmark, "as a Christian and a wise prince," would see no wrong done when his case was tried, but that in the meantime his place of custody must be changed. Showing no apprehension of the outcome, he pointed out that he could not prepare his brief in prison and asked leave "to send one of his servants to Scotland and France for letters, proofs and witnesses" of how the tragedy happened. He also asked for a copy of *Frederick II to Oxe, 1 Jan., 1568.* the Regent's letter. Both requests were granted with the proviso that he must show all letters to Oxe. The allusion to witnesses from France suggests that the whole truth of the Paris Plot might have been revealed if Bothwell's accusers had faced an investigation before an impartial court in a neutral country.

In preparation for his ordeal, Bothwell sat down with a Danish secretary to write a statement of his case. His opening may be quoted.

" To the end that the King of Denmark and the Council of his Kingdom may understand better and clearer the malice and treasons of my accusers, I have, as briefly as possible, included and truly declared the causes of the troubles and disturbances that have occurred from the year 1559 until to-day; for my accusers only are the principal authors and originators."

The memoir ran to six thousand words and was written by the 5th January, 1568, in Bothwell's room in the Castle of Copenhagen. On the whole he gives a very straightforward account of the main political events of his active life. Where he could not make a clean breast, he preferred suppression to falsification. He slides quickly over the murder at Kirk o' Field and ignores completely the blot on his honour, the kidnapping of the Queen. His tone throughout is of an injured, but quietly confident man. This spirit informs the firm peroration which avoids the extremes of defiance or apology.

"In this way I have been detained and imprisoned in one place or another for nearly four months and a half against all my expectation, for I thought I had come amongst friends, even if I had no passport. Not only that, but I have been slandered and unjustly accused by my enemies and deprived of the necessaries my rank demands. This I deem of far less consequence that the contumelies and indignities I have endured in prison. I am detained without cause by those from whom I expected help and succour; I am hindered from pursuing my business with various princes and nobles in certain countries for the deliverance of the Queen my Princess; this tends, I think, to our dishonour, injury and ruin."

This bold plea for freedom the prisoner hoped to deliver in person to the King and Council. But the last time Frederick and Bothwell had met was under happier conditions. The King may have felt that an interview with the man he had once delighted to honour, might be embarrassing. A few days after the brief was finished, copied in duplicate and corrected in Bothwell's own hand, orders came for the move to Malmoe.

As the disappointed prisoner crossed the Sound to the southern extremity of Scania, now part of Sweden but then an apanage of Denmark, he got a distant view of the town where he was destined to spend four and a half interminable years. A city wall, spires breaking the sky-line (the cathedral, however, had lost its steeple in a gale a hundred years before), low, half-timbered, pan-tiled houses coloured pink or yellow—the whole town was dominated by the high-pitched roof and staircase gable of the castle to which they hurried him.

The north wing of the building where he was housed stands to-day, though restored and converted into a museum. From the walls of the room in which he spent the next fifty-four months look down the slightly dyspeptic portraits of the local regiment of Hussars. But the vaulted ceiling which Frederick's letter to the governor mentioned, the doorway to the vanished closet which he had blocked, the iron lattices which he had strengthened, still exist.

The room is on the ground floor with two large windows that look south on the courtyard. Towards the sea is only the doorway to the closet, through which external wooden structure Frederick feared the adventurer might escape. Access to the large and airy apartment is by a big door in the west wall, where Bjorn Kaas could be relied on to post a sentry, day and night. Adjacent was a little guard-room with a large circular fireplace and a door that led down steps to the courtyard and to the soldiers' barracks below. Any attempt at escape had to pass a sentry, his mates in the guard-room and a courtyard liable to fill with the garrison. As a final insurance, the Governor's quarters communicated with the guard-room.

On the floor above was Frederick's royal suite, though there is no record that he ever used the bedroom over Bothwell's head while the prisoner was below. Such proximity might have spoiled a night's sleep.

If Bothwell was in a cage—and not all the "cunning and inventiveness" of the man who scaled the Castle Rock availed him to break its bars—the cage was honourable. Even more important, it was comfortable and (supposing he was given a brazier in winter) warm. Before the end, the consort of the Queen of Scots was to have worse lodging.

Seeing no hope of a prison break, the persistent Scot set to work to procure his release by policy. Within a few hours of his arrival he was penning a fresh appeal to the King's justice. This time he wasted less ink on current history. After a brief expression of his disappointment that he was not allowed to state his case in person, he bluntly announced two objects of the mission, which he declared the Queen and her loyal lords had entrusted to him.

"First I was to ask from the King's Majesty of Denmark, as the ally and confederate of the Queen, aid, favour and assistance both of soldiers and ships to deliver her from captivity. Secondly, to meet expenses which might be incurred, I was to offer the said monarch to return the Isles of Orkney and Shetland to the Crown of Denmark and Norway, freely and unconditionally, where they were in time past."

If his offer was accepted, Bothwell undertook to get any bond the King and Council cared to dictate, signed and sealed by the Queen, her lords and himself. To let him fulfil his promise to the Queen and tell her what hope of Danish help she had in her "extreme trouble and adversity," he asked for a quick decision.

Les Affaires
du Comte de
Boduel 29.

On the 13th January, 1568, the French Ambassador paid the author of this ingenious proposal a visit and took delivery of the two copies of the offer and of the earlier statement.   At Bothwell's request he gave Frederick's copy to Oxe and Friis, whom he found a little farther up the coast at Halsingborg. The answer, which was given on the 21st January at Copenhagen, has not survived. The offer of the islands by a man who could sign himself their Duke, and whose patent to that dignity had been inspected, can hardly have left the King of Denmark indifferent. It was only seven years since he had formally requested the restitution of territory which had belonged to Norway until Christian I had pledged it to the crown of Scotland in lieu of his daughter's dowry. Later offers to redeem the islands by the cash payment of Margaret's dowry had been ignored, but Denmark had not given up hope. Even if the *ci-devant* Duke of Orkney was in no position to implement his offer, even though Frederick took no steps to send soldiers or ships, hints in the diplomatic correspondence of the day suggest that the idea fell on fertile soil. Some part of Frederick's reluctance to deliver Bothwell to the hands of his enemies may have sprung from a sense of the finality with which an execution would close the Orkney offer.

It was not long before Moray reopened the attack. Sir William Stewart made a delayed return to communicate Frederick's disappointing reply, without convincing the Regent that the case was hopeless. Firm handling, he thought, was what the King of Denmark needed. With customary energy, he wrote to Cecil to bring up the big guns. If the Secretary could persuade Elizabeth to write, if he could get letters from France and Spain as well, "ye shall do a goodly work," he was assured, "and declare your affection to justice." Why justice could not be served by the impartial hearing that Frederick offered, the Regent did not condescend to explain.

Cecil extracted two letters from his mistress, a second *Queen Elizabeth to Frederick II, 29 March, 4 May, 1568.* in case the first miscarried. From certain phrases, it looks as if he played on her constant fear of assassination. All monarchs, she assured her old suitor Frederick, must *de la Forrest to Charles IX, 1 April, 1568.* stand together against regicides such as the one at present in his power. On every side his punishment was claimed. If he could be sent to Scotland, or better, to England, she would see that no harm came to him before the trial, which, if innocent, he must welcome. That, she promised on her royal word. Bothwell may be excused for preferring the solidity of the walls of Malmoe.

England, as usual, had responded to Moray's request. Elsewhere his efforts met less success. Spain made no move, and the agent he sent with strong representations to the French Court found no encouragement.

On the evening of the 2nd May, 1568, a star shot across the political heavens. Had Bothwell been free when Mary Stuart was rowed across Lochleven, history might have been altered. With him to lead her army victory would not have been outside her grasp. Her first move was to send the Laird of Riccarton to capture *Tytler vi. 37.* Dunbar and to carry the news of her freedom to her husband's prison. Surely, with that spur, he would contrive to hurry to her!

There was no time for the laird to fulfil his mission. In less than a fortnight the Queen risked all in the battle of Langside. Her forces were double the Regent's, but leadership was lacking. The incompetence of the loyalists threw victory away. On the 16th May, Mary committed the final imprudence of trusting Tudor magnanimity and crossed the Solway. In her restricted liberty at Carlisle she still did not despair of help from her captive husband and his outlawed followers. So, at least, Dandie Pringle, treacherous to the last, reported. "Please your Grace" (the Countess of Lennox was his *confidante*), "to wit that the Laird of Riccarton came over Tweed at Norham, was kept in the steeple, conveyed to Durham and eats and drinks at the Bishop's board, as I saw. He has brought money to furnish the Earl of Bothwell. I wish your Grace would pass unto the Queen (Elizabeth) either to stay him or get commission to Sir John Forster to take him. Also to get a letter to Lord Scrope to take Ormiston and Hob, his brother, who repair daily to the Queen (Mary) at Carlisle in secret."

Pringle to the Countess of Lennox, May 1568.

The collapse of Mary's hopes decided Frederick's policy. If there was now little chance of her restoration, a deal with the Regent was indicated. He sent one of his captains, Axel Wiffert, to offer Bothwell for trial in either Denmark or Scotland. The *quid pro quo* was a permit to recruit two thousand Scots for the Swedish war. Colonel Clerk knew of Axel's mission and supposed that Moray's attitude might need stiffening. He wrote reproaching the Regent because he had allowed Mary, "that cruel Jezebel, so much liberty and had not given her flesh and bones to the dogs to devour as prescribed by Holy Writ." Over her husband let no mistake be made. Wiffert should be detained and allowed to enlist no mercenaries (Clerk seems to have forgotten which king he was serving) until Bothwell was handed over, "for," he asserted, "they regard him as a holy relique and believe that you will buy him at a great price."

Drury to Cecil, 13 June, 9, 14 July, 1568; Wiffert to Frederick II, 21 Aug. 1568. J. Clerk to Moray, July, 1568.

Here was a fanatic after Moray's rigid heart. He promptly requested Clerk's royal employer to release the colonel temporarily from his military duties and let him pay a short visit to Scotland on urgent business. By October Clerk was home, hatching mischief against Mary and Bothwell.

James VI to Frederick II, 16 July, 1568.

Meanwhile Axel Wiffert received, so Moray assured *James VI. to Frederick II, 21 Aug., 1568.* the King, every facility in enlisting as many Scots as he liked. This concession was the more liberal, the Regent pointed out, because he could himself use every man. In return he expected the fulfilment of the Danish promise. The surrender of the regicide, driven "by the wind of God's goodness" on Norwegian shores, he reminded Frederick, had already been demanded: to leave no doubt of his guilt, copies of the deed of forfeiture pronounced against him in full session of the Scottish Parliament, were sent by the hand of Gavin Elphinstone. "But since (owing to the cruel wars which rage in neighbouring kingdoms and throughout nearly the whole of Christendom) the seas are beset by pirates, the prisoner could not be conveyed in safety to Scotland without a powerful naval and military escort. As that is not at present convenient, we have entrusted to the noble captain John Clerk, our minister, the execution of the said sentence."

The most informal and least conspicuous routine was suggested. With Frederick's permission, without any of the tedium of a trial, the colonel was to cut off the prisoner's head and bring it back to Scotland to stick on a spike at the scene of the crime—"If your Serenity allows it, you will have permitted an action most welcome to us and most honourable to yourself!"

Unfortunately for the beautiful simplicity of James Stewart's suggestion, the King of Denmark's ideas of "honour" were less positive. He wanted to know what his neighbours would think. He consulted his brother-in-law, the Elector of Saxony; his uncles Adolphus and John, Dukes of Schleswig-Holstein; Julius, Duke of Brunswick-Wolfenbuttel and Ulrich, Duke of Mecklenburg. To this august tribunal he posed the problem of his duty as a kinsman of his prisoner's wife, of his rights as a sovereign, of his royal reputation, and of the difficulty in guessing which way the cat would jump.

Only one of the princes took a line hostile to Bothwell. *Frederick II to Augustus of Saxony, 22 June, 1568.* Perhaps the Elector Augustus had been prejudiced by the story of Anna Throndsen which his brother-in-law

*Augustus of
Saxony to
Frederick II,
1 Sept., 1568.*

had passed on. In any case he reminded Frederick of Bothwell's anti-Danish bias, and lauded the principle of extradition. On most points the other magnates were non-committal, but they agreed that the case demanded a formal trial in the King's own dominions, before

*John Duke of
Schleswig-
Holstein to
Frederick II,
25 Aug., 1568.*

impartial judges, with counsel employed on either side. Duke John the Elder's advice was even more profound. Time, he opined, would bring wisdom.

Time indeed brought changes which made it less pressing to agree to Moray's demands. On the 29th September Eric XIV was forced to abdicate, and in November his rebellious nobles signed a treaty at Roskilde, surrendering their conquests and the claim to the triple crown. When Colonel Clerk got back to Denmark at the end of October with the most agreeably bloodthirsty anticipations, he met a vague reception. His private grudge against Bothwell, which earlier had brought him to Carberry Hill at the head of eighty soldiers collected for service against Sweden, looked as if it might be disappointed. The most he could effect, with Peter Oxe's permission, was the arrest of two of his enemy's remaining servants.[1]

These unfortunates were William Murray, a young gentleman who had once served the Queen as chamberlain, and Nicholas Hubert, nicknamed French Paris. On 30th October Clerk gave Peter Oxe a receipt at Roskilde for their persons to be taken to Scotland for trial and

*Clerk to
Cecil, 20
Nov., 1568.*

punishment. He communicated his success to Cecil and added that the King had allowed Bothwell " three months to justify his cause before the three Estates." When that formality had been indulged, the outlaw, he stated confidently, would be sent home for execution.

---

[1] Sixty-two names of Bothwell's followers figure on the Summons of Forfeiture of 1st October, 1569; only seven on the summons of 22nd December, 1569. These seven were therefore still at large. They were the two Ormistons, who are known to have found refuge on the Border; Patrick Wilson, who is known to have taken part in the siege of Dunbar, and four others, who may have been the "four or five" servants whom Bothwell was allowed to take from Bergen to Copenhagen. Their names are given as William Murray, brother of Adam Murray; Paris, the Frenchman; Simon Armstrong, called Wanton Sim; and Andrew Kerr, younger of Greenhead.

Four months passed and all that Clerk could chronicle *Clerk to Cecil, 10 March, 1569.* was that the Earl "had given certain articles into the Council." The zealous soldier sent a copy to Scotland and hoped for a surrender, "when the answer comes."

But Frederick was still playing for time. He *Dancay to Charles IX, 16 June, 1570.* objected that a colonel of his mercenaries was not a suitable plenipotentiary. Before May was out, Clerk had to give up hope of a happy voyage to Scotland carrying Bothwell's severed head. All he could do was to ship French Paris to Leith where he arrived in mid-June, 1569, to be taken to St. Andrews, tortured, examined, and hanged without a trial.

What happened to William Murray is not known. He was alive and well in the middle of May, under Clerk's *Peter Adrian to Cecil, 12 May, 1569.* eye but lodging with a merchant in Copenhagen. Staying in the same house was a Captain Peter Adrian, from Rye, Sussex, commanding one of the King of Denmark's ships. Noticing that Murray and Adrian had made friends, Clerk sent secretly for the sailor and suggested that "as he was a true Englishman," he might obtain the confidence of his young friend to "understand as much as he might the doings of the Earl of Bothwell and how he meant to proceed in his affairs." Adrian, bluff naval officer, found the request "honest and conformant to reason." He proceeded to encourage the Scot's friendship and "fed his humours with courteous talks, lamenting very much the present state of the Lord Bothwell." William Murray, who may have had ideas of an escape by sea, arranged a meeting with the prisoner, since visitors were humanely allowed at Malmoe.

Thus we get an interesting glimpse of Bothwell in the twenty-first month of his captivity. His talk and attitude of mind are recorded, and something of his way of life.

Adrian stayed four days—there was the room which Paris and Murray had left—and mentions that he "lacked no good cheer." At this time the Scottish Earl was certainly well treated and given every necessary—except freedom. At Copenhagen he had had to ask Peter

*Oxe to
Frederick II,
30 Dec., 1567.
Settlement of
Accounts,
2 March, 1569.*

Oxe for a loan of two hundred dollars to buy clothes; at Malmoe, Oluf Bagger, a merchant of Odense, had orders to supply him every year with English velvet and silk to the value of seventy-five dollars and to send the bill to Frederick. For a man who cared for dress, this mattered.

James Hepburn was glad to see Adrian and "after gratulations and divers courteous welcomes, made very much of him and promised so to recompense him that he should for ever after live by him." Clearly Murray had held out high hopes of escape or other advantage to be gained from his naval friend. In return Adrian "forgot not to feed him with all the gentlest and most courteous tales he could."

Bothwell showed himself *au fait* with current politics.

"I marvel," he said bluntly, "that the Queen of England should keep the Queen of Scots captive; it is against all good nature to show her such cruelty."

Other fugitives, he pointed out, like Moray and Morton, had received "good and gracious" treatment from Elizabeth. Bitterly he regretted his part in obtaining their pardons. Although he was talking to an Englishman, he declared that all his life he would be true to the policy of co-operation with France.

"I will not break that league for the amity of England," he declared.

Most of the Scottish nobility, he considered, were of that opinion, and the pro-English party could not be trusted. Even Moray had frequently said in his hearing that "the English were good companions, but too proud to be masters."

Turning to his own prospects, he professed his willingness to stand his trial in England, and complained of the injustice that kept him in prison in Denmark.

"No law has power over me, seeing I was acquitted by two assizes of the nobility of Scotland. I can only be touched by tyranny."

He wanted to know if Queen Elizabeth had written to Frederick for his extradition and mentioned his offer of the Orkneys. If he were handed over to the Scots (this is where he seems to have puzzled the sailor a little) he promised awkward disclosures.

"Those that mean to black my face, their own faces are as black," was his pointed remark.

Clerk had told Adrian that Bothwell had confessed to the murder of Darnley. This the prisoner utterly denied, but admitted "that it was with his consent." With a flash of his old fire he promised to have the colonel's throat cut, if ever he got free.

Cecil and Lethington were also singled out for unfavourable comment. "If the two secretaries were dead," he said thoughtfully, "both realms would be better." But Queen Mary, he related, had always "persuaded him to be quiet with Lethington."

"I answered her that if I made not an end of him, he would be my destruction. Now she has had good trial," was his regretful conclusion.

Presently his indomitable plans for the future took shape. His visitor was to carry letters to the French Court, to Charles, Catherine, the Cardinal, the Archbishop of Glasgow and to his old comrade-at-arms, de Martigues. They would get him out of prison, lend him some French soldiers and help him to land on the Clyde.

"Then," he boasted, "I will tread over the bellies of the Queen's enemies and my own."

Adrian agreed to take the letters, and of course arranged with Clerk to send them straight to Cecil. They were never written. Bothwell made his excuse (probably he had begun to suspect his visitor) that war had broken out between England and France. He requested Adrian to wait till he had further news. The sailor continued to wait.

Although Adrian's cruel game of raising Bothwell's hopes had no practical consequences, the reader must feel grateful to him for a last intimate glimpse of the prisoner. Captivity had not broken his spirit. But to watch behind prison bars the enemy flourish like a green bay tree is not a softening experience and hatred, even

437

tempered by a sense of humour, is unnourishing food for the soul.

It may be feared that Bothwell heard with unmixed delight of the murder of his life-long enemy, the Regent, at Linlithgow on the 23rd January, 1570. His death at the assassin's pistol is alleged to have been dramatically foretold.

"A devilish witch being condemned to die in the fire, Moray commanded that they should take a barrel of gunpowder to burn her with. When she understood the preparation of so much gunpowder, beside the tar barrels that was prepared for the fire, she burst forth, 'What needeth my Lord of Moray to prepare all this gunpowder? Less nor one ounce shall be his end.'"

CHAPTER THIRTY-SIX

PETER ADRIAN'S visit to Malmoe shows that "the Scottish King" was allowed considerable intercourse with the outside world. With dismay a later emissary from the British Isles warned Cecil of the ease of communication with Mary Stuart.

"Apperceiving the particular practices," the report ran, "that the murderer Bothwell hath daily with the King's Majesty's mother of Scotland, I give you advertisement hereof that all persons travailers betwixt them might in all times hereafter be stopped and punished, if men of great estimation be worthy of trust."

The implication is that Governor Bjorn Kaas was not the rigid disciplinarian that Bothwell's enemies could wish. A go-between was "one named Master Horsey" (a much-travelled man who later carried letters to Don John of Austria) employed by Frederick "to espy how all matters do proceed in England and Scotland." Another messenger was a Danish-born page of Bothwell's who could be mistaken for a Scot, so perfectly did he speak the tongue.

The letters that passed by their means between husband and wife have not survived. In one it is recorded that "she desired him to be of good comfort;" in another she intervened to try to save him from extradition; in another she helped the campaign he launched against Clerk. Some correspondence also passed on the subject of the divorce the couple had decided would prove to Mary's interest. As early as October, 1568, when the project of an alliance with the Duke of Norfolk was first mooted, from her prison at Bolton she authorised her representatives to consent, if necessary, to a legal separation. Next year Bothwell sent Lord Boyd an authorisation to procure an annulment, while Mary gave her agents at

T. Buchanan to Cecil, 19 Jan., 1571.

T. Buchanan to Cecil, 19 Jan., 1571.

Chalmers ii. 243.

439

the Convention of Scottish nobles at Perth a power to pursue "an action for divorce" in her name. The Convention, however, voted to take no further steps. Rather unkindly it pointed out that if Mary was in earnest she had only to write to Frederick and ask for her husband's execution.

Sir H. Norris
to Cecil, 29
Sept., 1570.
Sir H. Norris
to Queen
Elizabeth,
29 Nov., 1570.

About a year later fresh divorce gossip was gleaned by the English Ambassador in Paris. He warned Cecil of the danger of a marriage between Mary and the Duc d'Anjou, since the Pope (he declared) had just granted her an annulment. Her representatives at the Holy See were said to be one of the Kerrs and the Bishop of Dunblane, and the grounds for the dissolution "a rape committed on her by Bothwell, who by the Pope's sentence is banished Christendom and all Christian company. The bull is lately sent hence by a gentleman into Denmark, there to cause the said Earl to be executed for his heinous offence."

Henry Kerr did in fact present certain requests on Mary's behalf at Rome that summer; rape, by a decision of the Council of Trent, was an *impedimentum dirimens* as the Queen had been in Bothwell's power between the kidnapping and her marriage. But that the Ambassador's tale of divorce and bull was unfounded is proved by the negotiations for annulment that continued to be pressed.

Next March her party revived the idea of a marriage to Norfolk. The ill-fated Ridolphi was given a letter that was probably drafted by the Bishop of Ross to guide him on his mission to Rome. He was to remind the Vatican that Bothwell had captured the Queen and kept her captive "until he had procured a pretended divorce from his wife," when he obliged her to consent to an unwilling marriage. His Holiness was to be asked to take steps to relieve her "from so great an indignity" either by the ordinary process at Rome or by a commission of bishops. A memorial containing all the facts would be prepared by the Bishop.

But it was not until September, 1575, that Leslie presented his evidence to the Holy See. By then Don

John of Austria, a suitor more romantic than the Duke of Norfolk, had stepped forward.

To free Mary Stuart for the arms of the victor of Lepanto, the Bishop was bidden "to take good heed that *Cal. Eliz. ii.* *189.* the Holy Father shall publicly announce that the pretended marriage contracted without legality, but by a pretended procedure, is of no force. For although there are many reasons which make it clearly invalid in itself, yet the matter will be much clearer if His Holiness will come forward to annul it." The little-known evidence that Leslie produced to support his case is preserved at the Vatican and has been used in these pages.

Why, in spite of these repeated attempts to have her marriage dissolved, did Mary Stuart remain wedded to James Hepburn until death separated them? Is it sentimental to believe that she never wanted the knot undone and that each time the pressure of her advisers abated, she was glad to let her application drop? It is not unpleasant to imagine that this once beautiful lady (at her death at the age of forty-five she was "corpulent, round-shouldered, double-chinned" and wore an auburn wig) contrived to stay faithful to the memory of the derelict who had lost everything in her service.

The peace, which the rebellious dukes of Sweden had signed, was quickly repudiated by their new king and the war, with increasing unpopularity, dragged out its full seven years. Before the end was in sight with the Treaty of Stettin, King Frederick and Colonel John Clerk parted company. The man had become intolerable. However "dear" he might be to the rulers of Scotland "for his virtue and fidelity," he had earned his royal employer's whole-hearted dislike. When the second siege of Varbjerg cost the lives of two of the King's best generals, the colonel profited by the shortage of good infantry commanders to demand a fresh contract. He got it, but the King did not forget. When Clerk presented a statement of accounts alleging that he had made advances on the King's behalf to the extent of seventeen thousand dollars, Frederick indicated quite clearly that he did not mean to pay. Thereat the soldier demanded his discharge, muttering that somehow he would obtain what was due.

Lennox to Frederick II, 18 July, 1570. Buchanan to Frederick II, 19 March, 1571.

With relations at breaking-point, a Scottish soldier of fortune produced a report which fatally compromised the indignant colonel. Walter Aikman, the informer, had served Bothwell in France and Scotland before he enlisted in Clerk's Danish contingent. One of Clerk's subordinates, he stated, had been guilty of communication with the enemy. In vain Aikman had demanded his arrest, Clerk had shielded the traitor.

Simultaneously Gavin Elphinstone, recently a courier between Scotland and Denmark, produced a copy of the colonel's letter advising Moray to detain the Danish envoy, Axel Wiffert. The fat was in the fire. John Clerk was summoned to appear before a court of inquiry at Copenhagen on the 16th June, 1570.

As Aikman had been Bothwell's man, the hand of the prisoner of Malmoe may be suspected in the fate that threatened his persecutor. The Earl was a bad man to cross, however unhappily he might at the moment be situated. Clerk had boasted a little too loudly of his plans to take Bothwell's head to a spike at Kirk o' Field.

Oxe and Friis to Frederick II, 22 June, 1570.

The inquiry was held by Peter Oxe, John Friis, the Governor of the Castle of Copenhagen and others. Bothwell managed to send somebody from Malmoe to tell Frederick "that he could convict Captain Clerk of three rascally actions, the first against your Royal Majesty, the second against the King of France, and the third against the King of Scotland."[1]

Frederick II to Oxe and Friis, 24 June, 1570.

The Court consulted Frederick on this offer and obtained a ruling that a board of Scottish and German officers should visit the prisoner at Malmoe, "and learn by inquiry what accusation he can bring against Colonel

---

[1] That in 1563 John Clerk served in the English army at the siege of Le Havre would provide Bothwell with the rascally act against the King of France. Unless the killing of Charles Wilson, who was employed by the representatives of James VI, constitutes the remaining iniquity, the third accusation cannot now be verified.

Clerk." Bothwell's pleasure at the visit and his gusto as he enlarged on his enemy's lapses can be imagined. His story of Clerk's activities at Carberry Hill piled Pelion on Ossa and added to the charges already lodged the accusation that Frederick's soldiers had been used against the Queen of Scots.

On the 28th June a court-martial was formed of four German officers and three Scottish. One of the latter was Sandy Durham, late servant to Darnley, who was following the profession of arms in Denmark. The Court contented itself with investigating the original charge brought by Aikman that the accused had not punished a subordinate who had visited the Swedish camp to arrange desertion. On this count they found Clerk unfaithful to his military oath and recommended that he should give security not to escape.

So the unlucky soldier was held in the Castle of Copenhagen until he should be able to find the necessary sum, which Oxe complacently assured his master would be never. The technique of indeterminate sentences on indefinite grounds was well developed in sixteenth century Denmark.

Oxe and Friis to Frederick II, 28 June, 1570.

Bothwell had scored heavily. The luxury may have compensated him for the hornets' nest he brought about his ears. Word reached the British Isles that he had been given his freedom, a natural impression from his successful meddling in Clerk's affairs. Lennox, who had succeeded the murdered Moray in the Regency, promptly opened a fresh campaign for his extradition and agitated for Clerk's release. He wrote to Oxe asking his help and promising a new delegate with new and irresistible arguments. He wrote to Frederick expressing surprise at the Earl's apparent liberty and his success in procuring for others the pains he himself deserved. Lennox did his best to discredit Clerk's accusers, stating that one was Bothwell's man, while the others had robbed their masters or committed adultery. With even greater effect he induced the Queen of England to throw her influence into the scales.

Randolph to Sussex, 29 July, 1570.

Lennox to Oxe, 17 July, 1570.

Lennox to Frederick II 18 July, 26 Aug., 1570.

Queen Elizabeth to Frederick II, Summer, 1570 (Teulet, Lettres 207).

Good Queen Bess had never forgiven Bothwell. To Frederick she did not mince her words. If the prisoner was not to pay the penalty on the scene of his crime, the least she wanted was cells and chains. "It certainly does the King no honour that a regicide should wander free and large and live unpunished," she said tartly, "much less that he should boast of laying snares for the innocent." The letter ends with demanding Bothwell's punishment according to his merits and Clerk's release according to his. "The first is not only right, but prudent; the second merciful and just."

In the autumn arrived the new delegate whom Lennox had announced. This was Thomas Buchanan of Ibert, nephew of the more famous George. He was, unless his uncle helped him with his speech, himself no negligible Latinist. In that tongue on the 14th December, 1570, he delivered at Copenhagen Castle an elegant oration. It is the prerogative of public speakers to say nothing new in as many words as possible, and Thomas Buchanan's speech, for all its rolling periods, adds little to the reiterated demands for Bothwell's execution or extradition and for Clerk's release.

T. Buchanan's Contio (Teulet Lettres 208).

Such, however, is the stupefying power of oratory that Frederick was manifestly impressed. After a pause of three months, passed apparently in studying the copy of the speech that was supplied him, his answer contained important concessions. After praising the fluent and copious eloquence of the magnificent and generous Master Thomas Buchanan (the epithets suggest that Lennox did not rely exclusively on the persuasive power of reason) he remarks that the tragic fates of Darnley and of Mary must move all Christian kings, not merely to pity, but to contemplation of the vicissitudes in human affairs. Having shown that a Dane could turn a Latin phrase as well as a Scot, he added that if the Earl of Bothwell were guilty of the death of one or the ruin of the other, he would deserve the most condign punishment. That, however, the Earl constantly denied, claiming that the law had cleared him and that he had con-

Frederick II, to Lennox, 9 March, 1571.

444

sistently offered recourse to the arbitration of arms. Moreover, he would welcome a fresh trial, in Scotland or Denmark, if impartiality and a fair hearing could be guaranteed.

It is a pity, Frederick continues, that the Scottish envoy has not been given power to prosecute before a Danish tribunal. But so anxious is the King to oblige the authorities of England and Scotland, that he will consent to the extradition of his prisoner on three conditions. The rules of strict equity are to be observed at the trial; no precedent shall prejudice the rights of the Danish crown; and England and Scotland shall promise reciprocity. An answer to these conditions was requested before St. Bartholomew's Day (the 24th August); in the meantime the prisoner would be kept in stricter custody.

The use of the comparative disproves the stories of Bothwell's complete freedom. That his treatment now worsened is shown by a detail that must have distressed that "glorious young man." From this time forward the annual supply of silk and velvet ceased.

Some light is thrown on the change in Frederick's feelings by a conversation with the French Ambassador. Charles de Dancay learnt that the King would be glad, *Dancay to Charles IX, 16 June, 1570.* with all his heart, to be quit of the Earl, were it consistent with his honour. But until the charges were defined, he could not either try him or surrender him, since Bothwell denied "either killing Darnley or having had him killed *Dancay to Charles IX, 2 April, 1571.* nor having in any way consented to his death."

The war with Sweden was over. The possession of Bothwell's person was no longer a trump card. His existence produced little more than a twinge in the royal conscience. Nevertheless de Dancay thought that Frederick would delay the surrender until the last moment. From her prison at Sheffield Mary was doing what she could to save her husband. Master Horsey was to bring from her hand "letters of favour to the King of *T. Buchanan to Cecil, 19 Jan., 1571.* Denmark that Lord Bothwell be not delivered up to punishment, with some promises of a kindness of the

445

Isles of Orkney and Shetland." It may be feared, however, that the bait by now smelt a little stale.

Thomas Buchanan did not rest on his oratorical laurels and kept his employers fully posted. A letter which he wrote at the beginning of the year was intercepted on its way north by Morton who happened to be in London. He "took the boldness to open and read" it and found it contained too dangerous material to be trusted to the post. Some words and matters mentioned," he feared, "should rather have hindered than furthered our cause." When, therefore, Elizabeth inconveniently wanted to see this compromising paper, Morton "gave to understand that we had sent the principal away and delivered a copy, omitting such things as we thought not meet to be shown."

Morton, etc. to Lennox, 24 March, 1571.

The letter, like many inconvenient documents in the story, has perished and with it another chance of light. There remains only the evidence of the dishonesty of the prosecution.

T. Buchanan to Frederick II, 19 March, 1571.

After a little hesitation, the Scottish envoy assured Frederick that his country would accept the three conditions. The inevitable recapitulation of Bothwell's crimes followed, with the inclusion of witchcraft to explain his ascendancy over the Queen.

This burst of eloquence, the last of Thomas Buchanan's embassy, was reinforced by another letter from Elizabeth pressing for a trial in Scotland or England.

Queen Elizabeth to Frederick II, 22 Mar., 1571.

The attitudes of the interested parties on the question of reopening the murder case are instructive. Elizabeth, whose minister Cecil had no hand in the Kirk o' Field plots, wanted an investigation, provided it was held under favourable conditions. The King of Denmark, whose conscience was quite clean, consistently advocated an impartial tribunal. Bothwell himself proclaimed on every occasion his readiness to be tried in Denmark, England, or even Scotland. It was his Scottish accusers who wanted at any cost to avoid investigation and, on the principle that dead men tell no tales, to substitute summary execution. Frederick's stipulations pushed them into a corner. Their escape was adroitly managed.

In the middle of June the French Ambassador in London was allowed to hear that Lennox had accepted the King's conditions. This was a trick and it succeeded. The Frenchman, who did not know the truth and who feared lest Bothwell's revelations might compromise Queen Mary, was jockeyed into accepting the onus of stopping the trial. In the name of the "friends of the Queen" he begged his master to prevent the extradition which he considered would "complete the ruin of that poor princess." With a sigh of relief Lennox wrote to Frederick that, pending an answer from Elizabeth, he was content to postpone the Bothwell case until another occasion. *La Mothe Fenelon to Charles IX, 20 June, 1571.* *James VI. to Frederick II, 5 July, 1571.*

The King of France was under the influence of Catherine, who had not forgotten the secrets that had reached her about the Paris Plot. On the 15th July the French Ambassador to Denmark received his orders. By hook or crook extradition must be stopped. *Dancay to Charles IX and to Catherine de Medicis, 1 Sept., 1571.*

Six weeks later de Dancay sat down to write his report. His intervention had been successful, and for the time being Bothwell would not leave Malmoe. But the King, he pointed out, could not indefinitely refuse the prisoner a trial. Would Charles and Catherine consider whether they wanted him "liberated, if he was found innocent; or punished in Denmark, if he was convicted; or the sentence deferred during the French King's pleasure"? It was not impossible that Mary Stuart's cause might be best served by her husband's death. But all things considered, the Ambassador's advice was to play for time, intriguing neither for the prisoner's liberation nor execution. To this cold-blooded counsel de Dancay added in Catherine's ear a sinister hint that possibly a secret execution could be arranged.

St. Bartholomew's Day dawned without an answer from Scotland. With a shrug of his shoulders, Frederick dropped all talk of a trial, and the chance that the truth of Kirk o' Field might be known, for ever disappeared.

Bothwell, enjoying fewer privileges now, counted the useless days in the east room of the Malmoehus. No change in his condition had come when the bells of the next St. Bartholomew rang out their sanguinary signal. The anger in protestant countries that followed the massacre—in Rome a *Te Deum* was sung and in Spain Philip II was observed for almost the only time to laugh—extinguished the catholic Queen of Scots' last chance of restoration to her Calvinist throne. It slammed for ever the doors of Bothwell's captivity.

Lennox was dead, stabbed in the back; Mar, his successor, had died, exceptionally, in his bed. So had John Knox, after an escape from an assassin's bullet that bedded in the candlestick by which he was reading. In the spring of 1573 a man, "lately out of Sweden, reported that the Earl Bothwell was stark mad and had long been so."

Occurences in Scotland, March, 1573.

There is no official confirmation of this traveller's lamentable tale. But if four and a half years of disappointed hope and monotonous existence had ended in driving James Hepburn out of his senses, his condition will provide an explanation for Frederick's sudden severity.

In the summer of 1573 the King committed Bothwell to remote and rigorous confinement in the state prison of Dragsholm at the North of Zealand. Frederick was a humane man, but if Bothwell had fallen victim to maniacal attacks, medical science of the day would prescribe some such close captivity. Against this attempt to explain the change of treatment must be set Charles de Dancay's failure to mention insanity when he records the move. "The King of Denmark has until the present treated the Earl of Bothwell pretty well," wrote the Ambassador on the 28th June, 1573. "But a few days ago he had him put in a very bad and strict prison." The actual date of the transfer is given by a diary of contemporary events as the 16th June.

Eiler Brockenhuus Dagbog.